Getting the Whole Story

MARK:
Thanks for
helping us keep
the faith,

Terry
Wahl

The Guilford Communication Series

Getting the Whole Story

Reporting and Writing the News

Cheryl Gibbs • Tom Warhover

THE GUILFORD PRESS
New York   London

© 2002 The Guilford Press
A Division of Guilford Publications, Inc.
72 Spring Street, New York, NY 10012
www.guilford.com

Printed in the United States of America

This book is printed on acid-free paper.

Last digit is print number: 9   8   7   6   5   4   3   2   1

Library of Congress Cataloging-in-Publication Data

Gibbs, Cheryl K.
    Getting the whole story : reporting and writing the news /
Cheryl Gibbs and Tom Warhover.
        p.   cm. — (The Guilford communication series)
    Includes bibliographical references and index.
    ISBN 1-57230-795-1 (pbk.)
    1. Reporters and reporting. 2. Journalism.   I. Warhover, Tom.
II. Title. III. Series.
PN4781 .P525   2002
070.4'3—dc21   2002009759

Acknowledgments

It doesn't seem fair, somehow, for our two names to be the only ones on the cover of this book. Like newspapers, books are collaborative endeavors. Anyone who's written one could tell you that.

Were it not for Jay Rosen suggesting that we contact Guilford Publications with our textbook idea, for example, you wouldn't be reading this book. And were it not for series editor Theodore L. Glasser and former Guilford editor Peter Wissoker, who understood why and how to help us write a text that would be significantly different from other basic reporting tomes, you wouldn't be reading this either. They challenged us to make those differences *more* rich and meaningful.

We can also say with confidence that, were it not for current Guilford editor Kristal Hawkins and production editor William Meyer, who nudged, prodded and pulled us through various stages of the writing and production process, you would not be reading this book — at least not yet. As journalists who are accustomed to playing a part in publishing the equivalent of a book every day, it has been both humbling and enriching to see why real books take so much longer. We are grateful to Kristal, William and the many other fine people at Guilford who have helped us along.

We also could name dozens of people who have influenced our thinking as journalists by nurturing and mentoring us, challenging us and experimenting with us in our respective newsrooms. Without them, this book would be very different.

Many of them are journalists and journalism educators we have quoted within the pages that follow. In most cases we learned much more from them than we could convey with those brief passages. So if you, too, are excited by their ideas, we encourage you to seek out more of their writing, as we did. We especially recommend pretty much anything written by journalists Davis "Buzz" Merritt and Cole

Campbell, and by journalism educators Jay Rosen, Jim Carey, Ed Lambeth, Theodore L. Glasser, Roy Peter Clark, Lew Friedland and Phil Meyer.

We also are deeply grateful for the intellectual stimulation and support we received from people like David Mathews and Ed Arnone of the Charles F. Kettering Foundation in Dayton, Ohio; Lisa Austin, who worked with Kettering as research director of the Project on Public Life and the Press; and Jan Schaffer of the Pew Center for Civic Journalism.

Still others have helped with the preparation of this manuscript: Hugh Morgan, who will be sorely missed at Miami University of Ohio if he goes through with his threat of retirement, spent months carefully combing through the first draft of the book, and he gave us a wealth of important feedback. There's no way to adequately thank him.

Editor Steve Smith and editor-turned-ombudsman Dennis Foley gave us valuable feedback in the early stages of the writing process, usually accompanied by a good dose of humor. Journalist-turned-educator Kathy Campbell tested some chapters with her students and shared her insights about what worked and what didn't.

For years now, Earlham College journalism students have read various photocopied iterations of this manuscript. It is a rare sort of fulfillment that comes from identifying editing potential in students who can hardly disguise their glee at having found the teacher's typos or who — whether boldly or tentatively — offer their professor suggestions for improving something the professor wrote. Alex Davis, Anne Elisabeth Dillon, Sara Jenkins, Jason Long, Jon Jones, Ranjit Jose, Burke Josslin, Eric Kapenga, Danielle Cranin, Davin Coburn, Sarah Hampton, Ariel Hearne, Liv Leader, Alex Mayer, Lynelle Miller, Gerard Spears, Ryan Pirtle-McVeigh and Ilya Gurevic are among the students who have exhibited such potential. In some cases, they are now further developing that potential as working journalists.

Journalists at The (Norfolk) Virginian-Pilot, the Richmond (Ind.) Palladium-Item and the Columbia Missourian have been most generous in helping us with gathering photographs, granting us permission to use them and preparing them for publication. Special thanks are due to Drew Wilson of The Virginian-Pilot, who contributed several photos, and Nancy Young, also of The Virginian-Pilot, who gave us feedback and writing suggestions when we were particularly stuck.

Earlham College provided travel funds that allowed us to spend two weeks writing and editing together in the downstairs office/playroom at the Warhovers' beautiful home on the Outer Banks.

We also owe a great debt of thanks to our respective spouses and families.

Terri Warhover's support and enthusiasm for this project have been phenomenal, and her hospitality and thoughtfulness toward her husband's co-author (especially the "stress relief" lotion she sent after a computer software upgrade wiped out two weeks of work) have been greatly appreciated. Zach and Megan Warhover's excitement about daddy writing a book has been infectious all along. Terri's mother, Jacqueline Tucker, would put practically any proofreader to shame and, in our sprint to the finish, the rest of the Tuckers proved that it runs in the family.

Cheryl's husband, Mickey White, has been equally supportive and enthusiastic. In addition, when it appeared we faced a crisis with respect to the quality of the electronic versions of illustrations for the book, Mickey painstakingly inventoried the many problems and found ways to resolve every one of them. Cheryl's sister, Catherine Gedney, also a journalist, helped us to find stories for use as examples.

We are grateful to our friends who have hung in there as we've alternately enthused and vented about the book, and who have forgiven us for having turned down various social invitations when pushing to meet yet another deadline. We look forward to having more time to spend with them now.

We also are grateful to those of you who read the book and/or use it in your classes. We hope you find it a valuable alternative to the many fine craft-focused texts. Should you wish to offer feedback of any kind, we would be grateful to receive it.

CHERYL GIBBS
Earlham College

TOM WARHOVER
University of Missouri

Contents

x   Contents

Introduction

TO THE STUDENT

Maybe you're taking this class because you already know you want to be a journalist, writing about important news of the day, about issues that affect people's lives or about interesting people — like the president, let's say, or your favorite recording artist (if you're lucky). Maybe you just like to write, and you're considering journalism as a way of putting that English or philosophy degree to use in "the real world." Maybe you want to work in public relations for a corporation or nonprofit organization. Or maybe you just want to know more about how the media works.

Journalism is tremendously fascinating, rewarding work. For 12 years I worked full time as a reporter and editor in daily newspapers, and I dearly loved it. I learned so much about so many things that it made me feel truly at home in the world. I interviewed hundreds of people, from mayors to movie stars to murderers. I wrote about achievements, failures, triumphs, tragedies, hilarious situations, uncanny coincidences and utter depravity. I always, always felt my work could make a difference in people's lives — and often found out that it did. Teaching journalism for the past seven years has strengthened my conviction that this field has tremendous value, because I have learned from my students how greatly journalists have influenced their knowledge and views of the world.

From time to time, I still work part time at my local newspaper, because there's nothing — no thing — like the excitement of a newsroom. There, you can be one of the first to know about a breaking news event. You can experience the challenge of compiling information in the wonderful, inevitable dash toward a deadline. And you often find yourself laughing at an offhand remark someone makes amid the stressful final push to get the paper out on time.

If you've already written for your high school or college newspa-

1

per, you probably have a sense of that excitement. Maybe you remember a breathless student tearing into the journalism classroom with news about a change in the dress code or in the school's security system that was likely to be unpopular with students. Or perhaps, when you and your editor were in the newspaper office late one night going over the final printouts of a special story you'd written, you joked about whose pages had the most artistic arrangements of pizza stains on them.

If you haven't had any journalism experience, though, and the lure of late-night pizza isn't enough to convince you it would be a wonderful life, maybe these factors will inspire you to give it a try:

- No two days are alike — it's rare to hear journalists say they're bored.
- Journalists are constantly learning. Every interview is an opportunity to learn new things, often in a subject or field you know nothing about. You also learn a lot about the community where you live, the people in it, and what goes on there. You know what stores will open (or close) soon, what events are planned that might be fun to attend, and what developments in the community might affect you and the people you care about.
- Most reporters have a fair amount of freedom to set their own schedules, provided they get their work done and let their editors know when they'll be in the office. Few journalists work from 9 to 5. Usually, they work a combination of scheduled and "floating" hours. As a reporter, for example, you might be scheduled to cover a day-long meeting on Monday and spend the evening writing several stories about it, then work eight hours a day Tuesday and Wednesday and half a day Thursday, writing various feature and follow-up stories. You could have all day Friday off to help your best friend move, then work Saturday from 10 a.m. to 7 p.m. (At some papers, reporters take turns covering weekend shifts, so this would work out nicely.)
- It's almost a sure thing that you will work with funny people. Something about seeing human frailties and foibles up close, day in, day out, and working under deadline pressure draws funny quips out of even the most serious journalists.
- The more you write, the easier it gets and the faster you can write — and type. Think of it: If your job was to write stories for eight (or more) hours a day, on deadline, don't you think you'd get pretty fast after a while? If you ever then decided to go to graduate school, experience as a journalist would make writing a thesis or dissertation *much* easier. And maybe you've already noticed how many books are written by people who once worked for daily newspapers.

• The skills you hone in journalism — interviewing, researching, writing, editing, page layout and graphic design — are skills you can take into many other fields. In this era of frequent career changes, working in any form of journalism — whether print, broadcast or online — will give you skills that are transferable to other media as well as to many other occupations.

If all that sounds good to you, you're in the right class. If you aren't so sure, you're probably still in the right class, because what you will learn here will help you, as a media consumer, clarify your understanding of what good journalism is and how it can be achieved. As a citizen, it will help you understand how the media works, in case you ever want to make suggestions or write a letter to the editor about what reporters should cover and how, or to ask journalists' help in getting out a message about an event or an organization that matters to you.

Make no mistake: A *career* in journalism isn't for everyone. If you like structure and routine, the sometimes chaotic hours of journalism could test your sanity. If you slave over every word you write and become so attached to what you've written that you can't stand the thought of it being edited, you'd probably find it hard to adjust to life as a reporter. And if you enjoy writing lengthy academic papers, you might find the conversational writing style and length restrictions in journalism annoying.

But a *class* in journalism — that's another matter. As citizens, it's important for all of us to be aware of the essential role journalists play in our democracy; to know why we should protect the freedom of the press; to understand how we, as consumers, can assess whether a news report is accurate, fair and balanced; and to see how the many choices journalists make — whom to interview, which facts and quotes to include in a story and how the story is framed — can shape our understanding of what's happening around us.

These are areas worth knowing about, no matter what career you pursue.

CHERYL GIBBS
Earlham College

TO THE INSTRUCTOR (including editors who teach in their newsrooms)

Yup, it's another beginning textbook on reporting. If you teach journalism, either in the classroom or the newsroom, you've probably read at least a dozen of 'em, looking for just the right one — which is probably why you're reading this one.

So we'll cut to the chase and tell you how — and why — this book is different.

Both of us began our teaching careers in newsrooms, as editors. And both of us have interviewed many young job applicants who know how to write perfect inverted pyramid stories and lively features, but not as many who know why it's important to write those stories in the first place. Many are well-trained in the craft of journalism, but too few have an understanding of the important role journalists serve in our democracy. Ask them what journalists do, and they'll tell you they inform the public — which is certainly true. But as any good media lawyer or political scientist would tell you, journalists also play an essential role in sustaining our democratic way of life. And any good media critic or researcher would add that journalists don't just inform, they interpret, no matter how diligently they strive to report the news accurately, objectively and fairly. Reporters' interpretations influence how other people see the world and live their lives — but most young reporters don't understand that. They don't see how much is at stake in the work they plan to do.

Our hunch is that this lack of understanding is an indirect result of a natural tendency of educators to divide learning into manageable chunks, to separate theory from practice. In many journalism programs, students take an introductory course that gives them an overview of "the media" and touches on some of the issues we noted above. Students then spend most of the rest of their college journalism careers perfecting various aspects of their craft and developing a working knowledge of media law. By the time editors interview them for their first internship or job, those important issues have faded into the dim recesses of their memory.

Because of these curricular divisions, many beginning textbooks on reporting are excellent, extremely detailed "how-to" guides for developing the craft of journalism, rich with pointers and examples designed to help students master the finer points of reporting, beat coverage and news writing. These books leave it to other texts to cover the "whys" of journalism.

Our goal was to create a textbook that puts the "whys" of journalism together with the "hows." We have included sufficient "how-to" information on developing basic journalism skills, but we also discuss the journalist's role, the importance of press freedom and many ethical concerns that come up in day-to-day reporting. Additionally, we address changes in professional values and practices that have occurred in response to concerns among both journalists and nonjournalists about declining credibility in news coverage. Chapter

4 (The Community as a Context for the News), and Chapter 7 (Framing News Stories), reflect our most significant efforts in this area.

We also were guided by the lessons we have learned over the years working and teaching in newsrooms and classrooms, and through reading we have done about experiential education methods.

Because we believe that learning is most likely to occur when students build on what they already know, we wanted to create a textbook that serves as a bridge between what students have learned in the past about writing and journalism and what they will learn in early journalism classes.

One of the biggest obstacles to good news writing is changing the academic writing habits that have been instilled in students from the time they wrote their first research papers. In the newsroom, we have seen even experienced reporters fall back into those academic writing habits on occasion. In the classroom, we have learned that drawing clear distinctions between the conventions of academic and journalistic writing, as we do in Chapter 3: How News Writing Is Different, is an effective way to increase awareness and adoption of news writing techniques among newcomers to journalism.

In keeping with the "building on experience" theme, we also wanted to write a textbook that would incorporate specific classroom-tested exercises and experiences intended to lead students to significant discoveries and profoundly influence the way they cover the news. No exercise has resulted in more epiphanies for students than the "beat report" exercises "Learning from Experience: Community Knowledge" that follow Chapter 4. Not only do these exercises give students a greater understanding of the community they're writing about, they also help students to overcome some of their stereotypes about others and to uncover great story ideas.

Because we believe that the best journalists are constantly seeking to grow and improve, we wanted to write a textbook that instills in young reporters the need to balance the ability to think and act quickly on deadline with the ability to think and act in a more leisurely, reflective way when not on deadline. At several points in the book, we draw on the Quaker tradition of queries, or sets of questions, designed to foster thoughtful consideration of what we're doing and why. We use queries most heavily in the chapter on framing news stories, as a way of increasing students' awareness of just how many choices they make in reporting and writing about the events they cover, what their options are and how their choices shape both the story itself and its impact on the people who read it.

Because we believe many capable, committed journalists are out there, we introduce you to many of them in these chapters and provide samples of their work.

Because we believe that learning should be fun, we have tried to spice up the text by creating two fictional reporters — Jack Cutter and Jyll Upright — who make the most common mistakes of inexperienced reporters. We also have included optional readings and exercises throughout the book because we think they are especially good selections and we know that it often helps to give students supplementary articles to support what they've read in the basic text.

Because we both have print journalism backgrounds, and because most college journalists learn basic reporting skills by writing first for their campus newspapers, we have focused on sharing what we know and have not attempted to reach beyond our expertise.

But most of all, because we both love journalism, we wanted to write a book that would make it easier for all of us in classrooms and newsrooms to help bright young journalists "get it." We welcome your feedback.

CHERYL GIBBS
Earlham College

TOM WARHOVER
University of Missouri

Chapter 1

The Journalist's
Role in Society

Reporters often get special access to places and people in the news. Here, reporter Catherine Kozak of The (Norfolk) Virginian-Pilot got to take a look underneath the Cape Hatteras Lighthouse during the structure's move.

Photo by Drew Wilson. Source: The Virginian-Pilot

Key Concepts

- Journalists record and report the ongoing story of life in the community, state and country where they live.

- They provide valuable information that alerts people to events, opportunities, problems, possibilities and the meaning of those developments.

- They provide a "public space" for people to share perspectives and work through challenges.

- They play a key role in maintaining our democratic freedoms.

Journalists have a great job.

People open their lives and often bare their most important secrets to journalists. Politicians and people in power love to hate reporters but rarely refuse to return their calls. Doors open to writers armed with nothing more powerful than pen and paper or television camera or tape recorder. Reporters come seeking the truth, or facts or thought-provoking quotes to use in trying to convince their editors or producers that a particular story is worth printing. They work to become experts in what their stories are about — for a day or a week or a year — before moving on to become experts at something else. They listen and are listened to. They have the power to start wars and to end them, to make people famous and infamous, and to build communities and tear them down.

"What can I say about journalism?" journalist and novelist John Steinbeck once wrote. "It has the greatest virtue and the greatest evil. It is the first thing a dictator controls. It is the mother of literature and the perpetrator of crap. In many cases it is the only history we have and yet it is the tool of the worst men. But over a long period of time and because it is the product of so many men [and women], it is perhaps the purest thing we have. Honesty has a way of creeping into it even when it was not intended."

Our laws protect both the worst and the best examples of journalism, because the early leaders of our country understood how important it is in a democracy to allow the free exchange of ideas, including disagreement with those in positions of power.

Ironically, some of the worst journalism has made possible some of the best. In 1931, for example, long before the phrase "hate speech" was coined, officials in Minneapolis, Minn., tried to stop the publication of a tabloid that accused the Minneapolis police chief of failure to pursue an alleged "Jewish gangster" who was said to control numerous illegal activities in the city. The article went on to say, "Practically every vendor of vile hooch, every owner of a moonshine still, every snake-faced gangster and embryonic egg in the Twin Cities is a JEW." But the U.S. Supreme Court ruled that the state of Minnesota could not stop the publication.

In delivering the court's opinion on the case, Chief Justice Charles Evans Hughes wrote: "The fact that liberty of the press may be abused by miscreant purveyors of scandal does not make any the less necessary the immunity of the press from previous restraint in dealing with official misconduct."

That case set a precedent that, 40 years later, protected journalists working for The New York Times when the Supreme Court allowed the publication of the "Pentagon Papers," a secret government document that purported to show double-dealing and lying by officials during the Vietnam War.

Most of the time, journalists' stories are accurate. Still, from time to time, journalists get it wrong, most often through carelessness, ineptitude or arrogance rather than maliciousness or conspiracy.

Yet people respond to journalists. People open their hearts and minds. They unlock all manner of records, public and sometimes private. They invite reporters into their homes, businesses, places of worship and other gathering places.

Why?

Because journalists are the diarists of American democracy. They tell stories that make up the daybook of our common experience.

JOURNALISM AS STORYTELLING

The best of American journalism is consummate storytelling.

"Make it sing," longtime Virginia newspaper editor Ronald L. Speer often told reporters as they worked on their stories.

The "it" that sings might be a story about a person, or a neighborhood, or a city, or a state or a country. It might be a small feature story about a spelling bee tucked in the back of a newspaper's "Lifestyles" or "People" section or the lead story about the dramatic rescue of injured plane crash victims on tonight's newscast. The story celebrates the human condition: It makes us feel as though we were there, or leaves us outraged, elated, inspired or unsettled.

The reporter captures the deeper, often conflicted feelings we have about important issues — issues about which we have strong opinions, are deeply torn or have no idea what to think. The reporter writes the whole story, covering not just two sides, but all points of view.

We walk away from the story enriched in some way. It helps us to better educate or understand our kids, or take action in our city, or have a stimulating conversation over the backyard fence.

"The goal for the reporter," says Roy Peter Clark of the Poynter Institute for Media Studies, "is then not unlike the one [English novelist and short-story writer] Joseph Conrad described for the artist: 'My task which I am trying to achieve,' writes Conrad, 'is, by the power of the written word, to make you hear, to make you feel — it is, before all, to make you see. That — and no more, and it is everything. If I succeed, you shall find there according to your desserts: encouragement, consolation, fear, charm — all you demand — and perhaps, also that glimpse of truth for which you have forgotten to ask.'"

The very best of American journalism happens only rarely. Constrictions of time and space conspire against greatness. Daily newspapers publish the equivalent of a book every day, 365 days a year. Television and radio stations produce three or more news shows in just 24 hours. Editors and producers expect reporters to write on a daily basis. But, for all the stories they produce, there's little space or air time — stories in your local newspaper may have fewer words than are on this page, and radio or television reports rarely last longer than a few minutes.

The people who read and watch the work of journalists have little time to fit the news into their day. Studies show that most readers merely skim through their daily newspaper, reading very few of the stories through to the end. If they were to read the paper cover to cover, it could take hours.

Most journalism, then, is just like life — the truly interesting, unusual, surprising or shocking moments stand out from the more mundane or predictable events. Most journalism tells us things like, "The city council voted last night ..." or "A new bank president was appointed today ..."

The worst of American journalism distorts our common experience. It tells us rumors about celebrities' private lives or promises we'll lose 20 pounds in just four weeks on some new diet; it gives us the graphic details of the wrecked and the wretched; it distorts reality by giving us the illusionist's version of the truth with just enough fact to draw us in; and it lies not by spreading false statements so much as by cutting out that which makes the event whole and real and reflective of those who experienced it.

And still people respond.

Why?

Because journalists do more than create a diary of daily life. They also provide information that helps people improve their lives and the lives of their communities. They tell people what's going on in their cities or towns, their states, the nation and the world. They tell people about a neighbor receiving an award or retiring, or about a stranger who has opened a new business or has been charged with a crime. They provide information about interesting events or activities taking place on the weekend. They tell people when government officials and others are making decisions that could affect them — and about ways to influence those decisions. They provide information about problems in the community and about options for dealing with those problems.

JOURNALISM AS INFORMATION

The best of American journalism ferrets out information and presents it in clear, well-written stories. Sometimes, it seems deceptively simple: a straightforward story about changes in drivers' license laws, or an amusing feature about children using toy "Star Wars" light sabers to lead customers from a darkened department store during a power outage. Sometimes, it's much more complicated; making sense of confusing public issues and problems, then boiling them down into reports that people not only understand but act upon.

In a typical day, a journalist might write a story about a new theater company, a court hearing, a government meeting, or a local writer whose book will soon be published. In a not-so-typical day, the reporter might uncover corruption in the mayor's office, in the state Capitol or at the White House, or write about the aftermath of a tornado or other disaster.

Journalists report not just what happened but *why* and *how*. Stories about the troop movements in Afghanistan or Bosnia, for instance, are not complete unless they also explain the decisions behind shifting those soldiers.

From interviews and other research, journalists gather information that allows them to shed light on issues little known or little understood — like changing teen pregnancy rates or embezzlement by public officials. Reporters, photographers and editors set an agenda for public discussion of important issues in their communities that are sometimes unpleasant or difficult to deal with.

Journalists also keep powerful people honest. Perhaps the most famous example occurred when the integrity of former President Richard M. Nixon was called into question. Washington Post reporters Carl Bernstein and Bob Woodward revealed that the president had been involved in covering up a burglary of the Democratic Party headquarters in the Watergate Hotel in the early 1970s. Nixon eventually resigned in the face of impeachment proceedings. Some have said the Watergate story inspired many overzealous imitators, leading to widespread criticism of the media for sensationalism. However, both the public and the media continue to value journalism that uncovers real problems in our society and suggests solutions for these problems.

The best journalism always reflects citizens' aspirations for their communities to become better places to live and work, for government to work for the people, for democracy to give voice to people of all stripes and colors and opinions. "In its own way, the press — as part of the information and communication system of today's civilization — is a soul of the soul of all mankind," says Vaclav Havel, a playwright and dissident who became president of the Czech Republic. "It is a medium of self-understanding."

The worst American journalism panders to prurient interests and entertains at the expense of others. At the very worst, it fabricates an agenda only to sell newspapers. The Spanish-American War occurred in 1898 after two New York newspapers overdramatized Spanish injustices in Cuba. The term that was applied to their overzealous stories — "yellow journalism" — is still used today in describing overblown newspaper or television stories. Author Anne Lamott describes this phenomenon using a different metaphor: "Watching the media whip the small fires into giant forest fires so they can cover the result is infuriating."

And, while some people have simply tuned out, most people still want a media that is responsive. They haven't given up on journalists or supported restrictions on the freedom of the press in the more than 200 years of this country's history.

Why?

Because journalists do more than provide information. They provide a public space to keep the conversation going. They help people work through problems.

JOURNALISM AS CONVERSATION

James Carey, a highly regarded journalism professor at New York City's Columbia University, describes journalism as "the conversation of our culture." It embodies an ongoing public dialogue among the citizens, experts and officials quoted in news stories, and the writers whose views are published on newspapers' opinion pages.

Why It's Called "Yellow" Journalism

The phrase "yellow journalism" was coined in the late 1890s to describe the sensationalism that raged during a fierce competition between two New York City newspapers.

After purchasing the New York Journal in 1895, William Randolph Hearst soon was clearly trying to outdo Joseph Pulitzer's New York World, which at the time had the largest circulation in the country. Each paper fought to boost its readership through sensational reporting and crusades against political corruption and social injustice.

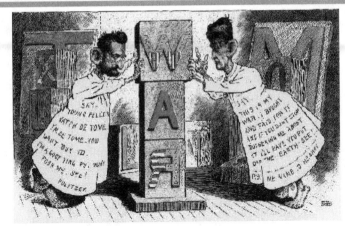

This cartoon, originally published about 1898, depicts New York Journal publisher William Randolph Hearst and rival Joseph Pulitzer of the New York World duking it out over coverage of the Spanish-American War. Each wears a yellow nightshirt like that worn by R.F. Outcault's cartoon character "The Yellow Kid," over which the two publishers also fought.

Source: The Richard D. Olson Collection

It was the first time newspapers used banner headlines, colored comics and abundant illustrations. A color reproduction test for a comic strip eventually led to the phrase "yellow journalism." An urchin drawn by Richard Outcault was printed wearing a bright yellow nightshirt in Pulitzer's paper in 1896. The boy was named "The Yellow Kid," catchy messages began appearing on the nightshirt, and the car-toon became enormously popular.

Later that year, Hearst hired Outcault away from Pulitzer. Pulitzer then hired Outcault back, then Hearst hired him away again. The competition over Outcault became a metaphor for the unscrupulous and sensational journalism that came to be known as "yellow."

Source: "Encyclopaedia Britannica Online"

The best of American journalism doesn't explain a problem or issue and then leap to another and another and another. It follows important developments over time, offering information about what's at stake, how people can get involved, and how well the community is doing as a whole. Responsible journalists see themselves as providing a service akin to a town square — a place to hear many opinions and to advance the debate of the day, a place where people can listen and be listened to, a place where considered judgments are made.

The best journalists do this by viewing their audience as people who can interact with the information in their stories, not just members of a market or consumers of information. These journalists' stories describe not only a problem but also where people stand in the process of solving it and what others have done in other times or places to solve similar problems. These reporters recognize that difficult problems don't have perfect solutions; rather, citizens usually must follow a path that meanders and forks through several possible solutions, with failures scattered along the way.

Author Daniel Yankelovich describes this kind of process as a bumpy road from snap opinion to public judgment. Yankelovich believes it's not enough to have information from experts at our disposal; real solutions in a community only come when its members have the opportunity to work through the competing values behind the facts. The best journalists envision their job as creating a public space for deliberation about important issues, not as providing a dividing line that forces people to move to one side or another. They know things are rarely that simple.

When journalists view their work as a catalyst for conversation, public debates are framed not according to who won but according to how the arguments advanced public understanding. Specialized knowledge by experts is valued, but not at the expense of the public's work of making decisions.

In today's hectic world, it's hard to keep our attention focused on one difficult issue or important event. Each new page of the daybook rapidly fills up with diverse problems. Journalists and citizens alike grow bored and restless for something new to capture their attention.

Still, people see journalists as holding jobs that are important not only to each of us as individuals but to the lives of our communities. Cole Campbell, a longtime newspaper editor, has likened journalism to "a three-legged stool" — its "feet" planted in a triangle that provides a steady foundation no matter what the terrain. In his analogy, the legs that support the stool are made of powerful storytelling, tenacious information gathering and the thoughtful nurturing of the conversations of our times. And he insists that these qualities are essential to our country.

Why?

Because democracy without journalism is no democracy at all.

JOURNALISM'S ROLE IN DEMOCRATIC LIFE

James Carey, addressing an incoming class of students, put it this way: "Here you will study the practice of journalism. Not the media. Not the news business. Not the newspaper or the magazine or the

Cartoon by John S. Pritchett

television station but the practice of journalism. There are media everywhere. Every despot creates his own system of media. There is a news business everywhere; there just isn't all that much journalism, for there can be no journalism without the aspiration for or institutions of democratic life."

The three legs of the stool, then — storytelling, information gathering and conversation — may support a seat called journalism, but it is democracy that sits upon it.

Something more than a desire for professional excellence drives the best of American journalism. The excellent journalists of our day master the techniques of the three-legged stool *for a reason*: They want to help people make their city and state and nation a better place. They know it's not enough to leave that task to elected politicians, and they know the health of our democracy depends on citizen participation.

People who travel abroad are often struck by how the news is reported in other countries. The difference is most apparent in countries where government-controlled media serve as a propaganda machine, framing every story so that the government is presented in the best possible light.

During the conflict that led to the 1999 NATO bombing campaign in Yugoslavia, for example, Serb officials waged war against the independent press as well as against ethnic Albanians. Many local radio and television stations closed rather than submit to government control or pay huge fines under a state-of-war declaration. Two newspaper reporters were jailed on charges of "spreading false information." Their paper, which had been critical of Yugoslav President Slobodan Milosevic and other Serbian officials, was banned in Serbia, and the paper's owner and editor-in-chief was gunned down in front of his home after government-owned media launched a campaign that accused him of "welcoming NATO bombs."

Even in countries without government-controlled media, journalists often face restrictions and dangers that are unimaginable to journalists in the United States. Journalists in many countries whose constitutions contain lofty words about press freedom have long been the victims of violence and threats. From 1986 through 1999, 55 Colombian journalists were murdered in reprisal for their reporting of events and actions others did not want known, according to the Committee to Protect Journalists in New York City. Drug traffickers were believed to have killed most of the journalists, but attacks have come from all sides, including corrupt politicians, leftist guerrillas, right-wing paramilitaries, and landowners, the organization said.

News organizations in many countries also have faced advertising boycotts and lawsuits designed to intimidate them into silence,

Journalism Dangerous in Many Countries

The tragic death of Wall Street Journal reporter Daniel Pearl drove home the dangers to journalists in other countries, but his was not an isolated case.

The Committee to Protect Journalists documented more than 500 cases of media repression in 140 countries in 2001 — including 37 journalists killed as a direct result of their work, up from 24 in 2002.

Eight journalists were killed covering the United States-led military campaign in Afghanistan, according to CPJ's "Attacks on the Press in 2001," released in March 2002. Many other journalists there were assaulted or censored.

However, most of those who died were not covering conflicts but were murdered in reprisal for reporting on such things as crime and corruption in Bangladesh, China, Thailand, Yugoslavia, and other countries.

In addition, the number of journalists in prison rose for the first time in five years, from 81 in 2000 to 118 in 2001. China added eight journalists to its prisons, bringing the total number of journalists behind bars there to 35.

Most chilling for many journalists was the ripple effect set in motion by U.S. State Department efforts to censor interviews with Al-Queda leaders.

"If the most celebrated democracies in the world won't allow their national interests to be tampered with, we will not allow it, too," Zimbabwean information minister Jonathan Moyo said. He then denounced as "terrorists" the country's independent journalists. Other countries also invoked national security in restricting or intimidating journalists.

Source: Committee to Protect Journalists

The Journalists Memorial, located near the Freedom Forum Newseum, honors reporters, editors, photographers and broadcasters who gave their lives reporting the news.

Photo by James P. Blair. Source: Newseum

according to the Freedom Forum, a foundation that supports press liberty.

By contrast, journalists in the United States enjoy an unparalleled degree of freedom, and no agency or officials regulate journalism's unique role in American democracy. The First Amendment to the Constitution gives the media vast freedoms without corresponding responsibilities:

> Congress shall make no law respecting an establishment of religion, or prohibiting the free exercise thereof; or abridging the freedom of speech, or of the press; or the right of the people peaceably to assemble, and to petition the Government for a redress of grievances.

Note that the amendment prescribes what Congress can't do, not what journalism *should* do. And yet, from the earliest debates and writings about the country, it was presumed that journalism would serve an important role in democracy. That tradition has served as an underpinning for two centuries of American journalism.

Thomas Jefferson, who wrote the Declaration of Independence and the Virginia Statute for Religious Freedom, said, "[The press] is the best instrument for enlightening the mind of man." He and the other founders of our country saw the importance of a citizenry that was informed on the issues of the day.

It wasn't as if they had any great love for the press; politicians in the 1700s were as pilloried by sharp-tongued editors as they are today. Still, they saw the press as a check on potential abuses of power in our government — the "watchdog role" — and, while it is not legislated that they perform this role, journalists hold it as a sacred trust.

Jefferson saw another purpose for the press: that of acting as a connector among government institutions, the civic sphere and private life. It is the people — the citizens — who hold the promise for America's continuing experiment in democracy. "I know no safe depository of the ultimate powers of the society but the people themselves," Jefferson said, "and if we think them not enlightened enough to exercise their control with a wholesome discretion, the remedy is not to take it from them, but to inform their discretion."

In today's world, Jefferson's definition of "the people" would include doctors trying to keep their heads above all the paperwork; middle-aged line workers on the graveyard shift; young mothers struggling to find time for both home and work; politicians and political handlers; even people who don't read the newspaper or listen to or watch newscasts. All of them need information to carry out their role in our democracy with "wholesome discretion."

These journalistic roles — watchdogs against government abuses and providers of information that connects government, civic and private spheres — fit the unique nature of American democracy, which depends on both representative democracy and something more basic: people governing themselves. David Mathews, the president of the Charles F. Kettering Foundation, a research organization that focuses on citizen politics, saw those two forms of democracy as interdependent. "Americans may have combined, in practice, two types of government that appear contradictory in theory: citizen democracy and representative government."

Consider, for example, how the two types of government can play out in the coverage of elections. Traditionally, journalists have covered campaigns as events in which citizens choose people to represent their interests in local, state and national governments. As part of that coverage, they have carried out their watchdog role by monitoring candidates' advertisements for false or misleading claims, checking the candidates' credentials and background, analyzing campaign finances and comparing the candidates' positions. The goal of that coverage is to help citizens make the best decision as to who can best represent them. But something else occurs during an election season, something that good journalists also cover:

Important concerns of citizens are aired in discussions about the election. Conversations occur about the most critical issues of the day.

"Democracy requires a lot more of us than being intelligent voters," Frances Moore Lappé and Paul Martin DuBois wrote in "The Quickening of America." "It requires that we learn to solve problems with others — that we learn to listen, to negotiate, and to evaluate. To think and speak effectively. To go beyond simple protest in order to wield power, become partners in problem solving. This isn't about so-called good work. It's about our vital interest."

Tony Germanotta, an editor at The (Norfolk) Virginian-Pilot, advises journalists to choose what to cover based on the answers to two questions: "Does it help the citizens decide? Does it advance the conversation?"

New York University professor Jay Rosen describes this type of democratic participation as the difference between "decision" and "discussion." In the 1996 presidential election, for instance, "Decision '96" played out in the choice to reelect President Bill Clinton. But "Discussion '96" also occurred: Journalists reported that people were talking about the declining standard of living and disappearing economic opportunity and security, the loss of the "American Dream," the rising number of absentee parents and the disintegrating values among young people. Candidates did not address many of these issues until journalists brought them to the fore.

It is important, then, for journalists to report on both the decisions and the discussions that are part of our democratic way of life in ways that foster widespread deliberation among citizens and candidates alike.

Why?

Because these deliberations are as important for our future as what happens in the voting booths.

THE CONVERSATION OF A NEWSROOM

These basic beliefs about the importance of journalism to our democracy are — or at least should be — deeply ingrained in journalists. But you won't hear much intellectual conversation about democracy or citizenship when you enter most newsrooms in America. Instead you'll hear people like Ron Speer.

Speer made a habit of waking up a lethargic newsroom by wandering around and prodding reporters out of their quiet reflections with his gravelly voice, saying, "It's a great day for the race." When asked what race, Speer would respond: "The human race."

He Traveled the World as a Journalist

Speer wore his suspenders around the newsroom of The (Norfolk) Virginian-Pilot for more than 20 years. He looked with suspicion on people with advanced academic degrees, and he believed that newspapers should hire more people who like to go bowling.

Speer didn't walk five miles through the snow to get to school. He rode a horse.

Speer was born in a sod house on the plains of Nebraska. From such humble surroundings, he went on to become a reporter, columnist and editor at papers including the Des Moines Register, St. Petersburg Times and The Virginian-Pilot. He has written for national magazines ranging from The Catholic Digest to Playboy, and traveled the world as a reporter for the Associated Press (AP).

For the AP, Speer covered big-time sports — the first major-league baseball game in the South, the Masters golf tournament, the 1968 Olympics in Mexico City — and history-making events in the civil rights movement of the 1960s. He interviewed Martin Luther King Jr. and five U.S. presidents. He talked with Soviet Premier Nikita Khruschev in the cornfields of Iowa.

His work as an editor at The Virginian-Pilot may have more lasting impact than any story he ever wrote. Speer believed that "newspapering" was fun and passed that conviction on to many reporters he helped train. His protégés are now reporting and editing for The Washington Post, The Los Angeles Times, The Philadelphia Inquirer and many other major newspapers. His achievements at the Pilot included directing the coverage of an economic development director gone astray; that months'-long investigation won a Pulitzer Prize for reporter Tom Turcol.

Speer finished his official career as general manager for the Pilot's North Carolina operations. He retired there on Carolina's Outer Banks, where he still writes a column weekly, gardens daily spring through fall, sails occasionally, and volunteers with several charitable organizations regularly.

Speer knew the conversation of the newsroom. He was an old-fashioned newspaper editor, the kind for whom the term "newspaperman" might still apply. He knew how to create the daybook of his community through great storytelling, solid news gathering and columns that nudged a sometimes sleepy city to wake up and keep talking through its problems and promises. He knew that covering a community "warts and all" meant knowing the size of the wart in relation to the size of the hand. He knew that, for each scofflaw, corrupt official or inept bureaucrat, there were 10 quiet heroes in and out of government.

He knew the song of his community because he was part of that community. Every Sunday morning, he held court at the local diner. He would go anywhere and do anything when asked, whether it was attending a quilting bee or stopping by the mayor's office.

And he knew that it was promise that drove him to work every day: the promise of a young reporter beginning to blossom; the promise of a great investigative story that would outrage his city or a well-told yarn that would make people laugh; the promise that his newspaper would have an impact.

Most days it didn't happen. But it's the idea of achieving a "more perfect union" that leads citizens and journalists like Speer to constantly search for a better answer.

EXERCISES

JOURNALISM AS STORYTELLING

1. Look through newspapers or magazines until you find a story you think is particularly well written. Think about why the story moved you, what makes the writing compelling, what purpose the journalist may have had in mind for writing the story, and what universal significance the story might have.

2. Look through newspapers until you find a story that seems sensationalized, biased or distorted in some way. (It may help to include supermarket tabloids in your search.) Analyze what makes the story seem distorted. For example, did the reporter convey innuendo by particular word choices? Did the reporter quote questionable or anonymous sources? Was important information omitted?

3. Think about the last spirited conversation you had with someone about an issue that affects lots of people. Try to remember if anyone told personal stories during the conversation, and if they mentioned specific ways in which they are affected by that issue. How could those stories be used as examples in a news story about that issue?

4. Talk to friends about how most news stories are written, then brainstorm with them about how certain stories could be written in much more interesting ways. Develop those ideas into a list of tips for reporters who want to make their stories more interesting.

JOURNALISM AS INFORMATION

1. Go to the library and compare two different newspapers. Look for differences and similarities, things you like and dislike about each. Make photocopies of two items from each paper (stories, photographs, informational graphics, elements of the graphic design, etc.) that illustrate the similarities and differences you identified.

2. Go through an issue or a section of a daily newspaper and analyze how the information in each story might be useful to people. For example, what meaning would a story about mortgage rates have for homeowners in the community? How might someone respond to a story about an upcoming community festival or a new restaurant opening? What value would people find in a story about construction delays on a new bridge?

3. Find a story in a newspaper about a coming event. Imagine that you were the reporter who was assigned to write a story. What kind of information would you like to have had in advance? How might you have gotten that information?

4. Talk to people in a public place (a shopping mall, your neighborhood, etc.) about whether — and if so, how — they stay informed about things that are important to them. Encourage them to give you examples of how they found out specific things that were useful or helpful to them.

JOURNALISM AS CONVERSATION

1. Skim through a week's worth of letters to the editor in a daily paper. How many letters are responses to news stories or news developments? How many are responses to other letters to the editor? How many seem unrelated to either local news or other letters? Did you see any published guidelines for letters to the editor? If so, do the guidelines seem reasonable? Why or why not?

2. If your local paper has a call-in line or e-mail bulletin board that allows people to make anonymous comments that are then printed, compare the anonymous comments in letters to the editor or local columns. Do the tone or content differ from one to the other? Do certain topics or comments come up more in one place or the other? Did you see any published guidelines for anonymous comments? If so, what are they?

3. Choose an issue about which you feel strongly. Plan what you would say if you were to write a letter to the editor, what facts you might use to support your argument, what kind of tone you would take in writing the letter, and what the purpose of the letter would be (for example, to persuade someone to adopt your point of view, to open a discussion about something, or to bring something to light).

4. Think of an issue you've seen covered in the news lately and talk to friends about it. After you're done talking, take time to think about the conversation. Were you and your friends clear and absolute about your positions on the issue? Or were there areas in which you felt ambivalent or conflicted? Once you've given this some thought, find newspaper stories covering the issue. Do those stories reflect the full range of positions you and your friends expressed, as well as the areas you were concerned about?

JOURNALISM'S ROLE IN DEMOCRATIC LIFE

1. Think of your mental picture of how our democracy works. Where and how do journalists participate in our democratic system? Where and how do citizens participate? Where and how do public officials and other influential people participate? Who holds what kinds of power in our democracy? What are the responsibilities that go along with that power? As a citizen, how have you been helped by information provided by journalists? Has this information influenced your views about political candidates, public issues or significant events? How has that information affected your actions?

2. Pick a country that is not a democracy. Find out what type of government the country has, who owns the major media organizations, how much freedom journalists have to report about problems, and whether journalists there have been the targets of threats or violence. If journalists' freedom is limited, what are the restrictions? If the government owns the media, does it control news content? If so, how? If journalists there have been threatened, hurt or killed, why were they were endangered? By whom?

3. Think about what kind of information you, as a citizen, would like to have at various points in a political campaign. Think about why that information would be important to you. What would you want to know about the candidates? What would you want to know about their supporters?

What kinds of things would you want reporters to write about? How often would you want them to cover the campaign? Create a timeline and map out when you would like to get what information, starting with the time the first person announces his or her candidacy.

4. Have a conversation with someone from another country about the media in each of your countries, what you like and dislike about the media, and how important you think freedom of the press is to the well-being of citizens. Go to the library (together, if possible) and read newspapers from each other's countries. Go over the newspapers together, looking for similarities and differences.

FURTHER READING

On the Web

The Annenberg Public Policy Center, Media and the Dialogue of Democracy: http://appcpenn.org/democracy/

The Center for Democracy and Technology: www.cdt.org

Committee to Protect Journalists: www.cpj.org

Freedom Forum Web site: www.freedomforum.org

International Federation of Journalists: www.ifj.org

Joan Shorenstein Center on the Press, Politics and Public Policy at Harvard's John F. Kennedy School of Government: http://ksgwww.harvard.edu/~presspol/

In Print

JOURNALISM AS STORYTELLING

"Best Newspaper Writing 2001: The Nation's Best Journalism," anthology edited by Keith Woods, published by The Poynter Institute for Media Studies, St. Petersburg, Fla., and Bonus Books, Chicago. (Issued annually)

JOURNALISM AS INFORMATION

"Mightier Than the Sword: How the News Media Have Shaped American History," by Rodger Streitmatter, published by Westview Press, Boulder, Colo., 1998.

"From Milton to McLuhan: The Ideas Behind American Journalism," by J. Herbert Altschull, published by Addison-Wesley, Reading, Mass., 1990.

JOURNALISM AS CONVERSATION

"The Conversation of Journalism: Communication, Community and News," by Rob Anderson, Robert Dardenne and George Killenberg. Published by Greenwood, New York, 1996.

"Letters to the Editor: Two Hundred Years in the Life of an American Town," edited by Gerard Stropnicky, Tom Byrn, James Goode and Jerry Matheny, published by Touchstone, New York, 1998.

JOURNALISM'S ROLE IN DEMOCRATIC LIFE

"Breaking the News: How the Media Undermine American Democracy," by James Fallows, published by Vintage Books, New York, 1997.

"Politics for People: Finding a Responsible Public Voice," by David Mathews, published by the University of Illinois Press, Urbana and Chicago, 1994.

"The Quickening of America," by Frances Moore Lappé and Paul Martin DuBois, published by Jossey-Bass, San Francisco, 1994.

INTERNATIONAL JOURNALISM

"Global Journalism: Survey of International Communication," edited by John C. Merrill, published by Addison-Wesley, Reading, Mass., 1995.

"News of a Kidnapping," by Gabriel Garcia Marquez, Alfred A. Knopf, New York, 1997.

Something to Think About:
The Loneliness
of the Street-Corner Orator

... American journalists and intellectuals have been traveling east in order to teach [the] newly liberated peoples [of Eastern Europe] the practical arts of writing a First Amendment, managing a modern newspaper or television station, or, more elementary yet, writing and editing Western-style journalism. We regularly assume these days that we have something to export to [them]. We are less open to the thought that we might have something to learn from them, that they might teach us something about democracy and civic culture. This curious astigmatism results from the fact that we assume that the liberation of the people of Eastern Europe resulted from something we did on their behalf and not from the internal dynamics of their own efforts. ...

Despite living under regimes almost as oppressive as that described by [George] Orwell [in "1984"], East Europeans, in country after country, managed to create a free public life. They had no help from the press; in fact, the press was their enemy. They created a life that, though it was submerged and clandestine, preserved, maintained, and developed public discourse, argument and debate. ...

We [in the United States] value, or so we say, the First Amendment because it contributes, in Thomas Emerson's formulation, four things to our common life. It is a method of assuring our own self-fulfillment; it is a means of attaining the truth; it is a method of securing participation of members of society in political decision making; and it is a means of maintaining balance between stability and change. ...

It is the third of Emerson's clauses, the clumsily expressed notion of political participation, that is critical here. If we think of the First

Note: This is an excerpt from the essay "A Republic, If You Can Keep It," by Columbia University Journalism professor James Carey, from "Crucible of Liberty: 200 Years of the Bill of Rights," edited by Raymond Arsenault, published by The Free Press, 1991.

Amendment against the background of recent East Europe experience, the interrelation among its parts becomes clearer. While the First Amendment contains four clauses — religion, speech, press, and assembly — one must think of them less as separate clauses and more as a compact way of describing a political society. In other words, the amendment is not a casual and loose consolidation of high-minded principles. It was an attempt to define the nature of public life [in the United States] as it existed at the time or as the founders [of the country] hoped it would exist. To put it in an artlessly simple way, the amendment says that people are free to gather together without the intrusion of the state or its representatives. Once gathered, they are free to speak openly and fully. They are further free to write down what they have to say and to share it beyond the immediate place of utterance. ...

The important thing about public conversation is that, in an old saw of E.M. Forster's, we don't know what we think until we hear what we say. Conversation not only forms opinions, it forms memory. We remember best the things that we say, the things that we say in response to someone else with whom we are engaged. Talk is the surest guide to remembering and knowing what we think. To take in information passively guarantees that we will remember little and know less, except for a trace of the passion of the moment. And soon we have no interest in information or knowledge at all. If we insist on public conversation as the essence of democratic life, we will come, as Christopher Lasch put it, "to defend democracy, not as the most efficient form of government but as the most educational one, the one that extends the circle of debate as widely as possible and thus asks us all to articulate our views, to put them at risk, and to cultivate the virtues of clarity of thought, of eloquence and sound judgment." ...

A press that encourages the conversation of its culture is the equivalent of an extended town meeting. However, if the press sees its role as limited to informing whoever happens to turn up at the end of the communication channel, it explicitly abandons its role as an agency for carrying on the conversation of the culture. Having embraced [Walter] Lippmann's outlook [on citizens as the object rather than the subject of politics], the press no longer serves to cultivate certain vital habits: the ability to follow an argument, grasp the point of view of another, expand the boundaries of understanding, decide the alternative purposes that might be pursued. A free press is a necessary condition of a free public life, but it is not the same thing as a free public life. If I am right in contending that we should value the press to the precise degree that it sustains public life, that it helps keep the conversation going among us, and that we devalue the press to the degree it seems to inform us and turn us into silent spectators, then there are two diremptions of the central meaning of the First Amendment against which we must be on guard. The first is the tendency of the press to treat us like a client, a group with a childlike dependence and an 8-year-old mind incapable of functioning at all without our daily dose of the news. The historian John

Lukacs has pointed out that one of the things that astonished Europeans about Americans in the 19th century was that we regularly overestimated the intelligence of ordinary men and women. These Europeans felt America expected more from its people than they could deliver. That, of course, was a mistake, but it is infinitely preferable to its opposite, namely, the systematic underestimation of the intelligence of people. Such an underestimation is the contemporary mistake made not only by the press but by all our major institutions — education, government, and business. ...

Second, the press endangers us when it disarms us, when it convinces us that just by sitting at home watching the news or spending an hour with the newspaper, we are actually participating in the affairs that govern our lives. At least the people of Eastern Europe never coined the awkward but apt phrase "narcotizing dysfunction" to describe the condition in which participation in the media becomes confused with participation in public life. ...

Paul L. Murphy noted that the decision in the libel case New York Times vs. Sullivan, and in many parallel cases, was an attempt by the Supreme Court to create a robust society of debate. We have, he concluded, secured freedom of speech for the street-corner orator. Unfortunately, the constituency of that orator is no longer on the corner, listening; it is at home watching television. However, if one looks at voting statistics and other evidence of participation in politics, or examines the knowledge people have of public affairs, or the declining attention to news on television or in print, one must conclude that the political constituency has disappeared altogether. Out there, there is no there there. The press has a great interest in the restoration of this constituency if only to assure its own financial survival. But that constituency will be found neither on the street corner nor in the audience until it has some reason to be in either place. Since there is no public life, there is no longer a public conversation in which to participate, and, because there is no conversation, there is no reason to be better informed and hence no need for information.

Chapter 2

What Journalists Do

Professional basketball player Jon Sundvold tells reporters about retiring University of Missouri head coach Norm Stewart, who was Sundvold's coach in college, at a 1999 press conference.

Photo by Chris Zuppa. Source: Columbia Missourian

▇▇▇▇▇▇▇ Key Concepts ▇▇▇▇▇▇▇

- Journalism is a collaborative enterprise. Many people help to shape the final form of every news story.

- Journalism today exists in many forms, but the basic process of reporting and writing for any medium is the same.

- Journalists in all media choose which news developments to cover and which should be given the most emphasis, based on their assessment of what is most valuable, important and interesting to the people in the communities they serve.

- Good journalists plan ahead, develop routines that help them stay on top of what's happening, and gather information carefully and thoroughly.

So you're thinking about becoming a journalist. You want to write stories that help people know what's going on in their communities, that shed light on society's problems and identify possible solutions, and that engage people with good writing about human triumphs and calamities, interesting people, important events and compelling issues. And — admit it — you wouldn't mind seeing your name on Page 1 of the newspaper, in bold letters, just above the title "staff writer." Or maybe you fantasize about saying your name on the air, just before the call letters of your favorite radio or television station.

Before you go further, consider this: The reporter is just one of several people who will touch the story in ways small and large, and the writing is sometimes the quickest (although most important) part of a reporter's task.

In fact, the final version of your story is never solely the work of the reporter. Many other people help to shape it:

- Assigning editors help reporters decide what to cover and keep track of all the stories in the works.
- City or metro editors and copy editors edit and proofread stories to make sure they contain no missing information or errors.
- Photographers take photos to run with certain stories.
- Graphic artists create charts or other illustrations that also may run with certain stories.

- Designers place stories, photos and illustrations onto the pages of the paper.
- News clerks check facts on occasion and routinely handle press releases and compile information into calendars and other listings.
- Senior editors oversee the entire news operation.

In other settings, such as broadcast or online newsrooms, people in comparable roles influence the final form of each news story.

One of the most exciting aspects of being a journalist now is that journalism can take so many forms. Newspapers, radio and television stations, online publications, magazines, organizations that publish newsletters, desktop publishing firms, book publishing companies, public relations firms — the list of organizations that hire people who know how to prepare a basic news story grows daily.

But no matter what the medium, the basic reporting process is the same: Stay alert to good story ideas, gather information, compile it into stories, then work with others to deliver the story in a way that catches people's attention and reflects the full significance of what happened.

Because of this basic reporting process, and because most beginning journalists start out writing for campus newspapers, this book focuses mainly on how stories are conceived, reported, written and edited in newspaper settings. But the basics we cover are universal. All journalists — print, broadcast or online — must understand the value of a good concept for a story or publication. All must understand the process of gathering information, organizing it logically and using it to write a story that, along with graphic and photographic images or background sounds, grabs and holds a reader, viewer or listener's attention. And all must work within deadlines determined by how often they have committed to presenting their work to the public.

In the case of newspapers, a journalist's work includes stories, headlines, graphics, photographs and newspaper page layouts. The newsroom is only a small part of a larger manufacturing plant that has hundreds of employees at many daily newspapers and thousands of workers at major metropolitan or national newspapers.

A newspaper with an average daily circulation of 200,000 readers might use 120 tons of newsprint to publish each weekday paper on printing presses that are as big as a two-story apartment building. The newsprint comes in rolls that weigh 1,900 pounds each and can be moved only with specialized heavy equipment. The number of newsprint rolls used would double on Sundays, when the paper is bigger and more people buy it.

The newspaper might collect $25 million a year in subscription sales generated by a circulation department that includes telephone marketers making hundreds of calls a week to residents who just got home from work or are getting ready to sit down to the dinner table.

The money from subscriptions, though, will be only a small portion of perhaps a $115 million annual budget. Newspaper subscriptions and sales from newspaper vending machines don't even pay for the cost of the newsprint used to print the paper. Most of the paper's revenue will come from an advertising department that has to sell enough ads to pay the salaries of nearly everyone who works there, as well as the costs of maintaining the building and other expenses.

A DAY IN THE LIFE

You aren't alone if the process of getting a news story into print seems somewhat mystical. To many nonjournalists — even those within the newspaper business — it also seems difficult to understand.

Take this example from a metro newspaper: A reporter wrote a story about a famous author who gave an evening speech at a local university, and the story appeared in the next morning's paper. Later that day, the reporter ran into the publisher, the newspaper's top executive in charge of the entire newspaper operation.

The publisher loved the story, and told the reporter as much. He asked the reporter how he did such a complete story about a talk that was less than 90 minutes long.

The answer: He didn't. Here are the steps he took:

First, he read the author's book. He researched the reviews. He called the author's agent to make an appointment for an interview.

He researched other articles and profiles written about the author. He spent 30 minutes interviewing the author by telephone. He discussed the story with his editor.

He wrote a "budget line" — a brief description that told his editors what the story was about, how long it would be, and whether it would have any photos or illustrations to go with it.

He filled out a form to arrange for a photographer to take photos during the speech. And he wrote a "shirttail" — paragraphs of background material compiled before a late news event, in case there would not be time to do it later.

He did all of that before covering the speech.

The result was a well-rounded story that gave the background and context behind the speech. It was the kind of story that was compelling to people who didn't know of the author as well as those who attended the speech. It was the kind of story the publisher took note of, even if he didn't know exactly how the reporter got it into print.

Of course, there was more that went into the story. The writer was a 25-year veteran reporter who had lived in the community for more than a decade. He knew the issues that were important and the people who were important to those issues. Over the years, he had developed an extensive network of sources, so that he probably knew about this speaker long before the public announcement was made. He also nurtured his working relationships within the newsroom. He convinced his editor the story was worth putting on the front page of one of the local sections of the paper, and his editor convinced other editors it deserved that kind of visibility.

The process of writing a story for a newspaper, then, is different from writing a paper for a class. It involves a lot more people and a lot more interaction between the writer and other people who edit and prepare the writer's story for publication. Journalists also have a much greater obligation to be accurate and thorough, because people depend on them for consistently reliable, understandable information about important developments in their world.

Let's say, for instance, that an election is coming up and a student at your school decides to run for city council. See what it would take and how many people might "touch" that story before you see it in print. ...

2 p.m. — A Story Hits the Radar Screen

Jack Cutter is the local reporter who recently began covering public life. He writes about the activities of local officials, elected and appointed. He covers the deliberations of the city council, trying to ensure that he knows and reports about important issues before the council makes decisions. He checks out tips from sources who might know about corrupt or wasteful practices at city hall. He roams civic league meetings and coffeehouses, listening for stories about people dealing with government.

Much of the job involves following paper trails — city council agendas, budget documents, committee reports, elections disclosure forms and the like — and spending time chatting with his regular sources — high ranking bureaucrats, party officials, secretaries, janitors and anyone else who might help him understand what's going on in the city.

It's election season, so one of his regular stops is the office where candidates file papers to make their candidacy official. Jack swings by the clerk's desk. It's cluttered. Piles of manila folders fill the desk, but the clerk knows where every piece of paper belongs. She's worked in this office for 32 years. She raised three kids on her modest bureaucrat's salary and now is looking forward to retiring. Jack asks about the grandchildren, and the two chat a bit. He eventually asks whether there have been any new election filings. "Just one," the clerk says. "A student at Real Smart University."

Jack's not happy. He usually knows before the official filing. Party officials aren't shy about letting reporters know. And it takes 1,000 signatures on a petition before you can run for council.

He knows he has a story for the next day's newspaper. He also has a lot of work to do. But he is a seasoned journalist, and he's discovered the news with plenty of time to get a fairly complete story — if he hustles.

He asks the clerk what she knows about the student, Jane Curic. Not much. The candidacy papers list an age, an address, a phone number and an occupation (student). That's about it. It's enough to start with.

Jack goes back to the newspaper office and picks up the phone. He starts at the source. Jack congratulates Jane and asks for an interview.

"Sorry," Jane says. "I'm in classes the rest of the day and have a recital tonight. Perhaps this weekend?"

Jack says that won't do; he needs to file a story for tomorrow's paper. Jane's stubborn, but at least Jack gets a few minutes with her by phone and an agreement from her to fax her resumé to the newspaper.

He then contacts other sources. He puts in calls, knowing that he probably won't get through to most of the people he's seeking on the first try. He calls the head of the political science department, because that's Jane's major; the "mom" at Jane's sorority house; the chairman of the Young Republicans campus chapter; and a couple of supporters whose names Jane provided. He begins a list of other people to contact later, if he has time.

He knows he won't be able to tell the "whole story" of Jane Curic on this first day, but he wants to get as much as he can. He wants to understand who she is and why she is running, and he wants to put her campaign in the context of current problems the city is facing.

3 p.m. — The Story Shifts — Not for the Last Time

Candidate Jane Curic is known only to one journalist so far. It won't stay that way for long.

Jack swings over to his assigning editor. She's the leader of a team of "metro" reporters covering local schools, government and public safety in the core city. The metro editor has covered 12 local elections in the past 10 years.

"I've got a new filing," Jack says. "A student at Real Smart U."

"What's a student doing running for council?" the metro editor wants to know.

"Says she's fed up with the current council. Says they don't understand the importance of RSU, or how to deal with the problems between the school and the town."

"Well, that's something to start with," the metro editor says. "We know some real issues exist between the two, and there's a lot at risk. RSU is our largest employer in town, but it also pushes local services to the max. It's likely to be an election issue this year. What else do you have?"

Jack tells her with whom he's talked and from whom he's still waiting to hear. The metro editor suggests they need more background checks. She wants at least a better statement from Curic about what the candidate hopes to accomplish. Jack knows he'll have to call Curic again. What about a photograph? Jack grimaces. If Curic won't cooperate more, he'll have to find a photo from a yearbook, perhaps, or swing by Curic's sorority and ask friends there. The metro editor also asks for a budget line before Jack does anything else; the afternoon budget meeting is in 30 minutes, and she'll need to get this story in play by then.

Jack bangs out what journalists call a "budget line" — a short description of his story:

JCRUN: Yourtown — Jane Curic, a senior majoring in political science at RSU, filed today for a council seat. We've now got six candidates running for two open seats. Curic is 22, with no real political experience (hey, she was student council president, big deal).

What it means: Not much. She doesn't have a snowball's chance of winning. But she could make things real interesting for incumbent Joe Sleaze, if she really pushes her pet issues.

Reporter: Jack Cutter.

Graphics? Info box on the field of candidates.

Photos? Trying for mug.

Length: 15 inches

Deadline to copy desk: 8 p.m.

The metro editor knows that if Jack writes the story the way he wrote the budget line, it will be a long night. She sends Jack an e-mail, asking him to rewrite the budget line. "Take out the sneer," she says. "It's not our job to say who will win at this point. Lay out the facts for the readers and they can decide for themselves. Besides, remember what we just talked about: Curic could have a real impact on the discussion about a big, big issue in this community."

Jack tries again. The new budget line reads: "Yourtown — Jane Curic, a 22-year-old political science major at RSU, has filed for a city council seat, saying she's fed up with the way the current council ignores the city's biggest employer and cultural center. Curic wants more attention and more money for the school, and she wants to do this by winning one of the two open seats on council."

The metro editor likes the new version and sends along the budget line to another editor, who adds it to dozens of others to form that day's budget of stories planned for tomorrow's newspaper.

3:30 p.m. — The Circle Widens

Jane Curic is now on the radar screen of more than a dozen journalists who, like Jack, routinely check for new candidacy filings. She is part of the discussion at the afternoon budget meeting. The managing editor is there. So is the photo editor, the night news editor, the copy desk chief, the Page One layout editor and several section editors.

They are trying to figure out what to put on the front page and on the cover of the local news section. Most of the council announcements have been placed on the first page of the local section, not A1. The managing editor — the highest-ranking editor at the meeting — wonders whether there will be enough room for Curic on the local front for tomorrow. The city has announced a major business expansion; the school board is deciding tonight whether to spend significant bucks on new school buses; the area hit a record high temperature today; and the metro staff has a weird story about a concert ticket counterfeit ring. But the metro editor argues for the Curic story, saying it's an equity issue if the other candidates make the front and her announcement does not.

Everyone agrees. The story about Curic will be on the local front in tomorrow's paper, with a small photo, or "mug shot," of her.

6 p.m. — A Story Is Born

Jack has been oblivious to any debate over the placement of his story. He's been too busy.

He's been working on background checks. First, he went to the newspaper library to look for past stories on Curic. Nothing. Then he went to Real Smart University. Bingo. Several stories in the university newspaper, including profiles on Curic's run for student council president. Jack won't use these stories in his report, but they will give him a better understanding of the candidate and help him ask better questions of the people he talks to. He swings by the university police station. Any outstanding tickets? Past arrests? Nothing shows up. He's not expecting anything, but it's a standard part of the background check. Next week, when he has more time, he'll check whether city and state taxes have been paid on time; whether Curic owns any real estate, and, if so, if the city has been notified of any enforcement problems; whether her economic interest disclosure with the state registrar's office has been properly filed, and if it shows any potential conflicts; and whether the items on her resumé actually happened (more than one candidate has claimed to have graduated from a university that has no record of the event). He doesn't have any grudge against Curic. Jack's not out to get her. But many of these document checks bear on her fitness for office.

Now Jack needs to get back to the office, make a few more quick interviews, and start writing.

By 6:30, he's got the "lead," which is what journalists call the opening paragraph (or paragraphs) of the story. Jack is satisfied with what he's got so far, and he still has 30 minutes before he has to deliver the story to the metro editor.

The story begins this way:

YOURTOWN — The race for City Council heated up Tuesday when political novice and Real Smart University political science student Jane Curic filed for one of two open seats, bringing to six the number of candidates for the Nov. 6 election, which has been marked by contentious ad campaigns and petty accusations.

While Curik agrees with political experts that she has little chance of winning, her entry marks support for the pro-University contingent and could force council front-runners to make concessions toward the school that has repeatedly and unsuccessfully asked for a laundry list of improvements in such things as streets, lighting, security and more.

The election will fill two seats.

One is currently held be Samantha Smith, who is retiring. The other has been open since last month's death of Jamie Midgette, who died while hiking through the Andes.

Political analysts contacted Tuesday agreed that the top candidates in the race to date are John Boutiski and Ron Scampi. Both are backed by their respective parties, both have a well-funded war chest and both have years of political experience.

But Curic could upset their well-planned campaigns by bringig up University relations. Boutiski, a former planning commissioner, has consistently voted against increased funding for the university. And Scampi, the "less government is good" candidate, is unlikely to support more funds.

Jack's happy with the progress. He can make his 7 p.m. deadline, get the story edited and get it to the copy desk long before the 8 p.m. deadline that was marked on the copy desk. Heck, he'll be home and watching reruns of "Friends" by then.

7 p.m. — It Isn't Soup Yet

As it turns out, Jack's been a little too optimistic.

The metro editor doesn't see his story quite the same way. She returns it to Jack for a rewrite. She begins by noting that Jack has made tremendous progress in finding more information since their afternoon's discussion. However, she believes Jack has strayed in the writing. She makes these suggestions in her note to Jack:

- *Remove "heat up" from the lead. It's a cliché and not supported by any facts. The lead is also too long; try to hold any lead to no more than 35 words. It also tries to do too much. Try to get one point across really well. This lead tries to announce a new candidacy, round out the campaign and characterize the nature of the dialogue between candidates. In trying to do all that work, it does none of it well.*
- *Where's Curic? The first five paragraphs tell me more about the council "front-runners" than about the new candidate. Why is she running? What are her issues? I know more about the political analysts right now than the candidate they are supposed to be analyzing.*
- *It would appear that Curic will be tapping the tension between the university and the city. That's where the controversy in this story should rest — not on the two front-runners.*
- *You have misspelled Curic's name in the second paragraph. In doing so, you break her trust, and the reader's trust, that you can get the facts right. How can they believe anything else in the story?*
- *Other specific editing notes:*

    Check your spelling throughout. Typos on "be" instead of "by" in paragraph 3, "bringing" in paragraph 5.
    As with "heated up" in the lead, "war chest" in paragraph 4 is a cliché best left to novels about pirates.
    "University" in paragraph 5 is not capitalized. Uppercase only when combined with the full title of the university. See the entry in the "Associated Press Stylebook" under "capitalization."

So much for "Friends." Jack starts rewriting.

8 p.m. — Deadline

Jack and his editor agree the rewrite is much clearer. It begins with Curic's plea for more cooperation and more response to RSU's pleas. The story adds context by summarizing the difficulty past councils faced in granting those requests. Jack includes a bit about Curic's background, her major in college, and what others have to say about her. He includes the political impact on the other major candidates, but not at the top of the story.

Jack and the metro editor talk about what worked, and what needed work. Even though he's been at this awhile, Jack knows that even the best writers need an editor with the distance to see mistakes and act as a sounding board for ideas. They end the conversation the same way they end most shifts: talking about possible "folo" election stories to work on tomorrow, and weighing those ideas against other stories he's developing.

Meanwhile, the photographer and photo editor are having their own huddle. Jane wouldn't agree to sit down for a photograph, but she did consent to being followed to class. Even better. The photographer has 30 or so images from the classroom, and another dozen or so as she walked to and from class. One picture of Jane Curic might make it into the newspaper. They look for the image that best captures the moment. Is it clear? Does it show action? Are the other people in the photo important to the moment? Dozens of questions are asked and answered in minutes. They agree on three pictures that have been scanned into the computer. A page designer will pick one of the three before the night's out.

So, Jack and his editor have sent the story to the copy desk. The photograph is with the page designer. Jane Curic's name is about ready to hit tomorrow's doorsteps, right?

Wrong.

10 p.m. — Deadline

It's time to move this Curic story, but the copy editor is worried. She's edited eight other stories tonight. She could only spend about 10 minutes on the Curic story. But she had to stop and call the writer: How old is Curic? The story never specifies which political party she belongs to — isn't that important to the race? Other problems with the story — subject/verb agreement problems, wordy sentences and unnecessary jargon — are cleaned up in minutes, all while trying to protect the writer's style.

But this call to the reporter is making her late.

And she still has the most important piece of the story to complete.

The headline could make or break the story. In a crowded page of competing words, the headline shouts for attention. It says "you must read me." Other words in large type support the headline. All serve to help a reader scan the newspaper quickly and efficiently and help decide which stories to read and which to skip.

She takes a stab at a headline and sends the story and headline on to the "slot" editor, the supervisor on the copy desk who approves changes to stories and OKs or rewrites headlines and other display copy.

The slot editor doesn't have much time. The headline is just so-so: "Real Smart U. student makes bid for City Council." Accurate but hardly compelling. He tries "Student offers Curic for City Council." Peppy, but too much like a campaign ad. Hmmm. Perhaps "Student's council bid centers on RSU complaints." Better. The slot editor ships the entire file to the page designer, who puts the photo, headlines and story on the computer screen. The Curic story is the last of the night for the front page of the local section. The designer sends the finished page to the printing plant.

WRITING AND "THE JOURNALISTIC FACTORY"

Of course, many more people will play a part in bringing the Jane Curic story to readers' doorsteps in the morning, from printing plate makers to press operators to truck drivers to delivery people. But even before they get involved, more than a dozen people have worked on this single story to make it come to life.

And the story will be displayed in ways that go beyond ink on paper. Most "metro," or metropolitan, newspapers maintain a Web site with at least a sampling of news stories. Jack Cutter might be asked to respond to citizens' questions posted on an Internet "chat board." Or he might later supply the online editor with Curic's complete campaign finance disclosure forms — information too long and tedious for the printed page but welcomed on an Internet database for those readers wanting more detail.

Jack also could find himself turning from the interviewer to the person who is interviewed. In several cities today, newspapers are forming partnerships with television stations or entering solo into cable television ventures. So a TV reporter could ask Jack about the story for the 11 p.m. broadcast, which would refer to his story in the next morning's newspaper. Another editor might take his story and rewrite it for television, or for radio, or for a "drive time" promotion for the newspaper.

Each medium requires different writing formats. But the story's building blocks — the way the story is conceptualized or "framed," and the reporting and interviewing techniques Jack uses — will form the basis for everything to follow. These concepts are discussed in more detail in future chapters.

Reporting and writing, then, are at once both a solitary pursuit and a collaborative process. Certain elements — photos, graphics, headlines, for instance — are added in other places along the way. Even the narrative story itself requires discussion between the editor and the reporter. Often — in any form of writing, not just journalism — the best act of writing is rewriting.

Still, a newspaper story begins with the reporter, and the reporter may get the idea for the story in one of several ways: a tip from a source, tripping across an interesting document, or listening to citizens talking about things that matter to them.

Although stories can be born in a thousand ways, they come to life in only one: through the skills of a journalist who does careful research and chooses the right words to communicate a message.

EXERCISES

1. Arrange to spend several hours in the newsroom of your campus or local newspaper, preferably observing the work of one reporter or editor. Try to be there when they are working "on deadline" as well as several hours before. Watch the reporters as they go about their work. What do they do? What is the process by which their stories end up in print?

2. Go through an issue of your campus or local daily newspaper and find a story you like particularly well. Then go through a week's worth of papers and find other stories by that same writer. What are the stories about? Does the writer focus on a particular subject or geographic area? What are the sources of information in those stories?

3. Call a reporter on the telephone and ask him or her about a typical workday. What is most interesting and most challenging about the job? What kinds of time management challenges occur when working on several stories, at once, while meeting deadlines?

4. Find fellow students or friends who have been interviewed by journalists. Did they feel the journalist did a good job of representing their point of view? Was the story written in a fair, responsible way? In the end, how did they feel about the experience?

5. In small groups or as a class, use one or more of the videos listed in a later section to start a discussion about the wide variety of experiences and opportunities open to journalists. You can either all watch the same video, or watch different videos individually or in small groups. Talk about what parts of the film(s) make the work of a journalist seem interesting, exciting and challenging and what parts make it seem tedious, boring or otherwise unpleasant. Consider how closely art imitates life in the film(s) — which aspects seem realistic and which seem embellished to make the film more dramatic. Compare the events in the film to any real-life experiences you have had talking to professional reporters or watching them work.

FURTHER READING

ON THE WEB

AJR/American Journalism Review: http://ajr.newslink.org   Includes articles from AJR about many aspects of working as a journalist.

CJR/Columbia Journalism Review: www.cjr.org   Includes articles from CJR about working as a journalist.

Jobprofiles.com: www.jobprofiles.com/bus.htm   Is a career information Web site with descriptions of a variety of jobs, including several in journalism, written by people who hold those jobs. Look under "Business and Communications."

The Washington Post's "Journalists in the Movies": http://jobs. washingtonpost.com/wp-srv/local/longterm/tours/newseum/journfilm1.htm#NEWS Describes numerous movies about journalists that author Matt Slovick deems "worth watching."

Workingreporter.com: www.workingreporter.com   Offers information about issues pertinent to working reporters.

IN PRINT

Biographies and Autobiographies about Journalists

"A Good Life: Newspapering and Other Adventures," by Benjamin C. Bradlee, published by Touchstone Books, New York, 1996. The story of Bradlee's Carrer with "The Washington Post," he rose from cub reporter to executive editor.

"American Journalists: Getting the Story," by Donald A. Ritchie, published by Oxford University Press, New York, 1998. Includes 60 essays about famous and not-so-famous reporters, editors, columnists, photojournalists, broadcasters and anchor people.

"Autobiography of Lincoln Steffens" (Vols. 1 and 2), by Lincoln Steffens, published by Harcourt Brace, New York, 1968. Steffens was a quintessential muckraker and socialist. The "New York Times" included this on its list of the greatest 100 books of the 20th century.

"Crusaders, Scoundrels, Journalists: The Newseum's Most Intriguing Newspeople," edited by Eric Newton, published by the Newseum, Arlington, Va., 1999. Brief biographies of 285 notable journalists, compiled by the managing editor of the world's only news museum.

"Ernie Pyle's War: America's Eyewitness to World War II," by James Tobin, published by the Free Press, New York, 1997. An homage to Ernie Pyle, one of America's most celebrated and beloved war correspondents, killed while covering World War II.

"Never Let Them See You Cry," by Edna Buchanan, published by Random House, New York, 1992. More of Buchanan's memoirs.

"Personal History," by Katherine Graham, published by Vintage Books, New York, 1998. Candid autobiography about the publisher of The Washington Post.

"The Corpse Had a Familiar Face," by Edna Buchanan, published by Random House, New York, 1987. Memoirs about Buchanan's days as a Pulitzer Prize-winning police reporter for the "Miami (Fla.) Herald."

"Writing to Deadline: The Journalist at Work," by Donald M. Murray, Heinemann, Westport, Conn., 2000. An in-depth description of the news writing process, along with interviews with experienced journalists.

Books about Broadcast and Online Journalism

"Designing Web Usability: The Practice of Simplicity," by Jakob Nielson, published by New Riders Publishing, Indianapolis, Ind., 1999.

"Web Navigation: Designing the User Experience," by Jennifer Fleming and Richard Koman, published by O'Reilly & Associates, Cambridge, Mass., 1998.

"Writing for the Web," by Crawford Kilian, published by Self Counsel Press, Bellingham, Wash., 2000.

"Writing News for TV and Radio: The Interactive CD and Handbook," by Mervin Block and Joe Durso Jr., published by Bonus Books, Chicago, 1999.

Truth Is No Stranger ...

If you're curious about journalism, you probably already know some of the titles on the lists below. All are fictional stories of journalists at work.

Although some say truth is stranger than fiction, when it comes to novels and movies about journalists, that's an arguable assertion. Most journalists don't get involved in the kinds of dangers and intrigues featured in the following works. But all of these books and movies are basically accurate in describing how reporters go about their work and some of the day-to-day challenges they face.

IN PRINT

"Act of Betrayal," "Contents Under Pressure," "Garden of Evil," "Margin of Error," "Miami: It's Murder," by Edna Buchanan. Buchanan's heroine in all of these mystery novels is Miami crime reporter Britt Montero.

"A Faint Cold Fear," by Robert Daley, published by Warner Books, New York, 1990. A thriller in which a central character, Jane Fox, as New York City newspaper reporter who goes on assignment to Colombia, South America.

"All the Dead Lie Down," "The Red Scream," "Under the Beetle's Cellar," by Mary Willis Walker. Her heroine is Texas investigative journalist Molly Cates.

"Still Waters," by Tami Hoag, published by Bantam Books, New York, 1992. A mystery in which the central character, Elizabeth Stuart, is the new publisher of the fictional Still Creek, Minn., Clarion.

"What a Woman's Gotta Do," by Evelyn Coleman, published by Simon & Schuster, New York, 1998. A mystery novel about a newspaper reporter who stumbles onto a sinister experiment while investigating her fiancé's disappearance.

MOVIES ON VIDEO ABOUT JOURNALISTS

"Absence of Malice" (1981): About a newspaper journalist who is unwittingly used in an ambitious prosecutor's misguided attempt to arrest a suspect in a murder case. In a subplot that raises an important ethical issue, the central character — a female reporter — gets romantically involved with the man who is being set up to take the blame for the murder. Stars Sally Field and Paul Newman.

"All the President's Men" (1976): Chronicles the work of the two "Washington Post" reporters who followed the story that eventually led to the downfall of President Richard Nixon. Stars Robert Redford and Dustin Hoffman.

"Broadcast News" (1987): A glimpse into the daily operations of a Washington, D.C., television news bureau, and the special considerations faced by broadcast journalists. Raises an ethical issue when an anchor-to-be presents a videotape that makes it appear that he was moved to tears by the person he was interviewing. Stars Holly Hunter, William Hurt and Albert Brooks.

"The China Syndrome" (1979): A TV reporter and cameraman happen to be at a nuclear power plant when a meltdown occurs, and the camera captures it all. A fast-acting engineer averts the crisis, so network executives decide not to air the film, lest it set off an unwarranted panic. The engineer then discovers the meltdown could happen again, and when another man is murdered to keep that information from becoming public, he seizes the control room. He asks for an interview with the reporter but is shot by security police before he can share his information. Stars Jane Fonda, Michael Douglas and Jack Lemmon.

"Citizen Kane" (1941): The story of a media magnate who aspires to political office. The title character is widely believed to have been based on William Randolph Hearst, despite the denials of director, writer and star Orson Welles.

"Eyewitness" (1981): A janitor who has a crush on a television reporter makes things up when she interviews him, along with other residents of a building where a murder occurred, just to talk to her. But his comments strike close enough to home that the murderers think he knows something and want to silence him. Stars Sigourney Weaver, William Hurt and Christopher Plummer.

"Foreign Correspondent" (1940): Directed by Alfred Hitchcock, this masterful thriller is about American crime reporter Johnny Jones, who is sent abroad in the hope that he can add some pizazz to the sleepy stories being sent back from Europe as war was brewing there. Good reporter that he is, he begins reporting about fascism and Nazi Germany's plans to take over Europe. While covering a peace effort, he witnesses an assassination, uncovers a spy ring and (of course) falls in love. Stars Joel McCrea and Albert Bassermann.

"His Girl Friday" (1940): The comedy in this film is enhanced by director Howard Hawks's instructions that the actors should talk fast and move quickly, to convey the rush-rush of old-fashioned journalism. A remake of "The Front Page" (1931), it's about an editor who plots to keep his ex-wife, a reporter, from leaving journalism — and from remarrying. Stars Cary Grant and Rosalind Russell.

"The Killing Fields" (1984): Based on the story of New York Times reporter Sidney Schanberg, who stayed in Cambodia after Americans were evacuated at the end of the Vietnam war. He and his translator are captured by the Khmer Rouge. The reporter is set free, but his translator is sent to sent to a "re-education camp." He later escapes and is reunited with Schanberg. Stars Sam Waterston, Haing S. Nor and John Malkovich.

"The Mean Season" (1985): A reporter gets an "exclusive" when he is contacted by a serial killer, who basks in the front-page attention he gets for each murder, until the reporter's notoriety eclipses his own. The killer than kidnaps the reporter's girlfriend. Based on the novel "In the Heat of the Summer," by former Miami Herald police reporter John Katzenbach. Stars Kurt Russell and Mariel Hemingway.

"Network" (1976): When a veteran newsman is fired after 25 years, he tells viewers he plans to commit suicide after his final broadcast. Ratings soar. He then gets swept into a series of ups and downs orchestrated by the network. First, he gets his own weekly show that does well for a while, then slips in the ratings. The network then has him assassinated and the lead-in to a new program. Stars Peter Finch, Faye Dunaway, William Holden, Ned Beatty and Robert Duvall.

"The Paper" (1994): A day in the life of a New York City tabloid. The central story line involves the arrest of two young black men in connection with the slayings of two white businessmen. The city editor thinks they were set up, but his managing editor wants to run the story regardless. It shows the hectic pace of a typical newsroom, but it goes a bit over the top in the scene in which the city editor tells the printing press operators to "stop the presses," and his managing editor tries to intervene. Stars Michael Keaton, Glenn Close, Robert Duvall and Randy Quaid.

"The Pelican Brief" (1994): A reporter comes to the aid of a law student who is nearly killed by a car bomb after she writes a brief that outlines a theory about the murder of two Supreme Court justices and her boyfriend, a professor, shows it to someone with the FBI. Together, they prove her theory to be true. Stars Denzel Washington, Julia Roberts and Sam Shepherd.

"Street Smart" (1987): A magazine journalist is assigned to write about the lifestyle of pimps, but he can't find one so he makes one up. The story is a hit, he gets his own television show and meets a pimp suspected of murder. Then a district attorney who believes the story was

Marisa Tomei plays a newspaper reporter married to the paper's metro editor, played by Michael Keaton, in the movie "The Paper." The film depicts journalists working on deadline to expose a scandal and free two innocent murder suspects.

Photo by Andy Schwartz. Source: Universal City Studios

about the murder suspect gets a subpoena that requires the reporter to turn over his notes — which, of course, don't exist. The pimp puts pressure on the journalist to produce notes that create an alibi for him. Stars Christopher Reeve, Kathy Bates and Mimi Rogers.

"Under Fire" (1983): An American photojournalist in Nicaragua captures the fatal shooting of a network news anchor by one of former President Somoza's National Guardsmen during the revolution there. The global response that follows helps end Somoza's oppressive government. The film was inspired by the real-life airing of videotape of the killing of ABC correspondent Bill Stewart by Somoza's troops, after which Somoza fled the country.

"The Year of Living Dangerously" (1983): An Australian reporter in Indonesia in 1965, when rebel unrest culminated in a coup against President Sukarno, gets romantically involved with a woman who works at the British Embassy. When she learns of an incoming arms shipment that is likely to make the country even more dangerous, she tells the reporter in the hopes that he'll leave the country. Instead, he decides to write about it. The script is based on real historical events. Stars Mel Gibson and Sigourney Weaver.

Chapter 3

How News Writing
Is Different

By the time reporters sit down to write, they've gathered information from interviews, public records and other sources. Here, reporter Chad Garrison draws on his notes and various documents to compose a story for the Columbia Missourian.

Photo by Jeff Inglis. Source: Columbia Missourian

Key Concepts

- Writing news stories differs from writing academic papers in three major ways: Most of the information in news stories comes from talking or listening to people, not from reading written materials; the sources of quotations are noted in the body of the story rather than in footnotes or citation lists; and information is organized primarily according to its importance to the public rather than according to the traditional introduction-thesis-body-conclusion formula.

- Accuracy should be a journalist's first goal.

- Personal opinion is used very judiciously in journalism. Although experienced journalists often include opinion in clearly labeled news analyses, editorials or reviews, opinion has no place in day-to-day news stories.

You've written a million papers for a thousand classes, and you know the drill: Figure out what you're going to write about, go to the library to do research, take notes from books and periodicals on a bunch of index cards or notebook paper or maybe even a laptop computer, print out a bunch of stuff from reputable sources on the World Wide Web, then organize all that information into a report that has an introduction, body, and conclusion.

If you have written some news stories, too, you probably realize that, in a broader sense, the process is similar. When you write news stories, you start by discussing a story idea with your editor. In the case of a sudden event like a fire or storm, the editor might simply give you a story assignment. Then you do the research and write.

But in journalism, you don't call it research — you call it reporting — and you do relatively little of it using books in a library. Instead, you gather most of your information by interviewing people. If you do in-depth reporting, you also spend time poring over public records such as official agendas, proposed ordinances, annual budgets, and agency audits. You also get information over the Internet. That's because these are the best sources of up-to-date information, and journalism is (obviously) all about bringing people up to date.

As a journalist, you don't write stories that follow the introduction-body-conclusion format common in academic writing. Instead, you call the parts of your stories by names like "leads" and "nut graphs," and you're expected to divide in-depth stories into "packages" of interrelated stories you and your editors call "mainbars," "overviews" or "cover stories," "sidebars" and "pullouts."

Most importantly, though, you don't write for just one teacher or professor who may or may not catch a misspelled name or notice that the words aren't exactly right in a quote. Your stories are read by hundreds or thousands of people — including the people you've quoted and others who have knowledge about the subject of your story. If you make errors or omissions, if you misrepresent what has occurred, or if you exaggerate or downplay the truth, someone always notices — and usually speaks up.

Journalism, then, is much more public than the writing you do in most classes or business settings. As a journalist, you draw on the public — citizens, public officials, public records — to get story ideas and information for stories. You filter that information through your understanding of what it means to the public. Then you write your stories and send them back to the very public from which you drew the information.

A Few Journalism Terms

Following are a few terms journalists use to describe aspects of their work:

Budget — A listing of all the stories planned for the next day's newspaper, with short descriptions about each and whether photographs or informational graphics are available to run with them.

Editorial — 1. All newspaper content that is not advertising. 2. An opinion article written to represent the institutional voice of the newspaper.

Graph — 1. Short for "paragraph." Alternate short form: "graf." 2. A type of chart used in informational graphics.

Lead — 1. The beginning of any story. May also be spelled "lede," to avoid confusion with the next definition. 2. A tip from a news source.

Mainbar — The main story in a major breaking news or enterprise story. If a story is called a mainbar, that means it is accompanied by one or more sidebars with supplementary information providing background and helping readers place the story into context.

Nut graphs — Paragraphs in news stories that tell the reader why the story is important now.

Pullout — A list or other "just the facts" information that runs with a story, usually in a format that sets it off visually from the rest of the story.

Sidebar — A story of lesser note that accompanies the main story, or mainbar.

Slug — A word or phrase used to identify a particular story. Comparable to what non-journalists would call a document or file name.

For a more complete glossary of journalism terms, see Appendix F.

GOOD NEWS WRITING IS ACCURATE

It is the public nature of journalism that makes accuracy so essential to good news reporting. News organizations — and the profession of journalism — earn the public's trust by reporting the news of the day accurately and thoroughly. If you make factual errors or leave out crucial information, you erode not only the public's trust in you as an individual reporter but also in your news organization and in journalism as a whole.

Misspelled names, incorrect times or phone numbers and bad math account for most errors. They occur on community listings, brief items and routine inside stories more often than on the big stories on the front page, but that does not make them any less damaging. Those listings, briefs and routine stories are among the most widely read parts of the newspaper.

Accuracy requires painstaking care in recording and repeating facts. It requires using the correct and complete names for people,

Why Accuracy Is So Important

Lack of accuracy was one of the key reasons people said they have lost faith in the media, according to a 1999 study, "Examining Our Credibility," by the American Society of Newspaper Editors.

The study showed that even the smallest errors undermine public confidence in the paper — and the public finds many of those errors.

The harshest criticisms came from people who had personal experience with the media, such as being mentioned in stories themselves or knowing people who were, and from people who had personal knowledge of situations reported in the press. Their experiences with the press frequently were negative, because they found many errors in news stories.

Although journalists offer a variety of explanations, ranging from deadline pressures to being overworked, the public believes there is no excuse for them, researchers found.

Running corrections in the paper helps to restore the newspaper's credibility, the study said, but it's always better to get it right the first time.

Other factors that reduced credibility:

• The public thinks newspapers don't know enough about, or demonstrate enough respect for, their readers and communities.

• They think journalists allow their personal biases to influence what they cover and how.

• They think newspapers try to sell papers by overcovering sensational stories that don't deserve so much coverage.

• They think journalists don't place enough value on holding stories until facts can be double-checked and on protecting the privacy of people in situations most journalists would consider "news."

Source: American Society of Newspaper Editors

places and things — and spelling those names correctly. If you misspell someone's name in a news story, it makes a bad impression not only on the person whose name was misspelled but on everyone who knows that person.

Misspelling a person's name can have far worse consequences than reflecting badly on you as a reporter. Let's say someone named Sara Smyth, 24, of Yourtown, was arrested on a charge of forging checks (note that we didn't say "arrested for forging checks," because that's as good as saying she did it). You remembered to ask how she spells her first name, because you know lots of *Sarahs* and *Saras* and even some *Serras*, but you never thought to ask how she spells such a simple last name as Smith.

After your story runs, a grocery store cashier named Sara Smith, who also happens to be 24 and lives in Yourtown, is suddenly fired, for no apparent reason (which is not very nice, but it is legal in most cases). The next day, someone points out your story to her. She figures that's probably why she was fired and calls her boss, who confirms it. Guess whom she calls next? If you're lucky, she'll call you, vent her anger and be satisfied by your offer to run a correction in the next day's paper. If you're not so lucky, she'll call a lawyer, who then will call the publisher of the paper, threatening to sue your paper for a large sum of money to compensate Sara for the pain, anguish and real-life consequences your slipshod reporting caused her.

Accuracy requires spelling words properly and using them as they're defined in the dictionary. Misspelled and misused words are,

An Honest but Libelous Mistake

As the police reporter for a campus newspaper, she was checking crime reports when she saw one about the arrest of a masked man who had jumped from a car, grabbed a female student's purse, then jumped back into the car and sped off. Another student who was with her had gotten the car's license plate number, and the police report said the case had been traced to a local man named John Thompson.

The reporter then asked the police chief if any more information was available about the Thompson case, and he told her, "Mr. Thompson was arrested just about an hour ago."

In her campus police beat column, she said John Thompson had been arrested, and she included the address listed for him in the police report. However, shortly after the story ran, Thompson's lawyer called to say his client, a well-respected restaurant owner, was not pleased with the story. The person who was arrested was his son, Peter Thompson, who was a student at the university and for whom he had purchased the car.

Source: Law of the Student Press

at best, a sign of carelessness. They also can be confusing: If you write about cats being *curios* when you mean to say they're *curious*, people will (understandably) misunderstand.

Accuracy requires getting facts and figures right, and checking any calculations you're using in a story. If the numbers don't add up, neither will your story.

Accuracy requires verifying addresses and the cities or towns where they're located. It means verifying locations or travel directions, to be sure they, too, are correct.

Accuracy requires verifying dates, times and phone numbers that are used in news stories and calendar items. Mistakes in this kind of information are especially problematic; people can show up for a play, public hearing or other event too early, too late or on the wrong day because you got it wrong. Chances are, they won't be too happy.

Accuracy requires never depending on someone else to catch your mistakes. Newspapers don't have fact-checkers and rarely use proofreaders. Editors often catch errors before stories end up in print, but not always — and it is always the reporter's responsibility to be sure his or her stories are accurate.

The most important habit you can develop, then, is that of checking and double-checking everything — become a skeptic of your own work. Proactive efforts to ensure accuracy should become a part of your routine each day. Here are four tips for doing that:

- Check the numbers.
- Treat names as sacred.
- When in doubt, take it out.
- Don't expect anyone but yourself — even a computer — to clean up your writing.

Check the numbers. Most errors in numbers are typographical, so it's essential to check things like phone numbers, street numbers, dates and times against your notes or other source material. Such errors are most commonly made in phone numbers, which are easy to check — just dial them. If your intent is to publish the rape crisis hotline number and the local Exxon station answers, you will make a correction that might save a rape victim from experiencing additional, unnecessary anguish. Web sites are easily checked in the same manner. Locate the site to find out if it's the same site you meant to publish.

Harder to find are errors in calculations — both those made by the reporter and those made by news sources. For this reason, a simple pocket calculator is a common tool among journalists. Doing the math not only ensures accuracy, it is also a function of clarity. It's better to tell readers how much the city budget will increase — $22.1 million — than to simply say last year's budget was $105.2 million and next year's will be $127.3 million. A more common problem is calculating percentages — things like misplacing a decimal point or using the wrong formula. The "Associated Press Stylebook," another essential tool of journalists, shows how to calculate percentages.

Treat names as sacred. Sources appreciate reporters who take the time to get names and titles right. Little is more important to a person. A common practice is to ask an interview subject to spell his or her name, then ask again at the end of the interview, then repeat it back. You also can ask for a business card — but be sure to ask if all the information on it is still correct. After the interview, you can check the person's name against a phone book or city directory. And

A Different Kind of Style

When professional writers talk about "style," they usually aren't talking about graceful turns of phrase or the distinctive characteristics of a particular author's writing. They're talking about a consistent use of language as designated by reference books called *stylebooks*, which are primarily used to ensure the linguistic "look" of a given publication, academic discipline or institution.

Most stylebooks are essentially a guide to word use, spelling, punctuation, capitalization, abbreviations, some points of grammar, and other aspects of writing.

Some stylebooks also specify a dictionary that is recognized as the universal reference for such matters as preferred spelling, hyphenation, etc., again for the sake of consistency.

Many newspapers also have style sheets or stylebook supplements that describe how various local words and expressions should be written and note any departures in that particular newspaper's style from AP style.

The most commonly used stylebook in journalism is the "Associated Press Stylebook," which also includes a manual about libel and other journalistic legalities. As you might guess, this stylebook was developed and is updated annually by the Associated Press wire service, which is based in New York City.

A few large newspapers and national magazines, such as The New York Times and The Washington Post, have their own stylebooks. Many magazines and book publishers rely on the "Chicago Manual of Style," published by the University of Chicago Press. Some magazines, such as U.S. News & World Report and Wired, have their own stylebooks — and Wired's stylebook is used by many online publications.

Graduate students writing research papers, theses or dissertations also use stylebooks — the "MLA (Modern Language Association) Style Manual," for example, or the "Publication Manual of the APA" (American Psychological Association).

Journalists use stylebooks to ensure consistency and uniformity within their publications. "The Associated Press Stylebook" is the most commonly used. Some larger or special-interest publications, like the New York Times and Wired, develop their own stylebooks. Many magazines and book publishers use "The Chicago Manual of Style."

Sources: The Associated Press ("Associated Press Stylebook"); Three Rivers Press ("The New York Times Stylebook"); University of Chicago Press ("The Chicago Manual of Style"); and Broadway Books ("Wired Style Guide").

be sure to check whether you have been given a nickname, in which case you should always get the legal name as well.

When in doubt, take it out. Editors always prefer stories to be accurate and complete. But accuracy comes first. Be sure of the quote before you put it in a story. Either confirm the facts or take them out. On many sensitive stories involving controversial subjects or alleging some misuse of power, most news organizations have adopted a rigid two-source rule, meaning the information must be independently obtained from at least two documents or interviews with separate sources.

Don't expect anyone but yourself — even a computer — to clean up your writing. Spelling and grammar checkers on word processors are helpful, but they miss many errors (if you use "their" when you should use "they're," for instance). Learn to spell and use grammar well. In addition, make frequent use of reference works such as the "Associated Press Stylebook," a dictionary or the local stylebook (if your newspaper has one) to check spelling and word usage. Even though other editors will review the story, it is never safe to assume that someone else will catch your mistakes.

It's good to do a "line-by-line" check by printing out the story and comparing every quote against the notes and every name against notes — and, wherever possible, another source such as a phone book or city directory. The same process is used to compare every significant fact against the document used. In a line-by-line, it's not enough to say, "Oh, yeah, I've got that in my notes." Look it up. If the fact is correct, mark it in some way on the printout.

This rigorous method is particularly important in checking investigative reports in which information is highly sensitive and could result in legal action against the news organization, unless it is irrefutably accurate and well documented.

Another simple trick, especially when deadline pressure doesn't allow time to do a line-by-line, is to read the story, sentence by sentence, back to front. You are likely to read your story so many times before giving it to an editor that your eyes will skim over inane mistakes, such as obvious misspellings. Reading this way makes you slow down.

Finally, when thinking about accuracy, think about what *isn't* in the story. It's not enough to check what will be published. Your readers will hold you accountable for what is missing. Your story is flawed if doesn't provide the appropriate context and background. Individual points in a story can be correct, and you still can be appropriately accused of writing an inaccurate story if the facts and quotes and opinions don't work together. The goal is clarity, not confusion. "Accurate but incomplete" is not always accurate at all. No story is ever complete, in that the issue or person or event is evolving and changing, even as the writer sits at the computer. But accuracy demands clarity, even in the most trying circumstances.

Remember: It's not only the newspaper's reputation on the line. Your name — and therefore your professional credibility — will be attached to that story.

GOOD NEWS WRITING USES QUOTES

As a journalist, you also weave quotes and attributions into news stories in ways that breathe life into the writing and lend credibility to the report. Quotes often add perspective or lively comments that make stories more thought provoking or surprising. They also indicate that you have done your research by speaking to the people who have a stake in the subject of your story.

Using quotes well poses many challenges. You must be able to write down the whole sentences people say, word-for-word, while simultaneously thinking of questions and follow-up questions. That alone is a tremendous challenge — and an essential skill.

Although a few reporters take the time to learn formal shorthand, it's more likely you will develop your own personal shorthand, using a combination of common abbreviations and notations of your own devising. You might use "S/B" in your notes to mean "should be," for example, or use brackets to mark off a word-for-word quote. It doesn't matter if anyone else can read your notes, as long as you develop a reliable and relatively consistent system for taking those notes.

Learning to think of appropriate questions and follow-up questions while taking notes is also something that comes with experience. The more automatic your note-taking becomes, the easier it will be for you to take notes and think of questions at the same time.

Once you learn to write down complete, accurate quotes, you should use the following guidelines for including quotes in your news stories:

• Use the person's exact words.
• Use complete-sentence quotations.
• Strike a balance between direct quotes and paraphrasing.

Use the person's exact words. Direct quotes — the ones that appear within quotation marks — should always be the actual words spoken by the people interviewed, exactly as they say them. Sometimes it isn't possible to use a full-sentence quotation, because people lose their train of thought or go off on tangents, or you may have been able to write down only a portion of the quote. When splicing together portions of sentences, use three ellipsis points (...) at each splice — but, as the "AP Stylebook" warns, be extremely careful in doing that. If the speaker describing a jungle expedition says, "It seemed like we were walking forever — just forever — before we came to the waterfall," for example, it would be OK to quote her as saying, "It seemed like we were walking forever ... before we came to the waterfall." The ellipses indicate that words were removed. Failure to include the ellipses would be questionable.

Use complete-sentence quotations. It is almost always best to use complete sentences when quoting people. Doing so makes it less likely that you will quote the person out of context or give him or her reason to believe that you did. Stories also seem fragmented if they have numerous two- or three-word partial quotes sprinkled throughout. In fact, putting quotation marks around one- or two-word quotes sometimes makes people think you're mocking their use of that word or phrase. Under certain circumstances, if all you were able to write down was a portion of what the person said, you may need to use a partial quote. But that should be the exception, not the rule.

Strike a balance between direct quotes and paraphrasing. Stories can get bogged down by rambling, vague or boring quotes. It's better to paraphrase those and use the most powerful, important or interesting points people made for emphasis and to add life to the story. It may help to think of stories and quotes as chocolate chip cookies: The dough is the information and paraphrasing that gives the story body, and the quotes are the tasty morsels of your interview subject's opinion, insight, humor or pathos interspersed throughout.

Here's an example of how to cull out the best part of someone's quote: Let's say you interview the head of the Student Activities Board for a story about a big, all-day music festival soon to be held on campus. In answer to your questions she says: "We're planning to have a whole lot of food — lots of clubs are having bake sales and lemonade stands and stuff. And we'll have games during the day Saturday, starting at 11 a.m. on the Commons. We've even got the college president volunteering to be in a dunking booth to raise money for scholarships. We've got bands set up to play in two-hour shifts from 1 p.m. until 9 p.m. And it's all free except the stuff where people are raising money, and even that won't cost much. Everyone's working really hard to make it all come together, and it's going to be great. If anyone says Monday they were bored over the weekend, it'll be because they wanted to be bored." Most of her comments involve straightforward information that could be stated much more directly if paraphrased. The best "chocolate chip" probably would be her spirited closing sentence. Another possibility would be the sentence about everyone working hard — especially if an exceptionally large

AP Style on Quotations: No Tampering!

The "Associated Press Stylebook" entry "quotations in the news" sets a high standard for use of quotes.

• Avoid fragmentary quotes whenever possible, and paraphrase cumbersome quotes.

• Use quotes *in context*, including modifying or qualifying passages and describing such factors as gestures or facial expressions that might indicate that a remark was intended as humorous or speculative.

• Do not alter quotations to correct errors in grammar or word use. Slips of the tongue may be removed — with great caution — by inserting ellipses.

• Do not use slang spellings like "gimme" or "gonna" routinely, but only to convey a desired touch in an occasional feature story.

number of people or organizations is involved, or the degree of hard work is unusual.

Be careful, however, not to make false or misleading assumptions when paraphrasing. If you aren't sure you understood what the person meant, call the person back. It never hurts to ask again. The same caution goes for quotes: Sometimes, it's tempting to use only the most lively quote, even if it was only a small part of what the person said. In such cases, be sure you include any relevant qualifying information, or you run the risk of being rightly accused of quoting the person out of context.

GOOD NEWS WRITING USES ATTRIBUTION

In news stories, you also must set aside academic conventions for using quotes and citing sources in favor of the journalistic convention called *attribution*, which may seem strange if you've never written a news story. In a newspaper, there's no place in the layout for academic-style footnotes; instead, information about where the quotes originated must be placed within the story.

Attribution gives credibility to your stories by indicating where you got your information. That allows readers to consider the source of the information, and it places responsibility for the information on the person or written material being quoted instead of on you or your news organization.

In general, you should report without attribution only those

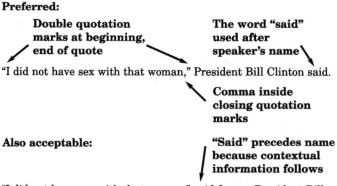

Preferred:

Double quotation marks at beginning, end of quote

The word "said" used after speaker's name

"I did not have sex with that woman," President Bill Clinton said.

Comma inside closing quotation marks

Also acceptable:

"Said" precedes name because contextual information follows

"I did not have sex with that woman," said former President Bill Clinton, who was impeached after having an affair with a White House intern named Monica Lewinsky.

The format for quotations in journalism.

physical events and details you personally observe. Other information must be attributed to some source: "The car was traveling at 120 mph, police said."

When quoting people, it is important to include not just the name of the person who is speaking but also explain that person's relationship to the story.

Sometimes, the relationship is clear by virtue of the person's job title. In a story about an arrest, for example, most people would understand Bill Johnson's relationship to the story if he were identified as "Police Chief Bill Johnson." Sometimes, the person's relationship to the story requires a clause, sentence or even paragraph of explanation. For example, in a story about a 20-year-old murder case that the chief helped to solve, it might be important to identify him as "Police Chief Bill Johnson, who was a rookie police officer when the murder occurred."

Never assume that the relationship is obvious, especially with famous people. It's better to identify Jennifer Anniston as "Friends" star Jennifer Anniston or as film star Brad Pitt's wife (depending on the context) than to leave some woefully out-of-touch readers wondering who she is.

Additional tips:

• Avoid fancy attribution.
• Use subject–verb construction.
• Keep the focus on the quote.

Avoid fancy attribution. Attribution should not be seen as an opportunity for creativity. Most editors prefer that reporters use the word "said," even if it seems repetitive, instead of distinctive words that creative writing teachers may encourage, such as "claimed," "retorted," "explained," "shouted," "speculated," "opined" or "continued." Using fancier words in journalism poses the danger of making stories seem biased or emotionally loaded. For example: "The mayor claimed he was innocent."

Use subject–verb construction. The most natural word order for attribution is "he said," "officials said" and so on. Verb–subject construction is better left to poetry or children's stories: "said he" or "said Pooh." However, when identifying a source's relationship to the story is cumbersome, the attribution can be altered. For example: "The sky is falling," said Chicken Little, a well-known storybook character.

Keep the focus on the quote. Whenever possible, the attribution should follow the quote. By putting the quote first and keeping the attribution simple, the reporter keeps the emphasis where it should be: on what the person said.

GOOD NEWS WRITING IS FREE OF PERSONAL OPINION

Most editors will expect you to be invisible in your news stories, presenting factual information about others without calling attention to yourself. That means you should avoid writing in the first person, unless you have a compelling reason to do so and have cleared it with your editor. The most likely occasion when you might be allowed to write in the first person would be if you witnessed a significant event or had personal experiences that are pertinent to related news stories. Otherwise, you will be encouraged to quote others' opinions but leave out your own.

Exceptions to the "no opinion" rule include specific types of journalistic writing found in daily newspapers, including news analysis, editorials, perspective pieces, personal columns, reviews and some types of in-depth reporting. Even in these kinds of articles, however, you are expected to draw on factual information to support your opinions.

This type of writing usually is reserved for journalists who have experience or expertise that lends credibility to their views. Experienced, respected reporters can gain that kind of credibility over time, as can people with expertise in different disciplines who contribute articles to newspapers. Writing that incorporates opinion is labeled clearly or printed in parts of the newspaper where readers expect to find opinion, such as on the editorial page or in the perspective section.

Other exceptions include articles written for community-of-

Doonesbury cartoon by G.B. Trudeau, © 2001, reprinted with permission

interest publications created by advocacy or activist groups, or by editors who are committed to telling the news from a specific political or philosophical perspective.

However, most news organizations will expect you to avoid making statements in your news stories that reflect your personal stands for or against issues, or your speculations about such matters as motives or what's really happening behind the scenes. Instead, they will expect you to present the facts so that readers can draw their own conclusions and form their own opinions.

The following journalism conventions will help you keep stories free of opinion:

- Use descriptive words instead of words that reflect individual judgment.
- Concrete language is a hallmark of journalism.

Use descriptive words instead of words that reflect individual judgment. Avoid adjectives and adverbs that imply that you personally have judged someone or something to be good or bad, dumb or smart, attractive or ugly: "She walked *gracefully* down the steps," "He *bravely* dragged the child from the river," "He gave an *interesting* speech about box turtles," or "The decision was *unfair.*"

This is another area in which the public nature of journalism calls for a different standard. In academic papers, you are often asked to take a position and gather information to support that position — much like editorial and opinion writers do in commentaries about current events. The purpose of doing that in academic papers is to help you develop critical thinking abilities and learn to articulate opinions clearly and effectively. The purpose of articulating opinions in editorials and opinions is to draw on your critical thinking abilities to foster public discourse. But the purpose of news stories has little to do with your personal opinion and everything to do with giving people the information they need to form *their own* opinions about what's happening in the community, who's affected, how, and why it matters. In such stories, your views are out of place because they divert readers' focus away from the public significance of the information. Once you state your opinion in a news story, you have made the story personal rather than public, and readers are forced to evaluate everything in the story in light of whether they agree with you and whether they think your personal views may have influenced the credibility of the information you provided.

It is OK, however, to use someone else's opinion in a news story. For example: "Several students at the hearing said they thought the decision was unfair."

One of the most common ways you can unwittingly inject your opinion into news stories is by choosing adjectives and adverbs that involve personal judgment. Words like "wonderful" or "interesting" reflect your personal judgment of a person or thing — which may differ greatly from someone else's judgment. If you were asked why you thought someone was wonderful or interesting, you might give an answer like this: "She's wonderful because she's enthusiastic, and in my opinion, enthusiasm is wonderful. She's interesting because she's traveled to so many places." In that case, it's better to use the descriptive words "enthusiastic" and "well-traveled" instead of the judgment-laden words "wonderful" and "interesting."

Descriptive words are easier to justify because they are based on observable facts and relative truths. A degree of judgment is still involved; however, the reporter could draw on observable facts to defend the assessment of that person. It's fairly safe, for example, to call someone enthusiastic if he or she speaks with energy and in positive terms.

Similarly, if you speculate about someone's emotional or mental state, it is always viewed as suspect. Better to describe his or her behavior in terms of specific physical details: "His sobs continued throughout the 21-gun salute," or "Her clothes were dirty and disheveled, and she muttered constantly to herself."

Another cautionary tip: Don't give things your seal of approval. Often, in an effort to make their writing lively, less experienced reporters will use enthusiastic exhortations to begin or end stories about coming events or organizations. Such invitations might sound like this: "C'mon over to the new Girls Club!" or "Put on your sunglasses and have a great time at the jazz festival this weekend!"

These kinds of comments have a promotional tone that is not appropriate for news stories. If journalists promote one event or organization in this way, it sets a precedent that will require them to promote all events and organizations in the same way — or face justified criticism that they are favoring some events or organizations over others.

If your newspaper becomes filled with nothing but enthusiastic stories, you will be rightly accused of *boosterism* — a word journalists use to describe news coverage so focused on promoting the good things in a community that problems are glossed over. If that happens, journalists can inadvertently forsake their important role of holding public officials and other community members responsible for the welfare of the community as a whole.

Concrete language is a hallmark of journalism. Reporters work to get specific details that not only remove personal opinion but also add life to a story. Describing a dog as a "big, unruly dog" might be

OK. Describing the dog as "a golden retriever that likes to jump on people and lick them" is better. Telling readers that the golden retriever's name is Fred is best of all.

In describing an act of bravery, it's much more powerful to give a detailed account of the person's actions, leaving readers to draw their own conclusions about whether the person was brave. Compare the following:

> "The man went into the river and bravely rescued the child."
>
> *versus*
>
> "As large branches rushed by in the churning river, the man half-walked, half-swam through chest-deep water to grab the child by the arms and pull him ashore."

MORE NEWS WRITING CONVENTIONS

Journalists have many other writing conventions that set their work apart from most academic and business writing. Here is a sampling of these conventions:

- Avoid beginning stories with questions, quotes or clichés.
- Keep the language simple.
- Use simple punctuation.
- Expect to have a length limit.
- Get over the idea that every story should have a conclusion.
- Get used to the idea of meeting deadlines.

Avoid beginning stories with questions, quotes or clichés. These leads are overused and rarely effective.

Even the kindest editors have been known to roll their eyes at stories that start with questions — especially when they've just edited four other stories that all started with questions. It's even worse when the questions are far-fetched, like this one: "Have you ever tried to jump rope and do back flips at the same time?" C'mon! Be honest? Have you ever done that? Heck, no! But the story forges on: "That's what Joe Schmoe did to win the World Rope Skipping Championship last week in Yourtown."

Editors also tire of seeing reporters turn in stories that start with quotes — whether they're pithy comments pulled from a book or dramatic statements made by a person the reporter interviewed. Opening quotes, which often pertain to only one aspect of a story, come from "out of nowhere" — no context has been established.

They also lend an academic tone to the story, which turns off many readers immediately.

Finally, editors tire of stories that begin with overused expressions and plays on words. At Christmastime, for instance, reporters inevitably submit stories that start off with twists on lines from Christmas carols: "'Tis the season to ... " [spend money, get your car winterized, bake cookies] or "Joy to the world, the [again, fill in the blank] has come." After the editor reads the first one or two of these, the cleverness wears off — if it was ever there.

If you can't think of any other way to start your story than with a question, quote or cliché lead, go ahead as a way of getting started on the story. But when you're done with the writing, go back and re-think the lead. Change a question into a declarative statement, add an opening sentence to set up a quote, and ditch the cliché. A straightforward lead is always better than a "groaner."

Keep the language simple. In news writing, fancy words are avoided, and sentences and paragraphs are kept short. Given the choice, journalists would rather use one- or two-syllable words — "use" instead of "utilize," "spit" instead of "expectorate," or "ringing" instead of "tintinnabulation." Common, descriptive language is used because news writing is expected to be closer to everyday speech than academic or business writing.

In addition, paragraphs are not arranged according to the same logic as in other kinds of writing. In fact, in many newspapers, every sentence appears as a paragraph. There are two reasons for this. Frequent indentations serve as visual points of reference that help readers' eyes track better as they're reading news stories in narrow columns. When copy editors shorten stories to fit them into the paper, it's easier to do if the paragraphs are shorter. That way, they can remove a paragraph at a time, here or there, to make the story fit into the space that has been allowed for it.

As you read these paragraphs, be aware of how easily you are able to keep you place.

This example has frequent paragraph indentations. The text block on the right is one continuous paragraph.

Which is easier to read? Which is more visually inviting?

This example show what it's like to have a long paragraph without frequent indentations. Studies say it is harder for our eyes to track from one line to the next when indentations are less frequent. The text also is less "gray" looking and more visually appealing when indentations are more frequent.

Use simple punctuation. Semicolons are rarely used in news stories (except to separate items in lists) because of the need to keep sentences short. In addition, if we are to be truthful, journalists in daily newspapers also tend to use punctuation less precisely than other writers. They also sometimes use dashes to excess and parentheses rarely.

Expect to have a length limit. Space on newspaper pages is always at a premium, so reporters are expected to keep most of their stories fairly short. If you've gotten good at padding academic papers to meet or exceed length expectations, this habit may pose a challenge for you. But if you still struggle to meet those expectations, it may be a relief. From time to time, an editor may grant you special permission to "write long," for stories that are especially important or compelling. Most of the time, however, your editors will reward you for keeping your stories short, concise and to the point.

Get over the idea that every story should have a conclusion. Less experienced reporters often struggle with the feeling that their story is almost done — it just needs a conclusion tying everything together. That feeling is an apparent holdover from the introduction-body-conclusion patterning in academic writing. It often prompts promotional-sounding instructions and proclamations, such as, "The tickets are going fast, though, so get yours soon!" or "With all of her talents, Williams is sure to go far." It's good to look for a particularly salient quote to end a story, or bring in a point that echoes the lead, especially in features and profiles. But don't devote an undue amount of time to writing the perfect conclusion. Some stories have wonderful endings. Some stories, especially hard news stories written on tight deadlines, just end.

Get used to the idea of meeting deadlines. Anybody who wants to be a reporter simply must be able to meet deadlines. Deadlines are different than due dates, which tend to be somewhat flexible. They also are much more absolute than goals. Timeliness is one of the key components of news. You can't very well tell someone what happened yesterday if you don't get the story done until tomorrow. In addition, in newspapers, it takes time to manufacture all of those bundles of inked newsprint, and still more time to deliver them to vending machines and subscribers' doorsteps. People expect their paper to be there when they wake up or get home from work, and if it isn't, they get cranky and sometimes cancel their subscriptions. For the paper to arrive on time, then, you have to get your story done enough in advance for the editors to read and edit it, for the page designers to lay it out on the page, for the pressroom staff to make the printing plates, and for the press operators to put the plates on the printing press and run enough copies of the paper for everyone who wants one.

To give you an idea of how serious journalists are about deadlines, it might help if you know that, according to "Webster's New World College Dictionary," the original meaning of the word "deadline" was "a line around a prison beyond which a prisoner could go only at the risk of being shot by a guard." Now, editors don't shoot people, but they do fire them. If, as a reporter, you miss your deadlines too often, your job will be literally on the line — the deadline. Although no editor would fire you for missing an occasional deadline when you've done everything in your power to get the story done, most editors are quick to spot patterns in your excuses if missing deadlines becomes the rule for you rather than the exception. Because it's never too early to instill in young reporters the importance of meeting deadlines, most journalism professors also build in penalties that will lower your grade if you miss your deadlines. They're a fact of life for journalists, and you just have to learn to live with them.

EXERCISES

1. Read an issue of a daily newspaper, paying attention to how routinely its stories incorporate the conventions described in this chapter. How consistently are the conventions followed? Do you notice any additional conventions?

2. Pick two stories out of a newspaper and photocopy them. Using highlighting pens, color each paragraph (or sentence) based on what kind of information it contains. Use pink for late-breaking information, blue for historical or background information, yellow for direct quotes and green for paraphrased information. Once you're done, think about how the story is organized. Which kind of information comes first? Where are quotes placed in the story?

3. Search through a daily newspaper looking for articles that contain opinion. Where do those articles appear in the paper? Does the paper make it clear who wrote those articles? If so, how? Does the paper use page headings, labels or other graphic devices to indicate that those articles contain opinion?

Further Reading

ON THE WEB

"Examining Our Credibility: Why Newspaper Credibility Has Been Dropping," prepared by Urban & Associates for The American Society of Newspaper Editors. Available online at www.asne.org/works/jcp/credibility2.htm or by going to www.asne.org, clicking on "Works," then on "Journalism Credibility Project."

Student Press Law Center: www.splc.org

IN PRINT

"The American Conversation and the Language of Journalism," by Roy Peter Clark, published by The Poynter Institute for Media Studies, St. Petersburg, Fla., 1994.

"The Essential Researcher: A Complete, Up-to-Date, One-Volume Sourcebook for Journalists, Writers, Students and Everyone Who Needs Facts Fast," by Maureen Croteau and Wayne Worcester, published by HarperCollins, New York, 1993.

"Law of the Student Press," published by the Student Press Law Center, Arlington, Va., 1997 (2nd printing).

"'Red Tape Holds up New Bridge' and More Flubs from the Nation's Press," edited by Gloria Cooper, collected and published by the CJR/Columbia Journalism Review, New York, 1987.

A SAMPLING OF STYLEBOOKS

"The Associated Press Stylebook and Briefing on Media Law," edited by Norm Goldstein, published by Perseus Books, Cambridge, Mass., 2000.

"Chicago Manual of Style: The Essential Guide for Writers, Editors, and Publishers," by John Grossman (preface), published by the University of Chicago Press, Chicago, 1993.

"Mastering APA Style: Students Workbook and Training Guide," by Harold Gelfand and Charles J. Walker, published by the American Psychological Association, Washington, D.C., 1990.

"MLA Style Manual and Guide to Scholarly Publishing," by Joseph Gibaldi and Herbert Lindenberger (foreword), published by the Modern Language Association of America, New York, 1998.

"The New York Times Manual of Style and Usage: The Official Style Guide Used by the Writers and Editors of the World's Most Authoritative Newspaper," by Allan M. Siegal and William G. Connolly, published by Crown Publications, New York, 1999.

"The Washington Post Deskbook on Style," by Thomas W. Lippman, published by McGraw Hill, New York, 1989.

Chapter 4

The Community as a Context for the News

When firefighters are called out to fires like the one at Cutshaw Market in Cambridge City, Ind., reporters usually follow soon thereafter. Firefighters from seven area companies helped put out this blaze.

Photo by Steve Koger. Source: Palladium-Item

- What qualifies as news varies from community to community. Good journalists know what matters to the citizens they serve — and why — and those are the things they write about.

- Good journalists hone their understanding of what's news in their communities by finding out about current conditions and issues, developing a civic map of the people and a historical overview of the area. They continually cultivate an understanding of their communities.

- Good journalists also rely on guidelines known as "news values" to help them determine what is news.

When a fire destroyed Cutshaw Market in downtown Cambridge City, Ind., on June 9, 1999, it was big news in the area.

It wasn't news because someone was killed or hurt (no one was). It wasn't news because foul play was involved (it wasn't) or because financial losses were in the billions (they weren't).

It was news because the fire engines' sirens woke up most people in the small Midwestern city. "I was up at four o'clock, out there in my pajamas to see what was going on," Cambridge City resident Jeanne Morse told Don Fasnacht, the reporter who covered the story for the area's daily newspaper.

It was news because in Cambridge, as the locals call it, the family-owned Cutshaw Market was more than a place to buy groceries. "I think half the people in Cambridge have worked here over the years," the market's owner, Bob Fortman, told Fasnacht.

"Everyone I've talked to is going to miss that place," Morse said.

And it was news because an estimated 100 volunteer firefighters from Cambridge and six neighboring communities in east central Indiana missed work while they battled the fire for $13\frac{1}{2}$ hours in record heat and humidity.

"Exhausted firefighters slumped on a nearby loading dock, eating sandwiches and drinking bottled water late Wednesday afternoon, while they waited for heavy equipment to get access to some stubborn hot spots," Fasnacht wrote in one of his stories about the fire.

The daily newspaper — the Palladium-Item in nearby Richmond, the county seat — ran front-page stories about the fire on June 9 and June 10. The paper also ran additional stories on Page 2 both days. On June 10, stories were put together with several photographs to make a full-page spread about the fire on Page 2.

A newspaper in a larger city would not have devoted nearly as much coverage to the fire. When placed in the context of a city's much larger population and geographic area, the fire's impact would be seen as less significant. As a result, news of the fire might run as a brief story on a page deep inside the paper, or it might simply be listed in a log of police and fire calls.

Journalists must know how to place stories into a context, based on what matters in the communities they serve.

In Myrtle Beach, S.C., or Ocean City, Md., where competition is stiff for vacationers' dollars and the economy depends on tourists, news of an attraction coming to town or of a federal grant to replenish the beaches would end up on Page One. In Jefferson City, Mo., or Springfield, Ill., the capital cities of their states, news about the government might be covered more heavily. But in a place like Richmond, Ind., a rural city of about 38,000 in a county of about 70,000, market fires and 4-H fairs are Page 1 news.

"I remember the parting words of an intern we had one summer," Fasnacht said. "He said, 'When I came, they should have told me the (county) fair story was the big story.' He thought that he was being dumped on all summer."

But if that intern had followed the suggestion in this chapter to cultivate his own understanding of the community, he would not have had to rely on the editors to tell him what "the big story" was.

IT'S ALL ABOUT COMMUNITY

Defining "Community"

Sociologists have long struggled with defining "community." George A. Hillery Jr. analyzed 94 definitions of community found in sociological literature. He determined that most define community as a group of people who share

- a geographic area
- social interaction
- a common tie or ties.

Modern mobility and new technology have prompted another definition. British sociologist David Clark has suggested that communities exist even if people don't live in the same locality or interact socially. Instead, he said, a community is a group of people who have a sense of solidarity and significance as a group. Such groups often are called "communities of interest."

The definitions are useful for journalists.

Most news organizations serve groups of people who live in well-defined geographic areas. It could be a small-town weekly newspaper or a large metro daily with "zones" to serve specific portions of the larger area. But many cities also have a variety of special-interest weeklies designed to appeal to computer users, minority groups, senior citizens, tourists, and other communities of interest. In addition, most magazines and some online publications are geared toward people who share certain interests or backgrounds but do not live close to one another.

Regardless of which type of community journalists serve, it is essential for them to have a sense of what is important to the people who will read their work.

How Community Knowledge Serves Journalists

Let's say you get an internship with your hometown paper, the Salisbury (Md.) Daily Times. Salisbury is only a 30-minute drive from the resort town of Ocean City, where you spent many summer days when you were growing up, basking on the smooth white sands, swimming in the Atlantic and passing time in the arcades and tourist shops along the Boardwalk. When you were old enough to work, you got jobs waiting on tables in both Salisbury and Ocean City. Then, when you were 17, you started living in Ocean City full-time and waiting on tables during the summer tourist season — something you plan to continue doing during your internship, even though you'll be working in Salisbury this summer.

Every morning, the editors, publisher and reporters meet to discuss what needs to be covered for the next day. This morning, they start talking about the need to write this year's version of a story that comes up every year: on the struggle to fill all the seasonal jobs in Ocean City. Since you have the most background information about the story, given your personal work history, you get the assignment. The next day, the following story appears as the lead story on Page 1, with your byline:

The Boardwalk at Ocean City, Md., has attracted hordes of tourists for decades. In recent years, it has also attracted growing numbers of seasonal workers from abroad. Observant reporters who know their communities can pick up on such trends.

Source: Ocean City Department of Tourism

Help Wanted

Resort businesses look to high-schoolers, overseas to fill empty seasonal positions

OCEAN CITY — Trying to ease the annual scramble for summer employees, resort businesses are hiring younger workers and foreign college students to fill empty positions during the busy summer season.

In the story, you explain that the thriving U.S. economy has resulted in more year-round jobs for high school and college graduates, making them unavailable for summer-only positions. In addition, most American colleges and universities now start school before Labor Day, making it impossible for students to stay throughout the tourist season. As a result, employers hire English-speaking college students from Europe — most of them from Ireland — because they don't start school until October and can stay through the season.

The person who actually wrote the story was Kathryn "Katie"

Soule, and it was her background we asked you to imagine as yours — a background that proved to be valuable to her and to the paper during her internship.

"Growing up in the ... area provided me with many advantages as a reporter. First of all, I had been a reader of the 'Daily Times' my entire life, so I knew what articles were interesting to me as a consumer. Secondly, I was familiar with much of the subject matter. I knew enough about the area to think of new ideas and sources, and I could suggest different angles to the other interns and reporters," she said.

In addition, her summer restaurant jobs helped her develop contacts that were useful in her reporting work. When she and City Editor Joe Weber conferred about possible sources for the story, for example, they included the usual contacts for tourism stories, additional sources from Joe's experience, and names of people Katie knew through her years of summer work in Ocean City.

But you're not Katie (obviously). What if that assignment came to you instead, and you had arrived for your internship knowing as much about Ocean City as you do about Timbuktu?

Well, let's assume you arrived in Salisbury a few days early, to give yourself time to settle in before starting work. During your interview for the internship, you asked the editors which communities the newspaper covers; when they mentioned you would be covering Ocean City, you were hardly disappointed. When you applied for the internship, let's just say it wasn't lost on you that you'd be only 30 minutes from the beach.

About Katie Soule

When last we talked to Katie, she was studying abroad in Copenhagen in the fall of 2000 and planning to graduate from Duke University in 2002 with a degree in public policy studies and economics.

She said her internship at the Salisbury "Times" gave her an opportunity to explore the possibility of going into journalism, which she was already doing by working on her student newspaper her freshman year at Duke.

Although she planned to continue working on her student paper after her semester abroad, she had decided to go to law school and pursue a career in public service.

"I found that I was not comfortable with everything a reporter's job entails, like trying to get someone to tell you something they shouldn't," she said. "However, I still love the media, both print and electronic, and I will probably work as a journalist or commentator of some sort later in life."

After her sophomore year, she interned in Washington, D.C., with Senator Barbara Mikulski, D-Maryland.

As you go about unpacking and making the inevitable runs to the store for cleaning and food supplies, you make a point of talking to a diverse assortment of people wherever you find them — while standing in the checkout line at the grocery or discount store, washing your clothes at the local Laundromat, eating at a corner cafe or lunch counter, or taking a walk in a public park when you need a break. You tell people you've just moved there and ask them what the area is like, what people do for fun, what they like most about the area, what they like least, what kinds of community issues concern them — questions designed to give you an overview of what's important to people there. While you're having dinner at a restaurant after your first day of unpacking, the high-school student who waits on you mentions that, in addition to this job, she's working in Ocean City to save more money for college. You mentally file that information away, along with many other interesting things you've learned by talking to people.

If you had time before you arrived, you called the Chamber of Commerce and tourism offices listed in the main communities the paper covers and requested information about the area. If not, soon after you arrive you make a point of visiting these offices and asking lots of questions. You read all the materials you've gathered and browse through the phone book's community guide (usually at the front of the book) and the Yellow Pages, looking for entries that pique your curiosity. If you've had a little practice cultivating community knowledge, it won't take you long to figure out that tourism is big business in Ocean City — especially in the summertime — which, in turn, means that businesses there hire large numbers of seasonal workers.

So when your editor asks you to write a story about the abundance of jobs and shortage of seasonal workers in Ocean City, you already have a context for the story as well as a possible source to interview: the Salisbury high-school student who served you dinner after your first day of unpacking.

The only thing that would be better is if you had come up with the story idea yourself, which could have happened this way:

The night before you start work, you decide to check out Ocean City. Enjoying the ocean breezes along the Boardwalk, you notice that the sunburned tourists are really out in force. The season is definitely under way. But you also notice that practically every souvenir store, french-fry stand, T-shirt shop, game arcade and caramel corn counter has one of those plastic, fluorescent, orange-and-black "Help Wanted" signs in the window. Your reporting instincts kick in and you start wondering: "Why are so many businesses still looking for workers? Is this normal? What's going on?"

If you made a point of asking questions about the signs while you were browsing in some of the shops or getting change back from purchasing your new Ocean City T-shirt, you'd probably get answers that would give you a great story idea to bring to your first morning story meeting. And your editors, no doubt, would be impressed by your ability to pick up on what's important in the area, even though you've only been there a few days.

In addition to helping you understand context and develop story ideas, community knowledge increases the accuracy of your stories and your credibility as a journalist.

For example, in Norfolk, Va., you're in trouble if you don't know the difference between an officer and a chief petty officer. That's because about 40 percent of the readers of The Virginian-Pilot are either in the Navy, retired from it or have a family member working for the service. Norfolk is home to the largest naval base of any country in the world. Reporters who cover the schools or local government and don't know their military terminology run the risk of making embarrassing errors and losing credibility with the military people who work and live in the community.

The value of community knowledge also results in insights that come from putting two and two together, which in turn lead to good story ideas. Think of it this way: A community is formed in the same way as ripples on a pool of water. Even the smallest pebble can start the waves forming and spreading.

Think about a place where you like to spend time — a local coffee house or movie theater, perhaps, or maybe the student union or campus library. Now think of all the people and institutions that are connected in some way to that place. If you have a favorite restaurant, for instance, in what ways is it connected to the rest of the community?

Well, for starters, it has to meet health and safety standards set by the local government. If it doesn't — the kitchen is found to be unsanitary, for instance — the city may shut it down. City officials who enforce those laws answer to you and other members of the public, because you basically hire, through elections, the mayor and city council members who make sure local laws are enforced. You pay their salaries when you pay your taxes. And you have a right to voice your opinion, if they're considering a ban on smoking in eating establishments.

The restaurant also competes with businesses in the area, so every time you go there instead of somewhere else, you are giving the business your personal economic support — and the more money you spend there, the more you're helping that business's bottom line. In turn, the restaurant may buy advertising in the local newspaper or city magazine, or on the radio or television station, which helps those businesses' bottom lines. The restaurant also buys things from various suppliers locally and outside the area.

These are just a few examples of how that ripple effect works. And if you make an effort to think about those ripples, you will be able to ask better questions, develop good story ideas and screen out faulty assumptions. Over time, you also will build a diverse network of contacts that can provide you with background information and ideas for stories.

Obviously, the longer you practice journalism in a community, the more shoe leather you will burn and the more you will learn about the people and places there. Journalists who make an effort to learn about a community often know more about it than some people who have lived there all their lives. Before you start gathering this information, however, you will need to learn your way around.

LEARN THE LAY OF THE LAND

Obviously, you can't dash over to the scene of a breaking news story or drive out to interview someone if you don't know where you're going.

Any time you move to a new town or city, you will acquire some of this knowledge quite naturally as you look for a place to live, arrange to have the utilities turned on, open a bank account, and find places to buy groceries.

Once you're on the job, however, you will need to increase that rudimentary knowledge as quickly as possible. Editors and other reporters won't mind giving you directions during your first few weeks on the job, but sometimes they may not be around to ask, and you will try their patience if you keep asking for directions after your first few weeks. Although really getting to know your way around takes time, here are a few steps you can take to speed the process:

Get maps. Get two sets of maps of all of the communities and counties covered by your publication — one for your desk at work and one for your car. Look for "through streets" (main thoroughfares) and back ways that locals take for shortcuts. If the maps don't help, ask; you can never go wrong by talking to people.

Find the landmarks. Make sure you know how to get downtown, to government buildings such as City Hall and the courthouse, to schools, colleges and hospitals. Find the shopping centers. Look for reservoirs, parks, golf courses, pools, community centers, convention centers, fairgrounds, prisons and cemeteries. Look for industrial parks, military bases and expanses of open land. Look for transportation hubs like airports, train depots, and bus stations. All of these are landmarks that people will refer to in giving you directions.

Get to know area names. Make sure you know the common names of any districts, areas, neighborhoods or sizable housing developments — for example, SoHo, Chelsea or Greenwich Village in New York City; the Kenwood, Dinkytown or West Bank areas of Minneapolis; or the Old Town, Myrtletown or Cutten areas in Eureka, Calif. Regional identities or nicknames also are important to know, such as the nickname "Delmarva" for the Delaware–Maryland–Virginia area or the "Tri-State area" for the region in which Ohio, Indiana and Kentucky intersect near Cincinnati.

Sometimes these names appear on maps, sometimes they're part of the names of businesses in the area, and sometimes they're just commonly used designations. Be aware that, when you're new to the community, you will no doubt have the experience of being corrected for your pronunciation of a proper name. It's inevitable. In Indiana, for instance, nobody pronounces the name of the city of Versailles the way people would in French class. They say "ver-SALES."

Get lost. Put your maps away and simply drive around until you find a part of the city or county that you've never seen before. Or get on a city bus and ride it until the route ends. It will force you to see new things. It also will force you to talk to people you might never talk to otherwise.

LEARN ABOUT THE PRESENT

Chambers of commerce, tourism bureaus, government offices, motorist club offices, and Welcome Wagon-type organizations are good sources of information for learning a myriad of facts: how many people live in your community, how many of them belong to which racial, ethnic, age and economic groups; the main industries and economic health of the community; overall educational level; and forms of local government. Much of this information is readily available in published materials prepared to encourage new businesses or conventions to come to the area.

Some newspapers also publish annual community guides. Keep an eye out for racks of tourism brochures in businesses that serve tourists, such as restaurants, truck stops, motels, outlet malls and gas stations just off the main highway. As you gather this information, pay attention to how people promote the community to prospective new residents and visitors, because that provides clues as to what they see as the area's strengths.

One often-overlooked publication is the phone book. Many have community information pages and give a quick overview of government services and utilities. Some also include maps. Browse through the Yellow Pages, looking for anything that strikes you as interesting. Are there more financial planners than farm equipment dealers? What kinds of ethnic restaurants does the community have? Do the nationalities of the restaurants provide clues as to immigrant groups that settled in the area, or to current demographics?

Another way to learn about the area is to take an informal tour. Your tour guides might include other journalists you meet at work, your neighbors, real estate or rental agents, insurance agents, or landlords. Offer to buy them lunch at their favorite restaurant if they show you around (which will also introduce you to a good lunch spot). In some cities, tours are offered by commercial organizations, or you may be able to go along on a tour sponsored by a tourism agency or the chamber of commerce.

One alternative to traveling tours is simply to find a spot where you can see the community's skyline. Look for tall buildings, which generally are located in economic centers; lower buildings, which generally connote residential areas or places where two separate communities grew together to become part of the same city; old church spires, which often are markers for older neighborhoods; and smoke and/or smokestacks, which often signify industrial areas. If you see something in the skyline that makes you curious, go find it and see what it is.

Spend an afternoon downtown, looking at the architecture and getting a feel for what goes on there. On a nice evening or weekend day, take a walk and talk to people who are out enjoying the evening. If you're not sure how to start the conversation, tell them you're new to the area and ask about the weather. You might be surprised by how many people will be eager to talk with you.

The quickest way to get up to speed on a community's most pressing issues is to ask — and the more people the better. The answers you get from your new co-workers are likely to be different than the answers you get from your new neighbors, elected officials or store clerks. Check what they say against stories in back issues of local publications. Many newspapers also publish "top 10" or "year in review" stories at year's end. Browsing through key pages of recent newspapers also can be helpful. If you look at the front page, the local section or page, and the editorial page for the past month, you should get a pretty good idea of which issues are on the front burner at the moment.

Another way you will learn about the present-day life in the community is by participating in it. Although, as a journalist, you must be careful not to align yourself with people or organizations in ways that could compromise your ability to be fair in the stories you write, it's a mistake to use that as an excuse for holding the community at arm's length. If you are too isolated, you'll fail to learn about important areas such as the community's social life, customs, and attitudes. You'll also have a boring life.

Many news organizations address concerns about community involvement in a formal way, by formulating policies designed to prevent conflicts of interest and the possible biases that may result. Those policies vary considerably, but most limit journalists to participatory rather than decision-making roles in nonpolitical community groups. They also restrict reporters from covering organizations in which they are involved, or getting involved in organizations they are assigned to cover.

In practical terms, that means you could probably audition for a community theater production (unless you're an arts writer), be a mentor with a youth organization (unless you're the youth page editor), or volunteer at a church-run food pantry (unless you're the religion writer). But you probably would be discouraged from serving on the board of directors for any of those organizations, or from helping with a political candidate's campaign. Many news organizations extend the designation of "political" to organizations focused on politically charged issues, such as abortion, gun control and the environment.

Even with such policies, however, participating in community life always involves taking risks. If you're a volunteer with an organization that suddenly is in the news when it doesn't want to be — one of the leaders of the group is charged with embezzlement, for example, or the organization's building is condemned as unsafe — you could face a dilemma. If you cover the courts, you might have to excuse yourself from covering the leader's trial. If you cover city government and therefore building code violations, you might have to excuse yourself from writing about the condemnation of the building.

Your involvement can result in other challenges. Well-meaning members of an organization you're involved with may want you to put something into the paper — or keep something out. But you don't have to belong to an organization to encounter that kind of request. Journalists get that even from perfect strangers.

No matter how much or how little you get involved in the community, you should expect at least some awkwardness that is tied to your work in journalism. It goes with the job.

Journalists who try to avoid such discomfort altogether live cloistered lives, socializing mainly with other journalists or with people who serve as their sources. When that happens, they can lose touch with the day-to-day concerns of people in the community — which, in turn, can lead to stories that no longer ring true for the majority of their readers.

No one yet has developed a sure-fire method for making the right connections. Just keep in mind the above considerations and the policies outlined by your news organization. Chances are both your life and your reporting will be much richer if you take a class, do volunteer work with a community organization, join a church, win a place on a local billiards team or become a "regular" at the lunch counter of your favorite local cafe.

LEARN ABOUT THE PAST

You don't have to become a local history buff to be able to cover a community well, but you do need to know key facts, like when the community was settled and by whom, and key events and people in the community's history.

Historical information and documents usually are available at public libraries, historical museums or locally owned bookstores. Back issues of local newspapers, past and present, can be helpful. You also can learn a lot about an area's history just by keeping your eyes open. Read historical plaques along roadways, and pay attention to streets, buildings and schools named after people who have been important in the community's history.

Architectural styles can give you clues. In parts of Florida and the Southwestern United States, many buildings clearly reflect the architectural heritage of early Spanish settlers. New Orleans is known for its French-influenced buildings. In the oldest neighborhood of

Ways to Get to Know a Community

- Get maps.
- Request tourism and newcomer information.
- Get newspaper community guides.
- Find the landmarks.
- Get to know area names.
- Get lost.
- Browse through the phone book.
- Take a tour.
- "Read" the skyline.
- Observe buildings for age, architectural style.
- Look for local history materials.
- Find past community research.
- Learn about all layers of public life.
- Talk to people, including a broad range of community leaders and a diverse cross-section of citizens.
- Get involved in community activities that don't conflict with your job.

Public libraries and historical museums often have copies of local history books, old city directories and other historical materials that can be useful in getting to know a community. This book, about Odessa, Tex., dates from 1952.
Source: The Naylor Co.

Richmond, Ind., German settlers built beautifully ornate homes and churches alongside Quaker settlers' elegantly simple homes and meetinghouses.

The ages of buildings in certain areas can tell you something about growth patterns. The usual pattern is for the oldest buildings to be in the center of town, with newer buildings radiating outward. Anomalies can provide important clues. Older buildings far away from the downtown area, for example, might once have been a part of a smaller town that has been absorbed into the larger city. Odd juxtapositions of new and old buildings can be the result of disasters, urban renovation projects, or other significant changes. Geographic barriers might have limited growth in one direction or another. Also important are transportation systems like waterways, railroads and canals, even if they are no longer used, because commercial development tends to occur along transportation corridors.

LEARN TO LOOK DEEPER THAN FACTS

So far, we've focused mainly on factual information. But good journalists' knowledge of the community goes beyond mere facts. Over time, they develop a deep understanding of what makes their community like others as well as what makes it unique. They know what people are proud of and what people wish were different about the places they live. They understand the challenges and opportunities that face the community.

In this era of increasingly sophisticated demographic research, methods of assessing and analyzing communities, audiences and markets abound. Government agencies, community groups and research organizations use a variety of methods in doing surveys and assessments that provide a wide array of information about communities. The focus of such studies can be very broad, as in quality-of-life studies or community visioning processes, or they can be very specific, as in environmental health or human service needs assessments.

Information from such studies can be helpful to journalists, and it usually is readily available in newspapers' in-house libraries or public libraries. If you know what you're looking for and who did the study, you also can request such information directly from the agencies and groups that sponsored the research. However, it is important to remember that such information usually tells only part of the story and may even be skewed for use in persuading others to go along with a particular plan or action.

When news organizations do research about their communities, they usually focus on demographic and purchasing patterns of those they consider their audience. This market research helps advertising sales staff work with advertisers to reach potential customers. It is also used by the news organization to plan its own marketing strategies.

The most common approach to such research, says journalist Michael J. Weiss, is called "cluster-based marketing," which categorizes people into lifestyle "clusters" based on age, ethnicity, wealth, urbanization, housing style and family structure. Depending on the system used — Claritas' PRIZM and Experian's MOSAIC dominate the industry — these clusters have names like "Shotguns and Pickups" and "Educated Cosmopolitans." "Cluster-based marketing is now used by corporate, nonprofit, and political groups alike to target their audiences," Weiss writes.

The use of such data by journalists has been the subject of controversy in recent years. Many journalists say this information helps them understand the interests and characteristics of people in their community. Others say using this information can cause them to increase coverage of "fluff" stories that pander to public tastes and, as a result, divert their attention from serious stories about important issues.

As with so many things, what's important is striking a balance. No good journalists would argue that, if they had to choose, it would be better to write a feature story about a new breed of dog that's become popular in town than to write a story about safety problems with an aging bridge. However, many journalists have lost touch with the interests of the people they serve to the point that they write stories about things that matter more to various groups of insiders than to the average citizen. Some stories about political infighting, for example, or about minuscule developments in various "hot stories" fall into this category.

Placed in the proper perspective, marketing research can help journalists begin to understand their communities in ways that help them improve their stories. But that kind of data does not get at the deeper levels of understanding that journalists also must cultivate.

For this reason, many journalists develop a variety of techniques that helps them gain community knowledge. These techniques build on what journalist David Broder, in a 1990 "Washington Post" column, described as "shoe-leather reporting, walking precincts, talking to people in their living rooms."

Many of these techniques are described in "Tapping Civic Life: How to Report First, and Best, What's Happening in Your Community." This publication, prepared for the Pew Center for Civic Journalism by the Harwood Institute for Public Innovation, details an approach to gathering community knowledge called "civic mapping."

This approach helps reporters see that civic life is much more complex than most of us think, with more layers and a broader range of leaders than the elected officials, prominent business owners and nonprofit executives we usually identify as people of influence. It suggests that reporters find new places to listen to groups of community members whose interests and concerns often are poorly covered. These are called "third places," after sociologist Ray Oldenburg's observation that places like eateries, barber shops, churches, parks and recreation centers are "the core settings of informal public life."

"Tapping Civic Life" also suggests that the listening done in these third places occur in the context of conversations rather than reporter-controlled interviews. It offers tips as to how reporters can learn to engage people differently and listen for things to which they might not otherwise pay attention — tips we will include in a later chapter on interviewing. It also helps journalists see how these altered goals and techniques pose challenges for them.

Often, when journalists start making calls and arranging interviews for their stories, they tend to gravitate toward elected officials

Expanding Our View of Civic Life

When we think of public or civic life, most of us think of elected officials holding meetings at the city building, with input from people we might call "movers and shakers" — prominent business people, directors of various foundations or nonprofit groups. But, according to the Harwood Institute for Public Innovation, it's not that simple. Important decisions and discussions occur in many more places, among a much broader range of people — some of whom are the kind of behind-the-scenes leaders who get things done without much notice from the media.

Here are the ways the Harwood Institute identifies the layers of civic life and types of leaders:

THE LAYERS OF CIVIC LIFE

• The official layer of government and public meetings
• The quasi-official layer of neighborhood associations, civic organizations and nonprofit groups
• "Third places," informal gathering places like cafes, coffee shops, recreations centers, churches and other locations where people often talk about what's important to them
• The incidental layer that takes place on sidewalks, in front and back yards, during lunch at work, or in phone calls
• The private layer, inside our homes

TYPES OF COMMUNITY LEADERS

• *Official leaders*: Elected or appointed government officials or heads of large institutions
• *Civic leaders*: People who hold important positions in the community, like church pastors, priests or rabbis; prominent business people; heads of civic groups and neighborhood associations
• *Connectors*: People who move between groups spreading ideas, often without having any official capacity
• *Catalysts*: Respected neighbors, coworkers, lay church leaders and others who encourage people to get involved in civic life
• *Experts*: People whose leadership takes the form of contributing specialized knowledge to other leaders or to the public discussion of various issues

Journalists tend to focus most of their coverage on the official layer of civic life — government meetings, public hearings, court trials, etc., and the organized interest groups that participate in those events in a formal way — and the private layer, the wellspring of human interest stories about individuals whose experiences are interesting, tragic, inspiring or unusual. "Tapping Civic Life" advocates that journalists expand their coverage of other layers of civic life by spending more time going to gatherings in the quasi-official layer — meetings of nonprofit groups and neighborhood organizations, for example — and spending time talking to people in third places, listening for what is important to them to enrich their understanding of the community and to get story ideas.

Source: "Tapping Civic Life," 2nd ed.

and experts. This is partly because it's efficient — people in these groups are easy to identify, tend to view talking to reporters as part of their job and usually provide good material for quotes. Although reporters' source lists sometimes include civic leaders such as religious leaders or prominent business people, they rarely include the behind-the-scenes leaders the Harwood Institute calls "connectors" and "catalysts." Also missing from many news stories are the voices of citizens, which is why Harwood advocates that reporters spend time cultivating relationships with citizens in third places.

"Journalists often [say] that when they call a source, they may ask a few questions, take a few quotes and go on to the next phone call. The goal is to obtain information quickly to write a story," Richard C. Harwood and Jeff McCrehan wrote in "Tapping Civic Life." "In civic spaces and conversations, your role is different. You are there to learn about the community and to understand it better. The goal should not be to 'find the quote.' Instead, it should be to discern patterns in what people are saying, to probe, to uncover meaning and figure out how people's thinking unfolds as they talk."

Although it will always be essential for reporters to be able to report the news quickly, it is important not to sacrifice quality. Reporters present an incomplete picture when they develop routines that help them meet deadlines but result in the exclusion of large segments of the population from their news stories.

"Journalists are confronted daily with deadlines and expectations that confound and exasperate even the best of them," Native American photojournalist Mary Annette Pember of the "Cincinnati Enquirer" wrote. "The average newsroom is not an environment that nurtures reflection on the complexity of the human race. It's a place that synthesizes a whole day's worth of local and world events into a few pages of newsprint in a hurry. It comes as no surprise, then, that in that haste to label, categorize and synthesize, the more complex aspects of real life can be overlooked."

Pember is among the many journalists who have expressed concern over the past dozen years or so about the media's continuing struggle to more accurately reflect the complexities of their communities.

One of the problems is that most of us naturally gravitate to people like ourselves, in terms of both general physical appearance and demographic characteristics. When reporters seek out news sources, then, they tend to gravitate toward people of their own race, class, gender, generation, and geographic area — what the late newspaper publisher Robert C. Maynard called the five "fault lines" that divide people in the United States.

His daughter, Dori J. Maynard, has carried on her father's work

Cartoon by Steve Greenberg

through the Maynard Institute for Journalism Education in Oakland, Calif. She urges journalists to become aware of the special challenges those divisions pose for them.

"My father believed that in order to bridge these fault lines, journalists must not only admit they exist but also learn to talk, report and write across them. Acknowledging fault lines compels us as journalists to seek out those who present a range of views on an issue," she wrote.

Although journalists, for many years now, have been making an effort to interview a greater cross-section of people, it remains a challenge.

The Poynter Institute for Media Studies in St. Petersburg, Fla., took on that challenge by sponsoring two year-long projects in the late 1990s to help journalists and their news organizations systematically connect with people and communities that were neither well covered nor well served by the media. Examples of these groups include Muslims, Asian-Americans, people who were wheelchair-bound, and gays and lesbians. These two projects, called "Making Connections" and "Push the Edges," had three objectives:

• To help journalists improve coverage by learning more about the people, history, concerns, and various cultures within their communities
    • To help journalists cover the community more fully by identi-

fying new "listening posts" where they could connect with people they had not been in the habit of talking with

  • To bring journalists together so that those who had honed these skills could share their discoveries with those still trying to learn

The results were described in a spring 2000 special issue of the institute's quarterly Poynter Report, with the theme "The Push for Connections: Covering the Untold Stories." In the opening article of that report, "Making Connections" director Keith Woods wrote: "Much of what we covered and discovered could be found in the tenets of solid journalism. But it's clear that journalists will need something more if they are to bridge the huge coverage gaps that allow people to go uncovered and stories to go untold. What the two projects sought to do was provide the 'something more.' In this case, it was introspection, exposure, continuing education, and a recommitment to basic journalistic principles."

Other articles in the report offer the following suggestions:

  • Journalists should be careful not to rely on the same news sources repeatedly, simply because they are people who are good at making quotable statements and don't mind being quoted.
  • Journalists should make a habit of going to a variety of places where they can listen to people who are part of the undercovered communities within their area. They should listen with all of their senses, observe what's going on, and engage in conversations, not interviews.
  • Before journalists talk with people who are part of an undercovered group, they should make an effort to learn about the people and their community. They should read old newspaper articles, check out relevant Web sites and search for novels, television shows, and films (or scripts) and other representations of those people in popular culture.

These representations often take the form of stereotypes that can result in inadvertent inaccuracies. Pember says journalists, like most people in this country, need to get past the stereotypes they have developed with the help of all those books, television shows and movies. In "Tapping Civic Life," the Harwood Institute makes a related admonition: "Watch out for preconceived views. ... Beware of possible preconceived views when engaging in civic conversations. Otherwise, it may be hard to hear and learn what these conversations have to offer."

In addition, it's important for journalists to recognize that diversity exists within every ethnic group. Pember wrote: "There are scores of Native American tribes in the United States located in varied environments with their own languages and cultures. Native Americans are not plugged into a collective consciousness, which they can access like a computer file whenever called upon to provide The Native American Perspective. To imply that they are is a subtle and insidious, albeit unintentional, form of racism."

Clearly, there's a lot involved in cultivating a depth of knowledge about a community and translating that knowledge into effective coverage of the community as a whole. Although most news organizations still are struggling with these issues, journalists are using the techniques and insights described above to ensure that they are telling the whole stories of their communities.

VIEW LEARNING AS AN ONGOING PROCESS

Good journalists understand that learning about the community they serve must be an ongoing process. They are always in danger of becoming too entrenched in familiar patterns — taking the same roads to work, talking to the same sources and hanging out in the same places after work every day. But no city or town is static. All communities are in a constant state of flux. That is the song of America. In the past few decades, the influx of ethnic populations has dramatically changed cities such as Miami, San Francisco, Boston, Chicago and New York. Sometimes a cataclysmic event, like the World Trade Center attacks or the tragic school massacre in Littleton, Colo., can change a community in wrenching, agonizing ways. Sometimes a fire in a small-town supermarket can have a profound impact over time.

The traumatic examples are obvious; staying alert to subtle changes is more challenging.

The act of "seeing" a community in different ways requires practice and experimentation. It's the difference between looking at an object straight ahead or out of the corner of your eye; the difference between seeing an object five feet in front of you and then looking at it from 50 feet away. Photographers make their livings doing this. Take a look at a sign indicating that parking is just ahead, for instance. You could drive by it every day and see the arrow pointing down the street. But stop someday and look at it while lying on the ground. You'll see that it points straight up into the sky. In the same way, journalists need to search constantly for the interesting people and places that make up the coverage area.

HOW COMMUNITY KNOWLEDGE BECOMES NEWS

Once you have acquired a basic level of knowledge about your community, you will be able to evaluate story ideas and news developments in light of what journalists call "news judgment," using a set of criteria called "news values" for evaluating whether stories are newsworthy.

Journalism textbooks generally include lists of these values. Traditionally, these factors have included:

Timeliness. Events that are occurring or just occurred.

Impact, consequence, significance or importance. Events that are likely to affect or be meaningful to a lot of people. Knowledge of the community is especially important with respect to this element of news judgment.

Magnitude. The "bigness" factor. If crowds were larger than ever, or the earthquake rumbled the Richter scale more than any others, or the entire county was flooded, it's bigger news than the usual-size crowd, ordinary earthquake, or spot flooding.

Prominence or celebrity, or their opposites. Events that involve well-known people, organizations, institutions or causes. Keep in mind that the newsworthiness of some stories is increased by a person's or organization's *lack* of celebrity — as when a person with little power or influence accomplishes something amazing.

Proximity. Events that occur close to home. "News is like a hurricane; the closer it gets, the more important it becomes to you," photojournalist and professor Jock Lauterer wrote in his book "Community Journalism: The Personal Approach." In evaluating how important proximity is, you should consider both geographic and emotional proximity. For example, many communities close to state lines or bounded by geographic barriers sometimes feel more closely tied to their state capital or a city 200 miles away than they do to the nearest city, which is in another state or on the other side of a mountain range. It's important to know what kinds of emotional ties people in your community have to neighboring locations.

Special interest. Stories targeted toward specific groups of readers, rather than to most people in a community.

Disaster or tragedy. Devastating events like natural disasters, accidents, bombings and other tragedies that cause great damage, injury or death. These are among the most challenging jobs journalists face. Providing accurate, timely news about such occurrences can be a great service, telling people where they can go for help and what they can do to protect themselves from further harm, and dispelling inaccurate rumors or fears.

Conflict or controversy. Public disagreements between people, organizations or institutions. When a conflict spreads beyond the actual people involved so that others begin taking up sides, it becomes a controversy.

Something extremely odd or bizarre. Stories that capture people's attention because they seem so unusual, far-fetched or strange.

Issues in the community. Important problems that become public. The issues can surface in a variety of ways. Sometimes they are identified during public discussions; sometimes, something occurs that calls attention to a problem. In response to a car careening off the road, crashing through a wooden guardrail and veering off a cliff, for instance, a group of citizens may mount a campaign to install stronger guardrails. Other times, public officials, reporters or citizen groups investigate tips or hunches about problems, which they later call to the attention of the public.

Currency. Things or situations people are talking about. Often this involves people taking a sudden interest in an ongoing situation. It may also occur in more subtle ways, as when people began noticing that tattoos and body piercings were gaining popularity with young people.

Human interest. People who have done something or are unique in some way most people would find interesting. These stories range from tragic to inspiring.

Helpfulness. How-to stories that help people cope with challenges or goals that arise in their lives.

Entertainment. Stories that are amusing or that focus on when and where people can have fun during their leisure time.

Humor. Stories written mainly to call attention to the absurdity or humor inherent in a given situation or activity.

Competition. The pressure from other media to get the story first. If the local newspaper breaks a story about the mayor being investigated on charges of accepting illegal campaign contributions, reporters for the local television station will take that as their cue to develop their own version of the story.

The essence of traditional news judgment is reporting things that are odd or unusual — breaks from the normal, everyday, expected course of events. However, there is a danger in emphasizing only the unusual, as "St. Petersburg Times" columnist Elijah Gosier wrote in a November 1997 issue:

> Newspapers are in the habit of routinely reporting the exceptional. Part of the definition of news is that divergence from the ordinary.

> Yet it is those offshoots from the routine — news — that many people use
> to form their perspectives on the state of the world around them. They form
> their opinions of the way things are from reading accounts of the way
> things usually are not.

Reporters who emphasize only the unusual run the risk of exaggerating the story's extremes and thereby creating false impressions and misunderstandings about what's really going on.

As a result of this tendency, some journalists and journalism educators have suggested that traditional news values be expanded upon by incorporating ideas such as the following, from University of Arizona journalism professor Rebecca Payne:

Cooperation/consensus. Stories about people who cooperate or reach agreement that enables them to achieve a common goal, sometimes overcoming serious obstacles or conflicts.

Common experiences. Stories about common experiences that have tremendous relevance to readers because they resonate with their personal experience.

By experimenting with expanded news values, reporters have covered more stories about ordinary people doing extraordinary things — stories like the woman in Wichita who couldn't get pizza delivered to her block, so she organized her neighbors to clean up the block and convince the pizza company to start delivering. Or stories like that about the gay student's transition into fraternity life, whose acceptance was made possible by cooperation among a few fraternity brothers.

Knowing the community is important for journalists because it helps them avoid overemphasizing the unusual and enables them to place stories into the context of most people's day-to-day reality. As Walt Harrington put it in "Intimate Journalism: The Art and Craft of Reporting Everyday Life": "The stories of everyday life — about the behavior, motives, feelings, faiths, attitudes, grievances, hopes, fears and accomplishments of people as they seek meaning and purpose in their lives, stories that are windows on our universal human struggle — should be at the soul of every good newspaper."

Although stories about unusual events, people and situations are certainly worthy of news coverage, many would argue that journalists have gone overboard with such stories. "It's long past time to ask American newspaper editors and reporters to rethink what they consider 'news,'" Harrington wrote. "It was decades ago that Herbert Gans, in his classic study of the American press, wrote, 'How ordinary people work, what they do outside working hours, in their families, churches, clubs and other organizations ... hardly ever make the news.' Changing that won't be easy."

In response to that concern, many news organizations are working to change their approach on two fronts: to place attention-grabbing stories into context, and to balance those stories with other stories that more fully reflect the richness of everyday life in the community.

EXERCISES

1. Look through a newspaper or news magazine and find three distinctly different stories that reflect the traditional news values listed above. Identify all the factors that make each story newsworthy. Are there several? Or only one or two? Which factors seem most dominant in each story?

2. Find an example of a newspaper or magazine story about an unusual event or person, and an example of a story about something or someone less extraordinary. What are the differences between the two stories? Are they written in different tones? Does one seem more dramatic or exaggerated than the other? Do they have different kinds of photographs or informational graphics with them? Does one of them appear to be more prominently displayed in the publication? Why do you suppose the stories are written and displayed the way they are?

3. Go to the library and search for books (usually in the sociology section) about community life or studying communities. Read one of these books and think about how you could use some of the ideas it contains in your efforts to understand a community.

4. With a group of other students (or possibly your entire journalism class), go to a place where you can spread out over a large expanse of open floor or ground. Figure out which way is north, then create an imaginary map of the United States. Mark off the four "corners" of Washington State, California, Florida and Maine. One at a time, briefly narrate the story of places that have been significant to you while moving from place to place on the "map." Start with where you were born, then go to the place (or places) where you grew up (if they're different), then go to any other places you love. When you're done, go stand either at the place you consider home or the place you would like to be your home. Students for whom places outside the United States are significant will have to go off the map, as it were. At each stop, say a little about what you remember most about that place (it's OK if your memories are sketchy), what makes it unique, and impressions or preconceptions you think outsiders have about that place.

Further Reading

ON THE WEB

City of Calgary, Alberta, Canada: www.gov.calgary.ab.ca/81/research/cdassess. htm   Online handbook on community assessment.

Claritas, home of PRIZM marketing research: www.stratmap.com/index.htm

Choose analysis and segmentation, then under "Choose an industry," choose "media and communications."

International Society for Quality-of-Life Studies: www.cob.vt.edu/market/isqols An organization for people interested in studying quality of life.

The Maynard Institute for Journalism Education: www.maynardije.org Information about fault lines and training sessions.

The Pew Center for Civic Journalism: www.pccj.org Ordering information for "Tapping Civic Life: How to Report First, and Best, What's Happening in Your Community" and other publications available online. The first edition of "Tapping Civic Life" also is available online, in the "Available only online" list toward the bottom of the publications page, or at www.pewcenter.org/doingcj/pubs/tapping/index.html.

The Poynter Institute for Media Studies: www.poynter.org.

IN PRINT

"Change and Tradition in the American Small Town," by Robert Craycroft and Michael Fazio (Eds.). Published by University Press of Mississippi, Jackson, Miss., 1983.

"Communities: A Survey of Theories and Methods of Research," by Dennis E. Poplin, published by MacMillan, New York, 1972.

"Community Journalism: The Personal Approach," by Jock Lauterer, published by Iowa State University Press, Ames, 1995.

"Covering the Community: A Diversity Handbook for Media," by Leigh Stephens Aldrich, published by Pine Forge Press, Thousand Oaks, Calif., 1999.

"From Main Street to State Street: Town, City and Community in America," by Park Dixon Goist, published by Kennikat Press, Port Washington, N.Y., 1977.

"Intimate Journalism: The Art and Craft of Reporting Everyday Life," by Walt Harrington, published by Sage Publications, Thousand Oaks, Calif., 1997.

"Studying Your Community," by Roland L. Warren, published by Russell Sage Foundation, New York, 1955.

"Tapping Civic Life: How to Report First, and Best, What's Happening in Your Community," 2nd edition, prepared by the Harwood Institute for Public Innovation for the Pew Center for Civic Journalism, Washington, D.C., 2000.

"The Community in America," by Roland L. Warren, published by Rand McNally, Chicago, 1972.

"The Great Good Place: Cafes, Coffee Shops, Community Centers, Beauty Parlors, General Stores, Bars, Hangouts, and How They Can Get You Through the Day," by Ramon "Ray" Oldenburg, published by Paragon House, 1989.

"Tupelo: The Evolution of a Community," by Vaughn L. Grisham, published by Kettering Foundation Press, Dayton, Ohio, 1999.

Learning from Experience: Community Knowledge

ASSIGNMENT 1: YOUR CAMPUS AS A COMMUNITY

The gist of the assignment. Interview a diverse group of at least six strangers on campus to find out what events and issues interest them. Then, write an 800- to 1,200-word report (usually three to five pages) that summarizes what they told you (one-half to two-thirds of the paper) and describes how you felt about your interviewing experience (the rest).

Why you'll be doing it. The purpose of this assignment is to help you:

• Get a taste of what it's like to gather quotes for news stories from a diverse group of citizens
• Focus on developing or improving your interviewing techniques
• Develop ways of learning about a community through informal conversations with people who live there
• Gather information that will help you develop ideas for news stories to write later in class
• Begin to think through some of the personal, philosophical and ethical issues that can arise when journalists perform an important part of their job: walking up to total strangers and asking them to spend their valuable time answering questions

Assignment Details

Interviews. Talk to a minimum of six people on campus and take notes on what they tell you. Try to write down at least some of their comments word for word. All should be people you do not already know, and no more than two should be people you find on "safe" territory, like down the hall in your dorm or in one of your classes. At least four of the people you interview must look substantially different from you, including at least one person of another race. For example, if you are a young, white, relatively sedentary person who wears jeans and flannel shirts, the people you interview might include a black , Latino or Asian-American student, someone with lots of tattoos or piercings, someone wearing a letter jacket, someone who is a lot older than you are, and someone dressed in really nice clothes.

Even though you will not use the information you gather for a published news story, you should still keep a record of each person you talk to and get his or her phone number. You may need that number later — as you develop story ideas from these interviews, you may want to interview one or more as news sources for your stories.

The fact that you won't be quoting them in a published story will have advantages and disadvantages — and part of the assignment is to reflect on that based on your experience. For example, some people may be more likely to talk because they know they won't be quoted; others may be less likely. The fact that you won't be quoting people may also affect some of your feelings about this assignment. Pay attention to those feelings, because they will be important in the part of your paper in which you discuss your feelings about your interviews.

Write your paper. As noted, half to two-thirds of the paper should summarize your conversations with the people you interviewed. Try to use at least some of the direct (word-for-word) quotations you wrote down. Be sure that you describe how each of the people you talked to were different from you. The remaining half to third of the paper should convey your feelings about doing this assignment. You can either divide the paper into two separate sections or blend these two categories of observation as you write. The paper should be written in a personal, not scholarly, tone. List the names and telephone numbers of all people you interviewed at the end of your paper.

Meet your deadline. Because deadlines are so important in the news business, you do not have the option of turning this report in late. If you have problems that cause you to worry that you will not meet the deadline, contact your professor as soon as the problems arise. That way, your professor can help you find a way to meet the deadline or, as a last resort, give you an extension of a day or two. The only other legitimate excuse for failing to meet the deadline is a note signed by a licensed medical practitioner.

Tips for Doing Interviews

• Start this assignment immediately or as soon as the weather permits. Don't wait for the weekend, then say you couldn't do your assignment because the weather was bad. The best way to meet deadlines is to start working on your assignments as soon as you get them, because you always have to work around other people's availability. The sooner you start trying to reach the people you need to interview, the greater the chances you will contact them in time to get your assignment finished by your deadline.

- The best time to talk to people is when they aren't rushing off to do something. Usually, mealtimes, evenings or weekend days are good. Finding the right time to catch people is an important part of this assignment.

- Experiment with different approaches to see what works best in getting people to talk to you. Some examples of ways other students have initiated contact include smiling, striking up a casual conversation, approaching people who are waiting or standing in line or passing time in a campus lounge, or taking an interest in something a person is doing, like hanging paintings in a gallery or juggling. After making contact, try various ways to get the person to answer your questions. A common approach is to ask if they'd be willing to answer a few questions for a class assignment you're working on. Another approach is to just start asking questions and, if people respond, explain why you're asking and see if they'd mind if you took some notes on the subject for your class project. If they are reluctant to be interviewed, explore ways of persuading them to change their minds. One option is to ask if they'd be willing to think about it and let you call them later. Be persistent but not pushy. Sometimes it helps to explain that you're not looking for an expert opinion, just the perspective of a typical student or citizen. Remember that each time you approach someone, you are as much a stranger to them as they are to you. As a reporter, part of your job is to get people to trust you enough to share information about themselves. If you can't do that, you won't have much of a future as a journalist.

- As you conduct your interviews, jot down notes and observations. When people say things that strike you as meaningful, try to capture the whole sentence, just as they said it, so you can quote them accurately. Also make note of any gestures or other indications of emotion that strike you — for example, if they shrugged when expressing confusion or laughed when saying something sarcastic.

- As with all interviews, be sure to get each person's full name, the proper spelling and, again, the phone number. If any of them go by nicknames, get their legal names as well. If anyone seems reluctant to give you this information, explain that you will only use it if you need to contact them again for more information or clarification for your report. (*Note*: It's a good idea to get into the habit of asking for this information as early in the interview as possible. That way, you won't find yourself having a bunch of really great notes from someone who had to rush off before you remembered you were supposed to get his or her full name and phone number.)

Tips for Writing Your Paper

Within a day or two after each interview, take some time to reflect on your conversations and jot down notes about what you found interesting in what people told you *and* about how you felt when you were talking with them. Here are some questions that may help.

• Did any themes emerge in your interviews? Did you uncover any new trends, interesting developments, unusual personal stories, simmering problems, strange developments or conflicting points of view? If so, what were they?

• What responses or ideas did people have that surprised you or seemed particularly interesting? Why did those things surprise or interest you?

• If you talked to people whose views were very different from your own, ask yourself this: Why might a reasonable person think that way? What might have led them to hold that point of view?

• What assumptions did you make about the people you talked to, based on their comments, behavior and appearance? Do you think those assumptions are accurate?

• How well did you understand their points of view? Did they describe things in the same words and contexts as you and your friends do?

• What assumptions might you make about the campus, based on your conversations on your beat? Do you think those assumptions are accurate?

• Was this assignment easy or hard for you? Why?

• How did you pick people to talk to? How did you feel about talking to people who don't look like you?

• Which approach(es) worked in getting people to talk to you? Which didn't? Were some people friendly and others not? What do you suppose caused the different reactions?

ASSIGNMENT 2: CITY BEAT WALK

The gist of the assignment. You will be assigned a "beat" consisting of a four- to six-block area of the community surrounding the campus. All beats will be within walking distance of campus, unless your professor grants your request to go to a particular, more distant neighborhood, and you have a way to get there. You then will "walk your beat," going up and down the streets observing physical details and recording them by drawing a rough map of what you find and by taking photographs of things that reflect the character and feeling of the neighborhood. Next, formulate a list of questions and use them to interview six people on your beat about what events and issues in the community interest them. Then write an 800- to 1,200-word report and turn it in along with your map and photos.

Why you'll be doing it. This assignment has many of the same purposes as the preceding exercise, with a few differences. In addition to furthering your experiences in the areas identified in the campus assignment, this assignment will help you:

• Begin to understand the basic characteristics that distinguish communities and, more specifically, neighborhoods. Through your own eyes, you will observe physical details that provide clues to such things as the general behaviors, lifestyles and political views (gotta love those lawn signs and flags) of people in your neighborhood. Through the eyes of people who live there, you will add their impressions to your own. *Note*: On this assignment, you should still strive to talk to as diverse a group of people as possible. However, since most neighborhoods are not demographically diverse, you may find that the best you can do is talk to people of different ages and styles of dress.

• Focus on developing or improving your powers of observation and your ability to develop and test hypotheses based on your observations.

• Begin to think about how maps (or other drawings) and photographs can be used as a way of providing additional information that complements your stories.

• Focus on developing or improving your ability to formulate articulate, open-ended questions.

• Begin to work through some of the fears and personal safety issues that can arise when reporters must go out and interview people in places that are unfamiliar to them. Although all of the neighborhoods identified as beats for this class are considered very safe, reporters must always be mindful of their personal safety. The following are good guidelines: Do your interviews during daylight hours and talk to people only in places where you remain in full view of the public, such as sidewalks or porches. If people invite you into their homes or other places where you will no longer be in full view and you feel at all uneasy about it, politely decline. If you follow these guidelines and still feel uncomfortable, ask a friend to go along and watch you from a distance so that if anything happens, they can get help. Do not, however, have your friend go with you to the interviews. Reporters need to develop the confidence to interview strangers on their own.

Assignment Details

Map. Draw a map of your beat. Artistic ability is not important here — it's sufficient to draw boxes, circles and stick figures and write words next to them to explain what they are. What matters is that you capture on paper the locations of houses, commercial buildings, overflowing dumpsters, lawn ornaments, children's tricycles, perfectly manicured bushes or other details that contribute to your impression of what your neighborhood is like. If it helps, begin with the grid on the page that follows this assignment sheet. You also may find it helpful to draw your map on graph paper.

Photographs. Turn in no fewer than 12 and no more than 24 photos. If you do not have a camera, borrow one or purchase an inexpensive disposable camera. Again, don't get hung up on whether you're a good photographer. Focus on content. Take photos that supplement the information on your map. Photos, for instance, can convey atmosphere or

An example of a grid used to make a community beat map.

movement in ways that nothing else does. A photo of a typical or un-usual house in your neighborhood, for instance, or a photo of a row of similar houses can give people a good idea of what the neighborhood is like. A photo of kids playing football in the street or of families washing their cars on a Saturday afternoon or of a fence covered with graffiti also can be very telling. Be sure that on the back of each photo, you make a note as to what you feel that photograph reflects about your neighbor-hood.

Questions. Before you go out on your interviews, formulate a list of questions to keep in mind. Draw on your observations about the surrounding community and concentrate on asking questions in a way that prevents people from answering simply "yes" or "no." For instance, if someone asks you if you like your campus, you're likely to tell them you do or you don't. But if they ask, "What do you like about your campus?" they'll get a much more complex (and therefore more quotable) response. Write your questions down — but don't carry them with you when you go. Try to keep them in mind as a general frame of reference for your conversations, and see how well you do at asking questions and follow-up questions on the spot.

Report. As in the campus assignment, your report should be written in a personal rather than scholarly tone, with one-half to two-thirds of the report summarizing your conversations and the remainder describing how you felt about this assignment. Again, try to use quotes, and list the names and telephone numbers of all people you interviewed at the end of your paper.

Meet your deadlines.

Tips for this Assignment

• Review the tips for interviews and for writing in the previous assignment.

• Before you do anything else, leisurely walk your beat. Do this alone for about an hour, without a notebook or camera or any other tools for recording what you see. It is important that you walk (rather than ride a bicycle or drive), so that you'll be going slowly enough to observe details. It's important that you go alone, so that you can concentrate. Pay attention to everything. What do you see? What do you hear? What do you smell? What are the textures and tastes of your beat?

• After taking your initial walk, think about what you saw. What hypotheses can you come up with about people in your neighborhood, based on your observations? Are you curious about anything you saw? Did anything disturb or delight you?

• In subsequent visits to your neighborhood, take notes not just when you're talking to people but also about things you see and hear. If you hear a factory whistle or church bells, write it down. If you smell fresh bread baking or some kind of chemical odor, write it down. Getting into the habit of writing down such observations can be very valuable to you as a reporter. Also record your impressions and responses — is there something that intrigues you? Disgusts you? Alarms you?

• Keep in mind that people in the community have different schedules from those of students. The best times to find people entering, exiting or otherwise outside their homes is during pleasant evenings or weekend days. These are also the times they are most likely to talk to you. If you go to many areas during regular business hours (9 a.m. to 5 p.m. Monday through Friday), you may have trouble finding people who will talk to you, because most of them will be at work. As in the previous assignment, finding the right time to catch people is important.

• Keep in mind that people in the community are less likely to be accustomed to seeing people who look significantly different from themselves. This means that if you are a person who has a distinctive personal appearance, either by genes, misfortune, or choice, you must be aware of that and work with it. If you are a hefty football player, you need to be aware that people may feel slightly intimidated by your size when they see you coming, and you will have to work a bit harder to put them at ease. If you're a petite or slender woman, they may be more willing to talk to you but also less likely to take you seriously. If, by your appearance, it is clear that you or your ancestors came from another part of the world, you also may encounter reactions based on people's stereotypes. If you have a physical disability for which you use a wheelchair or other apparatus, or a service dog, you might find that people will want to ask you questions about yourself — instead of answering your questions. And if you have cultivated a distinctive personal appearance by wearing vintage clothes or nothing but black and Doc Martens, or having multicolored hair, lots of facial piercings or abundant tattoos, you should remember that most "regular folks" who live near campus won't be accustomed to talking to people who look like you. Although your appearance probably would serve you well if you were interviewing performance artists for a trendy New York City magazine, you may discover that for this assignment, you need to either "dress down" to get people to talk to you — or be willing to explore people's reactions to your appearance as part of the assignment. The bottom line: Get six people to answer your questions (telling you to "bug off" doesn't count).

Chapter 5

Reporting Basic, Informative News Stories

Wisconsin's only state-sanctioned snow sculpting competition is among a flurry of activities in Wisconsin Dells' annual Flake Out Festival.

Source: Wisconsin Dells Visitor & Convention Bureau

▓▓▓▓▓▓▓▓▓▓▓▓▓▓▓ **Key Concepts** ▓▓▓▓▓▓▓▓▓▓▓▓▓▓▓

- Reporting news stories involves getting out into the community to observe people, places and events first-hand; conducting interviews; and gathering information from various written and online sources.

- The "five W's" (who, what, when, where, why) and the usually added "H" (how) can form the foundation for the most complex reporting assignments.

- Each story should include at least three sources who can give both information and context.

Most news stories begin with a simple premise: Something just happened — or will happen soon. Such "happening" stories are the mainstay of news reports. They can describe many types of events. For example:

- A holiday celebration: "Lexington's Fourth of July celebration ... was a gathering of thousands for food, fun, music and, well, sweat."
- Action by an official agency: "A suspected computer hacker made his first court appearance Wednesday after being indicted on charges of breaking into computers belonging to NASA and the U.S. departments of energy, defense and transportation, said federal prosecutors."
- Citizens participating in the democratic process: "The method used to calculate Greene County sewer bills might be causing thousands of customers to be overcharged unfairly, a Beavercreek resident told county officials Wednesday."

These are the most basic kinds of news reports: stories that help people know what's going on, how they might be personally affected by it, and how they can participate in events and public decision-making processes in their communities.

Such stories may be based on information the reporter receives from citizens or news sources, then verifies by interviewing people over the course of a day or two. The information may come in the form of a press release, a telephone call, or an e-mail message. The stories may be triggered by personal observations — a sign that says a new business is "coming soon," a recurring traffic jam caused by ill-timed traffic lights, a poster announcing a big concert, or a river of water coursing down the street from a broken water main. Or the stories may be based on what the reporter hears and sees while attending an event, with quotes added from on-the-spot interviews with citizens or people who have some official connection to the event.

These are relatively straightforward stories, and we read them with interest because they are about things that affect our daily lives. A story about streets being repaved might make us realize we should take a different route to work. A story about an expected heat wave might make us decide it's time to buy an air conditioner. A story announcing a public hearing about plans to build a new factory might inspire us to go to the hearing and comment on the plans.

Generally, such stories describe a clearly defined news development, public event, or activity of general interest. They fall into three categories:

- *What will happen.* These "advance" stories describe an upcoming event or occurrence, such as a concert or meeting, a business or organization opening, or a person who will do something of note. Information for such stories often comes from press releases as well as interviews with people involved in, or affected by, what will happen.

- *What's happening.* These can be "day of" stories reminding or notifying people of something due to happen that day, or they can involve something ongoing — like work being done by a person, organization or government agency, or a decision-making process that will lead to changes that affect many people. Information for these stories, too, often comes from press releases and interviews.

- *What happened.* Often, these stories are about unusual occurrences such as crimes, accidents, severe storms or unexpected announcements. They also might be after-the-fact accounts of events that were scheduled in advance, such as community festivals or government meetings. Whenever possible, reporters are expected to include in such stories information they gathered by actually going to the scene of the crime, accident or storm, attending press conferences where announcements are made, or being present during planned events.

The process of pulling together a good news story begins long before you open your computer to write. It begins with the first question. Ask the right questions, both of yourself and of others, and you'll get a complete story. Ask the wrong questions, or not enough questions, and some less-than-happy editor will likely send you back to your sources to ask new questions and rewrite the story.

For decades reporters have used a simple mnemonic to help them remember to ask the right questions. The five w's are "who, what, when, where and why." The list usually ends with an "h" — how.

You may have seen this list years ago in school, but you may not have realized just how powerful a tool it is. Some of the most complex or dramatic stories ever written were generated by information gathered by asking the same basic questions: What happened? When? Where? Why? Who was involved, or who should have been involved? What happens now? How can things improve in the future?

Use the five W's to guide you in gathering the information you need to write a thorough, accurate story that responds to the questions of the reader.

THE FIVE W's IN ACTION

One late Friday night, on a narrow, winding road, a woman lost her life to what has become the most deadly of weapons: the automobile. It happens every day in this country.

In Kill Devil Hills, N.C., a picturesque seaside village where the Wright brothers flew the first airplane, such a thing was rare enough to become a news story. The report began this way:

KILL DEVIL HILLS, N.C. — A 30-year-old Virginia woman died after a five-car accident Friday night near the intersection of Colington Road and the U.S. 158 bypass.

Deanna Marie Rhodes of Madison Heights, Va., was killed when the Jeep in which she was a passenger was hit from behind by a Ford Taurus and flipped over, Kill Devil Hills police said.

Her husband, Michael A. Rhodes, 42, and another passenger, William C. Goff of Rustburg, Va., were taken to Sentara Norfolk General Hospital. Michael Rhodes was driving the Jeep, which had stopped for traffic, police said.

Five vehicles and nine people were involved in the accident.

The story went on to tell readers in that community how long it took to clear the wreck and the names of the other people injured. It described the intersection's history as a common place for accidents.

But the reporter captured the most essential information in the top four paragraphs. This form of story organization is known as the inverted pyramid, where the reporter answers the most pressing questions right away:

- *Who was involved?* A Virginia couple, a passenger in their car, and six other people in four other cars. The Kill Devil Hills police responded to the accident.
- *What happened?* A woman was killed in a five-car accident. Others were injured.
- *Where?* Colington Road and U.S. 158 bypass. The "dateline" — journalists' term for starting a story with the name of the city where the events occurred — also cites location.
- *When?* Friday night.
- *Why?* This story doesn't say. It tells us the Jeep was hit after it stopped for traffic, but not why the driver of the Ford Taurus failed to stop. In paragraphs that follow those shown above, the story hints that alcohol may have been involved, but no definite conclusion is drawn.
- *How did it happen?* The woman who died was a passenger in a Jeep that was hit from behind by a Ford Taurus. The Jeep overturned, causing a chain reaction with the other vehicles.

The "why" of a story is often the most difficult and elusive element, because the root causes for many events are complex. Even in a straightforward story like this one, the police were unwilling to say that alcohol was the cause of the wreck, because no charges had been filed at the time of the newspaper's deadline. Later reports said that the driver of the Taurus was charged with driving under the influence of alcohol and second-degree murder.

To get answers to questions about an accident like this one, the reporter — you — would go to the scene of the accident to see firsthand what was going on. You would interview witnesses and talk to investigating officers, if possible, or call them later. You would call the hospital as near to deadline as possible to update the condition of the injured. You would read written police reports. You would check the files, which newspapers may call their archives, library or "the morgue," for information about previous accidents at the same intersection and any previous driving infractions of the drivers involved.

Each of those information-gathering methods gives you a different "take" on what happened.

Reporters who cover police news usually go to the scene so they can get information as soon as it is available. Here, some reporters chow down on pizza as they wait across the street from a home where a murder-suicide occurred in Manteo, N.C.

Photo by Drew Wilson. Source: The Virginian-Pilot

- At the scene, you can see who is involved and what role they are playing. You can see and possibly have a chance to interview participants or witnesses. You can watch what happens and recount with eyewitness vividness any dramatic moments that occur. You can make note of things that seem puzzling or interesting, so that you can ask about them later. You also can learn about customary procedures for handling the kind of situation you're observing.

- In your interviews with various sources — whether they be witnesses, investigators, hospital personnel, government officials, community organizers, or others — you can quickly obtain information from people who know things that you don't. They can give you the facts — but they can also give you much more than that. They may have expertise or training that enables them to evaluate and explain things; they may have a relationship to the story that helps you identify the emotional issues or tensions involved; or they may have supplementary information that helps you place the story into context.

• Written reports and records also serve as quick ways of getting information. Most events that have importance to the public are documented in some way. All public agencies, businesses and non-profit organizations are required to keep various records that are open to the public. Some are made available to reporters routinely; others require more digging. Whenever such records are available, it's a good idea to check them.

No matter what the subject of your story — fatal accident, community festival, government meeting, or profile of a notable person — you will rely on the same three basic information-gathering skills: observing, interviewing and researching. And in every case, the following guidelines apply:

• Be there — or be careful.
• Quote people precisely.
• Identify people fully.

Be there — or be careful. If you plan to use information from a meeting or event, make every effort to be there and stay as long as time permits. If you must limit your time, try to find out in advance

Research within the Newsroom

Most daily newspapers and some college papers maintain archives that are a valuable resource for adding background information, putting stories into context and spotting the larger story — a trend, danger or problem — as it is developing.

These archives usually are housed in a part of the newspaper building called the library or "morgue" (because "dead" articles were filed there while reporters worked on "live" stories).

Depending on the newsroom, archived stories might be available in electronic form from a reporter's computer, from designated library terminals or through a search of the newspaper's back issues online. At many daily newspapers, older sto-

ries are archived on microfilm or in file folders of clippings. In such cases, library staff usually can help reporters find information.

When archives are not available, it is often possible to ask an experienced staff member if he or she can remember whether, and hopefully when, the paper has run related stories in the past. You then can use that information to find those stories in back issues.

As a reporter, checking for past stories also can save you from embarrassment. Editors don't like to find that a reporter is pursuing a story that was published a month ago.

what will be going on and when. If you must leave before something is discussed, arrange to call people later to see what happened. Never assume that something that was expected to happen actually did.

Quote people precisely. When quoting someone, be sure to get the person's exact words. Never guess. And if you use quotes related to you by other people, make it clear who gave you the quote. For example: "Police said the bank robber calmly told the teller, 'Please give me all the money in your cash register and no one will get hurt.'"

Identify people fully. Be sure to get the full name and other identifying information about each person. It's always preferable to use a person's legal name, city or town of residence and that person's relationship to the story. If the person's occupation has something to do with the story, some or all of the following also may be important: the job, official title or employer. If the person is commonly known by a nickname, proper form is to put that in quotation marks (Jack "Bulldog" Cutter, for instance). Know your newspaper's policies for things like middle initials and honorific titles. In addition, when reporting potentially sensitive stories involving severe injury, death or accusations of wrongdoing, be sure to include as much identifying information as possible to prevent confusion about who is injured, dead or accused.

BEFORE YOU BEGIN REPORTING

One of the best ways to save time is to spend time planning before you even do your first interview. Good planning can save you from ending up with gaps in your stories that will cause your editor to send you back to your desk to make frantic, last-minute calls on deadline. It can prevent you from wasting valuable time calling people when they're not available or driving back and forth across town for interviews.

Choose your sources wisely. As a general rule, draw on at least three sources of information. Sometimes deadline pressures limit the sources available. Other stories — a report of an approaching snowstorm, for instance, in which only a meteorologist is quoted — can work with only one source. Generally, though, more is better.

Talk to people who are responsible, involved and affected. The source list usually includes at least one person noted as being in charge (or that person's designated spokesperson) who is organizing an event, leading an investigation, overseeing government action or representing a side in a controversy. Beside interviewing the person

Who Can Tell You What You Need to Know?

Knowing whom to contact requires first knowing what you're looking for. Make a list of the things you already know about your story. If it helps, use the five W's as an organizing tool. Then ask yourself:

- How sure am I that my information is accurate?
- Where did I get my information? How reliable is the source?
- Who would be the most reliable person to contact to clarify or confirm any information that seems shaky to me?

Make a list of the things you still need to find out, then ask yourself:

- What information do I need first?
- What information can I get only from one source, and what could I get from a variety of sources?
- Who is most likely to be able to tell me what I still need to know?

in charge, consider who is responsible (that may not be the same person), who might be involved behind the scenes, and who else has a stake in what's happening.

Talk to people in a position to know. A receptionist may be willing to tell you everything he or she knows and may prove to be a very reliable source of information. But make sure you differentiate gossip from fact. Take what you learn from the receptionist and use it to ask better questions of the person in charge.

Find out who has been most visible with respect to your story. Are some people or groups of people being portrayed as officials or experts whose knowledge should be respected? Is that appropriate? Are some people or groups of people being cast as villains, victims, heroes or scapegoats? If so, are they really? Also talk to not-so-obvious sources. Has anyone who has a stake in what's happening been excluded, in some way, from events or discussions? Are the interests of some people being marginalized or overlooked? If so, how can you get their views? And look for sources who can give you background information: a sense of the history and traditions of an area or event.

In other words, choose a mix of sources. If you go out to interview people on the street or in other public places, be sure you don't just talk to people who look like you — who are of the same race and age group and who dress (basically) like you and others in your family or social group. It's important to be aware that most of us tend to do that. Make a conscious effort to contact a more accurate cross-section of people in your stories.

In your planning, don't rely on friends or relatives to fill out your source list. If you feel you must quote someone you know well, be sure your editor knows about it before you start gathering information for the story. There's nothing wrong with gathering ideas from the people you know. But if reporters consistently quote their friends and family when they could quote others, it looks like they are either lazy or using their position to promote themselves and people close to them.

Also ask yourself whether your own biases or preconceptions might influence the fairness and balance of the story. If your personal interest is too strong, it's your obligation as a journalist to ask your editor to remove you from the story.

Work with sources' schedules. You'll have better luck reaching people and you'll get better cooperation from them if you're not begging for an interview at the last minute or at some odd time that suits only your schedule. In some cases the story may be urgent enough for you to contact them no matter what the day or hour. But when possible, fit your schedule to match theirs. Also allow enough time for them to gather the details you want. Although most reporters would love it if all information were available immediately, that just isn't so, especially if you're asking for information that requires some research.

Decide whom to contact first. Try to schedule this first interview with one person who can give you a general overview, which will lay a foundation for the interviews that follow. In an accident story like the example given earlier, that first person might be the investigating officer or the police department's public information officer. However, if the investigating officer is busy and the public information officer isn't in, gather information from whomever you can reach. Reporting is rarely linear. If the primary source isn't available, go to your secondary sources. Don't let one uncooperative or unavailable source stop you.

If you need to interview citizens for a story, where should you look for them? Are there scheduled activities where you could find either specific groups of people or a broad mix of citizens, depending on what's appropriate for your story? Are there public places (parks, sidewalks or government buildings) or businesses (stores, shopping malls or restaurants) where you could find people to interview? (Keep in mind that businesses are private property, which means you should ask permission of the person in charge before you approach their customers to gather information for a story.)

Make a list of all the other places you might find information. Consider what written press materials, records, reports, photographs, artwork, maps, or other materials might add to your story. Where can you get them? Common locations for such information include libraries, museums, archives, colleges and universities, chambers of commerce, tourism bureaus, Web sites, government and nonprofit offices, and businesses. If you feel you need to buy any photocopies or other materials for your story, be sure to ask your editor to approve the expense *before* you spend any money — unless you don't mind spending your own money.

Note the locations of offices, businesses or homes of people you plan to interview in person, as well as places you need to stop to interview citizens or pick up written materials. Are some locations clustered together? Are they spread out? Can you schedule your interviews either in clusters or along a logical route to reduce or eliminate the time you spend getting back and forth between locations?

A central goal of all these routines is to make sure your story is accurate. Each story offers opportunities to hone good reporting habits. Think about your strengths and weaknesses with respect to skills that are useful for reporters. How comfortable do you feel about interviewing? How good are you at taking notes? How well do you do research? How well and how quickly do you write? Are any aspects of this story particularly challenging for you? If you can't take notes quickly, for instance, and you've been asked to cover a speech, what can you do to make sure you get the information you need? You'll certainly want to work on improving your note-taking skills, but it also might be a good idea to take a tape recorder as a backup or ask if you can get a printed copy of the speech. If your story involves an interview with the governor and you feel nervous about interviewing someone so famous, what can you do to make sure you maintain your composure? It might help to prepare a checklist of topics you want to be sure to cover, or role-play the interview with a friend.

ASKING EFFECTIVE QUESTIONS

"The Q is the mother of the A," says Dennis Hartig, editorial page editor of The (Norfolk) Virginian-Pilot. And, as any reporter soon learns, if you don't ask good enough questions — or enough good questions — your story is likely to be incomplete or, worse, just plain wrong. For many people, asking questions is one of the biggest challenges of reporting.

Even Pulitzer Prize-winning reporters such as Edna Buchanan, former police reporter for the Miami Herald, learn the hard way about the importance of asking enough good questions. In her book, "The Corpse Had a Familiar Face: Covering Miami, America's Hottest Beat," Buchanan describes an experience that taught her the value of asking the right questions:

A man was shot and dumped into the street by a killer in a pickup truck. The case seemed somewhat routine — if one can ever call murder routine. But later, I learned that at the time the victim was shot he was wearing a black taffeta cocktail dress and red high heels. I tracked down the detectives and asked, "Why didn't you tell me?"

"You didn't ask," they chorused. Now I always ask.

We discuss more about asking questions skillfully in Chapter 8. Meanwhile, the following list can help you think through questions to ask your sources. Not every question will apply to every story, obviously, but many are questions commonly overlooked by beginning reporters.

Who?

- Who is responsible? Who is being (or should be) praised? Who is being (or should be) blamed? Who is being (or should be) held accountable?
- Who wasn't there? (If the mayor didn't show up at the annual city leaders' prayer breakfast because she overslept, it's mentionable but minor. But if she didn't show up because she didn't think it appropriate for the city to sponsor a prayer breakfast, then her absence becomes the story.)
- Who else might need to be involved? Who else do you need to call or visit to make the story complete?

What?

- What happened, or what will happen?
- What is the main theme of the story, or does it have more than one theme? (Ask this question of yourself during the reporting to make sure you are maintaining a sharp focus.)
- "What do you mean by that?" is an excellent clarifying question. (Inexperienced reporters often are afraid to appear unintelligent. Each time you ask this question, you give the person you're talking to another chance to explain and to elaborate on some important point.)

When?

- When did it happen, or when will it happen? (Be sure to get precise information, whenever possible. Get the day, date and time down to the minute. If the story involves a sequence of events, get that information for each event in the sequence.)

• When were things different? (This question is useful for stories about changes that have occurred over a period of time in a community.)

• When will you know more?

Where?

• Where did it happen? (Again, it's important to get precise information. Recall the story earlier about the fatal accident. The reporter needed to know the city and the street intersection.)

• Where is the common ground? Where are the differences?

• Where are you from? (Don't assume that a person interviewed in River City lives there. Ask.)

Why?

• Why is this happening? (Any 3-year-old can tell you the power of this question. That's how the child learns, by asking why or by asking its close cousin, "Why not.")

• Why now?

• Why should people care about this?

How?

• How did it happen?

• How could this change people's lives?

• How were things different in the past? How could things be different in the future?

In time, as Edna Buchanan has done, you will develop your own mental list of "must-ask" questions. Some questions are essential for any story, no matter what the topic; others depend on what kinds of stories you are called upon to write. For example, the question about what people were wearing can be very important for a police reporter. Noting what a woman wore during a court proceeding but not a man in similar circumstances could be a subtle form of inappropriate stereotyping in your stories. And a reporter covering government meetings rarely finds the information on what a public official is wearing to be useful. In any case, if you can draw on a mental list of questions like those above, you'll never be at a loss for what to ask next.

ASSESSING WHETHER YOU'RE READY TO WRITE

Once you feel you have interviewed all your sources and gathered all the information you need for your story, it's a good idea to assess whether you're ready to move on to the writing stage of news reporting.

Ask yourself if you are clear about what has happened, is happening or will happen — and why. If you feel vague or "fuzzy" about any aspect of the story, find more sources or ask more questions until you are certain everything is clear to you.

Ask yourself whether you have all the information you need. Have you been able to reach all the people you planned to contact? If not, have you found other people? Check for any loose ends.

Finally, ask yourself whether you could write a headline for your story. If so, what would it be? "Woman killed in five-car accident"? "Festival organizers expect record crowds"? "City council approves rezoning plan"? If you can't think of a headline, you may not be clear yet on what the story is about, which may point to a need for more reporting. Or it could be that you have gone beyond the original story idea, in which case you may need to change the focus of the story and discard some information or talk with your editor about funneling it into related stories.

As you are assessing whether you're ready to write, you may realize that you didn't get enough information to support writing the story the way it was originally conceived. Or maybe you uncovered something more important than the focus of your original assignment. What then?

You have several choices — all of which should involve interaction with your editor. Here's how such a situation might play out:

Are You Ready to Write?

Ask yourself:

- Am I clear as to what this story is about?
- Have I left any loose ends?
- What would be a good headline for this story?

If you can answer yes to the first question, no to the second, and have an answer for the third, you're probably ready to start writing.

Let's say an irate citizen calls one of Jack Cutter's editors to report on dangerous potholes that are snarling traffic at a busy intersection.

"Go out there and take a look at the holes," Jack's editor tells him. "We should check with the photo department as well, to see if they can free up a photographer."

Jack agrees and also suggests that he find out from the city how long those holes have been there and what the transportation people plan to do.

"Definitely," Jack's editor says. "Oh, and while you're in City Hall, you might want to check with the police department to see if there were reports about traffic accidents there in the past week or so."

Jack arrives to find a street crew repairing one of two basketball-sized holes that washed out near a clogged storm drain when a fierce thunder shower doused the city two nights ago. The other hole is marked with a warning sign. Not much of a photo, but the photographer takes one anyway and heads back to the office.

The street crew tells Jack they found out about the holes right after the storm, put up warning signs early the next morning, but had to wait a couple days for the holes to dry out enough to repair them. It doesn't appear to be a case of government neglect.

Jack goes back to the office and tells his editor, "There's no 'dangerous potholes' story. The city's fixing them as we speak, so I'm gonna go finish my profile of that new councilwoman, Jane Curic."

"Hold on, Jack," his editor says. "So there's no 'dangerous potholes' story. But is there another story there? Are those the only potholes they're fixing? Was there any other damage from that storm? And how 'bout other storms this year? We've already gotten record amounts of rain this year — have the street crews been busier than normal? How many drains have been clogged? And aren't we supposed to get some more storms later this week? How will all of that affect the Street Department's budget?"

"Hmmm, you've got a point," Jack says. "Maybe I should find out. And while I'm at it, I could get information about how the city decides what to fix first after storms."

"Yep, and we could include information about what citizens should do if they come across potholes or other damage that poses hazards. At some point, you might also think about writing a feature story about what it's like to work on the street crew, mashing gravel and tar into potholes all day long in the sweltering summer heat."

"Gotcha. I'll get right on it," Jack says.

Of course, stories can change in countless other ways in the reporting process. Sometimes it's enough to adjust the focus of the

Thinking about Rethinking

If you are wondering if you need to re-think your approach to a story, here are some questions that can help

- What didn't you find that you expected to find?
- What did you find that you didn't expect?
- If the original story idea was based on inaccurate information or assumptions, is the story still worth writing?

- Did you learn things that make the story seem more significant than was implied by your original assignment?
- Have you recognized any broader implications or human angles to the story that you could use as the basis for writing a different kind of article?
- What other kinds of articles could you write, based on what you learned in your reporting?

story slightly. Other times, simple stories can turn into major exposés. Consider, for example, the case of the two Berkeley High School journalists who decided to find out if an Indian teen-ager who died in her apartment two blocks from the school was a student there, so they could do a story on her. She wasn't. But a South Asian teacher told them that she believed the girl may have been sold into servitude in return for passage to the United States. The students then tracked down leads and exposed an illegal immigration scheme more than a month before any other news organization.

EXERCISES

1. Pair up with another student. Spend at least 15 minutes finding out as much as possible about the student by asking just three questions: Where are you from? What do you mean by that? Why? Don't ask any other questions, but you can ask those as many times as you like. Exchange roles with your fellow student, and use the same questions.

2. Find a full-page ad in your local newspaper. Using only the material in the ad, identify as many of the five W's and one H as possible. (You may assume that the ad is running for the first time.) Or do the same with a poster on campus announcing an upcoming event. Write a lead to a story from that information.

Further Reading

ON THE WEB

The Poynter Institute for Media Studies' Quick Click resource for reporters: www.poynter.org/quickclick/reporter.htm   Includes links to many resources available on The Poynter Web site as well as links to other sites.

Chapter 6

Writing Basic, Informative News Stories

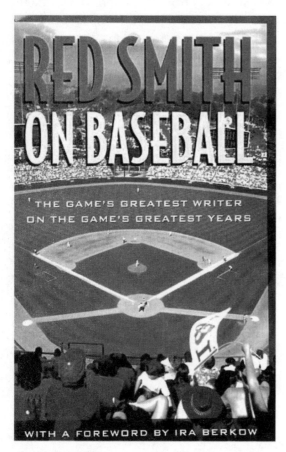

Source: Ivan R. Dee

▬▬▬▬▬▬▬▬ **Key Concepts** ▬▬▬▬▬▬▬▬

- After the reporting phase comes the writing phase. Good journalists spend time preparing to write, deciding how to organize the story and focusing the lead.

- It's important to make adjustments when the information gathered during the reporting process does not support the original story idea.

- *Importance* is the dominant organizing principle of news stories. Most news stories begin by focusing on the single most important piece of information, and the remaining material is added in order of diminishing importance.

When they talk about writing, journalists love to quote the great "New York Times" sportswriter Red Smith. "Writing is easy," he once said. "All you do is sit down at a typewriter and open a vein."

Most writers know the feeling. Whether you're writing news stories or term papers or fiction, you experience a moment of truth after all the research, reporting or other preparation is done. You sit down to write ... and realize you really should empty the trash first, or clear off your desk, or order a pizza, or go get a cup of coffee — anything but stringing together those first few sentences that commit you to the writing process.

Don't despair. Longtime writing coaches Roy Peter Clark and Don Fry, in their book "Coaching Writers: The Essential Guide for Editors and Reporters," say that those behaviors are normal — and can even be developed into routines that can serve you as a writer: "[The best reporters] develop idiosyncrasies that help them build momentum during the writing process: pilgrimages to the restroom, chain-smoking, pacing, daydreaming, junk food orgies, or self-flagellation."

If you haven't written news stories before, you might be tempted to start your first story with an introduction or thesis statement, as you would with an academic paper. If you've taken minutes in organizational meetings, you may find yourself writing stories about events by arranging the information in chronological order. But basic, informative news stories almost always should start with the news — the information that is most current, most important or most interesting.

Sometimes it's hard to decide what that is, especially if the story has several elements that seem equally newsworthy.

Sometimes it's difficult because the information you've gathered does not support your original story idea. In such cases, you might feel torn between trying to make that information fit the original idea and having the imagination and the confidence to revise the story idea.

No matter what the challenges, the basic process remains the same:

- Prepare to write by reviewing or organizing your notes and thinking about the relative importance of the material you've gathered.
- Be sure the information supports your original story idea — or revise the idea.
- Focus the beginning, called the lead, by deciding what's most important, most current or most interesting about your story.
- Think through how you will organize the rest of your information to flesh out the story.

PREPARING TO WRITE

Preparing to write is one of the most valuable things news writers can do.

"Experienced [news writing] coaches find that most writing problems occur in the organizing stage," Clark and Fry say. "Many writers with problems simply skip any form of organization at all. ... They may move directly from reporting to grappling for a lead, and then decide what they want to say."

A few minutes of planning can save hours of agony. Fry, for example, described the process he used in preparing a story about a speech. He went back through his notes, underlined the high points, eliminated bits he did not expect to use in the story, and wrote notes in the left margin. He then used two focusing questions taught to him by Christopher Scanlan of the Poynter Institute for Media Studies: "What's this about?" and "What's my point?" Using the latter question, he wrote a "point statement" that helped clarify what material he would use; anything that didn't support his point was then omitted. He sketched out a plan for the story by asking himself what the reader needs to know and in what order. At various stages of this process, he talked out loud to himself and scribbled down a list of whatever struck him. In all, he spent 10 minutes preparing to write.

For most reporters, the preparation process includes reviewing the information, spending some time thinking about their story, and "sketching out" the story in some fashion. The methods by which they accomplish these steps vary greatly depending on personal preferences and styles. In addition, most reporters find that, as they gain experience, their preparation process evolves.

Putting notes in order is key for many reporters, especially when they are working on in-depth reports about news with far-reaching impact. "The best reporters devote a lot of time to the mechanical drudgery of organizing the material, what Associated Press reporter Saul Pett describes as 'donkey work.' They make a fetish of creating careful filing systems," Clark and Fry wrote. Other reporters, like Fry, may mark their notes using symbols as simple as check marks or circles — especially if they are writing a relatively simple story. Still others index and categorize their notes, either by hand or using a computer program.

Thinking through how to write stories is an equally individualistic process. Some reporters, like Fry, scribble down notes and talk to themselves. Others talk to their steering wheels while running errands. Longtime newspaper editor Dick Thien, who went on to teach at the University of Nebraska at Lincoln, suggests that writers clarify the focus of their story by trying to summarize it in one sentence.

Thien also suggests that writers use a form of outlining. "Jot down key words or phrases from your notes to indicate the main parts of your story," he writes. "Then put them in the order [in which] you will use them." The next step, he says, is to make note of the facts or quotes you have to back up each part of your story. Kent State University professor and writing coach Carl Schierhorn suggests that reporters write "a three-minute outline" before sitting down to write every story.

Many editors require reporters to write their own budget lines and/or a possible headline, partly because that helps them focus the story. Veteran writing coach Donald Murray cites an example in which the only preparation a Boston Globe reporter seemed to need was some time to think:

> "How much time do I have?" the reporter asked his editor.
> "We want it in an hour."

"Great," he said, looking at his watch. "I've got time for dinner."

Murray followed him to the Globe cafeteria, watched him wolf down his supper and sit staring into space, his lips moving slowly for 10 minutes. Then the reporter returned to the newsroom and poured the story into the keys in nothing flat. Murray asked him later what he was doing while he sat staring in the cafeteria.

"Rehearsing," he replied.

TIPS FOR GETTING STARTED

If you've written news stories before, you may already have developed ways of preparing to write that work for you. If this process is new to you, however, or if you would like to explore ways of improving your abilities in this area, the suggestions that follow may help.

You can always fall back on the tried-and-true five W's. List as many whos, whats, whens, wheres, whys and hows as you can. If you're writing about a future event, for example, who's organizing it? Whom do they want to attend? Who else is likely to be affected by the event? What will happen during the event? When? When did the history of the event begin? Where will things take place? Why is the event being planned? Why are the organizers involved? How will it affect people?

If you go through your notes, as many editors and writing coaches suggest, develop your own system for marking key facts, pertinent quotes and questions that remain. Some suggestions:

- Get in the habit of making marks, writing comments or noting key words in one margin or the other.
- Mark your notes using ink of a different color.
- Use underlining or a highlighter. You can even use various colors to highlight different types of information — one color for quotes, one for historical information, and so on.

If you typed your notes into a computer, either during or after your interviews, always keep a copy of your original notes, either in print form or on disk. Then you can mark printouts of the notes as described above, use word processing options like underline and boldfacing to flag important points, or even pare down and reorganize the material to create a "skeleton" for your story.

While you are reviewing your notes, it is also a good idea to double-check your information for accuracy. Be sure you are solid on the spellings of all proper names, job titles of people you have quoted, dates and times of any events mentioned in your stories, and addresses and phone numbers you plan to include. (It may be helpful to take a few moments to review the section on accuracy in Chapter 3.)

After you have taken an initial pass through your notes, go back through them and mentally group together, or "chunk," pieces of related information. Be on the lookout for several kinds of information that can help you organize your story, or sections of your story. You won't use all of these in any story, but you can use some of the following for the simplest event reporting to the most in-depth piece.

Anecdotes

These little stories can be extremely valuable in helping you illustrate key points. They also can form the basis for your lead. Before you go through your notes, ask yourself if you remember any amusing, moving or interesting stories people told you. Was there one that seemed to say it all? If so, consider using that as your lead. Be careful, though. It is easy to become enamored with an anecdote or quote that doesn't quite fit the point of your story or that seems "tacked on." It's not enough to have a great anecdote if it doesn't illuminate the larger frame for the whole story.

Key Players

Who's who in your story? What is each player's role? Who has the power? Who has the information? Who has the money? Who's been most involved, or involved for the longest time? Who is relatively new to what you're writing about? Where and how do these people's lives and experiences intersect — or do they? If you're confused about the relationships or your story involves lots of people, it may help to create a who's who list, noting key facts about each person. This list can be useful as a reference or as a starting point for writing a "key players" sidebar, as described in Chapter 9.

Sequences of Events

Historical and background information is also important in many stories. Ask yourself how significant that information (no matter how recent the history) is to your story. Will your readers understand the story (or parts of the story) better if they have background information about what preceded the latest development? It may help to type out a timeline that gives a step-by-step account of what happened when. As with the key players list, this timeline can be useful either as a reference or as the start of a sidebar to your main story, if the history is extremely interesting or unusual.

Themes

Watch for recurring, unifying themes. Did the people you interviewed keep coming back to certain points? If so, what were they? What are the relationships, if any, between the themes? This is especially important in stories involving public policy issues like education, poverty, abortion, or responding to terrorism. Be sure you are mindful of the full range of perspectives expressed by the people you interviewed, not just the predictable polar extremes.

Cause-and-Effect Relationships

Did people tell you that one thing caused another? If so, make a list of these cause-and-effect relationships and, if appropriate, put them in order: *What* led to *what*, which then led to *what*? Are people in agreement about what caused what? If not, what are the areas of agreement and disagreement? Like the others, this list can be used as a reference or as a starting point for writing a segment of your story or a sidebar.

Series or Sets of Information

Details like research data, statistics, multiple examples, how-to tips, places to vote or get flu shots, or routine actions taken by governmental agencies make boring prose. Better to put such information in list form in your story. As you're going through your notes, think about whether anyone rattled off facts and figures or examples to support what they were saying, or gave advice in the form of how-to tips. If so, consider putting these related tidbits into list form within your story, using dashes or "bullets" to set off each item in the list.

You're Only as Credible as Your Sources

In the interest of accuracy, be sure you aren't accepting shaky information at face value.

As you go over your notes, pay special attention whenever anyone places blame for something on certain people or organizations.

Is it clear that those people or organizations were to blame? What factual evidence or expertise did the accuser cite to support his claims?

Does the person have any apparent biases? If so, are these biases influencing his or her judgment?

Does the person have anything to gain by pointing the finger at someone else? Might the accusations be a way of turning the focus away from his or her own responsibility? Does this person work for an organization that will benefit in some way from turning public opinion against the people or organizations being blamed?

Are you sure you know exactly for whom the person is working? (Remember that many organizations with vague or innocuous-sounding names are backed by special interest groups.)

How will you deal with issues of attribution and provide a sufficient explanation of this person's perspective so that the reader can evaluate the information?

What might the people who are being blamed have to say for themselves? Were they given an opportunity to respond?

Also be sensitive to the stereotyping that often creeps in when people make poorly documented allegations. If a speaker makes broad generalizations about teen-agers, college students, athletes, a minority group, women, computer enthusiasts or other groups of people, on what are they basing those generalizations?

All accusations are not groundless, but journalists must be sure that all information that appears in their news stories is well supported by factual evidence or expert opinion.

It's a matter of credibility. If you unwittingly pass along bad information because you didn't check it out, it doesn't make you look any better to place the blame on the person you quoted. Think about it: Is that any different from someone passing on juicy but untrue gossip about you, then denying responsibility for the fact that it hurt you? Doesn't the person have a responsibility to evaluate that information before passing it on?

DECIDE WHAT'S MOST IMPORTANT

After you've gone through your notes, it's a good idea to spend some time thinking about what's most important about your story. In the news business, *importance* is defined in terms of (1) breadth and depth of impact, (2) what is most current, and/or (3) what is most interesting.

Deciding the relative importance of various bits of information can be one of the greatest challenges for less experienced reporters.

It may help to ask yourself what people will want to know first when they read the story, and what they will want to know next. It may help to imagine having a conversation with a friend, relative or perfect stranger — what would you tell them first?

Filter what you've learned through your knowledge about the community. What will matter most to the people for whom you're writing? Why will it matter to them? Concentrate on which elements of your story truly are the most important, not just those that are most dramatic or unusual. Also think about how the subject of your story fits into the greater context of community concerns. Is it related to other issues or developments? If so, should you bring those points into your story?

It may help you to look back at the list of news values in Chapter 4. Assign importance to information that fits into any of the categories on that list. If your story involves any of the following elements, always include that information in the lead:

- Loss of human life
- Widespread destruction of property
- Obstruction or disruption of activity in the lives of a great number of people
- Decisions that will have broad, significant impact
- Corruption or other criminal behavior by people in positions of public trust

If you're writing about something that has been unfolding over time, it may be best to begin with what will happen next (including the expected impact of an event or decision). If no future activity is likely, focus on what happened most recently.

In stories with no obvious time or dramatic elements, however, deciding which information is most important can be more difficult. Journalists often disagree.

That was true in the account of how Jack Cutter developed his story in Chapter 2. After he learned that Jane Curic had filed papers to run for city council, he had to sort through what he thought was most important: Was it her status as a university student? The fact that she had little past political experience? That she was fed up with the current city council? That she thought more should be done to deal with the tensions between her university and the community? That much of the campaigning so far was marked by conflict and pettiness? That experts thought she was unlikely to win?

Initially, Cutter focused on Jane's status as a novice wading into a crowded field of contentious candidates. His editor, however, encouraged him to simplify the lead, placing less emphasis on the drama of the race and more on the issues Curic wanted to bring to light.

Those shifts in focus reflect differences in judgment as to what is most important about the story. Another editor might have been satisfied with Cutter's original story. From his current editor's perspective, what was most important in that story was not whether Curic would win but the issues she wanted to bring to the community's attention.

Sometimes, such differences of opinion won't surface until your story is being edited. If you have a chance to chat briefly with your editor before you begin writing, it will reduce the chances that you will be required to make unexpected revisions in your story.

COMMON TYPES OF NEWS STORIES

With experience, you will develop your own internal guidance system for writing news stories. Reporters like the one Murray observed at the Boston Globe often can sit down and dash off a well-written story without much apparent preparation, because they have done it so many times before that it comes automatically.

For now, however, it probably will be helpful to review the common types of news stories:

- The inverted pyramid
- Chronological and "hourglass," or "funnel," stories
- Question and answer stories
- Lists
- Segmented stories

Pay attention to how they are structured, how quotes are used, and how they place events and issues into community contexts.

Most of the stories here use *importance* as the overarching organizing principle. Some also use creative approaches to liven up the lead.

Consider these an "idea file" you can read through to help organize your own stories. It's also a good idea to start an idea file of your own, into which you put clippings of stories you think are well-written. Next time you feel sluggish getting started on a story, you may be able to get some ideas by looking through those clippings.

The Inverted Pyramid

Most news stories are written in what is called "inverted pyramid" form. In this type of story, the first sentence, paragraph or section contains the most important, most current or most interesting information. This is followed by a sentence, often called a "nut graph," that explains why the story is important now. Usually, this is followed by a bit of historical background or other information that puts the story into context. Remaining information is organized by theme, with the themes arranged in the order of diminishing importance. The story is described as an inverted pyramid because it's top-heavy with the most important information.

"The inverted pyramid organizes stories not around ideas or

The Inverted Pyramid

Long before the Internet changed modern communication, the telegraph revolutionized the way information was sent through time and space. Instead of giving a mailman a piece of paper to deliver to someone hundreds of miles away, people could go to the Western Union office, write out a terse message, and pay for the telegraph operator to tap out the letters in Morse code, which was then transcribed by another operator in a faraway town.

During the U.S. Civil War, the telegraph became an invaluable tool to reporters who were charged with sending in stories from the battlefront. The only problem was that the telegraph lines were often unreliable. Reporters started putting the most important information first, so even if they got cut off, their paper still would be able to report the gist of the story.

This inverted pyramid form also proved useful when it came to laying out the pages of a newspaper on a deadline. If a late-breaking story was too long to fit in the space that had formerly been occupied by a less important story, the people composing the pages could easily cut the story from the bottom — knowing they would be sacrificing the least important information.

Source: "A History of News," by Mitchell Stephens

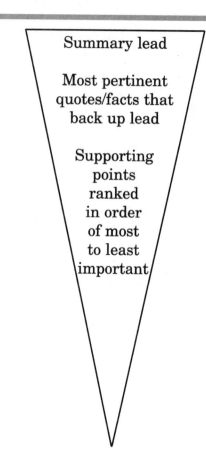

This figure illustrates the construction of the story format journalists call "the inverted pyramid."

Congressional reporters in Washington, D.C., race to the telegraph office to file their stories in this 1868 woodcut.
Source: Bettmann/Corbis

chronologies but around facts. It weights and shuffles the various pieces of information, focusing with remarkable single-mindedness on their relative news value," Mitchell Stephens writes in "A History of News."

Importance, then, is the dominant organizing principle for inverted pyramid stories. Within the pyramid, sections of the story are arranged according to their relative importance. These sections may contain the following:

- narratives — information that is engaging in terms of its storytelling value (especially anecdotes that illustrate what the story's about);
- sequential information — chronological storytelling, real-life dialogue, and cause-and-effect relationships
- similar items — multiple examples or lists

Every journalist must be able to write stories in the inverted pyramid form. Even stories that segue into other common story forms — hourglass stories, lists, segmented stories — usually begin with an inverted pyramid-style lead. It is therefore essential that, if you want to be a journalist (or understand journalism), you learn to write stories in this way before moving on to other forms of news writing.

Now, on one level, you already know what inverted pyramids are because, if you've read even a single newspaper, you've read at least a couple dozen such stories. If you haven't already written one, you may have parodied them in joking with your friends: "I can see it now: A 19-year-old college student was arrested Tuesday for writing the dumbest paper ever in the history of humanity."

The accident story in the previous chapter was a good example of a real-life inverted pyramid story. Here's another:

Internet bids for kidney race into millions before eBay pulls plug

By Jessie Seyfer
Associated Press Writer

SAN FRANCISCO (AP) — Internet bargain hunters bid into the millions for one of two human kidneys up for sale before online auctioneer eBay put a stop to the macabre sale.

Customers on eBay drove the price of one human kidney, offered up for sale Aug. 26 for $25,000, up to $5.7 million. The second kidney, posted Thursday afternoon with an asking price of $4 million, didn't receive any bids before it was pulled.

"Obviously these are pranks," eBay spokeswoman Kristin Seuell said Thursday. But, "we don't want to leave anything to chance."

The kidney auction was stopped because eBay's rules forbid the sale of body parts. Selling your own organs also is a violation of federal law, a felony punishable by up to five years in prison or a $50,000 fine.

The first seller, identified as "hchero" from Sunrise, Fla., advertised a "fully functional kidney for sale."

"You can choose either kidney. Buyer pays all transplant and medical costs," the description read. "Of course only one for sale, as I need the other one to live. Serious bids only."

A message sent to hchero's e-mail address was not answered Thursday.

Kevin Pursglove, an eBay spokesman, said the company lists 2.5 million items each day and has no system to spot questionable offers unless alerted by users.

"Any time you have an open trading environment with almost 6 million registered users, you're likely to see somebody who tries to bend the rules, or ... pull a prank," Pursglove said.

Dr. Thomas Reardon, president of the American Medical Association, was taken aback by news of the supposed sale.

"I'd question the ethics of any doctor who would participate in that kind of transaction," he said.

According to a 1999 study by the United Network of Organ Sharing, 44,000 people in the U.S. are waiting for kidney transplants.

"The need for organ donors is obviously great," said Barbara Hofstein, director of the National Kidney Foundation of Northern

California. "Attempting to sell organs opens up an enormous range of potential abuse."

Earlier this year, San Jose-based eBay banned the sale of guns and ammunition on the site, after people tried selling a missile, a bazooka, a rocket launcher and other military weapons.

Source: Associated Press, Sept. 3, 1999

You've read a zillion stories written in much the same way, right? But let's take a few moments to dissect the story above.

The lead. The lead is one sentence long and it's a straightforward summary-type lead, sometimes called a "direct" lead because it gets right to the point. It describes both the basics of what happened and what was remarkable about it. The writer clearly saw the high dollar figure as the most significant point about the kidney auction. Also included is the fact that the auction was stopped.

Nut graph. The second paragraph gives details to back up the lead and makes clear why the story is important now. It states the actual dollar figures, gives a little bit of history (when the kidneys were put up for sale), and pins down the day when the auction was stopped.

Quotes. The third paragraph is a quote that gives eBay's response to what happened. As eBay's spokeswoman, Kristin Seuell is (no doubt) a member of eBay's public relations staff who is authorized to speak for the company. It is common for stories to include a quote within the first five paragraphs, especially a quote that capsulizes someone's response to what happened. Additional quotes are woven into the rest of the story.

Remaining themes. After the first three paragraphs, the story answers the following questions, in the order listed: Why was the auction stopped? Who was selling the kidneys and where were they from? What did the seller's ad say? What did the seller have to say about all of this? How did eBay let this happen in the first place? What do people in the medical profession think of it? Why would people bid so much money for kidneys? Why shouldn't people sell their kidneys? Has anything like this ever happened before in an online auction?

Community as context. This story would be of general interest to many readers. It would be of particular interest for those involved in the Internet community, for those in geographic areas of the country with high concentrations of computer-related businesses (particularly the San Francisco Bay area and the Seattle area), and for people in the medical community. As a wire story, it was used by newspapers and Web sites throughout the country; however, it also was widely used in publications that serve communities of interest composed of people who use and work with computers.

Think Like an Editor

Take another look at the eBay story, imagining that you're an editor who has two minutes to cut that story to fit a small amount of space left on a page for the next day's paper.

Try cutting it from the bottom. What would go first? The information about eBay eliminating weapons sales is definitely expendable. Next would go the quote that backs up the information about how many people are waiting for kidneys and gives a clue as to why selling organs would be a bad thing — also expendable.

If you keep on cutting from the bottom up, you can see that you still get the gist of what happened even if all you have left is the first paragraph.

Obviously, the more of the story you read, the more complete is your knowledge of what happened. But the point is that, in writing inverted pyramid-type stories, you give people the basics before moving on to the details.

Delayed or Indirect Leads

Sometimes writers get a little fancier with the leads to their inverted pyramid stories. Usually this involves writing a clever opening sentence that often involves a play on words. The following is an example. The true lead is actually the second paragraph, which describes what the story is about. For this reason, many journalists would call this an example of a story with a "delayed" or "indirect" lead.

For Wal-Mart, a Soap War Looms against Mighty P&G

By Emily Nelson
Staff Reporter

Wal-Mart Stores Inc. is about to put the detergent business in a spin.

The giant retailer is introducing a private-label laundry soap called Sam's American Choice. The detergent began hitting Wal-Mart's shelves nationwide last week and should be in all 2,457 of its stores across the country soon.

The new product is likely to challenge Tide, a hugely important product from Procter & Gamble Co., one of Wal-Mart's most important suppliers. People don't wash their clothes more often or buy extra detergent just because they see a new brand at the store, so Wal-Mart will have to take sales from somewhere. The new Wal-Mart detergent is packaged in boxes and jugs whose background color is close to Tide's, but it's priced about 25% to 30% lower.

Stores sell more laundry soap than any other nonfood consumer product. Currently, Tide is the market leader in detergents, with 38.6% of the U.S. market, according to P&G. P&G calls Tide one of its top brands, and some analysts say it's the biggest P&G brand of all.

"Wal-Mart's really going after the family jewels with P&G,"

says Burt Flickinger III, managing director of Reach Marketing, Westport, Conn.

What makes detergent especially attractive to the huge discount chain is that Americans will often make a special trip to the store to buy more soap. They spend about $4.5 billion on laundry soap annually and buy it about every two weeks.

Wal-Mart, with its $137.6 billion in annual sales, accounts for about 20% of U.S. laundry detergent sales, analysts say.

"We saw a void in the marketplace for a product at that price point and quality level," says Mike Maher, a Wal-Mart spokesman.

Both companies insist that Wal-Mart's move won't smudge its close relationship with Procter & Gamble. Wal-Mart founder Sam Walton and the consumer-products giant pioneered the concept of a retailer and manufacturer sharing inventory responsibilities and sales data years ago. P&G, based in Cincinnati, was among the first companies to open an office near Wal-Mart headquarters in Bentonville, Ark., just to serve the retailer.

"They're a good supplier of ours and we expect to continue growing fully with them," Wal-Mart's Mr. Maher says.

Wal-Mart's action "in no way strains our relationship," says Molly Humbert, a spokeswoman for Tide. "We'll continue to actively market our brands."

[The story continues for several more paragraphs.]

Source: Wall Street Journal, Friday, Aug. 6, 1999, Page B1

If we go back and analyze this story, we can see it is organized in the following way.

The lead. The first sentence contains a light-hearted play on the word *spin*, while still signaling that the story is about the detergent business. The second sentence completes the lead by explaining what the writer meant by the first. Another option would have been to write a "straight" or "direct" lead, such as the following:

> Wal-Mart is introducing a private-label laundry soap called Sam's American Choice. The detergent began hitting the giant retailer's shelves nationwide last week and should be in all 2,457 of its stores across the country soon.

Although nothing is wrong with writing a straightforward lead that just "tells it like it is," especially if you're writing under a great deal of deadline pressure, this example shows that many stories can benefit from a little creativity.

The nut graph. The rest of the second paragraph explains the gist of the story.

Remaining themes. The third paragraph explains why the introduction of a new detergent is significant in the business world, which is the Wall Street Journal's primary audience. This information leads into an exploration of several interrelated themes. The writer notes that Wal-Mart's new product will put that company in competition with Procter & Gamble, then she describes both companies' responses to questions about whether that competition will affect their existing cooperative relationship. Several additional themes are explored in the portions of the story that are not included here.

Quotes. The story's first quote is in the fifth paragraph. It capsulizes what people who are knowledgeable about the business might be thinking about Wal-Mart's new product. Other direct quotes in this story are the response quotes from people associated with both Wal-Mart and Procter & Gamble. By including these quotes, the reporter has (1) let the companies speak for themselves and (2) demonstrated that she spoke with them.

Community as context. Although the Wall Street Journal is published in New York City, its "community," or audience, consists of business people throughout the United States. As a result, the writer focuses not on this story's significance in New York but rather, in the fourth paragraph, she cites information that shows detergent sales to be big business countrywide. The story is also of general interest because most people buy detergent, and Wal-Mart and Procter & Gamble products are sold from coast to coast.

Style variations. Depending on how familiar you are with Associated Press style by now, you may have noted as you were reading the above example that the Wall Street Journal style is somewhat different. For instance, the "Associated Press Stylebook" calls for the use of the word "percent" instead of the "%" symbol, and no use of courtesy titles like "Mr." Both "%" and "Mr." were used in this story. In addition, the Wall Street Journal has its writers use "says" instead of "said" in attribution, and the paragraphs are longer than in many newspapers. It's important to remember that the editors, not the individual writer, always determine these differences. The goal is to achieve consistency within any given publication.

Anecdotal Leads

Many inverted pyramids begin with what journalists call "anecdotal leads," which use a narrative, or storytelling, approach to describe a person or people whose situation typifies the story. After introducing these people, the writer segues into the inverted pyramid format. The following is a good example:

Hundreds brave snow and ice to take home free holiday food

By Richard D. Walton
Staff Writer

The sign just inside the West End Conference Center noted that there was no smoking inside the building.

And there Helen Griffin stood, huffing and puffing.

It wasn't cigarettes, but a three-block walk through ice and cold, that caused it.

"It's bad, sooooo bad," the 69-year-old said, between gulps of air. "*Lord*, it's bad out."

Bad out, but not bad enough to keep this hardy Indiana resident from making the frigid journey to claim some groceries at the annual We Can Feed the Hungry Christmas Food Giveaway, sponsored in part by Indiana Black Expo and radio station WTLC.

Griffin, pulling a rusted metal cart, said she had no choice.

"I need the food," she said.

So many do. And volunteers stood ready to help some 1,000 people Tuesday before Mother Nature rudely interrupted.

By day's end, only about 400 had come to claim their bags of food and their frozen turkeys. Many also trudged away with sweat shirts, caps and jackets donated by area businesses.

[The story went on to describe other people who received help and other programs that dispensed it. A paragraph in small type at the end of the story explained that the giveaway had been extended due to the weather, and it gave information about how and when people could come later for food.]

Source: Indianapolis Star, Wednesday, Dec. 20, 1995, Page A2

The lead. The writer takes a narrative approach in describing Helen Griffin as she huffs and puffs after coming in from the cold. Instead of writing a straightforward lead that focused on the fact that a bitter snowstorm prevented hundreds of needy people from receiving much-needed food, he draws readers into the story by describing one woman who braved the ice and cold.

Nut graph. The sixth paragraph tells you why the reporter is telling us about Helen Griffin — that she was there to participate in a holiday food giveaway. Three paragraphs later, the reporter also tells us that only 400 of an expected 1,000 participants showed, due to the harsh weather.

Remaining themes. Although the writer begins by focusing on one woman in one location, he eventually broadens the story to include the other holiday giveaways in the city.

Quotes. The writer makes excellent use of quotes. His use of the extra letters in the word "so" and italicizing the word *Lord* give an almost audible quality to the quote. The description he tags on to the attribution also adds to the vividness of the verbal picture he creates.

Community as context. This story's local significance is abundantly clear: It describes how the bad weather that gripped the area posed special problems for the needy and the programs that serve them. This is probably not a story that would hold much interest for people outside Indianapolis.

Chronological and "Hourglass," or "Funnel," Stories

Just as journalists have created the visual imagery of an inverted pyramid to represent stories in which the most important information comes first, they use the pyramid to represent chronological stories in which the information that is presumed to be most important — the culmination or result of a sequence of events — comes last.

Journalists usually write purely chronological stories only as "day-in-the-life" features or sidebars to other news stories. Such stories generally focus on a sequence of events that unfolds in a dramatic or interesting way.

The chronological form generally should be avoided when writing about public meetings or other events, because such stories read like minutes and force readers to wade through a lot of introductory information before they get to the important stuff.

However, many inverted pyramids include chronological segments. And a hybrid story form that combines an inverted pyramid-type lead that transitions into a chronological account is fairly common. This way of organizing material is especially useful in stories about crimes, accidents, severe weather, or other catastrophic events in which it's important to present information in sequence for readers to understand what happened.

Because this kind of story is basically an inverted pyramid perched on top of a pyramid, some journalists call this an "hourglass" or "funnel" story.

Vigil to honor biker killed in hit-run

Bicyclists from around Chicago plan a vigil Sunday in memory of Thomas McBride, a cyclist who was run down by a motorist this week, according to police.

The group, which will meet in Chicago's Daley Plaza at noon Sunday and then ride bikes to the West Side intersection where McBride was fatally struck Monday, wants to draw attention to the perils facing cyclists on the city's streets, according to Adam Kessel, one of the event's planners.

McBride, 26, of Chicago was riding in the 5300 block of West Washington Boulevard around

8:25 a.m. Monday when he got into a dispute with a man driving a 1997 Chevy Tahoe, police said.

They said the motorist let McBride ride on, then slammed him repeatedly with the Tahoe and ran over him when he fell from the bike. The motorist fled, police said, but later turned himself in after he realized that he had lost one of his license plates near McBride's body.

Carnell Fitzpatrick, 28, of the 3800 block of West Warren Boulevard, has been charged with first-degree murder.

Source: Chicago Tribune, May 1, 1999

The lead. This story starts with a straightforward summary-type lead announcing a vigil planned to honor a fallen bicyclist.

Nut graph. The lead explains why the story is important now, but that information is fleshed out in the second paragraph about why the vigil is being held.

Remaining themes. After giving the basic information about the vigil, this story transitions into a chronological retelling of the events that led to the vigil.

Quotes. Quotes are not used in this story — only paraphrasing.

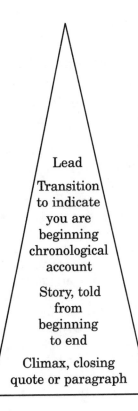

Lead

Transition to indicate you are beginning chronological account

Story, told from beginning to end

Climax, closing quote or paragraph

This figure illustrates the construction of a chronological story or story segment. In many cases, reporters combine the inverted pyramid style with this style, resulting in what they then might call an "hourglass" story.

Note, however, that the information still is attributed to sources. Sometimes, in extremely brief stories like this, quotes are not used or are edited out in the interest of cutting the story to fit the space.

Community as context. This story would be of interest to people in Chicago, and especially those people concerned about safety issues and bicycling. It also would be of interest to bicycle enthusiasts (and therefore to bicycling publications) outside the area, as well as to public officials who are responsible for ensuring bicyclists' safety in other cities. It also is a variant of road rage, which is an issue of increasing concern nationally.

Question-and-Answer Stories

Another essentially chronological reporting form is the question-and-answer story, which works well with stories that focus on the views or experiences of one person. .

Both the questions and the answers are expected to be pretty much word-for-word, arranged in chronological order, although they may be edited for length using the conventional guidelines and notations described in Chapter 3 and later in this chapter.

Again, these stories generally begin with an inverted pyramid-type lead that puts the important information first. Then they segue into the Q-and-A.

A bohemian rhapsodizes about Gotham

When is a tour guide not a tour guide? When he's Timothy "Speed" Levitch, the 28-year-old, Bronx-born showman who's part madman, part madcap. Levitch has been leading double-decker bus and walking tours of Manhattan for seven years. His colorful, anachronistic style assures him a place among the fellowship of New York eccentrics who have given the city its soul.

A street-corner philosopher and urban poet, Levitch is as likely to spout e.e. cummings as tourist factoids, and he's the subject of "The Cruise," a documentary directed by newcomer Bennett Miller that premieres in New York today, opening nationwide

Nov. 6. USA Today's Cathy Hainer gets a first-hand preview.

Q: Will you explain how the film's title, "The Cruise," refers to your philosophy of life?

(The cruise is) the art of crafting moments. People get caught up in the trip (of daily life); they forget that each one of us is sculpting moments in collaboration with time and space. At the end of each day, we've all created an art gallery of moments. The cruise is an effervescent homage to the present tense.

Q: What is it about New York that appeals to you?

New York is a teacher, a sage teaching life lessons. For instance, I've learned to notice carefully. The city is only persecuting those who try to control it. To enjoy life in New York is to be an associate of chaos.

Q: What is it about New York that repels you?

New York is a portrait of the humanity that built it and struggles in it. And as Leonardo da Vinci said, any portrait is a self-portrait. That's true of all cities. All cities are a profound opportunity.

Q: How would you describe New York to an alien?

New York is a giant sculpture where the streets are chiseled from rock, just like Michelangelo carving out a block of marble, and every human being is part of this sculpture.

Q: New York has been described as a city of neighborhoods. Which are your favorites?

I'm pretty fickle. I love the ground wherever I'm standing. The other day it occurred to me that all the concrete in the city is actually flesh. That makes the city really exciting.

The Jewish Lower East Side is a living Diaspora. Today a tour of the Jewish Lower East Side is an aerobic workout of the muscles of the imagination.

I call Greenwich Village the landmark of neurotic genius. It's unbelievable what a vortex of creative thinking and radicalization has taken place there. Edgar Allan Poe wrote "The Fall of the House of Usher" at 61 Carmine St. Thomas Paine died nearby. Melville lived two blocks away. Two doors down lived James Fenimore Cooper. The essential litany of American literature was written on those streets.

Gramercy Park is so quiet, luxurious and voluptuous. It's a dinosaur left behind from the Victorian past, when all parks had gates and locks. I always discuss that in Central Park, which was one of the first big public parks where everybody was invited. That was a real cultural revolution in the 1860s. It was the first place where women dared to exhibit their ankles publicly. That's where I would have been hanging out in 1868.

Q: What can tourists do to get the most out of New York?

Surrender. That's what the city demands. So much of the world havoc is caused by our attempts to know things that we're not meant to know. When somebody on a tour asks me the exact height of the Empire State building, they're limiting the limitlessness. Instead of discussing the (impact) of the building on our lives, it's easier to know it's 1,476 feet tall. Stop trying to control what is beautifully out of control.

[The story continues through six more questions and answers.]

Source: USA Today, Oct. 23, 1998

The lead. The lead to this story is actually at the beginning of the italicized introductory paragraphs, which follow the inverted pyramid form.

The nut graph. The second italicized paragraph explains why the story is newsworthy now: because someone has made a documentary about Levitch, and it's scheduled to open soon.

Remaining themes. After the introductory paragraphs, the theme of the story switches from describing Levitch himself to describing how he feels about New York.

Quotes. Always abundant in a Q-and-A, no?

Community as context. This story obviously would have the greatest appeal for people who live in, visit or like reading about New York City. It also would be of interest to people in the tourism business in many communities and so might be picked up by tourism trade publications, were it a wire story.

Lists

Lists often are inserted into the bodies of news stories. Pure list stories also appear, often as sidebars to other news stories. Lists work especially well for summarizing research findings or describing how-to tips or other similar bits of information.

Caller ID reels in criminals
But new technology also can foul the work of unwary officers

By Mark Fritz
Los Angeles Times

A scientist named Terry Spontarelli met a girl on America Online, set up a tryst in a Tulsa, Okla., motel, then engaged in three hours of sex acts that violated eight laws.

She was 13, he was 35, and she'd skipped school by pretending to be sick. Sometime during her encounter with the Ph.D., who had brought his camcorder, she made a preemptive phone call to her mother at work. She pretended she was still at home.

Like a lot of people who pick up a phone these days, the girl underestimated the endlessly mutating power of the technology she was using. She didn't know that her mother's company, a collection agency, had installed caller ID, and that police would soon be banging on a door at the Microtel Inn.

Spontarelli, an explosives analyst at the Los Alamos National Laboratory, pleaded guilty to various state and federal crimes against having sex with a minor. He was sentenced in June to 10 years in a federal penitentiary and another 10 in an Oklahoma state prison.

"If the mom hadn't had caller ID at her work, we wouldn't have known where this girl was meeting this adult, this child molester," said assistant U.S. attorney Susan Morgan in Tulsa.

The caller ID box — and the even more widely available keystroke services that copy what it does — is only one part of a brutally competitive communications industry that is moving faster and marketing harder than lawmakers, lawmen, lobbyists and civil libertarians can control.

As it has exploded across the country, caller ID is having an almost daily effect on police work, in some cases putting sleuthing powers once held by police in the hands of the victims, sometimes even entangling cops when they go carelessly undercover.

The fluid ease of caller ID has, likewise, opened up a new set of moral debates in some communities about supposedly confidential hot lines for suicide, rape, domestic abuse and drugs.

"How many people think about that when they call somebody? That the person on the other end instantly has their phone number and possibly their name and address?" said Peter Crabb, a Penn State psychologist.

Here, from the last month alone, is a sampling of true crime stories from the world of caller ID:

• A New Jersey high school teacher who claimed she took a phone call from somebody who threatened to blow up the school was arrested after caller ID showed there was no such call. Schools nationwide have scrambled to install caller ID because of the rash of copycat threats after the April massacre at a Colorado high school.

• A 15-year-old boy with a long juvenile record of crime told his father he was spending the night at his older brother's house. Caller ID indicated otherwise, and the man tracked his son to a hotel in downtown Cleveland, where the boy had spent the night having sex with his state-assigned social worker. Suzanne Smithers, 47, was sentenced to two years in prison for corrupting a minor.

• In Galveston, Texas, Mark Dixon went on trial for helping his girlfriend kill her husband. Barbara Holder was convicted of capital murder in March. Police said the pair conspired to make the stabbing of Curtis Holder, 47, look like a robbery, but their story unraveled three days later when Barbara Holder told a neighbor watching one of her children that she was calling from the police station when caller ID showed she was really at a local hotel.

[The story lists two other examples, then returns to further information about caller ID's usefulness in criminal investigations.]

Source: Los Angeles Times, July 1999

The lead. The anecdotal lead illustrates, with a timely retelling of a recent case, a growing trend.

Nut graph. In the third paragraph, the writer explains that technology is extending its reach in ways many people are not aware of.

Remaining themes. After the nut graph, the story uses a quote to transition into a discussion of how use of caller ID is booming, both benefiting and posing problems for police. It describes the moral dilemmas that caller ID raises and uses a quote to give an example. It then lists several other crimes in which caller ID has played a role. Note the set-up sentence used to introduce the list. The themes in the last section of the story (not included here) demonstrate how oblivious many people are to technological changes, how police are working to outfox the technology, and what is being done to protect people from harmful consequences of caller ID use.

Quotes. The quote from the assistant U.S. attorney makes clear the cause-and-effect relationship between the use of caller ID and the arrest. The attorney's repugnance at the scientist also is clear: "this adult, this child molester." The second quote points to an interesting moral dilemma that arises from caller ID use.

Community as context. This story has widespread general appeal because caller ID is available in most areas of the United States, and people might not be aware that it is used to solve crimes. The story also would draw particular interest in communities where caller ID has been used to solve crimes and in places that are home to telephone company headquarters, law enforcement training facilities or companies that manufacture caller ID equipment.

Segmented Stories

Segmented stories usually begin with inverted pyramid-style leads and then break information into chapter-like segments. Some of these stories are written in what could be described as an "expanded list" form. The following story is an example.

Try these 60-second bites for health

By Linda Marino
Prevention

Got a minute?

Good. That's as long as it takes to do something that can save your life. If you can spare about eight minutes, you can do every one of these proven death-defying feats.

Order the salmon

• How long it takes: A few seconds.
• Lifesaving potential: In a study of more than 20,000 men, researchers found that eating 4 to 6 ounces of fish once a week reduces by 52 percent your risk of dying from a heart attack within an hour of the onset of symptoms ("Journal of American Medical Association," Jan. 7, 1998).
• The details: Scientists speculate that the omega-3 fatty acids in fish work the magic. No fish packs more omega-3s than salmon — about 3.7 grams in a 6-ounce cooked serving. That supplies a week's worth of omega-3 fats.

Have your bones scanned

• How long it takes: One minute, two tops.

• Lifesaving potential: Up to 20 percent of the 300,000 people who suffer a hip fracture annually will die within a year, according to the National Osteoporosis Foundation in Washington, D.C.

• The details: A DEXA scan, the gold standard for detecting osteoporosis, is recommended for all women over age 40. But for a quick, cheap and fairly accurate test, you can get a scan from one of several portable devices that measure bone density at the heel, forearm or finger. After a minute or two, you have the results. It costs about $30 and may be available in your doctor's office. Depending on results, your doctor may want you to get a DEXA scan as a follow-up.

[The story continues with 10 more segments about health tips, all written in the same format.]

Source: Charlotte Observer, Aug. 2, 1999

The lead. This story has a delayed inverted pyramid-style lead written in a very conversational tone, as though the writer is talking to the reader.

The nut graph. The second paragraph makes it clear that this story is about health tips.

Remaining themes. The story doesn't say much before it transitions into segments that take the form of standardized lists. Remaining segments describe the benefits of flu shots, checking bread and pasta labels, eating vegetables, being screened for colon cancer, flossing your teeth, taking vitamins, buckling your seat belt, taking aspirin, changing your smoke alarm batteries, and washing your hands.

Quotes. Only one quote is used in the story, in the segment on aspirin (not included here); however, all information is attributed.

Community as context. This story would be of general interest to people throughout the United States. It would be of special interest to people in the health care profession.

The above story, which appeared in the Charlotte Observer, was provided by a magazine that gives papers reprint rights because the magazine's editors believe the exposure among newspapers' broad audiences may encourage people to buy their magazine. Many magazines do this, and newspaper editors traditionally consider these stories for inclusion in their pages, using the same criteria they use for evaluating every other story.

WRITE YOUR LEAD

After all the preparing, thinking and reading you've just done, you should have a good idea what comes next: writing the story.

Start by identifying what is most important or interesting about your story. If you're writing about a speech, was it something the speaker said? If you're writing about a concert, is it the notoriety of the artist or that a nonprofit group will benefit from ticket sales?

Pick one aspect as your focus and use it as the basis for your lead. Don't try to tell the whole story in the lead. Use general, descriptive words, not details — unless the details have unusual significance or are likely to mean something to the majority of people reading the story.

You can't go wrong if your lead is no longer than one sentence of 25 words or less. Some professors, editors and newspapers will accept longer leads; however, few will object if you keep your lead short, so long as it captures the essence of the story.

Look back at the leads in the preceding stories in this chapter. Each writer picked one point to emphasize, then included only as many other facts as were needed to give you the gist of the story.

Here's another familiar example — the first paragraph of the accident story in the previous chapter:

> KILL DEVIL HILLS, N.C. — A 30-year-old Virginia woman died after a five-car accident Friday night near the intersection of Colington Road and the U.S. 158 bypass.

Those 26 words give you the gist of the story. The woman is described rather than named because most people reading probably don't know her. The fact that she was only 30 and that she was from Virginia is much more likely to be significant to them. If the woman had been well known — someone like Hillary Clinton or Britney Spears, for example — her name would have been important enough to put in the lead. The time of the accident also was generic — just "Friday night." The exact time is probably less meaningful to most people than the general time frame, which might have been when they heard sirens, drove past the accident or wondered what took their daughter so long to get home from the movies.

DEVELOP KEY POINTS

Once you've identified what's most important, imagine that someone has told you just that much about the story. Think through how the story should unfold from there by asking yourself what you would want to know next, then what you would want to know after that, and so on. If you feel muddy about it, ask a friend or relative, "If I told you this, what would you want to know next?"

Writing Tip: Dissolving "Writer's Block"

If you find yourself experiencing "writer's block" when you're trying to write your lead, try these ideas.

Start by typing this sentence: "You'll never believe what happened (or is going to happen)." Then continue as though you're writing someone a letter instead of a news story.

Very often, this sentence will prompt you to think of the most compelling information. Once you get rolling, just delete that opening sentence and revise what you've written into the news writing style.

Or type "Lead goes here," then start writing the body of your story. Many times, as you organize the rest of the information, an idea for the lead will come to mind.

It may help you to make a list of the questions you develop, in order; beneath each item, list what information you have to answer that question. You also can number these questions and write corresponding numbers in your notes beside the material that answers the questions you come up with. This can make it easier to pull that information into your story.

Keep in mind that the paragraphs that follow the lead are extremely important. Be sure you use them to provide information that fleshes out the lead and to "ground" the story with a nut graph that makes clear why the information is important now.

Readers should know the point of your story no later than the fifth paragraph. Some editors put this in terms of the "so what?" test: With each paragraph, readers will be asking, "So what?" If you keep them waiting too long, they'll abandon your story and move on to the next one.

It also works well to include a quote that supports the lead within the first five paragraphs.

Sometimes it works to write a transition or secondary lead that draws the reader into each successive section of the story, then develop that point fully before going on to the next. In developing each point, include quotes, explanation and details, as appropriate.

Be sure that, as you develop the story, you place it in context. Always give enough background information so that readers understand the story's importance and how it relates to other events and issues in the community. Such background information may include:

- Historical facts
- Known or potential effects of what you're writing about
- Whether what you're writing about is tied to other events, situations or issues in the area your newspaper covers

- How information in your story compares to what's going on in other places, or to what went on in the past
- Any other context that gives the reader insight about the significance

Also be sure that you eventually include all pertinent information, such as the time and date something occurred (or will occur), the location (including the name of the building, room number and/ or street address), any cost involved for participants, and when appropriate, a phone number for people who want more information.

A last bit of advice: Be selective. Not everything you *could* put in the story *should* be in the story. Beware of going off on tangents or letting your story get bogged down by too much detail about minor points. As thriller writer Elmore Leonard says, "I try to leave out the parts that people skip." Also be prepared to give up some of your best quotes or most interesting facts because they don't have much to do with the rest of the story.

QUOTES REVISITED

Remember that quotes add life to your stories by making them seem more conversational.

"The language of journalism is not like speech, but it is closer to speech than most other forms of writing," Roy Peter Clark writes in "The Language of Journalism." "This is what (Hugh) Kenner means in describing it as populist. It also explains the journalistic obsession with quoting, with the attempts to represent speech in prose. ... When eyewitnesses, especially everyday folks, are given their voices in print, the effect can be powerful, moving, puzzling, funny or outrageous."

As you incorporate quotes into your story, remember these guidelines (also presented in Chapter 3):

- DO use the person's exact words, in the order in which they were spoken within each block of speech you are quoting.
- DO use complete-sentence quotations.
- DO strike a balance between quotes and paraphrasing.
- DO intersperse quotes throughout the story.
- DO use ellipses (...) to connote where you have spliced together parts of a quote.
- DO put quotation marks around direct quotes longer than a few words, and attribute them. Unless you paraphrase what someone

said, using their words without crediting them is no different ethically from plagiarizing something from a printed source.

- DON'T put quotation marks around things people didn't actually say. If your editor or professor says your story needs more quotes, don't just put quotes around things you may have paraphrased, no matter how close you think they may be to what the person said. Go back to your notes and double-check, pull out additional quotes or call the person back to get quotes you can use.
- DON'T borrow quotes from another source (another newspaper, a magazine, a televised interview, etc.) without acknowledging both the person who is quoted *and* the origin of the quote. Otherwise, it's yet another form of plagiarism, and it can damage your credibility with your readers. They assume that, by quoting someone, you talked to them. If you didn't, you always should make that clear.

Good Setups

Remember that using complete-sentence quotes makes it less likely that you will quote the person out of context or give them reason to believe that you did. There is an art to using full-sentence quotes. It often helps to precede the quote with a transition sentence that essentially sets up (but does not repeat the information in) the quote, as follows.

> A GOOD SETUP:
> Coach John Nelson said the team has been working hard lately.
> "We've been practicing two extra hours a day for the past two weeks, trying to get ready for the semifinals," he said.

> POOR SETUPS:
> Coach John Nelson said the team has been spending extra hours in practice.
> "We've been practicing two extra hours a day for the past two weeks, trying to get ready for the semifinals," he said.
> *Why it's poor:* The setup sentence is redundant.

> Coach John Nelson said that "we've been practicing two extra hours a day for the past two weeks, trying to get ready for the semifinals."
> *Why it's poor:* The quote appears to be fragmentary, because the writer made it part of a larger sentence.

When asked what the team has been doing to prepare for the semifinals, coach John Nelson said that
"we've been practicing two extra hours a day for the
past two weeks."

Why it's poor: The "when asked" approach is too
self-conscious. It makes the reporter a player in the
story, which is unnecessary. As in the previous example, the quote also looks like a fragmentary
quote.

Working with quotes can present a variety of challenges. Sometimes you just weren't able to take notes fast enough to get down everything you realized later you would want to use as quotes in your
story. In addition, some people are very terse or tend to speak in sentence fragments, which makes it hard to get good, full-sentence
quotes from them. Still other people are very wordy or they ramble,
making it difficult to get succinct quotes. Here are some examples of
ways to deal with each of those problems:

When You Weren't Writing Fast Enough

Take a look at the fragmentary quotes you *were* able to write down.
See if the addition of a word here or there will make any of the best
quotes usable. For instance, in the course of interviewing Sheriff Jonathan Jones about an accident, you wrote down the following:

"still collect'g evid and try'g to det what caused"

You know, because you're starting to develop your own shorthand, that those notes translate into:

"still collecting evidence and trying to determine
what caused"

You could insert a couple of words, putting them within parentheses to connote that they weren't what he actually said — or at least
you're unsure if they were. That would enable you to use this quote:

"(We're) still collecting evidence and trying to determine what caused (the accident)," Sheriff Jonathan
Jones said.

It's obviously better if you can get to the point that you write
down the whole sentence in your notes. But while you're still developing basic note-taking skills, the above technique can be useful.

When People Ramble

Some people take forever to get the point, and others never do get there. Sooner or later, every reporter interviews people who are long-winded or who jump from topic to topic, making it difficult to quote them.

In these situations, you may have no choice but to severely edit their quotes, in spite of the "Associated Press Stylebook" admonition about changing only a word or two.

When editing to this degree, the most important point to remember is to preserve the basic meaning of the comments. If you splice together portions of sentences, always keep the fragments in the order spoken and use ellipses (...) at each splice, as follows.

What the person actually said:

> "We've had tornadoes here before — I think the last big one was back in the '70s, or maybe ... hmmm ... yeah, it was '78, because that was our last year of high school, isn't that right Betsy? (He turns to his wife, who nods) — but this one was bigger than any I've ever seen before," lifelong Yourtown resident John Perkins said.

A better way to use this quote:

> "We've had tornadoes here before ... but this one was bigger than any I've ever seen before," lifelong Yourtown resident John Perkins said.

If, in editing a lengthy quote, you need to substitute a word for a pronoun or add words to make a person's meaning clear, be sure to put the substituted or added words in parentheses, as follows.

What the person actually said:

> "He has been thinking about this a really long time. Really long. He has been trying to get this festival started for the past five years, so we're really glad the community finally got behind him," festival organizer Joan Smith said.

A better way to use this quote:

> "(The mayor) has been trying to get this festival started for the past five years, so we're really glad the community finally got behind him," festival organizer Joan Smith said.

You also have the option of paraphrasing some of what the person said, especially if the quote is rambling or vague. You can then use the most powerful whole-sentence quotes for emphasis.

What the person actually said:

> "I always knew there was something not quite right about Jimmy — sort of like an ax murderer waiting to happen. Just little things he did, you know. But Ma and Pa thought he was the best kid ever. They always liked Jimmy better than me or the other kids. He could do no wrong," Billy Jones said.

A better way to use this quote:

> Billy said his brother Jimmy was a favored child and could do no wrong in his parents' eyes. But Billy sensed darker forces at work. "I always knew there was something not quite right about Jimmy — sort of like an ax murderer waiting to happen," he said.

Be very careful when revising your story or editing others' words not to put quotation marks around comments that were paraphrased.

Partial Quotes

Although it's generally best not to use what's called a "partial quote" — a sentence fragment, sometimes that's the best you can do.

Using partial quotes always involves writing a setup that leads into, or wraps around, the quote. It's best to avoid setups that lead into the quote with the word *that*, because the word is unnecessary. It's also best to avoid setups that begin with the such phrases as "when asked about" or "with respect to."

A problematic way to use a partial quote:

> Of the mayor, festival organizer Joan Smith said that "he has been trying ... "

A better way to use a partial quote:

> Festival organizer Joan Smith said the mayor "has been trying to get this festival started for the past

> five years, so we're really glad the community fi-
> nally got behind him."

Note that the subject of the quote is pulled out and placed into the setup. This is a common solution when using partial quotes.

The worst use of partial quotes:

> Billy said he "always knew" his brother was "an ax
> murderer," but his parents didn't notice because
> "they always liked Jimmy better" than their other
> children.

Note the inaccuracy that crept into this patchwork quilt of frag-ments above. Billy didn't actually say he thought his brother *was* an ax murderer; he said he always thought his brother was "an ax mur-derer waiting to happen." Hacking up his quote also diminished the impact of the quote because "an ax murderer waiting to happen" is a powerful bit of language. Additionally, the clause "they always liked Jimmy better" could stand as a full-sentence quote.

Last of all, if you are thinking about using quotes of only two or three words, make sure the words themselves are unusual or inflam-matory enough to merit the attribution. In Billy's mangled quote, for instance, "always knew" could have run without the quotation marks.

When using quotes, you also will use attribution. Although cov-ered in Chapter 3, here's another recap to make sure your attribution is as well done as your quotes:

- Report without attribution only those physical events and details you personally observe.
- Attribute both direct quotations as well as paraphrased informa-tion.
- Keep attribution in subject–verb order whenever possible.
- Keep it simple: Just say "said."
- Make clear the sources' relationship to the story.

TAKE ONE LAST LOOK

After you've written your story, page through your notes to make sure you haven't overlooked any important information. If you find something you've missed, work it in.

Check one last time to make sure there is logic to the order in which you have introduced each chunk of information, and that your story flows. If not, reorganize it or add transitions that lead the reader from one topic to the next.

EXERCISES

1. Look through a copy of a daily newspaper. Count how many stories fit into the categories of basic, informative stories described above, and how many don't. What percentage of the stories fits into one of the categories? What percentage does not? If stories don't fit, what sets them apart?

2. Find an example of a story told in inverted pyramid form. Read through it, paying attention to how various pieces of information in the story were ranked in terms of their importance. Why do you think the information included in the lead was considered the most important? Do you agree with the way the information was ranked? Were there aspects of the story you think should have been given more importance? Why?

3. Find an example of an hourglass or chronological story. How much of a preface does the story have before it becomes chronological? What kind of transition is used in the chronological account? Would the news value of the story have been clear without the preface?

Further Reading

ON THE WEB

HealthPro Computer Services: http://members.home.net/hlthpro/cano98/ net_09.html "Consider the Source: Who Is Providing the Information?"

Media Awareness Network: www.media-awareness.ca/eng/webaware/tipsheets/ w5.htm "Knowing What's What and What's Not: The 5 Ws (and 1 H) of Cyberspace," a guide to evaluating credibility of information on the Internet.

The Poynter Institute for Media Studies: www.poynter.org/dj/index.htm Select articles such as "Components of a Good Story" or "The Practice of Writing" under the "Reporting & Writing" heading; www.poynter. org/Research/rwe.htm Select articles such as "An Editor and Writer at Work," by Donald M. Murray, or "A Message about Reporting Methods: Make No Mistake," by Bob Steele.

IN PRINT

"Using Quotes: A Practical Guide," by Fred Fedler, published by the Journalism Education Association, Manhattan, Kan., 1983.

Story Portfolio:
Basic News Stories

The following two articles are typical of the kinds of stories written by beginning reporters. They were chosen because each has strengths and weaknesses. The following set of questions can be helpful in analyzing and discussing the strengths and weaknesses of these and other news stories

- The lead: What kind of lead does the story have? Is the lead effective?
- The nut graph: At what point in the story do you know why the story is important now?
- Remaining themes: How are other themes organized in the story?
- Quotes: Are quotes used well? How are they spaced within the story?
- Community as context: Where and to whom would this story have the greatest interest? Does anything about this story give you a sense of the uniqueness of the community?
- Credibility: How accurate does this story seem? What sources are cited, and how credible are those sources?

STORY 1: MU'S COACH SMITH BLOWS OFF STEAM

Football coach implements new policy on injuries

From the Columbia Missourian

Short practice, short press conference, short fuse.

Coach Larry Smith was more intent on lecturing about player access, press relations and the new injury policy in Monday's after-practice press conference than on the state of his football team.

Threatening to ban a reporter from practice for violating the Tigers' interview policy, Smith finished his conference with a black-balling diatribe about coach and player interviews, demonstrating his overt objection to question and answers unfiltered through the MU sports information director's office.

"I'm not going to turn this into a circus," he said. "We have rules and any professional journalism person or media person has rules. If you don't cooperate with those rules, then there will be no cooperation from this end."

Incensed by a recent "Missourian" article on Travis Garvin's drug-related suspension, Smith berated a "Missourian" reporter for attempting to contact players and coaches at home.

NEW POLICIES: MU's new injury policy, ad-libbed by Smith during Monday's opening remarks, states that the condition of injured players will not be discussed. Their presence on the field is now acceptable evidence that they are well and ready to play, Smith said.

Because of the new policy, the condition of offensive lineman Rob Droege, quarterback Jim Dougherty and linebacker Antwaun Bynum are unknown.

Droege was carted off on a stretcher after Friday's scrimmage with an ankle injury. Dougherty is expected to undergo elbow surgery this week to repair a torn ligament. And Bynum, who was left dizzy after Aug. 22's practice, was in pads Monday.

"I am not going to comment on any injury," said Smith.

LEATHERNECK PREP: Wearing numbers of Saturday's opponent, the Tigers emulated the expected offenses and defenses of the Western Illinois Leathernecks.

The Leathernecks run a similar zone defense as MU, adding one more defensive lineman, creating a five-lineman, two-linebacker set.

The defense is piloted by Edgerton Hartwell, a 6-foot-2, 245-pound linebacker, who is expected to plug many of Western Illinois' holes.

LAYING THE LUMBER: Expected to run through those holes are Tiger tailbacks Zack Abron and Zain Gilmore.

The two will split time on Saturday as running backs coach Chris Tabor sees fit, Smith said. They share the No. 1 spot on the depth chart.

"We are going to probably do it by feel," said Smith. "They are both going to play about 50 percent of the time, to keep them nice and fresh."

SHORT ADDITIONS: Freshmen 5-foot-8 Marcus James and 5-foot-10 Octavious "Tay" Jackson are slated as No. 5 and No. 6 on the receiver depth chart.

James continued to go airborne after wayward passes Monday and with quick hands, he continued to pull them down.

James will return punts and kickoffs.

Jackson shimmied and cut upfield Monday with the deftness that helped him gain nearly 1,600 all-purpose yards in his senior year at Pahokee (Fla.) High.

Published Aug. 29, 2000
Columbia Missourian, University of Missouri
www.digmo.com

STORY 2: LECTURER DISCUSSES RAPE ISSUES

Speaker talks to students about sexual aggression

From the Indiana Daily Student

Steve Thompson hates zebras.

He doesn't really have a problem with the striped African mammals, but he can't stand the lax attitude they have when another zebra gets attacked. Thompson sent many people home Thursday night with a similar anti-zebra feeling.

Thompson spoke to nearly 200 people, men and women, about the origins of our current ideas of sexual assault, and how to stop the cycle.

"As a man, I am sick and tired of rape being a women's issue," Thompson said. "As long as we think it is a women's issue (rape) will not stop."

Thompson got his start in the field by teaching women self-defense. After one of his students got attacked and suffered serious injuries, Thompson reevaluated his approach.

"I had betrayed her trust. She trusted me to teach her to do something with her that would make her safe, and I let her down ... I just taught what was traditionally taught," he said.

Thompson's first discovery came from the reading he had done on the subject. He discovered that most of the information he was reading was about the victims, and not about the rapist.

Subsequently, Thompson decided to take an active approach.

"I realized that what people thought was the reality of the street was in fact not true," Thompson said.

Even today, Thompson works with local police and the FBI to create profiles of rapists and to learn from victims.

He also researched where the common conceptions of a rape victim and rapist originated. Thompson referred to Lord Hale, an English chief justice in the 1600's who recognized the difficulty of convicting a rapist. He also mentioned psychiatrist Sigmund Freud, who said women were confused about sex, and a man named Amir who cultivated the phrase "victim precipitated" in the 1960s.

"Now our job here is to overcome this myth, this attitude that is not founded on fact," he said.

Thompson separated men into three separate categories. The good men, the spectators and the predators. The good men respect themselves and others, the spectators or "zebras" simply "don't have the guts to stop it," and the predators take from other people.

"We have to eliminate this spectator mentality ... it's men who rape, it's men who can stop rape ... we have to place the burden where it should be," Thompson said.

Thompson also said the majority of rapes are premeditated, and whether it is an acquaintance rape or stranger rape, the rapist always has his goal in mind.

Because rape is the ultimate goal of a rapist, a certain strategy must be employed. Thompson warned the audience that oftentimes, the rapist will use conventional tools such as alcohol and drugs, particularly gamma-hydroxybutyrate or GHB. This drug is easily made from household materials and is tasteless when mixed with a citrus based liquid. In addition to drugs and alcohol, Thompson said the rapist will make an effort to separate the victim from the pack.

Thompson said one of the reasons a rapist might be difficult to identify is because he most often sticks with a pack. This type most likely plays a team sport, is very egocentric and thrives on being in control, he said.

"He is not like good men, not at all, but he appears to be," Thompson said. "This guy doesn't respect himself, he doesn't respect women."

Just as there is a distinct type of man who rapes, there is a distinct type of victim that he looks for, Thompson said. Two of the top three victim groups can be found on college campuses. Statistically, the most vulnerable group are freshmen females pledging sororities, followed by freshmen females in general. The third group includes freshmen and sophomores in high school. Thompson suggests exuding an image of confidence as a deterrent to rapists.

Nonetheless, Thompson stressed that the responsibility still lies in the hands of males.

"We have to separate responsibility from judgment," he said.

Thompson then opened the floor to questions. The crowd pressed Thompson from many angles, from confrontation of the predator to the duties of a bartender in the prevention of sexual assault.

Debbie Melloan-Ruiz, co-chair of education for the Commission on Personal Safety, introduced Thompson at the beginning of the speech. She said she hoped those who attended walked away with more than they expected.

"Our culture is permeated with myths about this issue, I hope that some of those myths that people came in with got broken down," she said.

Freshman Mark McGarrah said he was pleased with Thompson's speech.

"He is a really great speaker, I feel like he really informed the people, if they asked questions he gave great answers or he just told them point blank he couldn't give them answers," McGarrah said.

McGarrah said he came away with a new sense of what could be done to stop the problem and plans on volunteering at the Middle Way House.

"I really didn't know about rape before now, because I come from a really small town," said freshman Kelly Burton. "It really made me think about how I maybe need to pay a little more attention to my surroundings."

Thompson sent out a message to the students, faculty and Bloomington residents who attended the lecture.

"I want you to talk to other people. Simply talk," he said. "When you are in a residence hall and you hear someone make an ignorant comment, take that time to educate."

Published Monday, Sept. 25, 2000 Indiana Daily Student and Indiana Digital Student www.idsnews.com

Chapter 7

Framing News Stories

Drawing by W.E. Hill. Source: Puck magazine, Nov. 6, 1905

▓▓▓▓▓▓▓▓▓▓▓▓▓▓▓ **Key Concepts** ▓▓▓▓▓▓▓▓▓▓▓▓▓▓▓

- All of us, journalists included, interpret events in ways shaped by our perceptions, experiences, knowledge and relationship to the event.

- These interpretations influence the choices journalists make in creating news stories — choices such as who is interviewed, what questions are asked, how people are portrayed in news stories, what information and quotes are included, and the tone of the story.

- Whenever time permits, journalists should evaluate how they are interpreting news events and framing their stories as part of their writing process.

- Because deadline restrictions do not always permit journalists to reflect on how they are framing their stories as they write them, internal critiques, done after-the-fact in many newsrooms, evaluate how stories are framed and other elements of good news writing to assess the accuracy and quality of the overall news report.

Take another look at the drawing on the previous page. What do you see? A young woman? Her face is turned away as she gazes into the distance, showing her cheekline and jaw. Her black hair covers just half of her ear. She wears a long, flowing bonnet. It looks expensive. Got it?

Now look again. It's not a young, attractive woman; it's an old peasant woman, with a large bulbous nose, bags beneath her eyes, jutting chin and a scarf wrapped around her hair. Her thin lips are pressed together and her eyes turned downward

Same ink, same lines, same drawing. Two different images. Your interpretation of various pieces of the picture — the way you saw one line as a nose rather than a jawbone, for instance — defined the picture for you. The black ink didn't determine what you saw; you did.

Reporters and editors see and define stories in a similar fashion every day. It's not just facts that determine how a story is told — it's the reporter's perceptions, assumptions, and choices. Any two reporters will write the same story in different ways. Look at any national or metropolitan newspapers, for instance, from the same day. You'll see the same event described differently — sometimes dramatically so — in The New York Times and USA Today and The Christian Science Monitor and The Washington Post and the Wall Street Journal and the Chicago Tribune and the Los Angeles Times.

Why? Partly because each paper takes a different "angle," or "framing," in its coverage so that each paper's news report remains distinctive. These diverse angles and frames are partly due to the fact that each paper is geared to a slightly different audience, as described in Chapter 4, but also because, like the rest of us, the way in which reporters and editors see things and then pass on to others what they have seen is shaped by their individual experiences, knowledge and opinions. Each of us is equipped with our own unique "filter," similar to the filters professional photographers put over the lenses of their cameras to cut the glare or bring out the blues in a particular photo. The filter changes both what the camera sees and the final images it produces. We usually can't see our own filters as well as we see those of others. We might perceive someone else as "cynical" or "overly sensitive" or "hyper," for example, but we don't often think about the fact that the person might describe us, from his or her perspective, as "a Pollyanna" or "callous" or "lethargic."

Sociologist Erving Goffman, in his book "Frame Analysis: An Essay on the Organization of Experience," describes how we interpret our perceptions by filtering them through various cultural, sociological and personal frameworks. "It seems that we can hardly glance at anything without ... forming conjectures as to what occurred before and expectations of what is likely to happen now," Goffman wrote.

When we watch a play, for instance, we know that the events onstage are fabricated (even if they're based on real-life events), that the outcome is predictable, and that the purpose of the event is to entertain us. What happens onstage has real-life consequences for the actors only if their ability to enact their roles affects the demand for their services, or if they carry things from their stage roles into their personal lives (as when onstage romances bloom offstage). When we watch a football game, we know that it, too, is a fabricated event, with rules that affect but do not determine the outcome because the game is a contest. The stakes are real, because both teams, their players, and many other people experience consequences determined by who wins. Similarly, when we watch news events, we know whether the event is fabricated, whether the outcome is predictable, and what the purpose of the event is. We have a sense of what rules or rituals are involved — at some point during a presidential inauguration, for instance, the new president will raise his or her right hand and take an oath of office; or during a criminal court hearing, at least one lawyer is likely to cry "Objection!"

Goffman's work makes it clear that facts don't frame themselves. People do. We draw on our perceptions and experiences to interpret what Goffman calls an "actual, untransformed activity." If we see someone taking a pill, for instance, we could draw one of many possible conclusions, depending on what we saw, in what context. We could conclude that the person has a medical condition, is simply taking vitamins, or experimenting with drugs, or participating in a scientific experiment or a number of other things. Later we might realize that it wasn't a pill, it was an M&M — or nothing at all — he or she was removing a tiny piece of paper that came from a soda straw.

The problem is that we usually frame things quickly and unconsciously. As we go about our daily lives, we don't often think about how our conjectures and expectations shape what we see and how we interpret it. To use Goffman's terminology, we don't think about how we frame things.

Journalists are no different from the rest of us. Most, in the crush to meet their deadlines, don't stop to think, "We're framing the story this way or that way." But that's what they do every day — they frame stories by making selective judgments about what information to emphasize and include and how to present that information. Journalists who are honest with themselves know it is impossible to report "just the facts, ma'am."

This chapter describes how stories are framed and how this framing affects everything about the stories that result: whom the reporter interviews, what information is sought, how questions are asked, which quotes and facts are selected for inclusion in the story, and the order in which those facts are presented.

A DEFINITION OF FRAMING

Framing is the way we picture something in our heads. It's an act of imagination that journalists use every day, often unconsciously. Framing allows journalists to give shape and meaning to the stories they write.

"News is created, like any other brand of story-telling, fictional or otherwise, through selection, framing, and editing," Yale University sociology Professor Joshua Gamson wrote in Current magazine. "Reputable news institutions thus depend less on the claim that they are transmitting the truth (news as a window on the world is an increasingly hard sell) than on the notion that they can be trusted to select, collect and present information honestly and well. They will

not make things up, they will collect all sorts of significant information, and they will tell the story as they see it. This is, after all, medi-
ated information, and the mediator must be trusted for the
information to be believed."

The judgments reporters make about how to frame a story are
based on a number of factors:

- Their understanding of their communities and what is important to the people there, which affects how widely the story will be
read and whether people become engaged by the ideas or issues it
presents
  - Their views of what elements of the story are most significant
in historical, geographical and other contexts
  - Their publication's policies or norms for writing various kinds
of news stories
  - Practical considerations like how long they have to write the
story between the time they learn about it and who they can reach
by deadline
  - Their personal preferences and values with respect to reporting and writing

Framing decisions influence whether stories are read at all,
whether citizens will see how stories affect them and other people
who are important to them, whether citizens are likely to respond to
those stories, and how various stories affect public life in the communities where they are reported.

What does framing look like? Election coverage offers perhaps
the best documented and most researched example. For years, election stories were framed as updates in a horse race, a winner-take-all
game. That attitude drove the stories that were written — the news
was dominated with up-to-the-minute polls on which candidate was
ahead, "behind the scenes" coverage of campaign strategies and
strategists, and regular tallies of mud-slinging through television and
print advertising. The coverage was built around the competitive aspects of politics, in which the politicians are on the field of play and
the citizens are spectators in the stands. But most citizens are less
concerned about the competition and candidates' strategies than
they are about what the candidates stand for — and whether the
candidates have some sort of track record that proves they know
how to translate their positions on issues into actions that benefit
their constituents.

Various researchers and authors have suggested that the gap between the values and concerns reflected in election coverage and the
values and concerns of citizens is partly to blame for the fact that

Journalists Emphasize Conflict

When citizens complain that news media are biased, they often back up that assertion by saying that reporters tend to overemphasize or exaggerate conflict and controversy in their coverage of the news.

As it turns out, that was exactly what the researchers from Project for Excellence in Journalism and Princeton Survey Research Associates found when they studied the front page stories of three national and four regional newspapers.

Researchers in the 1999 study looked at journalistic storytelling techniques from four perspectives: what topics were placed on page 1, what triggered coverage of each story, what narrative device or "frame" was used in composing each story, and what the underlying social or folkloric message of the story was.

They found that about a third (30 percent) of the stories presented the news through a combative lens, framing stories in terms of conflict, focusing on winners and losers, or revealing wrongdoing.

It was about half as likely that the story would be written to explain how things worked or place the story into context. And it was less than half as likely the story would be a "straight" news account that stuck to the who, what, when, where and whys.

Underlying messages communicated by stories framed as conflicts — for example, that the government can't be trusted or that the little guy deserves a break — contribute to citizens feeling that reporters are biased, the researchers found.

"What ultimately deserves more reflection by journalists is whether their use of frames is balanced," the researchers wrote in a report about the study. "The data suggests a perhaps unconscious bias in journalists toward approaching certain types of news the same way over and over.

"There may be too great a tendency to view the news through a combative lens. Explanatory frames are underused, points of agreement are undervalued, and (reporting about public) policy is undernourished."

In addition, they suggested that journalists take another look at the underlying messages embedded in the ways they frame stories.

"The element of underlying message may help journalists to begin to address the more elusive question of bias in a less defensive and more open-minded way," the researchers wrote.

Source: "Framing the News: The Triggers, Frames and Messages in Newspaper Coverage," a report by The Project for Excellence in Journalism and Princeton Survey Research Associates

---

many people in recent years have been disillusioned with the political process. In response to this disillusionment, a new frame for election coverage began to take shape in 1988. Politics was redefined, in a sense. If politics was more about shared problems requiring common solutions, then citizens could no longer be mere spectators. Many in the media began their election coverage by conducting surveys or convening small-group discussions to ask the public which issues were important to them. These news organizations then made sure their coverage of the election focused mainly on those issues and where the candidates stood in relation to them.

In the 1996 election, some news organizations expanded on this idea by presenting election coverage as though it were part of a hiring process, with candidates asked to submit cover letters, resumés and references — just like most citizens do when they apply for jobs. These materials were then published along with candidates' responses to questions posed by citizens, so people could decide whom to "hire" at the ballot box.

The old frame: elections as a horse race. The new frame: elections as a job search, in which citizens interview candidates about the things that matter most to them and pick the applicant with the best qualifications. The frame changed from one of competition among those wishing to be elected to collaboration among those doing the electing.

Research shows that when news organizations adopt the new frame, readership and reader satisfaction have increased in many communities. In some cases, the impact on public life has been reflected in other ways as well. After an issue-based election project in Wichita, Kan., in 1990, a greater number of voters turned out at the polls. A 1997 study by the Pew Charitable Trusts showed that citizens in communities whose media have provided issue-based election coverage feel more strongly that they should vote in every election.

To understand the power of framing, consider this update from the election example: A decade after the new frame began to be formulated, some news organizations were still struggling to understand how to execute the frame in their news columns and during airtime. Other newspapers and television stations were openly hostile to it, declaring that the old frame is still the correct one.

Framing affects everything, not just elections. In 1996, for example, church burnings in the South gained national attention. A few burnings showed signs of racial hatred against African-Americans. That theme became the frame for all stories involving torched churches — even after several news organizations ran investigative stories debunking the idea that there was a rash of race-based burnings. "The church-burning story is a classic example of media framing so strong that it can ward off even a sturdy set of actual facts," veteran journalist John Leo wrote in his column in U.S. News & World Report. "Once the story was seen as a startling new epidemic of classic racial hatred, it was very difficult for the media to drop this powerful narrative line, even though evidence piled up very quickly that it was exaggerated to the point of being a hoax."

University of Texas journalism professor Stephen Reese says that *persistence* is one of the components of a frame. "The significance of frames lies in their durability, their persistent and routine use over time," he says. Other attributes, according to Reese, include:

- "The frame is based on an abstract principle, and is not the same as the texts through which it manifests itself." For journalists, the frame isn't the same thing as a story angle or idea; a frame is the thing that drives the story idea.
- "The frame must be shared on some level for it to be significant and communicable." Journalism's job is to enter the conversation of a community in a way that reflects where people are at; if journalists fail, people won't find their stories relevant.
- "Frames organize by providing identifiable patterns or structures, which can vary in their complexity."

Consider another example from John Leo — how the media frames coverage of the gay community. "Almost without exception, the media tend to look at stories about gays and lesbians through the familiar lens of the black struggle for civil rights," Leo says. "Whatever the actual news, these narratives are told in terms of bias, exclusion, tolerance, and rights." So when Ellen DeGeneres became the first television character to "come out" as a lesbian in 1997, "the Ellen story was told as a social breakthrough against prejudice, often with reference to other firsts — the first black to get a television series, the first frank references to sex, and so on.

"This is certainly a valid narrative line. Bias and the denial of rights are real, and straights have a lot to answer for in their historic cruelty toward gays. But rights-and-bias is only one way of framing a broad, continuing, and confusing story."

Leo says that most Americans — who, polls show, have conflicted feelings about issues such as gay marriage and teaching tolerance for homosexuality in the schools — don't frame the story on gays the same way journalists do. Citizens, Leo says, "are mostly concerned with questions of substance, all centering on the question of what homosexuality is (or what homosexualities are) and what the social impact is likely to be as we glide rather casually from social tolerance to social approval." These kinds of questions, however, are too often dismissed as prejudice by reporters because the issue is framed as one of civil rights.

The effects of framing go beyond whether stories speak to citizens' experience. If a reporter writes not only about a problem but also about its possible solutions, for example, citizens are much more likely to see ways they can get involved in helping to solve the problem. Likewise, a story that presents only two highly polarized positions on an issue, about which many people have mixed feelings, may cause citizens to feel the story has been sensationalized or that no room exists in the public discussion about that issue for people who don't have strong feelings one way or the other.

Beneath it all is the fact that the choices reporters make in framing stories reflect the values that they hold dear. A story that presents an issue as highly polarized would imply that the reporter values competition and clearly articulated political positions — power struggles fought by opponents who state their positions strongly. A story that describes a variety of approaches to solving a community problem and encourages public participation in finding a solution would imply that the journalist values collaboration and citizen involvement. A story that describes a person's triumph over adversity would imply that the reporter values the human capacity for survival and transcendence. And so on.

Given that so much is involved in framing decisions, how can reporters and editors make the best choices in this regard?

Byline: Ted Rall. Source: Universal Press Syndicate

CHOOSING THE BEST FRAMING

No story framing is inherently good or bad. What matters is whether the framing is appropriate to the story. Let's revisit the Watergate story, for example. When reporters Bob Woodward and Carl Bernstein unearthed the connection between then-President Richard Nixon and a break-in at the Democratic National Committee headquarters in the Watergate hotel, it was appropriate to frame the story as a political scandal of great significance. The president had abused his power by trying to cover up the connection, misusing the FBI and IRS, falsifying documents, and paying witnesses to keep quiet. The Watergate story was so significant, culminating in Nixon's resignation from office, that since then journalists have overused the scandal frame, adding the suffix "gate" to any story that has even the least hint of controversy.

"These days a Girl Scout can't scam a box of cookies without triggering a flurry of Cookiegate coverage. Scandals, semi-scandals and pseudo-scandals that hardly register on the Richter scale of corruption — it doesn't matter, they all get the 'gate,'" Suzan Revan wrote in the September 1997 issue of "American Journalism Review."

In many cases, journalists unconsciously exaggerate the conflict, competition or controversy in the story as a way of trying to capture the attention of readers — and of judges in journalism awards contests. These pressures to make stories falsely dramatic can easily tempt reporters to focus on who is being victimized by whom and who is triumphing over others' attempts to do them in. Over the long term, however, this approach backfires, just like in the children's story about the boy who cried wolf.

"One of the principal deformities of journalism — and, for that matter, the public's most frequent criticism of the media — is that it suffers from a kind of hypnosis with novelty and conflict," Guido Fernandez wrote in the book "La Agonía a la Hora del Cierre: El Minuto de Silencio que Puede Hacer Cambiar al Periodismo" ("The Agony of Deadline: The Minute of Silence That Can Change Journalism").

When journalists exaggerate conflict, they are stretching the truth in ways that are detrimental not only to their own integrity as self-proclaimed truth-tellers but to the health of public life in their communities as well.

"Clearly, people are drawn to conflict, but where obviously contrived or transparently partisan conflict stands in the way of resolution of important problems, citizen tolerance for it — and those who convey it — becomes strained," Buzz Merritt wrote in "Public Journalism and Public Life: Why Telling the News is Not Enough."

The overemphasis on conflict and competition has also led

some journalists to routinely frame stories as having only two sides, when many issues in our communities are far more complex. These journalists use an on-the-one-hand/on-the-other-hand approach, striving for balance by quoting people on opposite ends of the spectrum. However, the majority of citizens do not see the issue in such starkly contrasted terms.

"Framing the issue at the extremes creates more than the deficiency of inaccuracy. On issues of more than one dimension, it defines most people out of the discussion. 'If that's what the argument is about,' they say, 'I'm not in it; my views aren't reflected' — thus they opt out. The quoted sources (and the journalist who presents them) become participants in a closed cycle," Merritt wrote.

Take the issue of abortion, for instance. Reporters typically quote, on the one hand, those who oppose abortion, usually on religious grounds; and, on the other, those who support it, usually on grounds that a woman should have a right to make that choice. Rarely does a reporter quote someone who has mixed feelings — yet that is where most citizens find themselves.

"There are a number of issues in this country where there seems to be very little gray area. ... If you're not for it, you're against it," a Los Angeles man told The Harwood Group, which reported his comments in a report titled "Meaningful Chaos: How People Form Relationships with Public Concerns."

He and others who participated in the Harwood discussions said that such polarization and the animosity it usually fosters keeps them from discussing public policy issues with other citizens, because they have no other model for talking intelligently and calmly to work through the tensions involved in addressing those issues.

Consider, for example, how difficult it is for people to discuss racial tensions in the United States. Then read the following two leads from stories about Americans' reactions to the acquittal of O.J. Simpson, a former professional football player and film star, on charges of murdering his ex-wife.

This was a wire story that appeared in many local newspapers:

> There is no avoiding it.
> Lurking in the aftermath of the dramatic O.J. Simpson verdict — as it did throughout the trial — is the question of race in America.
> Will this bizarre "trial of the century" provide a wedge of distrust to further divide us? Or will it lead to a healthy discussion of differences between blacks and whites?
> The great fear of many who deal with daily racial issues is the former.

Clearly, this story focused mainly on how the verdict will affect racial tensions, and it pits whites against blacks in a mistrustful relationship. The following story in The Christian Science Monitor described the significance of the verdict very differently:

> Though the O. J. Simpson case is over, the United States justice system is just beginning to go on trial.
>
> Two days after the acquittal of Mr. Simpson cast a panorama of stunned white faces and jubilant black faces in America's living rooms, talk has not subsided about the kind of justice served by the verdict and the lessons to draw from it.
>
> Few Americans believe anything about this trial was normal. Still, aberration or not, the Simpson case could have a lasting effect on U.S. law enforcement and society at large. Experts say perceptions about the verdict could produce a kind of slippery slope of distrust — in the area of race relations, trust in police work, gender relations, and the American legal system.

This story acknowledged the issue of race, to be sure, but it also put the response to the verdict in the context of a range of issues involving the fair treatment of all Americans.

In the view of The Harwood Group and other researchers, stories that present only two extremes of a complex issue are not only superficial and inaccurate; they also foster polarization among citizens.

Double murder defendant O.J. Simpson listens to not-guilty verdict with his attorneys F. Lee Bailey, left, and Johnnie Cochran.

Source: AFP/CORBIS

Stories that present a range of perspectives, however, lead to more constructive public discourse.

In her story about a controversy over land use in Virginia Beach, Va., for example, Virginian-Pilot reporter Karen Weintraub focused not on the power struggle between city council members over one member's proposal to build a golf course but on a variety of proposals for developing the land — and several approaches the community could take in resolving the controversy. Resolution could come through a simple vote, through hiring an outside consultant or through a public design process. An accompanying graphic showed a map of the land in question, with a total of five proposals represented as possibilities. The story, in its published form, appeared under the headline, "Is Golf the Best Course?" and essentially posed that question to the citizens of the Norfolk area.

Instead of focusing on who was winning and who was losing with respect to the golf course proposal, she focused on the range of possible uses for the land in a way that clearly showed how citizens could get involved in both the discussion and the decision about what would be done with that property.

You could call this the "competing goods" frame, in that it presents a variety of options — each good in its own way — so that citizens can see the full range of possibilities.

Yet it would be awfully hard to imagine telling the Watergate story by presenting a range of competing goods for citizens to consider and act on. The framing must be appropriate to the situation to work.

HOW STORIES ARE FRAMED

To understand how reporters make framing decisions, it may be helpful to think of the decisions we each make in taking a simple photograph. As we peer through the lens, we decide who or what will be in the picture, what action we will capture within the frame, and where we will stand in relation to the subject of the photo. Those decisions usually are determined in part by our purpose in taking the photo — whether to create a historical record of something that occurred, or a compelling close-up of an interesting person or captivating moment in time. Our decisions also are influenced by our personal preferences as to what makes a good picture.

In a similar way, reporters frame stories partly based on their purpose in writing the story. At times, they write simply to chronicle day-to-day events in their community — what is sometimes called the "newspaper of record" approach to news coverage. At other times, they examine issues in depth or they write to entertain. Story framing decisions also are influenced by the reporters' and editors' personal preferences and values, as well as by their news organization's policies or norms for reporting various kinds of stories.

Because framing decisions are so often made under the pressure of deadlines, when there is little time to think through various alternatives, it is important that journalists periodically evaluate the habits and assumptions they make in writing stories. It is also important to allow time during planning and staff meetings to discuss story framing for non-deadline stories, and to evaluate story framing during periodic self-critiques.

THE PURPOSE OF THE STORY

A good starting point for deciding on a frame is to consider the story's purpose. Is your goal to create a record of a significant event? To make people aware of a problem or issue that affects their lives? Or do you want to give them information about someone who has done something unusual or inspiring?

The purpose of the story has a tremendous impact on the kind of reporting you do as well as on the story you write. If your goal is to record an event, you probably will plan to be there, take notes about what happens and interview others who are present. If you're writing about a problem facing your community, you probably will seek out comments from a number of people who have an interest in the issue, as a way of finding out exactly what is involved as well as what the alternatives are. If you're writing a profile of someone, you may interview only him or her.

In considering the purpose of a story, here are some questions you may find helpful:

• *Do you want your story to convey basic information about an event that occurred?* If so, why is it important to cover this event? Why is it important now? What are people most likely to remember about it 10 years from now? Was it an isolated event or a step in a long process? If it was part of a process, what is important about that process? What place does this event have in the history of the community? What's the next step in the process?

• *Do you want your story to inform people about a pressing issue that affects them?* If so, why is this issue important? What will people be able to do with the information you provide? What reaction do you

Whom Should You Interview?

Choosing the people you interview can have a tremendous impact on your story.

If you interview only public officials about public problems, you are likely to get a very different kind of story than if you interview only citizens. What's important is to find a mix of people that includes a representative cross-section of people who have a stake in what's going on.

A good rule of thumb is to interview a minimum of three people about every story: at least one person who has an official connection to what happened or is happening, and at least two people who are affected in some way by what is happening.

It's also important to look beyond the obvious sources. Communities have many different types of leaders, according to the authors of "Tapping Civic Life: How to Report First, and Best, What's Happening in Your Community."

As you think about whom to interview, include official leaders who hold high-level positions in government, businesses or nonprofit organizations; civic leaders who hold recognized positions in religious and civic organizations, chamber of commerce or neighborhood associations; and, when appropriate, experts who have specialized knowledge pertinent to your story.

Don't overlook two less obvious types of leaders who can frequently add a great deal to your stories, described as follows in "Tapping Civic Life":

• Connectors: people who move between organizations and civic conversations, often with no official capacity.

• Catalysts: respected neighbors, co-workers and church lay leaders who encourage others to get involved and provide community expertise or historical perspective.

want people to have to this story? How can you write the story in a way that makes that kind of process likely? Is the process you want to initiate the most constructive process for the community to deal with this issue at this point in time?

• *Do you want your story to educate people about a problem or process* they seem not to understand as well as they should? If so, why is it important for them to understand this problem or process? Is it something they can have an impact on? What do they need to know to affect what happens?

• *Do you want your story to engage people in a tale of human triumph, tragedy or travails?* If so, what good will it do to tell this story? What kind of emotion do you want the story to evoke? If you decide to present the people in this story as characters in a drama, will it require that you exaggerate their strengths, weaknesses, thoughts, actions and reactions? Will this story raise questions about anyone's integrity? If so, have they done something that merits raising those questions?

Additional elements that enter into framing decisions, with questions that can help you think through those decisions, are presented in the sidebar. These questions can lead to useful insights if you review them throughout the process of planning, reporting and writing your stories.

Do Journalists Give Peace a Chance?

Some journalists would tell you that, as they cover wars and other violent conflicts, they can unwittingly make things worse.

Advocates of "peace journalism" believe they can increase the chances of a peaceful resolution if they explore the broader causes of conflict rather than simply reporting on the violence, demonizing some of the participants and oversimplifying conflicts.

Taking lessons from conflict resolution theory, they encourage journalists to pay more attention to underlying political factors, multiple causes, possible compromises and effects on civilians.

"Journalism does not only legitimize violence but is violent in and of itself," says conflict resolution guru Johan Galtung.

In several Peace Journalism Forums held in England, journalists who cover events in war-torn countries studied and reworked various stories.

They then reworked those stories, seeking to create accurate, fair, balanced stories that included "sides" usually left out.

They also experimented with other ways of broadening the range of discourse in such stories.

Jake Lynch, a television news correspondent based in London and Sydney for Sky News and The Independent, has written a great deal about peace journalism.

He suggests that journalists go beyond reporting on the visible effects of war (how many missiles were fired, how many people were killed or wounded, etc.) and examine the deep structural origins of the conflict. This deeper examination avoids reducing the number of parties to two — us vs. them, good vs. evil.

Reporters also should look for and acknowledge that winning always involves trade-offs and exacts a price on the winner as well as the loser, he said.

And they should be aware that presenting people in war-torn countries as passive victims can have unintended consequences.

He cited a United Nations report on a massacre in Sarajevo. The report implied that Bosnian forces fired a shell at their own people to win international sympathy.

"Victim journalism ... may even lead one party to play upon its existence by acting in the most appalling way to generate sympathetic headlines of a sort calculated to hasten intervention on their behalf." He wrote in his online publication, "The Peace Journalism Option."

Journalists received copies of the report about the massacre but didn't report it at the time, Lynch wrote.

POSITIONING PEOPLE IN YOUR STORIES

If a reporter frames a story, he or she also frames the people in it — positioning the sources in relation to one another, in relation to the reporter's biases, and in relation to the story frame itself. The framing of a story even positions the reader of that story.

"News stories position us in a wide variety of ways — as spectators or as participants, as insiders or outsiders, as voters, as consumers, as fans, as victims, as celebrants, as sentimentalists. Take the sort of story we commonly call a 'tear jerker.' It puts us in the position of the jerkee, the one from whom tears are pulled," New York University Journalism Professor Jay Rosen wrote in "Public Journalism Theory and Practice: Lessons from Experience."

How you position a source determines the questions you ask. The questions determine the answers, which in turn drive the story.

Try this: Imagine interviewing someone you think is lying to you. The questions you would ask this person will likely attempt to catch him or her in the lie — "But didn't you say ... " or "Doesn't that contradict ... ." In investigative stories, reporters try to make sure they have a "paper trail" of documents so that the source can't squirm away with half-truths. Now imagine that your interviewee is the most honest human being on the planet — or the victim of another's lies. Wouldn't the questions you ask be entirely different?

In almost every community, for example, you'll find someone who shows up and generally antagonizes the city council of school board by describing what a lousy job they are doing.

Here's an example of how one California paper described such people in an August 1996, Page One feature:

Headline: Activists annoy some, inspire others

[*Summary paragraph:*] Gadflies show up at every meeting and speak their mind. They slow the process, and they pester politicians. But, some say, they're necessary.

[The first paragraph after the summary describes how one such "gadfly" tried to have an entire county board arrested for cutting off his speeches. The story then continues:]

The Summit Valley man has been called a thorn in the side. Pain in the neck. Gadfly. And, like many other activists in the Inland Empire, essential to open government.

"That's democracy. It's a messy business, but you have to tolerate it," said Michael Clarke, professor of public administration at California State University, San Bernardino.

The rest of the story describes the many problems caused by this and other gadflies, quotes another expert who says such people are a necessary evil in our democracy, then presents a gallery of gadflies along with descriptions of their many run-ins with various public officials. The substance of their comments — the issues they are fighting for — are given short shrift, sometimes summed up in two or three words, such as "tax reductions" or "environmental activism."

Obviously, a reporter who positions such people as gadflies does not give any credibility to their views. A reporter who positions them as concerned citizens will listen to what they are saying. Both approaches have their dangers — one can lead to not hearing what could turn out to be an important story; the other can result in precious time wasted on conspiracy theories or other dead ends. But it is important to avoid positioning people hastily and without thinking about the implications.

Positioning shows up in small ways. Giving a person with a degree in medicine the title "Dr." before his name positions him as an expert. That may be appropriate in a story about health, but not appropriate if that doctor is protesting the construction of another Piggly Wiggly store in his neighborhood.

Positioning can even have legal repercussions. A reporter who positions someone as a scoundrel or thief — without proof to back it up — opens his newspaper to a libel case that can result in costly legal bills, no matter what the outcome.

The trick here is to try to avoid boxing people into roles or oversimplifying their positions. Remember: You don't want to be thought of in one-dimensional terms, so don't position your sources that way.

In considering the positioning that occurs in telling a story, here are some questions you may find helpful.

• How have you acknowledged the power relationships between the people in your story? Have you presented some people as villains or victims? If so, could you make a convincing case that certain experiences, advantages or disadvantages have made them truly powerful or powerless?

• Have you presented some people as experts? If so, what knowledge and experience qualify them to be positioned that way?

• Have you presented some people as crusaders or activists? If so, what have they done that indicates they have clearly taken a stance in favor of a particular approach to an issue?

• How have you described the personal relationships between people in your story? Have you considered a variety of levels in those relationship, including personal and family ties as well as professional ones?

POSITIONING YOURSELF

We all tell our own story. In effect, we position ourselves as reporters as well. We might think of ourselves as blue-collar or white-collar, as African-American or Anglo, as working stiffs or public servants. Go into a newsroom and ask the journalists there to describe themselves. Some may say they are reporters, others writers. It's a self-defining distinction.

Here are questions that may help you think about how you're positioning yourself.

• Are you positioning yourself as an expert? Authority? Teacher? Crusader? Mobilizer? Bystander? Observer? Eyewitness? Fellow citizen? Veteran of some personal experience?
• If your position is based on knowledge, expertise and/or opinion — expert, authority, teacher, crusader, mobilizer — do you have the qualifications to assume that position? If so, how will citizens know you have those qualifications?
• If you are interviewing only experts or only citizens or only the people on one side of an issue, are you implying that you support that group's position or that you have allied yourself with them?
• If your position is based on detachment and objectivity — bystander, observer or eyewitness — are you truly detached and objective?
• If your position is based on involvement and personal experience, is your involvement and experience recent enough to be relevant to the story?

These definitions, built on your life experiences, can affect your story. It is inevitable that you will position yourself in some way; the important point is to be aware of how you're doing it and whether it is affecting your ability to see the story fairly.

PUTTING THE STORY IN CONTEXT

You also will put your story in context in terms of your community's history, current situation and process. Just as in photography, reporters can capture a panoramic or long view of the big picture, a snapshot of a moment in time, a close-up of an individual, or a variety of other perspectives on an issue or event.

Here are questions that can help you think about how you have contextualized your story:

• How have you positioned the story on the historical timeline of your community? Is it a pivotal event? A routine step forward? A renewed effort to deal with something that has come up before?

• How have you positioned the story in terms of its importance outside your area? Have you considered how various aspects of your story might tie in to things that are happening on regional, state, national and international levels?

• How have you positioned the story in terms of process? Have you told the story at a point in the life of the community that is likely to be the most beneficial? Have you included information in the story about the related developments that preceded and will follow what you're describing in your story?

SELECTING NEWS SOURCES

Choosing the people who appear in your stories is one of the most crucial decisions you make as a reporter. When covering events, reporters generally choose whom to include from among those people who attend. When writing stories about issues or ideas, reporters basically assemble a group of people they think will help them best tell the story. Some reporters choose the sources for their stories based on who is the official source of information about the event or issue they're covering, and who is likely to have knowledge or expertise about the subject of the story. Other reporters look at who will be affected by the event or issue and focus more on citizen perspectives. Still other reporters incorporate a mix of people in various categories.

In considering the people to interview and describe in a story, here are questions you may find helpful.

• Who has a stake in this issue or event? Who is affected (or could be)? Why do they care? In what ways could your story affect their lives? Whom should you contact to be sure your story accurately reflects what is at stake? Whom will you choose not to contact? Why?

• Of all the stakeholders you just considered, for whom is the story most significant? Why? Whom should you interview?

• Who has the power in the situation you're writing about? Who stands to gain? Who stands to lose? Who would be unaffected?

What people or groups hold positions that give them an official role in connection with the story? What people or groups are involved in nonofficial capacities? Which of these people should you talk to?

• Are some of the people affected by this issue or event commonly viewed as disadvantaged or marginalized, or commonly stereotyped? Has anyone been "cast" as the villain(s), accomplice(s), victim(s) or hero(es)? If so, how do you see them? Can you think of other ways to view them? Which of these people should you contact? How will you depict them accurately and fairly?

• What kind of "buzz" has this story generated so far? Who's talking about it? Who has commented publicly about it? Should you include any of them in your story? If so, what can they contribute? Is the buzz among isolated pockets of people, certain interest or demographic groups, or communitywide? Who can help you assess and convey how people in the community are talking about the issue or event in your story?

• If the story involves complicated ideas and/or extensive background information, who can help you understand those things?

• For whom are you writing the story? If you are writing the story for a general audience, are you using language and descriptions that people will understand? Are you using technical language or the kinds of words, phrases and descriptions used by experts, politicians, officials or academics? If so, will most people understand what you're saying?

• Who can be a sounding board to help you assess whether you're using words that are understandable to the average reader? If you are writing the story for a specialized audience about a subject outside your expertise, who can help you check your facts and learn how to write for that audience?

• Do you know how the people for whom you're writing view the issues and concerns at the heart of your story? Are you describing those things in ways that resonate with their understanding of those concepts?

• Who are the experts in this story? Who is well informed? If certain people claim to be well informed, how can you be sure they are? Who is underinformed or misinformed? Who says they're poorly informed — and how can you be sure they are?

TESTING YOUR FRAMING

Sometimes it's hard to see the pitfalls of the framing we have chosen for a particular story. Here are questions that can help you assess whether your framing is aligned with the story you should tell.

• What values are implied in the way you have framed this story? What aspects of the story have you emphasized at the beginning? Why? What other information are you including, and why is it valuable? To whom is it valuable? What will people gain from having this information? Why is that important?

• Is the purpose of this story compatible with your sense of responsibility as a citizen and as a journalist? What about this story is most important to you personally, as a citizen? Would other citizens view it in a similar way? Why or why not? What about this story is most important to you professionally, as a journalist? Would other journalists view it in a similar way? Why or why not? Is there a gap between what is important to you as a citizen and what is important to you as a journalist? If so, why do you think that gap exists? Is there a way for your story to better address your concerns as both a citizen and a journalist?

• Does the framing you have chosen serve as a good vehicle for accurately and fairly portraying the people, events and issues involved in your story? Have you talked to a variety of people affected by the subject of your story? Have you captured the essence of everyone's comments and not just used the most extreme quotes? Have you exaggerated or downplayed any aspect of the story? If so, for what reasons — and are those reasons valid?

EXERCISES

1. Select a news story that is being covered by several different publications available in your area. This can be a national, state or local story. Clip out several versions of the same story and write a short paper evaluating how each publication framed the story in terms of purpose, positioning and people. Also evaluate how effective each framing is and suggest other ways the story might be framed.

2. Over a designated period of time, read a given publication and clip stories that show a range of approaches to framing. Look for consistencies and differences from one story to the next. What kind of framing is used most often? Least often? Write a paper describing the publication's approach to framing stories and evaluating those framings in terms of purpose, positioning and people.

3. Find an example of a story that is framed in a way that is particularly interesting to you. Call the reporter who wrote the story and ask why he or she framed the story that way in terms of purpose, positioning and people, whether other framings were considered, and what the general story framing process is in his or her newsroom.

4. Find a story that is framed in a way you don't like and use the information in it to either rewrite the story with a different purpose, different positioning and different people, or describe how you would frame the story differently. If reframing the story would require additional reporting, describe how you would go about gathering additional material.

Further Reading

ON THE WEB

"Framing the News: The Triggers, Frames and Messages in Newspaper Coverage," study by the Project for Excellence in Journalism and Princeton Survey Research Associates: www.journalism.org/framing.html

"Frame Wars over Elian Gonzalez," by L. Michael Hall, Ph.D.: www.neuro-semantics.com/Articles/elian.htm

"Gender in Political Science: Framing the Issues," by Pippa Norris, Kennedy School of Government, Harvard University, presented at the Political Studies Association annual conference in Glasgow, April 1996: www.soton.ac.uk/~psd/1996/norris.html

"Outgunned: How the Network News Media Are Spinning the Gun Control Debate," special Media Research Center report by Geoffrey Dickens, the center's senior media analyst: www.fulton-armory.com/MRC2.htm

"The Middle East — War Journalism and Peace Journalism," by Jake Lynch: www.mediachannel.org

"The Peace Journalism Option," by Jake Lynch: www.conflictandpeace.org/6pub/3pub.html

IN PRINT

"Frame Analysis: An Essay on the Organization of Experience," by Erving Goffman, published by Harper & Row Publishers, New York, 1974.

"Framing Public Life: A Bridging Model for Media Study," by Stephen D. Reese, a synthesis keynote review prepared for Framing in the Media Landscape, the inaugural conference for the Center for Mass Communication Research, College of Journalism and Mass Communication, University of South Carolina, Columbia, S.C., Oct. 12-14, 1997.

"Journalists, Framing, and Discourse about Race Relations," by David Domke, Journalism and Mass Communication Monographs, No. 164, published by the Association for Education in Journalism and Mass Communication, Columbia, S.C., December 1997.

"Lies My Teacher Told Me: Everything Your American History Textbook Got Wrong," by James W. Loewen, published by Touchstone Books, New York, 1995.

"Steps to an Ecology of Mind," by Gregory Bateson, published by Ballantine Books, New York, 1972.

Branding the News

A segment from National Public Radio's
"All Things Considered" news program,
Friday, Sept. 21, 2001

SUMMARY

Facing the same news from the same sources, major news organizations are trying to distinguish themselves from one another: From "Attack on America" to "America's New War," some critics say that the "brand names" the networks have chosen to distinguish their coverage may be a force in directing their coverage. NPR's Rick Karr reports. (4:00)

THE REPORT

Noah Adams: From NPR News, this is "All Things Considered." I'm Noah Adams ...

Robert Siegel: ... and I'm Robert Siegel. Within hours of the strikes on the morning of September 11, each of the television news organizations began labeling its coverage. In the ensuing 10 days, the labels have evolved. NBC, for example, is now going with "America on Alert," while CNN has chosen "America's New War." TV news executives say giving brand names to big stories is standard practice. Media critics argue that it can subtly shape news coverage. NPR's Rick Karr reports:

Karr: A brand is a kind of story, according to Jim Twitchell, who teaches English and advertising at the University of Florida.

Twitchell: Branding is the attachment of a story, a myth, a saga, to ... usually, it's an object that's interchangeable with some other object.

Karr: Take bottled water, for example. It's all pretty much just H_2O, Twitchell says, yet one brand identity might say, "This water comes from a pure glacier." Another, "This water makes you sexy and cool." And yet another, "This fits into a healthy lifestyle." In the same way, Twitchell says, the networks' brand identities for their coverage of recent news events are intended to heighten the differences between them.

Twitchell: The stories all are interchangeable, just like bottled water. In other words, if you're a television network, you're showing the same images — they're almost like wallpaper — that your competitor is. And so the only way for you to distinguish yourself — the only way for you to say, well, this bottled water is different from that bottled water — in other words, that CBS's coverage is different from NBC's — is to somehow get in there with some other story.

Karr: The brand identities are those other stories, Twitchell says. For example, ABC chose "A Nation Challenged." That brand promises a story told cautiously, without judgment. And in fact, media critics have generally praised ABC's coverage of last week's events for what they say is its even tone and careful reporting. On the other hand, the 24-hour cable news networks have selected more aggressive brand identities. Fox News chose "America Stands United." Here's a Fox anchor using the tag line before a commercial break:

Anchor: The cleanup efforts continue in lower Manhattan as they continue to look for many of their own friends and neighbors inside the rubble. This, as "America Stands United."

Karr: This kind of branding was pioneered by CNN during the Gulf War, when the network completely revamped its graphics and theme music. For this crisis, the brand identity is "America's New War." CNN uses it in onscreen graphics and promotional spots.

Sound clip: Bringing you the latest reports as events unfold in "America's New War." Stay with CNN.

Karr: Television news organizations say branding like this is something they've done with most big stories, from the Gulf War to O.J. to the disappearance of Chandra Levy. A representative of one of the 24-hour cable networks said, on background, that they do it to inform viewers of the topic at hand and give viewers some idea of the content of the coverage. The representative said senior news editors choose the tag lines. But Dara Williams, director of the Newswatch project at San Francisco State University, says the CNN brand, in particular, shows subtle bias. It neglects alternatives to war by accepting without question the Bush administration's assertion that war is inevitable. Williams says she understands the ways in which the story has put pressure on journalists.

Williams: But at the same time that doesn't mean that we throw out the ethics and the standards that we have set for ourselves, and for what readers and viewers expect from us, and that is to be the eyes and ears and yet be skeptics and to ask questions and to make sure that we're getting the whole story, not just the story that the source wants to tell us.

Karr: The broadcast networks' brand identities have become less visible over the past few days as they've returned to more normal schedules. Meanwhile, CBS has changed the brand identity of its coverage from "Terror Hits Home" to "America Strikes Back." Rick Karr, NPR News.

Copyright 2001 NPR

For the record: The brand identity on NPR's Web site at the time this segment ran was "America Transformed."

Chapter 8

Interviewing

Reporters must develop good interviewing skills for use in a variety of settings, including press conferences and one-on-one interviews by telephone or in person.

Cartoon by Daniel McCoy

- Interviews are the primary way of gathering material used in most news stories, so good interviewing skills are essential for journalists.

- Good reporters develop their own distinctive styles for approaching people to request interviews as well as for interviewing itself.

- Careful preparation can build trust in the people you are interviewing and make interviews more fruitful.

If you read a story that captures and holds your interest, you can bet it was written by a reporter who is good at conducting interviews. Usually, these stories cut right to the heart of what is important. The only way reporters get to the heart of any story is by earning the trust of the people they interview, asking the right questions, listening attentively to the answers, and being very observant.

The best interviews are done in person, either by appointment or spontaneously. Some interviews are done by telephone, if time is limited or the person being interviewed is far away or has limited time.

The reporter may ask questions designed to gather factual information as efficiently as possible, or the questions may be more open-ended and probing, to flesh out stories, reflections and opinions that help to clarify the meaning of the story. The reporter usually takes lots of notes.

Interviews are the most efficient way for reporters to gather facts for their stories. Interviews also provide a focused, in-depth look at one person's perspective or experiences.

SETTING UP THE INTERVIEW

For some reporters, the most challenging part of interviewing is making the initial contact. Sometimes this will involve phoning the person and asking to make an appointment for an interview. Sometimes you'll approach someone in person — possibly a stranger — and either get him or her to talk to you on the spot or make an appointment for an interview.

Both situations can seem intimidating, especially to beginning reporters who are the least bit shy. It may help if, before you call or approach the person, you clarify in your own mind the value of your story and why the person's contribution to it is so essential. If you believe it is important for someone to be interviewed, that person will be more likely to believe it, too.

It is also helpful to begin consciously developing a variety of methods for approaching people. You need to experiment, drawing on your own personality and unique characteristics to find ways of approaching people in a variety of circumstances. Calling the police chief to ask for an interview about a new evidence lab, for example, is pretty straightforward. Talking to disaster victims or their grieving relatives requires much more sensitivity. Nevertheless, any two reporters probably would approach each of those situations in a slightly different way. What's important is to learn how to use your distinct characteristics and interests to your advantage.

If you saw the movie "Erin Brockovich," which was based on a true story, you saw an example of a born interviewer who does exactly that. Although she was an investigator for a law firm, not a reporter, she convinced people to give her vast amounts of information that proved the Pacific Gas & Electric Co. tried to cover up its poisoning of a town's water supply and the resultant devastating health problems. As portrayed by Julia Roberts, Brockovich used her intelligence, her natural empathy, her tenacity and her willing-

The real Erin Brockovich, left, documented a power company's contamination of a California town's water supply in much the same way that an investigative reporter might have, through public records research and extensive interviews. Brockovich, whose mother was a journalist, describes how she came to spearhead the fight against the power company in her 2001 autobiography, "Take It From Me: Life's a Struggle But You Can Win."

Photo by Stewart Cohen, reprinted with permission.

ness to talk to people on their turf and their terms. She even consciously used her sexy wardrobe, which threw many people off-balance and caused others to underestimate her. She knocked on doors and interviewed people in their homes, talked to a farmer as he was hosing down the concrete floor of the stalls where he milks his cattle, and sweet-talked a painfully shy young man at the water district office into letting her go through all of the town's water records.

She wasn't the first person to interview someone while they were working or sweet-talk his or her way to information. But if you've seen the movie, you'll probably agree that it's doubtful anyone has ever done those things quite the way she did. And that's the point: Find the way that works for you.

Sometimes it helps to get to know people a little before asking them for information, according to Peter Wasson, longtime police reporter with the Wausau, Wis., Daily Herald.

"When I walk into a source's office, I stop and look around," he wrote in an article about reporting. "Pictures of the source's spouse and kids on the wall, the 45-inch muskie he caught on vacation, her skiing hobby — all tell me something personal about the sources. Sources hate reporters who come in and want nothing but information. They love to talk about themselves, their hobbies or their children — and only then, their jobs."

Sometimes, however, it's best to remain businesslike, especially if the person you're interviewing is extremely busy, used to dealing with the media, and has limited time for the interview.

No matter what approach you use, it is important to behave in a professional, respectful manner, because your behavior may be the only basis on which they decide whether to trust you with their information.

THE INTERVIEW ITSELF

Once you begin the actual interview, your behavior will set the tone for the discussion and determine the richness of the information you receive. Most people will know whether you're truly interested in understanding them or if you're just looking for a few quotes so you can rush off to your next interview. In addition, if they feel you're being careful and thorough in the way you ask your questions, they will be more likely to speak freely. This is true even in interviews in which you must ask about unpleasant subjects: The person accused of wrongdoing or caught up in a controversy will be more likely to talk if that person feels you will listen carefully and treat him or her fairly.

The following material contains specific suggestions that will help you build the basic level of trust that is needed for successful interviews.

Plan Ahead

Schedule interviews as much in advance as possible to show consideration for the person you want to interview. It also helps ensure that you will not find out, two days before your deadline, that someone you need to talk to is on vacation or can't fit you in until four days after your story is due. As a reporter, you have a responsibility to yourself, your editors and the people in your community to be organized in such a way that you do not repeatedly call upon others to drop everything to talk to you so that you can meet a deadline you've known about for weeks. Last-minute interviews should be requested only for stories that must be written on deadline about things that just happened.

It also may help to plan your interviews in a logical order. If you're writing an in-depth profile of someone, for example, it may be best to interview the person last — after you've heard what others have to say. If you're writing about something that will call for a response to various allegations, make sure you have all the information before you interview the person or people who must respond to those claims. You may also want talk to some people to get the basic facts and to others to clarify the significance of those facts. It helps if you're clear about what you want from each person.

Allow enough time for the kind of interview you need with each person. If you just need a brief overview of the facts, or you've got most of the information for your story from other sources, you may need only a 15-minute or half-hour interview. If the person you are talking to is one of the key sources, allow an hour or even two — and don't rush.

By planning your interview well, you can avoid having to make numerous follow-up calls or interviews. Although most people will be glad to verify or clarify information later, or to answer additional questions in a follow-up phone call or interview, they are unlikely to politely endure repeated requests for information you could have gotten in the initial interview. Always remember that, unless talking to the press is part of their job, they're essentially volunteers who are helping you write your story. Value their time.

Be Persistent

Don't be offended by getting disconnected, being put on hold, never getting called back, or other frustrations that may or may not be intentional efforts to avoid you. If you take those things personally, you'll be miserable and won't get the information.

Former police reporter Edna Buchanan is a great role model for persistence. Part of her job involved calling people who were accused of, or the victim of, extremely unpleasant things. When people would hang up on her, she would simply wait a minute, call them back, and say they must have gotten disconnected. She found that most of the time people would not have the guts to hang up on her a second time.

If someone isn't returning your calls, be creative — so long as you don't lie or misrepresent yourself. If you're tired of waiting, make another call. Then try calling the person back again. Explain that you've been on your phone and you were worried he or she might have tried to call and couldn't get through.

Another approach: Try calling about a half-hour before you have to leave the office. Say you're getting ready to leave and wanted to try again, in case the person might try to call you back, only to find that you've left.

Obviously, you can overdo it, and you will learn to gauge when you're bordering on becoming a pest. But calling more than once sends the message that you're persistent. If the person is trying to avoid you, sooner or later he or she will decide to talk to you and get it over with.

If you're having a hard time reaching someone in person, try waiting. If the person is holed up in an office, just wait. Spend the time thinking through how to organize a story, or start writing a lead. Sooner or later, the person you're waiting for will have to come out of the office. You also can find out when he or she usually comes in to work or back from an appointment, then wait wherever you need to be to catch the person in transit.

Identify Yourself

Be clear about who you are, who you're working for, the purpose of your interview, and how long you think the interview will take. (A good rule of thumb is that most interviews take one-half hour to an hour; however, this time frame may vary greatly based on the type of story you are doing and how much time the person you are interviewing has available.)

Think about What You Want to Ask

Prepare as thoroughly as possible. Ideally, you'll have time before the interview to check your news organization's files or other resources to gather background information that will help you formulate good questions. If you are called upon to cover a breaking story in a geographical or subject area that is unfamiliar to you, take a few minutes — no matter how urgent the story is — to get at least some context from your editor or someone else with knowledge in that area. Preparing in this way will ensure that you get the bulk of the information you need during the initial interview.

Think about the general topic you want to cover and, if it's helpful, make a list of these topics to refer to during your interview. You may also want to think through *how* you will ask those questions. When you're seeking factual information, the questions should be more focused and specific. When seeking to understand the meaning of the story, the questions should be more open-ended and general. (We'll talk more about that later in this chapter.)

Pay special attention to questions you think you might feel uncomfortable asking. For important stories and if time permits, it may even be helpful to try different ways of asking "tough" or uncomfortable questions by rehearsing with a friend or colleague, or even just by talking to your steering wheel while you drive to the interview.

It's OK to make up a list of "must-ask" questions, especially when you need to get responses to specific allegations in uncomfortable circumstances. However, don't read the list to the source during the interview. Doing so makes an interview unbearably stilted. More importantly, getting locked into a list of prepared questions can cause you to miss asking follow-up questions about important points that come up spontaneously during the interview.

Leave Your Desk

Although telephone interviews are often necessary, it is always better to conduct an interview in person, and in the normal environment of the person you are interviewing. Gestures and facial expressions provide important clues about a person's attitudes and feelings, and adjusting your questions to respond to such factors can lead to a deeper discussion. In addition, seeing someone in his or her office, home or favorite restaurant can provide additional clues about what is important to the person, as well as giving you physical details that could be included in your story.

Avoid Stereotyping

Before you go out on an interview with someone who is different from you in some significant way, think about whether you have any preconceived ideas. Do you expect athletes to be all muscle, no brains? When you think of someone who is blind, do any stereotypes come to mind? What are your notions going into an interview with someone of another religion or race? The point isn't to berate yourself for having such preconceptions, because most of us do. But unless you are aware of them, they can intrude on your interviews in unfortunate ways. "Reporters may find their Native American source suddenly turn uncommunicative if they blurt out, 'Gee, you don't look Indian to me,'" Native American photojournalist Mary Annette Pember of the "Cincinnati Enquirer" writes. People who are disabled might get understandably annoyed if you ask lots of questions about their disability (especially if that's not what you came there to interview them about) or if you assume things about what they can't — or can — do.

If you find you have preconceptions or curiosity about the things that make people different from you, do a little research or try to think of people who defy the stereotype. "When interviewing Native Americans, reporters should bring with them: solid research, basic human respect, genuine curiosity and a healthy skepticism for anything that doesn't ring true. These guidelines for interviewing Native Americans are otherwise known as The Basic Tenets of Quality Journalism," Pember writes. Don't expect everyone to cheerfully accept the challenge of educating you and everyone else in the world about their ethnic group, disability or other distinguishing characteristics.

Blend

Dress and behave appropriately. If you're going to interview a high-profile business person or government official, wear conservative clothing and be prepared to get to the point. If you're going to interview a country farmer or people at a family reunion, wear casual clothes. Certainly, there is room for individuality here. But if you are strongly attached to creating an extremely distinctive physical appearance, you may find it will limit the success of your interviews with people other than those whose general appearance resembles yours.

Be Prompt

Nothing is seen as a greater indicator of respect than promptness. If you are late, it is seen as an indication that you view your time and priorities as more important than those of the person you are interviewing. Although you may discover that people from other cultures have a different attitude about promptness (Latin-Americans, for instance, tend to be somewhat looser about arriving "on time"), it is always better to err on the side of punctuality.

Be Aware of Your Body Language

No matter how hectic your day is, take a moment before each interview to relax and focus, then begin the conversation as though you've got all the time in the world. Sit relaxed but not lazy in your chair. Speak slowly. Don't fidget — you could send cues that make the person you are interviewing assume you're in a hurry, and he or she therefore gives you rushed, superficial responses. If you're under deadline pressure, say so. If you seem rushed, at least it's best to let the person know why.

If you don't believe in the value of the story you are there to ask questions about, your body language may communicate that. If you don't believe there is value in getting your questions answered, the person you're interviewing probably won't either. If you feel at all uncomfortable about your story assignment, talk to your editor about it before you get to the interview. Talk through why the story is important, or what value it may have for the people who will read it.

Be Honest

Don't lie about who you are, who you work for or the purpose of your interview.

Some journalists argue that deception is justified in extreme cases in which they believe it is the only way to gain access to important information about things that threaten public well-being. Others believe such an approach is never ethical. This is an area of tremendous ethical concern, and news organizations generally must weigh the potential threat to society against the potential damage they may do to their credibility by using deception.

If you find yourself in a situation in which you believe deception is warranted, always talk it through with your editors first. Chances are they will call in the newspaper's attorneys before approving such a course of action. Without your editors' and attorneys' approval, you will be risking dismissal and possible legal repercussions for violating fraud and employment laws. (U.S. courts have offered no protection for reporters who use deceit to gain access to information.)

In general, tell the person what your story is about. How specific you should be usually depends on how far along you are in your story. Many times, the story idea you start out with turns into a very different story as you gather information. When doing investigative reporting, it is especially important not to state accusations you cannot yet prove. Telling the person what the story is about has the secondary advantage of making it less likely the interview will go off on tangents.

Don't bluff or sidestep certain questions in a vain attempt to avoid appearing stupid. If you don't know or don't understand, ask for more explanation. Otherwise, your vanity may result in incorrect assumptions in your story — and then you really will appear to be stupid. For example, one reporter, asked to do a story on buildings in downtown Knoxville, invited an architect to tour the main street with him. The architect repeatedly referred to "Italianate" designs; the reporter, not wanting to appear stupid, didn't ask what that meant, and instead published a story describing all those "Italian 8" buildings.

As the Chinese proverb says, "He who asks is a fool for five minutes. He who does not is a fool forever."

Avoid Making Promises

Don't make promises you can't keep. Don't tell someone when a particular story will appear, because there's a good chance the schedule will change. Don't agree to let the person you have interviewed read the story before it appears. Aside from the logistical problems it would create to let every person who is quoted read every story, the implication when they ask to "read" a story is not just that they want to know what's coming — they also want the right to approve it. This opens you up to the possibility that they will ask you to change things in ways that compromise your understanding of the story and their role in it. An alternative used by some reporters is to agree to call the person and read back to them only their words, as they will appear in quotes, or to read passages involving complex technical information, to verify that what they've written is accurate.

Also be very careful about promising to quote someone as an anonymous source. Because of ethical breaches in recent years, most newspapers are very reluctant to quote unnamed sources. Before you waste a lot of time talking to someone you ultimately may not be able to quote, check with your editor. Is this a case when the information the person has to offer is so compelling that the paper would consider using it without naming the source? In addition, once you guarantee anonymity, you have made a verbal contract you can't go back on. If you use the person's name, he or she can sue — and win.

Establish Ground Rules

In a similar vein, be careful about accepting information "off the record." If you agree to do that, you must be meticulous about making sure you remember what's "on" and what's "off." One way to ensure you don't confuse matters is to put your pen down when a source starts talking off the record. That way, if you can't find it in your notes, you know it wasn't on the record.

It is especially important to explain "on the record" and "off the record" to citizens who have not had much experience in dealing with the media. If it's on the record, it means you may quote them. Do not assume they know you're planning to quote them, even though it may seem obvious to you. A graceful way to do this is by simply asking, "May I quote you?" This question makes your intentions clear to them and will save you from ending up in the uncomfortable position of having someone say to you, after a long conversation, "Now, I don't want you to quote me on any of that." Conversely, don't assume people know they can speak to you "off the record," which means you will not quote them. This can be especially important if you are writing about a sensitive subject, the person has seemed reluctant to talk to you, or they don't want to be quoted. "I was surprised to learn when I started my job that very few people know the 'rules' of talking with a reporter," police reporter Peter Wasson wrote. "Many clerks or other low-level employees thought that if they talked to me, their names would appear in the newspaper. I took the time to explain that the clerks could safely give me tips because I would confirm the information from other sources before I printed it, and thus avoid using their names."

If you talk to people off the record, however, be careful to explain that you need to know beforehand when they're telling you something they don't want you to report, so you can honor their request. Otherwise, if some of the interview is on the record and some of it is off, you may become confused about exactly when they went off the record. In addition, as a reporter you always should consider whether you want to take on the responsibility of knowing something you cannot print (more in Chapter 14 on journalism as public discourse).

Get Off to a Good Start

You will find it enormously helpful in the long run if you develop the habit of gathering basic information at the start of every interview. This habit will not only ensure that you gather essential information about the person you are interviewing, it also will tend to put the person at ease by starting the interview on a neutral, non-threatening note and giving them an idea of what to expect.

Here are effective start-up questions.

• Ask how the person would like his or her name to appear and how to spell it (even if it's a common name like Smith — or is it Smyth? — or Matthews — or is it Mathews?). If the person gives you a business card, be sure to ask if the information on it is still current. It doesn't matter how you do it. Just be sure to check the spelling of the name and be sure to get both the legal name and, if appropriate, nickname.

• If one of the reasons you are interviewing the person is because of his or her position, ask for an exact, official job title. If the title is confusing, ask the person to explain in plain language.

• If you are interviewing the person as a citizen, ask where he or she works, lives, and any other personal information that helps you describe the person's role in various parts of the community.

• Be sure you fully understand the person's relationship to the story and his or her stake in it. What experiences has the person had that are relevant to your story? What, if anything, does the person stand to gain or lose? If you're writing about the schools, does the person have school-age children or not? Either way, does he or she pay taxes to support the schools? Use your judgment as to whether to ask these questions at the start of the interview or as the conversation proceeds.

• Ask the person's age if there is a reason to distinguish him or her from other people who may have the same name (as in crime and court stories, so as not to get hard-working delivery driver Pete Jones in trouble with his family, friends and employer if the other Pete Jones is arrested on a drunken driving charge); if it is relevant to the story because the age would give the person a particular perspective or set of generational experiences; or if you want to be sure you're talking to people of all ages. Ask the reluctant source to pin it down as much as he or she is willing.

Listen Well and Check What You've Heard

Throughout the interview, listen carefully to what is said and how the person says it.

Be sure to get the correct spelling of all proper names — and if interviewees don't know, ask them who would. Never guess about how a name is spelled.

If someone is telling you about an important event or experience, keep asking questions until you can picture what happened as vividly as if it were a scene from a movie.

At various points in the interview, check to make sure you've heard correctly. You can do this in several ways: Repeat back, in your own words, what you believe the person said, and ask if you've got it right; compare or contrast what the source is saying with a different point of view and ask if the comparison or contrast is appropriate; or ask the person to repeat things you aren't sure you understood.

In addition, think about what the person is *not* saying. Your interview subject may be making incorrect assumptions about what you want to know, avoiding uncomfortable subjects that are pertinent to the story, or even dropping hints as to things he or she wants you to ask about. Ideally, you will identify these missing pieces during the interview and ask about them at the time. However, if you don't see them until later, be sure to call or go back for answers.

Wait for an Answer

As you ask your questions, allow time for the person to reflect a bit, then respond. Although some people will answer quickly — especially people accustomed to dealing with the media — many will feel better if they have a few moments to think before answering. If you jump in with another question or start talking because you are impatient or uncomfortable with the silence, you may be cheating yourself out of a well thought-out answer. This is especially true in interviews with people who are under a lot of emotional stress or who are accused of some wrongdoing.

You can also use silence intentionally, as a way of drawing people out if, for some reason, they have been reserved or even secretive in their answers. If you wait in silence because you have not yet gotten the answer you want, their discomfort may prompt them to break the silence and begin speaking more freely.

Ask the Source if There's Anything to Add

Near the end of the interview, ask if the person has any questions of you or if there's anything you haven't asked. There may be important aspects of a story or new developments that you would not know to ask questions about. Asking this very open-ended question gives the person you are interviewing a chance to offer that information. It also builds trust by communicating that you want to be careful not to miss anything in writing the story.

Plan on Calling Back

Leave the door open for a follow-up phone call or interview. At the end of the interview, it is a good idea to suggest that you may call back for additional information or to check your facts, once you get into writing the story. At this time, you may ask for a home telephone number, if you think you may need it. You may also suggest that the person you have interviewed should feel free to call you if he or she thinks of something else that is relevant to your story. If the person you are talking to is someone you happened to meet in gathering information for a story, be sure to ask for a telephone number, and give yours (handing the person a business card is an easy way to do this).

Again, all of these guidelines are designed to help you build trust as a way of getting the most out of your interviews.

"What it all boils down to, in the end, is old-fashioned courtesy," writing coach Jack Hart wrote in the "Portland Oregonian"'s monthly newsletter "Second Takes." "Honest, interested, respectful interviewers score the biggest prizes almost every time. Hard-boiled, macho journalists who pride themselves on their cynical, tough-minded questions end up with more doors slammed in their faces than good stories. And cagey manipulators sometimes outsmart themselves."

THE QUESTIONS YOU ASK

Nothing shapes a news story more than the questions a reporter asks, and nothing distinguishes an experienced reporter from a novice more quickly than the skillfulness in asking the right question at the right time.

Broadly speaking, general, open-ended questions usually bring out general answers. Questions about specific facts help fill in gaps. And truly closed-ended questions are those that can be answered with a yes or no response.

When gathering factual information in interviews, the reporter often begins with a few questions as a way of prompting the person being interviewed to lay out the basic facts for the story. If you're writing about a robbery, for instance, you may ask the police sergeant, "So, what happened in that convenience story robbery last night?" If you're writing about a new program for pregnant teenagers, you might say to one of the organizers, "How did your program start, and what are your plans?"

Cartoon by Mike Ritter. Source: North America Syndicate

Hopefully, you will be able to sit and listen, making note of things you will need to ask the person to clarify or expand on. Sometimes it may seem appropriate to interrupt for a clarification or additional information; sometimes it may seem best to wait until the person has finished talking, then ask.

When you need to fill in gaps or clarify what you've been told, you may need to ask questions that are narrow in focus.

Be careful to avoid close-ended questions as much as possible. Anything that can be answered with a simple yes or no is an invitation *not* to talk — and the goal of any interview is to get the subject talking. If I ask, "Is it warm outside?" the best I can hope for is a yes or no response. But if I ask, "What is the weather like outside?" I might get an answer about cool breezes and puffy clouds and sun slicing through the new buds on trees.

Open-ended questions are usually best because they get people talking and allow you to find out, relatively quickly and easily, what they think is most important about the subject of your story. But asking a good open-ended question is not as easy as it appears.

An open-ended question should be a sincere invitation for the person you are interviewing to provide information and perspective

Tips from the Toolbox

There's a difference between getting a good quote and getting a good story.

In the rush to get stories written on deadline, reporters can be tempted to "go for the quote," asking pointed questions designed to elicit colorful or pithy responses. With public officials and others accustomed to talking to the press, this can work well. But with less press-savvy people, it can lead to stories that just don't ring true, according to reporters and others interviewed in the video "Interviewing: New Questions, Better Stories," one of four videos in the Pew Center for Civic Journalism's "A Journalist's Toolbox."

Politicians, for example, expect pointed, "big" questions that essentially demand that they immediately summarize their beliefs or their stand on an issue. But those kinds of questions cause most "regular folks" to tense up, and that shuts down the interview.

When talking to people unaccustomed to dealing with reporters, it is better to ask "small" questions and give people time to try on ideas, talk at their own speed, and explore what often turns out to be a web of concerns they have about something.

Examples of big versus small questions:

Big: What's your position on crime in the schools? What should be done about it?

Small: What do you make of crime in our schools these days? What might the causes be? What do you struggle with when you think about it?

It's also important to probe below the surface to be sure you understand what people are saying.

"I'm finding very often that when I say, 'Tell me more about that' or 'What do you mean by that?' that they didn't mean what I thought at all," Orange County Register reporter Kimberly Kimby says on the video.

It's important to listen more and allow for periods of silence while people formulate their answers.

In their answers, look for patterns that reveal things about the issue or situation that you might not have considered going into the interview.

When Norfolk Virginian-Pilot reporter Karen Weintraub spent time listening to striking shipyard workers, expecting to hear how hard it was for them to not go to work every day, she discovered instead that their working conditions were so miserable and their wages and pensions so low that they had welcomed the opportunity during the strike to spend time at home and with their families.

"I didn't get a quote, I got a story," she says in the videotape.

on the subject of your story. Your goal should be to understand the story as the person sees it.

In the book "The Seven Habits of Highly Effective People," Stephen R. Covey talks about this point in a chapter on listening, "Seek First to Understand, Then to Be Understood." He advocates something he calls "empathic listening": "Empathic listening gets inside another person's frame of reference. You look out through it, you see the world the way they see the world, you understand their paradigm, you understand how they feel."

Effective open-ended questions, then, are phrased in ways that are free of assumptions, opinions or accusations.

If you ask, "What do you think about the huge amount of severance pay they gave the high school principal?" you are revealing that you have judged the amount of the severance pay to be "huge" (although it is unclear by what standard you have made that judgment — in terms the school budget? how tax dollars should be spent? or in relation to similar payments made by other school boards?). And implied is your belief that the amount was too high. It would be better to ask, "What do you think about the high-school principal's severance pay?"

If you begin an interview about how a controversial decision was made by asking, "Why weren't more citizens involved in making this decision?" you are communicating your position that a higher number of citizens should have been involved. A better approach would be to ask, "Who was involved in making this decision and why?" The question about why citizens were not involved can then become a follow-up question, such as: "Some people have said that more citizens should have been involved in this decision. What do you think about that?"

Loaded questions can cause problems on several levels. They can cause the people you are interviewing to become uncooperative or even angry. They also can have an effect social scientists call "contagion bias," in which the response of the person you are interviewing is affected by the feelings you are telegraphing in the way you word the question.

In one experiment, for example, a group of people watched a film of an automobile collision and then was asked to estimate how fast the cars were going. Their estimates varied from 31 mph to 41 mph, depending on what words the researcher used to describe the impact. If they were asked at what speed the cars "contacted" each other, their estimates were lower than if they were asked the speeds at which the cars "hit" each other. The estimates were highest when they were asked the speeds at which the cars "smashed" together.

Your choice of words, then, can greatly affect not only the way you frame the story but also the accuracy of responses you elicit from those you interview.

Examples of Open-Ended Questions

Here are examples of effective open-ended questions that can be useful in various types of settings.

To draw out ideas, opinions and feelings:

How have you been you affected by ... [any event or issue]?
How have other people been affected by ... ?
What have you heard people saying about ... ?
What are their concerns?
What do you [or they] think caused or led to this?
What connections do you [or they] see between these and other con-
    cerns?
What do you [or they] feel you stand to lose if things don't change?
What do you stand to gain?
If you had a chance, who would you talk to about this issue? What
    would you ask them?
What kinds of things could you or other people do to address these
    concerns?
As it is, who is likely to respond to this situation? How would you ex-
    pect them to respond?
What do you like most about ... ?
What do you like least about ... ?

To draw out details, personal stories and anecdotes:

What's your earliest [or best] memory of ... ?
What conversations have you had with people about ... ?
What's the funniest thing you remember about ... ?
What was the hardest thing about ... ?
Can you tell me about a time when ... ?
Could you describe for me what _____ looked like? [Or sounded
    like, smelled like, or felt like. For instance, if they're telling you a
    story about something that happened in a bus depot, could you
    smell the diesel fumes? Was there noise from the engines?]
Was there a time when things could have gone in a different direc-
    tion?
When did you realize that ... ?
How did you decide to ... ?
Would it be best for you to just tell me the whole story, from the be-
    ginning?

Asking Tough Questions

Sometimes, especially in one-on-one interviews, you may have to
ask questions that make you or the person you are interviewing feel
uncomfortable. Imagine talking to grieving relatives about a family

member who was murdered, or confronting a business person or public official about something shady or illegal the person is accused of doing.

Reporters develop various techniques for asking these questions.

In the case of talking to grieving relatives and other people who are in pain, a compassionate approach is obviously best. One option is to say something like, "I'm sorry to bother you at such a difficult time, but I wanted to be sure you had an opportunity to make comments for my story, in case there's anything special you'd like people to know about your brother." A surprising number of people will welcome this opportunity. If they say they don't want to talk, don't push — but consider calling them back later, to see if they have changed their minds after having a chance to think about it. (For more detailed information and suggestions, see the section in Chapter 11 about interviewing trauma victims.)

Reporter Toni Wood, in an article in the March 1993 Writer's Digest, described a situation in which, writing a story for the Kansas City Star, she spent an hour talking to a homeless man and woman while their three small children played nearby, before getting around to asking the toughest questions:

> "How have you found food for your children during the past year?" I asked.
>
> The man dropped his head and took a deep breath. He then told me how he rummaged through McDonald's dumpsters for meals. I hung on every word, listening as he described the best time to scavenge for food and how to kill germs in a microwave oven.
>
> "That was the first time I'd ever tried McDonald's breakfast burritos," the wife said brightly.
>
> The couple was teaching me about a lifestyle I knew little about; I, in turn, would teach readers about urban poverty. In my years as a reporter, I've found that my most discomforting interviews have yielded some of my best articles.

Some of the toughest questions to ask are those that involve confronting someone about something shady or manipulative he or she may have done.

Wood recommends asking these types of questions directly — but after building up to them.

"By the time you reach the climax of the interview, your subject will probably be relieved to get to the point. After all, he knows why you are there. He expects it. So look him in the eye, and ask your questions clearly and directly," she wrote.

Other reporters use variations on the off-handed approach used by Columbo, Peter Falk's 1980's television detective. The character had a knack for finishing an interview, saying goodbye, then sticking his head back through the door and saying something like, "Oh, just one more thing. You wouldn't have any idea how that million dollars got into your briefcase, would you?"

Another approach is to ask the person to respond to accusations or criticism from others: "Your opponent in this election says you have spent campaign funds in illegal ways. What is your have a response to that?"

In any case, be sure to keep your composure when asking tough questions. Don't get rattled if the interview subject gets angry — let the person vent or cry or threaten without reacting. Your job is to understand the source and get the answers to your questions.

Another thing that may happen when talking to people about sensitive subjects is that they will ask you to give them a list of your questions in advance. You should feel free to do this — although it may be better to give them your list of topic ideas instead of explicit questions. Your editor can help you make that decision. Make sure they know that the listed topics are not the only things you will ask about.

POSSIBLE CHALLENGES

No matter how well you plan or how carefully you conduct yourself, you are likely to run into certain challenges that all reporters encounter at one point or another. Typical situations you should be prepared for include uncooperative sources, overly talkative sources, and vague sources.

An Uncooperative Source

Sometimes you'll find yourself interviewing — or asking to interview — someone who is extremely uncomfortable, uncooperative, angry or evasive. Such a stance is sometimes obvious from the beginning, as when someone says, "No comment," or gives terse answers. At other times, you may become aware of it through the responder's nonverbal cues or changes in voice tone during your conversation.

In such cases, try to put the person at ease. Otherwise, you may have to ask a series of very focused questions to draw information out piece by piece.

If the person is resistant for other reasons, you can try to persuade the source of the benefits of talking.

I (Cheryl Gibbs) once interviewed a former local defense attorney who had been convicted of criminal charges and then disbarred for bribing the local prosecutor to dismiss drunken driving cases. He had asked the paper to run a story about his new business venture — a real estate development project — and balked at the idea that his past, about which he had never talked publicly, was pertinent to the story. I explained that this information was very pertinent because he was essentially asking the public to support his new venture after having violated the trust the public had placed in him as a representative of the court. I encouraged him to talk about it as a way of putting his past actions into perspective, but he still resisted.

Finally, I said, "Well, let me tell you what's going to happen. You can talk to me now, or we can get that information from the stories we've run in the past."

"That sounds like a threat!" he protested.

"It's not a threat, it's a fact. We're going to talk about your past, one way or another. It's just the way we do things, and wouldn't you really rather have people know what you've learned and what you think now about everything that's happened?"

Reluctantly, he agreed to talk — and the interview was memorable, resulting in a compelling story about why he'd engaged in criminal behavior and the consequences he had experienced as a result.

If you find yourself in a situation in which someone becomes resistant in the middle of an interview, you can try explaining the importance of your questions; if that fails, back off a bit. Change the subject to something a bit more neutral until the person has a chance to get over the fact that you've asked him or her to talk about something difficult. Giving a little time before getting back to those sensitive questions can make all the difference.

The most difficult interviewing challenge, however, occurs when someone is knowingly, skillfully resistant or evasive. Sometimes such interviews can seem like a game of wits, impossible for novices and difficult even for experienced reporters. In these instances, if the person has something to hide, it may not be worth your time to talk to him or her until you have dug out the facts from another source, so that you can then present that information and ask for a response.

A Real Talker

Every reporter eventually winds up in an interview with someone who gets bogged down in details, talks about minor points at great length, or repeatedly goes off on tangents. In such cases, about all you can do is to gently bring the conversation back to the focus of your story as soon as you feel it veering off course. If the situation is extreme to the point that you're getting little or no valuable information, the best thing may be to draw the interview to a close, thank the person for his or her time and look for someone else who can more effectively help you with your story.

Vague Answers

Vague answers to your questions may indicated that sources honestly don't know the answers themselves, or they may not have thought about the subject you're asking them to comment on. You can give them more time to find the information or formulate their thoughts, or you can move on to another source.

EXPECT THE UNEXPECTED

Despite the occasional frustrations of interviewing, it is the most common way reporters gather information, and it also is the source of the quotes and details that Ron Speer would say make stories sing.

Even interviews that don't seem promising at the outset can have unexpected outcomes — especially when reporters reveal their own vulnerability to the people they're interviewing.

In his book, "Creative Interviewing," Ken Metzler tells about "San Jose Mercury News" reporter Nora Villagran showing up on Joan Baez's doorstep looking extremely disheveled and embarrassed, having clumsily fallen down a flight of steps on her way to the interview.

Baez welcomed her with concern, put ice on her swollen ankle, urged her to take off her shoes and stockings, then suggested that they wouldn't have an interview — they would instead be "just two barefooted women talking." Villagran later said it was one of her best interviews.

Her candidness, then, helped Baez relate to her on a human level, not as an intrusive reporter. The same could be said about Truman Capote's interview with Marlon Brando for a New Yorker profile, which is well known among writers.

Brando abandoned his usual tight-lipped demeanor and told Capote all about his life — even mentioning his mother's alcoholism. When someone asked Brando why he had said so much, he responded, "Well, the little bastard spent half the night telling me about his problems. I figured the least I could do is tell him one of mine."

EXERCISES

1. Play the following game, focusing on open-ended questions and un-cooperative interview sources: Find a partner and take turns being interview subjects. The subject should try to answer all questions with yes or no responses, or with one-word responses. The first interviewer to go five minutes without asking a close-ended question wins.

2. Go through a copy of a daily newspaper, looking at how quotes are used in stories. Think about what questions the reporter may have asked to get those answers — the "Jeopardy" approach, if you will. Imagine what the tone of the interview was like, how long it may have taken to get to the level of conversation reflected by the quote, and whether the reporter may have talked to the person more than once.

3. Watch a television interview program and make note of how questions are asked and how people respond. Are the questions open-ended, closed-ended — or both? When are which kinds of questions used? What is the apparent goal of the interview? What values does the interviewer reveal in the questions he or she asks? Does the interviewer appear to be seeking any kind of emotional response? If the person responds with emotion, how does the interviewer react?

4. Strike up a conversation with a total stranger about what he or she thinks the media should do or not do in interviewing people for stories. What kind of ground rules does the person think should apply? What kind of things would a source want to know about how his or her quotes will be used? What does the person think about the way people are interviewed in various types of television or radio shows?

Further Reading

ON THE WEB

CMC Magazine: "Interviewing and Information in a Digital Age," by I-chin Chang: www.december.com/cmc/mag/1997/jul/chang.html

The Poynter Institute for Media Studies:
"Rules to Interview by, Part I": http://poynter.org/dj/080200.htm
"Rules to Interview by, Part II": http://poynter.org/dj/080300.htm
"Interviewing Juveniles": http://poynter.org/dj/tips/broadcast/bj_kids.htm
Interviewing bibliography: http://www.poynter.org/research/biblio/bib_int.htm

IN PRINT

"Before the Story: Interviewing and Communication Skills for Journalists," by George M. Killenberg, published by St. Martin's Press, New York, 1989.

"Covering Violence: A Guide to Ethical Reporting about Victims and Trauma," by William Coté and Roger Simpson, published by Columbia University Press, New York, 2000.

"Creative Interviewing: The Writer's Guide to Gathering Information by

Asking Questions," by Ken Metzler, published by Prentice Hall, Englewood Cliffs, N.J., 1989.

"Interviews That Work: A Practical Guide for Journalists," 2nd ed., by Shirley Biagi, published by Wadsworth Publishing, Belmont, Calif., 1992.

"Interview with History," by Oriana Fallaci, translated by John Shepley, published by Houghton Mifflin, Boston, 1976.

"The Craft of Interviewing," by John Joseph Brady, published by Vintage Books, New York, 1977.

"The Journalist and the Murderer," by Janet Malcolm, published by Vintage Books, New York, 1990. (Malcolm focuses on the relationship between journalist and subject, exploring the interpersonal and moral dimensions of their interactions.)

A Poem by R.D. Laing

From "Knots"

There is something I don't know
       that I am supposed to know.
I don't know *what* it is I don't know,
       and I am supposed to know,
and I feel I look stupid
       if I seem both not to know it
           and not know *what* it is I don't know.
Therefore I pretend to know it.
       This is nerve-wracking
       since I don't know what I must pretend to know.
Therefore I pretend to know everything.

I feel you know what I am supposed to know
but you can't tell me what it is
because you don't know that I don't know what it is.

You may know what I don't know, but not
       that I don't know it,
and I can't tell you. So you will have to tell me everything.

Chapter 9

Observation, Curiosity and Note-Taking

Be good + you will be lonesome.

Clemens

Mark Twain

3–15–

Mark Twain, aka Samuel Clemens, was a journalist before he became better known as the leading American humorist of his day.

Source: © *Bettmann/CORBIS*

208

████ **Key Concepts** ████

- Your story almost always will be better if you leave the office to do your reporting.

- Good journalists are observant. They learn to pick up on things like patterns or repetition, things that seem out of place or don't make sense, or things that seem meaningful or significant, either literally or symbolically.

- Good journalists also are curious, so when they hear or see something that catches their interest, they can't help but ask questions about it.

- Note-taking is much more difficult during interviews than during public meetings or class lectures, because you have to be able ask questions (and follow-up questions) while continuously writing down what the person is telling you.

In 1868 journalist Samuel Langhorne Clemens wrote an eyewitness account of the public hanging of convicted murderer John Millian.

"(Millian) skipped gaily up to the steps of the gallows like a happy girl. I watched him at that sickening moment when the sheriff was fitting the noose about his neck, and pushing the knot this way and that to get it nicely adjusted to the hollow under his ear," Clemens wrote for the Chicago Republican.

Using the first-person style that was customary at the time, he went on to capture the rest of the grisly event with vivid detail: "I can see that stiff straight corpse hanging there yet, with its black pillow-cased head turned rigidly to one side, and the purple streaks creeping through the hands and driving the fleshy hue of life before them."

Years later, Clemens became much better known as Mark Twain, author of "The Adventures of Tom Sawyer" and "The Adventures of Huckleberry Finn." A few words of advice show why his writing, fiction and nonfiction alike, was so powerful: "Don't say the old lady screamed — bring her on and let her scream." Other journalists have expressed the same idea in a simple mantra: *Show, don't tell.*

Imagine, for instance, that you're covering the World Championship Wrestling event being broadcast live from a sports arena in your area. You could begin your story in the following way:

> People of all ages attended Monday night's World Championship Wrestling event at Colorado Springs' World Arena.
>
> Even though they all had reserved-seat tickets, hundreds of people waited in line for hours, excitedly hoping to catch glimpses of their favorite wrestlers.

That does the job, right? It covers the five W's and tells us that anticipation was in the air. But that's the problem: It only tells us; it doesn't "bring on" the people and let them speak for themselves. The writing could be much livelier, as Colorado Springs Gazette reporter Katie Johnston illustrates:

Mason and Evan Walters were too busy to talk, intently pressing their faces against the World Arena glass in search of World Championship Wrestling star Goldberg.

"I see him, Dad," said Mason, his dimples deepening. "C'mere!"

Dad, who admits he's not much of a fan, gamely pressed his face against the glass beside his sons, ages 6 and 8.

Inside the arena, a pony-tailed girl dragged behind her mother. "We have to wait for Grandma!"

Teen-agers and toddlers, senior citizens and Gen-Xers alike were among the 7,000 enthusiastic fans lined up clear to Venetucci Boulevard an hour before Monday's show. Even with tickets for reserved seats, they arrived early and braved the scorching 5 o'clock sun to be a part of Turner Network Television's WCW "Monday Nitro," televised live from the World Arena. ...

To write that kind of lead, Johnston had to pay attention to things that a less gifted reporter might not notice and a less talented writer might not think to include.

She started by using the image of people with their faces pressed to glass to convey a sense of anticipation. Then, in the process of attributing that first quote to Mason Walters, she mentions his dimples growing deeper, which tells you not only that he was smiling but that his excitement was growing. When she quoted him, she captured both his exuberance and his youth by writing "C'mere!" instead of going for the grammatically correct but much more sedate, more adult "Come here!" By mentioning that the boys' dad was "not much of a fan," she skillfully added yet another dimension to the story: Even those people who weren't totally sold on wrestling got swept up in the excitement. Then she described the pony-tailed girl who wanted to wait for Grandma, which told us it wasn't just school-age kids and their parents eager to witness the event.

Reporter Katie Johnston focused on fans like 5-year-old Ariel Hall in her story about the public response to a WCW wrestling match that was being televised from Colorado Springs, Colo.

Photo by Jerilee Bennett. Source: Colorado Springs Gazette

THE VALUE OF PERSONAL OBSERVATION

That Johnston was there is clear from the story. She witnessed the things she described. Although it is possible to gather such details by interviewing others who were present, nothing is better than being there, soaking in the sights and sounds yourself, because that allows you to hone in on the details that strike you as most interesting, most telling and vivid.

"That's one of my favorite things to do — descriptions and 'color' pieces and crowd things," Johnston said. "Observation's one of my strong points."

Gathering such information through observation, however, does pose certain challenges. The most obvious one is that you have to be able to function on several levels at once. Specifically, you will be better at making and recording observations if you

• Cultivate a high level of *awareness* of the sights and sounds around you, including the ability to spot patterns and inconsistencies.

• Develop your natural *curiosity* so that when you see things that are unusual, inconsistent, contrasting, or meaningful, you immediately start wondering about them.

• Incorporate into your *recording skills* a way of remembering which sensory details, at which moments, made those sights and sounds distinctive.

As Johnston arrived at the arena, for instance, she noticed the long line outside the stadium. That observation provided colorful detail for the story, but it also activated her curiosity — and therefore prompted several questions that yielded important factual information:

Q: Exactly how long was the line?

A: Clear to Venetucci Boulevard.

Q: How long had it been there?

A: Lined up ... an hour before Monday's show. [Not a very precise answer, because it doesn't say exactly when the line began forming, just how long the line was an hour before the show. However, that may have been about as accurate as anyone could get.]

Q: What was it like to wait in that line?

A: "[they] braved the scorching 5 o'clock sun."

Once Johnston got closer, she started looking for people to talk to.

"I just started picking people at random. The boys were an obvious choice," she said.

By "the boys," she means the Walters boys, whose faces were pressed against the glass. And when she heard Mason Walters call out to his dad, he obviously wasn't talking to her.

"Eavesdropping is a particularly good way of reporting," she said. "Just walking around listening to people."

While she was writing down what Mason was saying, she noticed his dimples and what happened to them as he spoke.

She then talked to the family — getting their names, the boys' ages, obtaining permission to quote them, and finding out that the boys' dad is not particularly fond of wrestling.

She also overheard the pony-tailed girl telling her mom to wait for Grandma. Uh ... wait a minute — Grandma at a wrestling match? This, too, was a clue — and evidence that the event of interest to several generations.

"There were probably five or six people I talked to who aren't in the story. Obviously, everybody you talk to isn't going to give you a gem," she said. "The best thing is to talk to a lot people and then you can sort 'em out."

Johnston also takes voluminous notes.

"I probably write down 99 percent of the stuff that gets into my story. I've gotten good at writing everything down and using about an eighth of what I've written," she said.

It's possible that Johnston could have gotten some of this information from interviewing people, but it's very unlikely she would have gotten it all — or gotten the degree of detail she captured by being there. And if she had merely called up the event's promoters and gotten the facts — how many people were there, what happened, etc. — the story would not have been nearly as interesting to read.

IF YOU CAN'T BE PRESENT

Realistically, you won't always have the opportunity to witness the events you write about. You may be asked to write a story that conveys the emotional impact or human drama of an occurrence you had no way of knowing about in advance, such as an arrest, crime, accident or catastrophe. You may be asked to write about a planned event you did not attend. Or you may be asked to write about someone you are unable to meet or something you are unable to experience personally.

Gathering second-hand information is almost always less reliable, because people vary in their ability to recall such details. It also is more time-consuming, because it may take several interviews to piece together enough information to write a lively story. But skilled reporters can do an amazing job of capturing the essence of what happened, especially if they ask questions that help them picture what went on.

Edna Buchanan, who won a Pulitzer Prize as a police reporter for the Miami Herald in 1986, was known for her attention to detail:

> What a reporter needs is detail, detail, detail.
> If a man is shot for playing the same song on the jukebox too many times, I've got to name that tune. Questions unimportant to police often add the color and detail that make a story human. What movie did they see? What color was their car? What did they have in their pockets? What were they doing at the precise moment the bomb exploded or the tornado touched down?

Knowing what was in the victim's pockets may seem like a strange question. But Buchanan gives two examples of times it yielded valuable information. The first concerned a killer who hacked off a victim's hands and head to keep the person from being identified but overlooked a receipt bearing the victim's name and address, tucked deep into one of his pockets. The second concerned a 75-year-old veteran from Key West who was killed as he rolled down

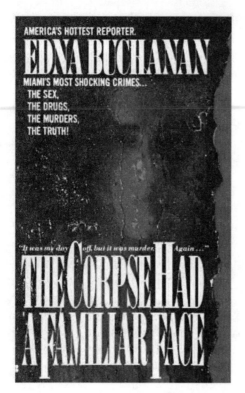

Edna Buchanan won the Pulitzer Prize for her crime reporting in Miami. She now writes detective novels in which she draws on her years of reporting.

Source: Diamond Books.

a Miami highway in his wheelchair at 1 a.m. What was he doing there at that hour? In his pockets were discharge papers from the Miami VA hospital and forms from social service agencies rejecting his appeals for help in returning home. It turned out a social service agency in Key West had put him on a bus to get treatment in Miami but made no arrangements to get him home. After his requests for help were denied, he decided to make it back on his own. He had covered about seven miles of the 156-mile journey when he was killed by a young man in a Corvette.

Just as details can give you a more thorough understanding of the story, they can give you the raw material for compelling writing. Imagine, for example, being one of the many reporters from all over the world who was assigned to write about the April 20, 1999 shooting rampage at Columbine High School in suburban Denver. All of the reporters had to get the facts about the tragic events at the school — who was shot, who did the shooting, how it happened, when and where in the school and why. But the reporters who wrote the most moving stories — the stories that most fully conveyed both the tragedy and the heroism that made the shooting such a powerful symbol of so much that is wrong and right in our society — included the kind of detail that brought to life what happened. And they gleaned this detail from interviews with witnesses.

Consider the following excerpt from a story by New York Times reporters James Barron and Mindy Sink:

When he heard the noise in the hall, Adam Foss leaned out of the choir room, the room where the confident singers of Columbine High School in Littleton, Colo., rehearse the kinds of songs that student choruses have sung for generations.

Hours later, he remembered seeing the barrel of a shotgun. He remembered seeing a flash of fire. He remembered seeing a teacher go down. He realized he was trapped in a school under siege.

Mr. Foss, 18, scrambled back into the choir room, he said, and herded the other students into a closet, an 8-by-8-foot room, the kind of musty, stuffy place where robes or sheet music are stored. Not knowing whether the gunman was poised to blast the closet or had gone away, Mr. Foss and his friends barricaded the door with a filing cabinet and waited.

The boys peeled off their shirts — the closet was hot, and they dared not open the door. They lifted one or two classmates with asthma who had trouble breathing toward the ceiling, where the ventilation seemed better. Together, they waited as the minutes ticked by until the police swept the school and shouted that it was safe to come out.

Or consider this story excerpt from the Denver Post:

The library was a scene of carnage, with bodies crumpled everywhere. Tables and chairs were overturned. Computer screens were shot out. Blood-spattered books were tossed about the floor.

Only one student was rescued alive from the library at Columbine High School in Littleton, the site of Tuesday's worst carnage.

Troy Laman found her.

It was his job to find living, breathing people among the dead. About mid-afternoon Tuesday, the paramedic for Denver Health Medical Center entered the second-floor library with members of the Metro SWAT Team.

The bodies of four victims lay to the left of the library door. Nearby, a female student lay on her side.

"She was awake. She started to scream," Laman said.

He hurriedly radioed authorities outside that one student was down but alive. Then he moved on, touching bodies but staying clear of packages that might contain explosives.

In minutes — the grisly task finished — Laman and partner Robert Montoya whisked the student to safety.

The student turned out to be Lisa Kreutz, an 18-year-old senior, now in serious but stable condition at Denver Health Medical Center with multiple gunshot wounds. She underwent surgery later that day to repair severe injuries to a shoulder and forearm.

As Kreutz was being carried out of the library, Laman said she pleaded, "Help me. Help me."

At one point, she closed her eyes. Laman said he implored her to keep them open so she wouldn't become unconscious. She had lost a lot of blood and was pale with a low pulse, Laman said.

Twenty-four hours after the rescue, Laman and Montoya said they still were in shock. But both said they felt glad to have helped save one life.

"There are so many times when you can't make a difference," Laman said. ...

The reporters who wrote these stories clearly went beyond the basic facts. Barron and Sink described the shooting from the vantage point of Adam Foss, who provided a very detailed account of what he had experienced — right down to the size of the choir room and what they used to barricade the door. The Denver Post reporters set the scene with details others had described to them.

A cafeteria surveillance camera released months after the Columbine High School shooting gave a chilling look at the terrible experience the schools' students endured that day. Writing about such an event is one of the biggest challenges a reporter can face.

Source: Jefferson County Sheriff

CULTIVATING AWARENESS AND CURIOSITY

When you first arrive on the scene of an event, take a few moments to look around, listen, even smell. Draw on your powers of observation and natural curiosity. What things look as if they belong there? What looks unusual, disrupted or out of place? Who is there? What are they doing? Who seems to be in charge? What sounds do you hear? What seems to be creating those sounds? What do you smell? Where do the smells come from?

Take detailed notes about the things you notice, for possible use as scene-setting details at some point in your story. Make note of physical details, but also pay attention to such things as hand gestures, facial expressions, tones of voice and nervous habits like throat-clearing, finger-tapping or pacing. Develop your own shorthand or other method for jotting down those moments when people's words are punctuated by expressions or other behavioral clues that you can use to add life to your story. You also may be able to use your observations as springboards for good questions, like, "I noticed you were smiling when you mentioned that baseball game. Why was that?" Such questions often draw out wonderful anecdotes that can make your stories much more interesting — anecdotes you would never learn about if you hadn't notice the smile or didn't ask.

And it's the asking that is at the heart of curiosity. The best reporters ask about everything. If they are assigned to write a story about a stray pebble in the street, they can think of dozens of questions to ask about that pebble, which may lead to four or five pretty good story ideas.

They might start by asking where the pebble came from, for instance.

Do they see any deteriorating patches in the road surface near the pebble? If so, could the pebble be the starting point for a story about road conditions?

Or ... are kids playing nearby — kids who might have thrown the pebble? If the reporter talked to the children, they might describe a new pebble-throwing game that's become popular, or they might complain that pebble-throwing fights are becoming more common. A story about the game would describe an interesting new trend, and a story about the fights could point up an emerging problem the community should address.

Or ... the reporter might look around to see if any construction in the area could be the source of the pebble. If so, what about a story about the side effects of construction, how neighbors cope, and how construction companies manage?

Or ... what if the pebble is left over from when road crews scattered dirt and pebbles on ice-covered roads the previous winter? If so, why is it still there — and are there more pebbles nearby? Could the reporter do a story about how well (or not well) the city cleans up the debris after winter subsides? Or about how the city is preparing for road treatments for the following winter?

The reporter also could take the pebble to a scientist for analysis — is it made of a kind of stone normally found in the area? Is there anything particularly interesting, geologically speaking, about the pebble? In either case, that pebble could be a starting point for a story about what types of rock and soil are found in the area and how that has affected construction, farming and water quality.

The ability to muster curiosity about such mundane things as stray pebbles is an extremely valuable trait to have as a reporter. Obviously, most pebbles are of limited interest. If you were to write strictly about a pebble, about all you could do is report what kind of stone it is, whether it's got any dirt or other substance on it, and where it is or was located. What snags good reporters' curiosity and makes something interesting is wondering about what the thing *signifies* and how it fits into the *larger picture*. Their curiosity serves them well, whether they're writing about a pebble or a new organization or a community event.

BUILDING ON YOUR RECORDING SKILLS

Good reporters learn to write fast. There are no two ways about it. A rare few actually learn formal shorthand. Most just develop their own form of shorthand or speed-writing as they gain experience. They also learn their limitations, and compensate for them, perhaps making a habit of going over their notes within hours after their interview while they can still remember what word they meant when they wrote that snake-like squiggle or wavy line suspended between two consonants.

What matters is finding a way of capturing accurately and thoroughly what people tell you. Sometimes that gets pretty challenging — especially if the person talks considerably faster than you can write. The following ideas may help:

• Take extra pens, pencils, paper and any other backup supplies you might need. (If you're using a tape recorder, for instance, take extra tapes and batteries.)

• Don't try to write down every word. Distinguish between background information, which often works better if paraphrased anyway, and good quotes — the things people say that are especially eloquent, distinctive, revealing or insightful. Over time, you will develop an internal monitoring system that will let you know when you're getting close to a really good quote. (Subjects' comments may start to get more interesting, or they become more expressive.) Learn to work with this internal system. Learn when to write something down and when to let it go. Sometimes the best tactic is to let the person go on talking while you keep focusing on getting down a previous sentence or two that was really great. If you can keep half-listening as you write, you may develop the ability to listen and write at the same time. Sometimes you'll abandon writing one quote for another that's even better. Ultimately, you'll develop a "flow" to taking notes.

• Remember that you can control or at least influence the pace of the interview. If you find that the person is talking too fast, consciously slow down the pace of your questions. Don't rush — or let the other person make you feel rushed. Getting thorough, accurate information and quotes should be your top priority, no matter how long it takes.

• Develop some way of distinguishing in your notes between direct quotes, partial quotes and paraphrasing or other information. Some reporters put big quote marks at the beginning and end of each quote. Others bracket them or write "quote" beside them. It doesn't matter how you do it — just that you do, so you can be sure that you're quoting people accurately.

• Never hesitate to ask for time to get it right. It's easy in an interview to feel pressured to keep things rolling. However, sometimes it's so important to get a key quote right that it's best to say something like, "Wow! That was really important, and I'm just going to take a moment here to make sure I get the whole thing written down." Chances are the person you're interviewing will be glad you are being so careful.

• Keep a separate sheet of paper handy for jotting down additional questions that occur to you during the interview, so you're sure to ask them later.

• Develop a way of marking your notes so that if you become confused about something but feel that asking for clarification would break the flow of the interview, it will be easy to go back and find it. Some reporters write in a big question mark or circle the confusing information. Then, make a habit of closing every interview by flipping through your notes, making sure you've cleared up your confusion.

• Formally transcribe your notes only for important or in-depth stories. Otherwise, you will spend far too much time on a task that just won't be worth it.

Many journalists use tape recorders. If you are a radio journalist, a tape recorder is an essential tool of your trade, allowing you to capture quotes and ambient noise for use on the air. But for print reporters, tape recorders can have serious drawbacks, so it is important to be clear about why you want to use them.

If you think it will be easier than taking notes, think again. After the interview is done, you will have to listen to the tape and write down those quotes you want to use. That takes much more time than taking notes during the interview, and there's a good chance you also will be tempted to transcribe much of the tape, which takes forever. When you're done transcribing, you usually have much more material than you can possibly use, and you may tend to overwrite as a result. (An often overlooked advantage of note-taking is that our human limitations naturally force us to edit as we go.)

Tape recorders work best when they're used as backups in interviews that are particularly sensitive for one reason or another. If you're interviewing someone about some alleged wrongdoing, for instance, it will be very important that you quote that person accurately. In such cases, it's a good idea to use a tape recorder with a counter, use a fresh tape, and set the counter to zero at the start of the tape. Then, take notes as you would without the recorder, but jot down the numbers that appear on the counter at key points during the interview. That way, it will be easier for you to locate a quote on the tape so you can check your notes against the recording.

Also, consider tape recorders when you intend to use long passages: question-and-answer formats, for instance, or transcripts of important or historic speeches. Author and journalist Studs Terkel recorded oral histories of everyday people living through momentous times in books such as "Working: People Talk about What They Do All Day and How They Feel about What They Do" and "The Good War: An Oral History of World War II."

In most cases, it's your choice whether to use a tape recorder, and many newsrooms do not provide them. If you use a recorder, no matter what the circumstances, make sure it is in good working order before every interview — and do a short sound check after you first arrive.

Another method of note-taking, used most often during telephone interviews, is typing notes directly into the computer. Most reporters develop the ability to do this. Although this is a perfectly good way to take notes, be aware that it always makes you vulnerable to the usual snafus that can affect computer files. Save your file often while working in it, and be sure to print out a paper copy of the notes as soon as the interview is done. Even if all you do is file the printout, it could be important if your notes on disk are inadvertently deleted or corrupted.

PROTECT YOUR NOTES

You should save your notes and tapes. Most newsrooms expect reporters to save their notes for a year for legal reasons. If someone is going to sue your paper on grounds that you made a mistake in your story, in most states they have a year to do it. However, it may be wise to save notes about controversial or ongoing stories for a longer time. Before you start throwing away notes, ask your editors how long you should save them.

During note-taking, don't write your own opinions in the margins that could come back to haunt you if your notes became part of a libel suit. If you write "he's lying!!!!" or "she's guilty as sin," a judge and jury may determine you weren't exactly impartial during the interview.

That said, don't just turn your notes over to anyone, even if they have a legal document that demands you do so. If anyone asks you for your notes or presents you with such a document, immediately talk with your editor. Our laws protect journalists from such intrusions, so that they can continue to carry out their important task of investigating and reporting without interference from the government.

Such requests most often come from lawyers who believe the reporter's notes contain information that will help them prepare a better case for their client. Many also come from officials who seek to uncover unreported facts or the identities of reporters' anonymous sources. Although these requests may be innocent and well intended, they are at best a time-wasting hassle for the reporter and, at worst, attempts to extend the power of the state in ways that undermine the freedom of the press.

EXERCISES

1. Find a newspaper story about a place that is familiar to you. Clip out or photocopy the story and set it aside. Then go to the place that is the subject of the story and spend time observing and gathering details about it. Look at the story again and see if you can think of ways that additional details could have been used to make the story more interesting.

2. Write a "verbal video clip." Choose a spot on campus that strikes you as interesting in some way. It can be a busy meeting spot, a quiet corner for studying, a distinctive-looking building — whatever stands out for you. Stand or sit there in a way that you can observe and write comfortably.

Spend about half an hour writing down details — what you see, what you hear, what you smell and, if applicable, what you taste or touch. Use these notes to create a verbal video clip, written as though it will set the scene in a movie. If it helps, you can start with the phrase, "As the scene opens, the camera focuses on ..."

3. Pair up with another student from class and take turns interviewing one another about your most embarrassing childhood experience (or another subject of your choice). Stand as you do this, so you can practice taking notes standing up. (A variation: Do the same assignment but by calling the person on the phone while seated at a computer, so you can practice typing your notes as the person speaks.) As you are conducting your interviews, experiment with some of note-taking techniques described in this chapter. Afterward, type up your notes and ask the person you interviewed to look them over and give you feedback on how accurately you captured what was said. (A variation: Work in groups of three, with one person interviewing and taking notes, the second person acting as the subject and the third person just taking notes. Rotate roles. Type up your notes and go over them as a group. How accurate is each set of notes? What are the differences between the interviewer/note-taker's notes and those of the person who was solely taking notes?)

Further Reading

ON THE WEB

AJR/American Journalism Review: "Details, Details: Meticulous, Exhaustive Reporting Is as Essential to Compelling Narrative Journalism as Sparkling Prose": http://ajr.newslink.org/ajrbradjan00.html

IN PRINT

"Word Painting: A Guide to Writing More Descriptively," by Rebecca McClanahan, published by Writers Digest Books, Cincinnati, 1999.

Chapter 10

Adding Photos, Graphics and Other Visual Elements

This is the kind of photograph that becomes an icon of our times. In this moment, U.S. women's soccer player Brandi Chastain celebrated her winning penalty kick at the Women's World Cup in July 1999.

Photo by Mike Blake. Source: © Reuters NewMedia Inc./CORBIS

Key Concepts

- Text is only part of any story. Journalists use photographs, graphics and an assortment of other visual elements to make stories interesting and clear.

- Arranging for photos, graphics and other visual elements, and writing text to accompany many of those elements, is an essential part of a reporter's job.

- Reporters also are responsible for writing "budget lines" that tell their editors what stories they're working on, how long they expect those stories to be, and what visual elements will accompany them.

How does this chapter begin? Most reporters would say it begins with the previous sentence. But that was not the first thing you read. The "story" of this chapter began with the headline (in this case, the chapter title). In the same fashion, a newspaper story rarely begins with the first sentence. The headline, photographs, graphics and information boxes serve as "points of entry" to draw readers into the subject. Photographers, copy editors, designers and graphic artists work to make a whole package that provides readers with emotional impact, context, and understanding.

Sometimes the graphics, headlines and photos are even more important than the story because they may be the only part consumers read. A newspaper is a "skimming" medium — readers skim headlines and other big type to get the gist of community and world events, stopping only at the few stories that interest them.

To consider points of entry as only typographic billboards for your story would be a mistake. These presentation devices help *tell* the story — often in ways that are more effective or dramatic than narrative prose. It is, after all, a visual world. The old saw describing a newspaper as "black and white and read all over" hasn't been accurate for some time — today's newspapers are black and white and red and every other color. With rare exceptions, newspaper consumers expect the newspaper to contain many different formats of information delivery.

In fact, information displayed graphically sometimes *is* the story. Just as, for years, newspapers have run photographs without

narrative stories (sometimes called "standalone" photos), graphic de-
pictions increasingly have been considered whole reports. USA Today pioneered the concept by running a daily chart on its front page
with a graphic snapshot of America. At The Virginian-Pilot, reporters
for the public safety team developed periodic pages showing the in-
cidence of crime at a neighborhood-by-neighborhood level. These
reports sometimes ran with no more than a lead-in paragraph of nar-
ration.

Gathering the information, however — no matter what its final
form — starts with the reporter. In addition to writing strong stories,
today's reporters are expected to arrange for photographers to take
pictures to go with their stories; to work with staff artists who create
illustrations; to provide graphic designers with information for interesting charts or maps, and to help copy editors and page designers
select nuggets of information to be set apart from the main story in
special type.

Along the way, reporters provide information to everyone who
will be involved in getting the story into print. They give their editors brief summaries of the narrative report being gathered and inform them about all the related items that make up a single
newspaper story.

Some newspapers use a group brainstorming strategy called "the
maestro concept" to plan stories and visual elements simultaneously. This approach was developed in the early 1990s by journalism professor Leland "Buck" Ryan in collaboration with journalists
at the Logansport (Ind.) Pharos-Tribune. Editors, reporters, page designers, photographers and artists meet about individual stories, after enough reporting has been done to get a sense of them. In each
story meeting, a person designated as the maestro uses a story planning format to help the group (1) think through questions readers
would have about the story, (2) refine the story concept, (3) picture
it on the page and (4) identify challenges. In picturing the story on
the page, they consider what kinds of photographs and/or informational graphics might be appropriate, what kinds of sidebars or pullouts could be written, and whether series logos or other graphic
elements will be needed. In these discussions, the journalists sometimes go so far as to sketch out possible page designs.

Such discussions can be very valuable, especially for beginning
reporters. But time considerations in most newsrooms usually do not
permit reporters to participate in this manner on every story. In
many cases, the job of developing ideas for photographs and other
visual elements is left to the reporter, so it is important to understand how to do that well.

Pharos-Tribune Story Plan

Story Slug _____ Projected Run Date _____

Special Deadlines _____ Copy: _____ Art: _____

Story Idea _____

_____   _____   _____
Reporter   **Display Editor**   **Photographer**

Think Like A Reader

I. Reader's Questions

1. Why should I Care?

Your Best Answer _____

_____

Other Questions That Immediately Come To Mind

1 _____

2 _____

3 _____

II. Refine The Angle

1. What is the single most important element in the story?

_____

2. Headline Ideas:

A. Main Head _____

B. Subhead/Summary Graph _____

_____

_____

III. Picture It On The Page

Sketch Presentation So Readers Questions Are Answered In The Highest-Visibility Points. Decide on Best Tool–Type,
Photo, Artwork or Graphic to make the point.

Checklist for High-Visibility Points

1 Head/Deck .... ❑
2. Caption .... ❑
3. Pull Quote ...... ❑
4. List .... ❑

Other Graphic Elements

❑ Q&A
❑ Facts
❑ Bio
❑ What's At Stake
❑ How Does It Affect You?
❑ What Can You Do?
❑ What's The Next Step?
❑ How Can You Learn More?
❑ How Can You Get Help?

IV. Defining Challenges

1. **Reporting**

A. What Do We Need To Find In A Hurry? _____

_____

2. **Photo**

A Ideas For One Photo Or Multiple Photos _____

_____

3. **Was There A Reader Action Element?** _____

This is the form developed for use in maestro sessions at the Logansport (Ind.) Pharos-Tribune.

Source: Logansport Pharos-Tribune

ARRANGING FOR PHOTOGRAPHS

One of the most important tasks for which reporters are responsible is arranging for photographers to take photos to go with their stories.

Take a moment and picture the member of the U.S. women's soccer team who pulled off her top after her team won the World Cup or Princes William and Harry walking solemnly behind the casket of their mother, Princess Diana. Or the late John F. Kennedy Jr., as a toddler, saluting at the funeral of his father, whose presidency had been ended by an assassin's bullet only days before.

These images burned themselves into the American consciousness and are remarkably potent symbols of memorable events.

Most stories, with or without photos, are not so important or eventful. Some stories don't require any photos at all. However, when you set out to write a story, it's extremely important to consider whether a photograph is appropriate.

To tell the whole story, it's important to think about how photos will work with your report *while* you are reporting. Too often, the photography is an afterthought — and, when that happens, the photograph often looks like an afterthought as well.

At most newspapers, reporters aren't expected to have the knowledge and skills of a trained photojournalist. But it doesn't hurt to think like one. To take a good news photo, you have to think differently than you would in taking a photo at a family gathering or during your vacation. The goal of those photos is simply to record who was there and what they did. News photos must also be compelling visual images. With a little imagination, you can always do better than taking a photo of the person you're interviewing as they sit on the sofa or at their desk saying "cheese" for the camera. To increase the chances of getting a good photo (or photos) to run with your story, consider the following tips:

- Natural is best.
- Shoot people, not things.
- If you can't shoot people, shoot art.
- Mugs are always good.
- Don't blow it off.
- Work with the photographer.

• *Natural is best.* Ethically speaking, journalism is all about truth and reality — it is not appropriate to ask a person to "recreate" an action or pose in a way that makes the picture appear that it was taken during a spontaneous moment. Posed photos — the businessman at his desk, for instance — are ethical but often dull; photos of real people doing real things are simply more interesting. The worst posed photos look stiff and static, with people smiling at the camera, looking off into space, or pretending to be busy. Think through who are the most important people in your story and what situations they might be in that would capture the essence of the story. It's always best to talk with the photographer before making the assignment, although that's not always possible because of tight schedules and deadlines. Such conversations work best if you think beforehand about what events, activities, locations or objects can be photographed and have dates, times and locations available to give to the photographer.

• *Shoot people, not things.* It's always best to include people in photographs — preferably people doing things that are visually interesting. Instead of arranging for a photograph of the high-school principal and choir director pretending to put up a poster about the upcoming fund-raising breakfast, get a picture of people stacking bags and bags of potatoes that were donated for the event. Instead of setting up a photo with the head of the local community foundation handing the head librarian one of those big, phony-looking checks, look for a picture of people going down the steps to illustrate the grant that will make the library handicapped-accessible.

Creative photographers find interesting ways to shoot otherwise mundane photographs. The motion of the truck in this photo adds interest to what might otherwise be a boring photograph of a dangerous intersection in Richmond, Ind.

Photo by Steve Koger. Source: Palladium-Item

- *If you can't shoot people, shoot art.* If it's absolutely impossible to include people in the photo, try to think of an essentially "artsy" photo idea. Look for interesting angles, like an unusual spot from which to take a photograph of the building that was just added to the National Register of Historic Places or a close-up of one of the new parking meters installed by the city. Another option is to look for interesting visual patterns, like angular lines in the steel frame of a new discount store that is under construction or the repeating shapes of paintings hung along the wall for an art exhibit at a local gallery or museum.

- *Mugs are always good.* Thumbprint-sized portraits, which journalists call "mug shots," often can be used instead of, or along with, other photos. Always consider assigning mug shots or checking to see if one is available in the archive of mug shots that most newspapers maintain for use in breaking news stories. When in doubt about whether to assign mugs, ask your editors if they would like them. In addition, many newspapers keep simple "point-and-shoot" cameras handy for reporters to take mug shots when all of the photographers are out on assignment.

- *Don't blow it off.* Don't neglect to arrange for photos just because you don't think there's anything worth shooting. Check with your editors or photographers before you make that call. They may decide they have enough other photos to run, without one for your story.

- *Work with the photographer.* If both you and the photographer are in a situation that requires you both to gather the notes and pictures at the same time, be sensitive to each other's needs. Sometimes the interview process conflicts with the picture-taking process, and vice versa. A team approach will produce better copy and pictures. It can be disastrous if the reporter and photographer are competing for time; the unprofessionalism can be palpable to the interviewee. The best reporter/photographer teams discuss each other's objectives and are gracious not to step on toes.

Newspapers have a variety of systems for setting up assignments for their photographers to shoot. Some maintain schedules in their computer systems; others keep the assignment schedule on paper. Some require reporters to fill out paper photo assignment sheets; others use computerized forms or e-mail. Whatever system is used, the information they need from reporters is the same: when can the photographer take the photo? Where should the photograph go? How will the photo be used? Who are the contact people?

- *When can the photographer take the photo?* Be specific, especially if you have arranged for people to be someplace to have their photo taken at a certain time. If there's some flexibility, as is the case with many events, provide a time frame — and include any suggestions you can about what will be happening when. If a newsworthy equipment auction includes a viewing hour before the bidding, for example, the photographer might think that context would present a better photo opportunity than the auction itself. Or the extra hour could give the photographer more flexibility to shoot another assignment that day.

- *Where should the photographer go?* You will need to give a specific address, obviously. But you also may need to tell the photographer such details as which entrance to use or what office to go to, or give street directions if it's an out-of-the-way place.
- *How will the photo be used?* Will it stand alone with just a caption — or, as journalists say, a "cutline"? Will it appear with a story? If so, what's the story about? Will it appear as a mug shot? Is it for a particular section of the paper? Will the photo be used with a larger graphic?
- *Who are the contact people?* Be sure to include all pertinent names and phone numbers, in case the photographer has a conflict and needs to reschedule the appointment.

ARRANGING FOR GRAPHIC ELEMENTS

Most newspapers expect reporters to routinely provide certain types of information in concise form for use as points of entry — those visual elements that attract readers' attention and encourage them (so to speak) to "enter" a story. Headlines and photographs are considered points of entry. Other elements are called by a host of names — graphics, pullouts, pull quotes, sidebars, bio boxes, "if you go" boxes and marginalia boxes, to name a number of them. What the points of entry are called may differ from one newsroom to the next.

Informational graphics are created at most newspapers by graphic artists who use computer-scanned images and computer drawing programs to combine text with photos or illustrations to create visually interesting charts, maps and diagrams. Such elements should always add something to the story, not just serve as a decorative way of presenting unimportant information.

Other elements, such as "if you go" boxes and quotes from a story put into display type, are created by the people who lay out the pages of the paper, usually using computer pagination programs. Since many of these elements are used on a recurring basis, the newspaper usually has set formats. For example, most stories about events, activities or other opportunities that are open to the public now run with boxes that list dates, times, locations, prices, parking information, contact names, phone numbers and so on. These boxes may contain information such as when and where a performance will be held, how to help victims of a fire or other tragedy, or when the city council will meet about a controversial zoning proposal.

On the next page is a newspaper page with examples of these elements, to help you imagine the possibilities and sample formats for writing them.

Reporters are expected to type this information in the newspaper's established format and submit it with their stories. Some newspapers also routinely ask reporters to identify interesting quotes in their stories and even to write suggested headlines.

"Pulled quotes" may be run with our without mug shots. With each quote, the reporter should include the speaker's name, identifying information appropriate to the story (job title, for instance, or age and town of residence, or the date of the quote) and what was said, word for word. In choosing quotes, look for those that reflect the essence of the story, not just the comments that are the most colorful or surprising.

Reporters in most newsrooms are expected to make suggestions and provide information for graphics for their stories. They also are expected to break up longer stories into several related stories, some of which will be presented as boxed elements that serve as points of entry.

It is important to talk with your editor about ideas for graphics and dividing long stories into several related parts so you don't end up wasting your time and energy on great graphic ideas and stories that won't be used. The editor can tell you whether the graphic artist or page designer will have time to create a graphic for your story and whether enough space will be available in the newspaper to accommodate all the information you want to provide.

It's also important to learn your newspaper's preference on whether to include information in the narrative story. Should a story on the 2000 census include population trends in the graphic only, or in the graphic *and* the narrative story? Should the election night story include vote totals if there's an accompanying graphic showing the same thing? Editors differ on the answer. Generally, though, a graphic should allow a reporter to take most of the tedious numbers out of the narrative, but not so many that the context is damaged. That election night narrative, for instance, might include the percentage of the win ("Jones won 52 percent of the vote last night") while leaving the actual numbers to the graphic.

Who's who in court

The judge: Superior Court 2 Judge Alex Davis, 50, of London. Current post 14 years; previously deputy district attorney 4 years, private practice 3 years.

The defendant: Norma Miller, 19, Clear Creek. Accused of killing 17-year-old girl in gas station robbery; had been fired from job there.

The prosecutor: District Attorney Bernie Renner, 38, of Westwood. Elected to current post four years ago; previously, deputy district attorney 7 years.

The defense: Defense attorney James Gerald, 53, of Boston. In private practice 20 years; previously, deputy public defender 6 years.

①

This is just dummy text, to show how these graphic elements can be inserted onto a page. It says absolutely nothing, so if you keep reading you will simply read the same paragraphs over and over again.

If you are obsessive-

Violent crime down

Centerville police responded to fewer violent crimes last year. The statistics:

④

	2000	2001
Murders	2	1
Assaults	12	10
Rapes	1	1
Robberies	2	1

The Larson file

⑤

Born: Aug. 28, 1950, Knox Dale, Pa.
Age: 52
Education: B.A., High Ridge College, 1980
Family: Wife Angela; daughters Josie, 21, and Sylvia, 19
Career: U.S. Navy, Vietnam War; taught in New York City schools, 1980-85; formed YouthBank with former students, 1986.

compulsive, it might be fun for you. Otherwise, you'll probably get bored.

This is just dummy text, to show how these graphic elements can be inserted onto a page. It says absolutely nothing, so if you keep reading you will simply read the same paragraphs over and over again.

Mission has grown in past 10 yers

Nov. 3, 1982: Bountiful Kitchen opened
May 1985: Expanded with bequest from John Andrews
January 1991: Name changed to

②

Oasis Help Center
July 1998: Homeless shelter opened in building next door
May: Local churches, community groups organized celebration to mark 20

If you go ...

What: Jones County 4-H Fair
When: Thursday through July 23 (schedule: Page A7)
Where: Jones County Fairgrounds, Wilmington Pike at Jennings-Euphrenia Road
Admission: $2 per person, $3 parking, midway rides extra

③

If you are obsessive-compulsive, it might be fun for you. Otherwise, you'll probably get bored.This is just dummy text, to show how these graphic elements can be inserted onto a page. It says absolutely nothing, so if you keep reading you will simply read the same paragraphs over and over again.

simply read the same paragraphs over and over again.

If you are obsessive-compulsive, it might be fun for you. Otherwise, you'll probably get bored.This is just dummy text, to show how these graphic elements can be inserted onto a page. It says absolutely nothing, so if you keep reading you will simply read the same paragraphs over and over again.

Of course, if you've read this far, here's a quote to reward you: "As far as I'm concerned, *whom* is a word that was invented to make everyone sound like a butler," Calvin Trillin said in The Nation.

⑥

"The public is the only critic whose opinion is worth anything at all."
— *Mark Twain, humorist*

Examples of graphic elements: 1. Key Players; 2. Timeline; 3. Go Box; 4. Chart; 5. Bio Box; 6. Pull Quote.

Cartoon by Bill Watterson. Source: Universal Press Syndicate

Common Points of Entry

After "if you go" boxes and pull quotes, lists are the most common points of entry for which reporters compile information. If you're writing about schools recommended for renovation during the summer or the most dangerous intersections in your community, for instance, you should consider typing out a list of school names or cross-streets at dangerous intersections. Depending on the focus of the story and what information is available, you can include such additional information as what renovations are needed or planned and how much money they will cost, or how many accidents occurred at the dangerous crossroads.

Use a method when listing the items. For example, you might decide to list schools alphabetically, or by neighborhood, or by ranking from the greatest need of repair to the least, or from the most to least costly. Be sure the information you emphasize is appropriate to the focus of your story. If your school renovation story focuses on some residents' concern that the schools most in need of repair have received the least money, don't just list the schools alphabetically. Assuming that the facts support the residents' concerns, help readers see the problem by starting the list with the most run-down/least-funded school first, with a description of needed repairs and amount of money allocated, and ranking the rest of the schools by the same criteria.

If comparisons are an element of the story, be sure you compare similar sets of information. It would be meaningless if not harmful, for instance, to compare how much was spent on repairs on one school five years ago with what is being spent on another this year. Compare spending during the same time periods, whether five years ago or today or both, but don't mix the two.

If rankings are an element of the story, be sure to cite the source of the information at the end of the list. The list carries different implications if state officials have listed a nearby landfill as among the 10 most environmentally safe (or hazardous) landfills in the state than if the company or agency that operates the landfill tells you that.

Other lists might include short, concise summaries of the facts of the story, set off with dashes or bullets; or tidbits of surprising or unusual information that you discover during the reporting process.

Reporters also are often asked to provide information for the following elements to run with their stories:

- *Number charts.* Percentages, dollar figures, employment statistics, weather data and other numbers often work better in chart form. Using this format also saves writers from getting bogged down in trying to drape interesting prose around a bunch of numbers — and saves readers from falling asleep while reading the results of such efforts. Stories about government spending and personal financial planning, for example, often include budget figures broken down by expense and income categories.
- *What's next.* Information about whatever is likely to happen next helps readers keep track of an ongoing story. Perhaps a judge is expected to rule within the next day or next week. Or the issue will be considered at the next city council meeting. Or the accused murderer's lawyers plan to put him or her on the witness stand the next day.
- *Bio box.* In some stories, background information about a person is important. A bio box usually includes biographical and other information that is pertinent to the story.
- *Maps.* Maps are perhaps most useful with stories about some change that will affect an area's geography, such as creation of a new subdivision, construction of a new factory or a petition to abandon a road. They also can be used with stories about activities occurring in out-of-the way or hard-to-find places, or with stories about how conditions differ from one location to another. If your story compares crime rates in various neighborhoods, it's a good idea to show readers where those neighborhoods are. Don't assume your readers know every neighborhood or voting district. Locator maps are relatively easy additions that help readers make connections and understand the context of your story.

Additional Points of Entry

Additional kinds of information reporters are sometimes asked to provide include timelines, key players, quotes, further reading boxes, diagrams, and actual documents.

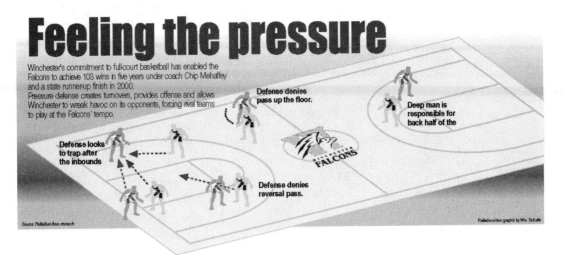

Feeling the pressure

Winchester's commitment to full-court basketball has enabled the Falcons to achieve 103 wins in five years under coach Chip Mehaffey and a state runnerup finish in 2000.
Pressure defense creates turnovers, provides offense and allows Winchester to wreak havoc on its opponents, forcing rival teams to play at the Falcons' tempo.

Defense denies pass up the floor.

Deep man is responsible for back half of the

Defense looks to trap after the inbounds

Defense denies reversal pass.

FALCONS

Source: Palladium-Item research

Palladium-Item graphic by Wm. Schulte

Graphic by Bill Schulte. Source: Palladium-Item

• *Timelines.* If you're writing a story about something that occurred over a long period of time, it can be helpful to create a timeline. Following a timeline can help your readers understand the history and sequence of the issue. It can also be used as a reporting tool to help you keep the sequence of events clear, especially in a complicated story. Timelines are nothing more than chronological listings of key developments. Sometimes they begin with the first official development that occurred; sometimes they begin with a general paragraph that describes conditions that precipitated the first development in the story. More detailed timelines can be especially useful with stories in which split-second timing caused things to happen. One common use of timelines is with stories involving police dispatcher's calls in police shootings or high-speed chases.

• *Key players.* Stories in which numerous people are important, either as historical figures or "key players," can benefit from a cast-of-characters listing that explains who is connected to the story and how. Descriptions can include biographical information or other relevant details. These lists are especially useful when relationships (past or present) are an interesting aspect of the story, or when so many key people have been or are involved that readers could have trouble remembering who's who.

• *Quotes.* Sometimes what people say is so central to the story, or people say so many valuable things, that it can be useful to arrange a series of quotes in list form. This format can be especially useful in a story involving accusations and counter-accusations, people entrenched in various positions, or changes of mind or heart. It also works well when you want to include additional points of view. But be careful. This kind of grocery store list of quotes can lead to superficial opinions. Many newspapers ask reporters to do what once were called "man on the street" interviews, especially for reactions to various news developments. Although such comments can be valuable in capturing people's initial or top-of-the-head thoughts about something, it's important to remember that they usually do not reflect the deeper feelings that often prove to be more influential in their decisions regarding issues raised by those developments.

• *Further reading boxes.* These list books, Web sites or other sources readers can consult to get more information. It's usually a good idea to include whether these sources are available at local libraries and bookstores.

• *Diagrams.* Three-dimensional, encyclopedia-style diagrams or floor plans can be extremely valuable in helping people picture things like planned construction or office relocation or where people were when something happened in a given building. Diagrams also can help people understand scientific concepts and procedures such as surgical techniques, stages of plant growth, or how information is relayed by satellite from objects in space back to earth. Diagrams are normally created by graphic artists who may either do additional research themselves or ask the reporter to help them learn enough to create an accurate, informative diagram.

• *Actual documents.* On some stories, one or two critical documents serve as the catalyst for the entire report. In that case, it's often useful to run the complete document, excerpts or paraphrasing of key points. Perhaps the most famous example in recent years dealt with the impeachment proceedings of then-President Bill Clinton. In 1998, independent prosecutor Kenneth Starr released a report containing allegations against the president. These allegations were used as the basis for impeachment proceedings in Congress. Many newspaper editors decided the document was so important — it was such a momentous event in our nation's history — that they published it in its entirety, even though doing so used massive quantities of the nation's newsprint supply the day after the report was released.

In fact, newspapers used several graphical methods during the controversy surrounding the proceedings against the president. Several newspapers ran *lists* of every person who voted for or against impeachment; lifted *pull quotes* of what would become famous denials ("I did not have sexual relations with that woman"); and published *what's next* boxes describing the precedent-setting impeachment.

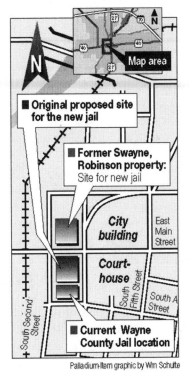

Palladium-Item graphic by Wm Schulte   *Graphic by Bill Schulte. Source: Palladium-Item*

KEEPING EDITORS INFORMED

One of the most important but undervalued tasks reporters do each day is to write and update budget lines, which are brief summaries of their stories and the photos, graphics and illustrations that will accompany them.

Budget lines serve many purposes. They are valuable communication tools that allow reporters to get feedback from editors on their plans for upcoming stories. They let editors determine, at a glance, the important stories of the day. They help the editors determine whether there are enough stories, photos and other materials to create informative, visually interesting newspapers during the coming days. And editors who have up-to-date budget lines from all reporters can do a much better job of making sure appropriate amounts of staff time — including reporters, photographers, graphic artists and page designers — can be devoted to each story.

Newspaper editors rarely have the luxury of making decisions about the next day's paper based on completed stories. The budget lines, then, become the most important means of determining which stories will wind up on the front page versus the obit page.

Newspaper partners also scan the budget lines looking to fill their needs. On a given day, the budget (the document combining all the budget lines) might be viewed by an online editor, a television producer, and even a marketing representative looking for good stories to promote during drive-time radio.

The budget, then, becomes a mini-version of the newspaper for the next day (or the next weekend or beyond, depending on each newspaper's needs). It is a synopsis of the collective work of the newsroom.

The reporter's budget line is sometimes called a "pitch" or a "tout" because it is as a reporter's best sales tool. If you want the best play for your story, with the most time and space, with the best effort at photos and graphics, you have to pitch the merits of the work you're doing. Why is it interesting or entertaining or important? Why is it important *now?*

Writing or revising budget lines also can help reporters focus or refocus a story.

As with procedures for arranging for photo assignments, newspapers have various methods for maintaining budgets for upcoming editions. Most keep such information in their computer systems, some keep it on paper, but as with photo assignments, all require the same basic information:

- Story "slug" or name. Every story has some kind of one- or two-word name that is used as a quick way of identifying it and sometimes indicating when or where it will run in the paper. Formats for such names vary greatly and can be influenced by matters as diverse as tradition and computer system consideration. Examples: CITYCOUN-0105 (a story about the city council's Jan. 4 meeting to run Jan. 5); TJSNOW (Tom Jones' story about snow).
- Name of the writer
- Expected length of the story
- A list of photos, graphics or other visual elements that will accompany the story
- A brief description of what the story will cover

If you are writing more than one story, list the main one (sometimes called the "mainbar") first. Near the beginning of the description, be sure to refer to it as the mainbar or main story. List other stories (often called "sidebars") in descending order by timeliness, importance or interest. A story about related developments, for instance, should be near the top of the list. Excerpts from official documents, timelines or other background information should go toward the bottom of the list.

EXERCISES

1. Go to the library and spread out several different newspapers on a table. Take a step back and look at the photos on Page 1 of each paper. Which are the most interesting and eye-catching? Why? From what distance are the photos taken? What kinds of moments do they capture? How big a role does the size of the photo play in drawing your eye?

2. Go through a newspaper looking for stories with information boxes. Read the stories, then think about how the boxes enhance your understanding of the story. What do you like about each? How would you improve upon them? What kinds of information does the paper put in those boxes? Can you think of any other kinds of information boxes that would be useful to you?

3. Start a scrapbook or "idea file" of your own, clipping photos, information boxes and informational graphics that seem especially attractive or helpful. Use this book or file as a place to go for ideas when writing your stories.

Further Reading

ON THE WEB

The Poynter Institute for Media Studies: Tip sheets on "Incorporating Visual Thinking into Courses":

Part 1: Getting your students to think visually: www.poynter.org/dj/061900.htm

Part 2: How to incorporate news audience ideas: www.poynter.org/dj/062000.htm

Part 3: Teaching Informational Graphics: www.poynter.org/dj/062100.htm

Tip sheet on "Diversifying Illustrations: Some Points to Keep in Mind": www.poynter.org/dj/042700.htm

Tip sheet on "How W.E.D. (Writing, Editing, Design) Works": www.poynter.org/dj/071000.htm

"The 'Journalism' in Visual Journalism," by Monica Moses, a downloadable Adobe Acrobat PDF file: www.poynter.org/Visual/MVJ/Index.htm

IN PRINT

"The Best of Newspaper Design," published annually by the Society of News Design, North Kingston, R.I.

"Contemporary Newspaper Design: A Structural Approach," by Mario R. Garcia, published by Prentice-Hall, Upper Saddle River, N.J., 1993.

"Eyes on the News," by Mario R. Garcia, Edward Miller and Pegie Stark, published by The Poynter Institute for Media Studies, St. Petersburg, Fla., 1991.

"Eyes on the News," by Pegie Stark and Mario Garcia, edited by Edward D. Miller, published by The Poynter Institute for Media Studies, St. Petersburg, Fla., 1991.

"The Newspaper Designer's Handbook," by Tim Harrower, published by McGraw Hill, Boston, 1998.

"Newspaper Layout and Design," by Daryl R. Moen, published by Iowa State University Press, Ames, Iowa, 1989.

Chapter 11

General Assignment Reporting

Reporters often are assigned to cover community celebrations like the Beardstown (Ill.) Fall Festival. And few such celebrations are without Shriners, who at the Beardstown in 2000 rode a bicycle built for 25. The parade included 22 different Shriner parade teams, or about 400 to 600 Shriners.

Photo by Steve Warmowski. Source: Jacksonville (Ill.) Journal Courier

- Most reporters get their start doing what is known as general assignment reporting — writing stories about a variety of subjects and events, often assigned by an editor.

- The kinds of events most commonly covered by general assignment reporters include speeches, fund-raisers, festivals, parades and other activities sponsored by community groups; accidents, disasters and unusual weather developments; and neighborhood news.

- General assignment reporters also are often asked to write stories from press releases and to "localize," or add local information to, international, national, state or regional stories that come to the paper through various wire services.

As a general assignment reporter, you could end up anywhere on a given day. Your editor might send you to a last-minute press conference, called by the mayor, because the person who covers city government is on another assignment. You could be told to cover the volunteer fire department's annual spaghetti dinner Friday night at the high school, or to head toward the rain-swollen river to talk to people who are evacuating or putting sandbags around their homes.

That's part of the fun of being a general assignment reporter, or "GA" — but it's also one of the challenges. You have to be able to handle any story at a moment's notice. That's one of the reasons so many newspapers have new reporters start on the general assignment beat: There's no better way to build basic reporting skills.

Amid the unpredictability, however, is a certain degree of sameness. General assignment reporters do cover many planned events that don't fall into institution- or issue-based beats. GAs often are asked to write stories about accidents, disasters and unusual or extreme weather. They serve as backups for other reporters. They get pulled in to help cover major stories when extra reporting power is needed. They often are asked to contact local people for quotes and information that can be added to stories that come in from various wire services. And they write stories from press releases, usually after doing telephone interviews with people connected with the news development described in the release.

Interns at both large and small papers normally serve as general assignment reporters. Larger papers tend to have several full-time

Wanted: General Assignment Reporters

Following are typical ads for general assignment reporters, as posted online.

GENERAL ASSIGNMENT REPORTER WANTED

The Inyo Register is now accepting applications for a full-time general assignment reporter. Applicants should possess basic writing and grammar skills plus a drive for exploring all facets of life in the Owens Valley including sports, government, personalities and events. Flexibility and a strong work ethic a plus. 35mm camera work required. Hourly wage plus medical benefits. Send resumé and clips to Barbara Ferrey-Laughon, Inyo Register, 450 E. Line St., Bishop, CA 93514 or fax to (760) 873-3591. [Posted to a journalism jobs board April 28, 1998]

REPORTER WANTED

The Yankton (S.D.) Daily Press and Dakotan," an award-winning six-day daily located in a historic South Dakota river town, is seeking a general assignment reporter. Applicants must have strong writing skills. Knowledge of photography, computers and newspaper design is helpful. Competitive benefits. Please send resumé, clips (no fiction or poetry) and references to:

Kelly Hertz
Managing Editor
Yankton Daily Press and Dakotan
P.O. Box 56
Yankton, SD 57078

general assignment reporters. Smaller papers may not have any; instead, all reporters might do a certain amount of general assignment work.

WHAT GAs DO

Most of the stories written by general assignment reporters are about planned events. As a GA you may be asked to write an "advance" story, alerting people that an event is coming up. You also might be asked either to attend the event or gather information so you can write about it after the fact.

Much of the information about these events is available in printed form from the people planning them. Sometimes your editor will give you this information — perhaps a press release, a schedule or a brochure — when assigning the story. Sometimes you'll have to track down the information yourself by contacting the event's organizers and doing background research, as you would for any story.

Types of Advance Information

Biographical information. Event planners and publicity agents often provide printed copies of resumés or biographical information for speakers, presenters, performers, parade marshals, and others who will be in the spotlight during certain events. Photographs also might be available, which you can use as mug shots with your story.

Printed copies of speeches, scripts or musical scores. If a speaker is going to read from a printed speech, it may be possible for you to get copy — sometimes in advance. People who perform in Christmas pageants, plays or similar events might work from scripts that also may be available. And musicians rely on musical scores that can be helpful if you can read music. Remember, though, that many live performances involve ad libbing, so it is unwise to use the printed material as your primary source of information. Always tell people what happened, not what was supposed to happen.

Press releases, press packets or informational materials. People who organize events, especially press conferences, typically prepare press releases and other materials for reporters. They also may prepare programs, schedules or brochures for distribution to the public. How much material is available depends on the size and sophistication of the event and the organization sponsoring it. Community organizations planning relatively small-scale events may prepare only a press release. Detailed schedules often are printed for festivals and fairs. Public relations agencies for major motion picture studios send out fat press packets containing a wealth of information and photographs or slides, usually packaged in colorful, jazzy-looking folders and envelopes.

Get whatever materials you can, but don't publish the information without first verifying it. Press releases are notorious for containing incomplete or inaccurate information, and they always present the point of view of the sponsoring organization. If incorrect information is published, readers won't and shouldn't accept an excuse that the press release was wrong.

Following is an example of a press release that is typical of what you might receive for a local event:

FOR IMMEDIATE RELEASE

Sept. 27, 2000
Contact: Jim or A.J. Daggy, (765) 962-2142

PLANT EXCHANGE PLANNED
    Gardeners interested in swapping or giving away flowers, trees and house plants may do so at the plant exchange in Richmond on Saturday, Oct. 7.
    The free event will be from 8 a.m., rain or shine, until all material is gone. The first 10 minutes will

be devoted to exchanges among people who brought things. After that, it's open season and all plants are free.

The exchange will be held in the parking lot of the old railroad depot, on North 10 Street at E Street. Participants are encouraged to be there right at 8 a.m. (no early exchanges, please) for the best selection.

In the past, participants have swapped flowers, vines, trees, shrubs, ferns, grasses, flower and vegetable seeds, house plants, garden tools and pots. Many have been willing to give away plants to beginning gardeners who have nothing yet to trade.

The event is sponsored by the Vision in Progress Beautification Committee. For more information, contact the committee president, Dr. Jim Daggy at (765) 962-2142.

Following is an example of an announcement of a new kind of press conference made possible by changing technology — a telephone news briefing. Although the format has changed, the basic information in this announcement is the same as it would be for a traditional in-person press conference.

Press conference announcement

FOR RELEASE: Immediate
Wednesday, December 2, 1998

Advisory to General Assignment, Education and Labor Editors and Reporters

University of California UAW Academic Unions to Hold Telephone News Briefing at 1:00 p.m. Pacific Time Today (4:00 Eastern Time)

Striking teaching assistants at University of California campuses will hold a telephone news briefing at 1:00 PM Pacific Time today. Also joining the call will be faculty and student supporters.

UAW Vice-President Elizabeth Bunn, who directs the union's Technical, Office and Professional (TOP) Department, will also participate from her office in Detroit.

Reporters can access the call at 1-888-422-7101; participant code 740287. For questions or further information, please contact Frank Joyce at 313-926-5297.

The best thing about most prepared materials is that they usually include the name of a contact person who can give you additional background material. In this case, if you called Frank Joyce, he would no doubt offer to get you that material by mail (if there were time), e-mail or fax.

Books and recordings. Sometimes, speakers or others in the spotlight will have published books, made musical recordings available on tape or cassette, or appeared in television shows or films available on video. It may be valuable for you to go through some of these materials.

Information from key people. In some cases, it may be worth your time to call people for background information — especially if you've gotten any of the above information and noticed something that seems incomplete, confusing, unusual or unfamiliar.

If you cover an event for which you wrote the advance, you will have good information to use as background in your story. If someone else wrote the advance, get the materials that person gathered and go over them — in advance.

As you're preparing for the event, figure out the best time to go. If it's a computer expo at the local convention center, for instance, find out if any major companies are planning to unveil new products. If so, that would be a good time to show up. If it's a political rally, find out when the main speaker is schedule to take the podium. If it's a community festival, weigh whether it would be best to go during the parade or when a well-known entertainer is being featured. If you aren't sure when to go, get help from your editor, another reporter, the event's organizers, or someone in the community who could tell you what's likely to be most interesting.

Tips for Covering Planned Events

Write background in advance. If you have time before you go, copy and rewrite the background information from the advance or use information you have gathered to write a few paragraphs of background material you can work into your finished story.

Arrive early. Arriving early gives you time for interviews and valuable observations. If you find out when certain things will be happening and arrange to be there — when sound equipment checks will be done for concerts, for instance, or when the speaker is scheduled to arrive — you may be able to "ambush" people for interviews or arrange to interview them later. Arriving early also gives you a chance to read the program or schedule, if there is one.

Write down observations. Take notes about the environment in which the event is occurring. If you're covering a presentation, for instance, jot down descriptions of what's on the stage. Also check out the audience. How many people are there? Although event organizers often can give you a fairly accurate head count after the fact, especially if they've sold tickets, sometimes you will want to count the crowd members — or groups within the crowd — yourself. Who are they? Elderly people? Parents with small children? Protesters carrying signs? Why are they there? For inspiration, look back at what Katie Johnston did for her wrestling story in Chapter 8.

Vacuum the scene. Writing coach Don Fry advises reporters to "vacuum the scene" when they are writing stories. What he means is that you should pick up any and all available posters, fliers, promotional photos or other materials (including three-dimensional freebies like political candidates' buttons, candy bars with specially printed wrappers, etc., which can be photographed and used as art elements with your stories).

WRITING THE STORY

Most stories you write as a GA should follow the guidelines for news writing in Chapter 3, for good reporting in Chapter 5, and for writing basic, informative news stories in Chapter 6. Here's a brief review:

- Do whatever it takes to make sure your story is accurate.
- Get information from a diverse, balanced mix of reliable sources as well as from credible written materials and personal observation.
- As you're gathering information, be on the lookout for photo ideas or other ways to add visual elements to your story.
- Put the most important information first — except in cases when your editor expects you to write a piece that complements another story that puts the important stuff first.
- Devote extra effort to making the lead of your story lively or compelling.
- Mix exact quotes and paraphrasing, all with attribution that properly identifies the source of the information and the source's relationship to the story.
- If the information you gather is different from what you expected, change the focus of your story to match the information.
- Use a stylebook as a reference.
- Keep language and punctuation simple.
- Write within your length limit.
- Meet your deadlines.

Advance Stories

Following is an example of a very brief advance that appeared in the Columbia Missourian on the day former Associated Press correspondent Terry Anderson spoke at the University of Missouri. Earlier stories gave more detailed information, but this one covers the basics.

Terry Anderson to speak tonight at MU

By Jae-Hee Lee
Columbia (Mo.) Missourian staff

Terry Anderson, a former chief Middle East correspondent for The Associated Press, will speak at MU's Middlebush Auditorium at 7:15 tonight in celebration of the 40th anniversary of the Freedom of Information Center.

Anderson was a captive for seven years in Lebanon. Since being released in 1991, the U.S. government has denied Anderson information about the terrorists who kidnapped him, saying the release of information would violate the terrorists' privacy.

In his speech, Anderson will talk about his unsuccessful attempts to gain information about his captivity through the Freedom of Information Act. He also will discuss foreign journalists in peril in various parts of the world.

Former MU professor Paul Fisher and former Journalism School Dean Earl English founded the FOI Center in 1958 as the first clearing house of information about access to government records.

The lead. This is a straightforward, direct lead that includes most of the five Ws.

The nut graph. In this case, the writer includes the information in the lead that makes clear why the story is important now — that the speech is tied to the 40th anniversary of the university's Freedom of Information Center.

Remaining themes. The second paragraph gives background information about Anderson, and the third summarizes what he is expected to discuss.

Quotes. None. Be aware that quotes are often the first thing to go when editing stories for length. Had there been more room, this story could easily have included a quote or two from Anderson (taken from prepared materials provided by his agent or from a telephone interview) and from the MU professors associated with the FOI Center.

Community as context. This story would have the greatest interest to students at the university, especially journalism majors. It also would have interest for journalists elsewhere.

Covering speeches like that given at the University of Missouri by Terry Anderson, a former Associated Press reporter, is a common responsibility for general assignment reporters.
Photo by Matthew Ratajczak. Source: The Columbia Missourian

Style note. Note that this newspaper's style permits the use of MU (short for University of Missouri) on first reference. Also note references to the Freedom of Information Center. It is spelled out on first reference, then referred to as the FOI Center on second reference. This is a sign that the newspaper's style permits the use of acronyms on second reference. Some papers follow a similar rule; some prefer that acronyms never be used, instead using a phrase like "the center" or spelling the name out in full; and some would expect reporters to put the acronym in parentheses earlier in the story.

Speeches

Giving people the highlights of a speech works a lot better than giving people a chronological account of what the person said. As with other news stories, start with the most important or interesting information you've got — something the speaker said or did.

Before you start writing, think of one point or gesture that seemed to get the biggest response, or that has stuck with you the most. Find a way to use that as your lead — but avoid the common temptation to begin with a direct quote. For people who didn't hear the speech (and that includes the majority of the people you want to read your story), the quote comes out of nowhere.

Also consider the speaker's credibility. If a speaker were to say, for instance, that men are less intelligent than women, would you take that information at face value and pass it along without attempting to check it out? Or would you ask the speaker to cite evidence to support such a claim or contact experts for responses? Remember: You put your own credibility on the line with every person you quote. If you fail to critically evaluate the information offered, you run the risk of mindlessly perpetuating misinformation that can be damaging in a variety of ways.

In every speech story, be sure the speaker's occupation and/or reason for speaking, the date of the speech, and where the speech was given also appear in the first several paragraphs. Speech stories can include excerpts from question-and-answer sessions held after the speech and comments from audience members you interview afterward.

The following story, about Terry Anderson's speech at the University of Missouri, is an example of a well-written speech story.

Anderson decries barriers to free flow of information

By Jae-Hee Lee
Columbia Missourian staff

Since his release in December 1991, Terry Anderson has been fighting the government for information about the terrorists who captured him in Lebanon. He's been told the information is classified.

"My favorite reply was 'We can't give you any information about the individual you requested because of the Privacy Act,'" he said. "The CIA told me to get notarized releases from the kidnappers."

But he said under the Freedom of Information Act, the government must disclose what information it has. In case the information is classified, the government must justify why it is being withheld.

"It is the nature of the bureau- crats to withhold information," Anderson said.

Anderson addressed a packed auditorium on the MU campus Thursday night in honor of the 40th anniversary of the Freedom of Information Center, an agency founded by journalists to provide public access to government documents.

Anderson, former chief Middle East correspondent for the Associated Press, was captured by terrorists in Beirut, Lebanon, in 1985.

There are 2 billion to 10 billion pages of secrets in Washington, Anderson said, and it costs $5 billion a year to maintain those secrets.

"Forty thousand new secrets were created last year," he said. "It's breeding; it's multiplying."

Anderson said secrets are kept because people are rewarded, encouraged and not punished for keeping government information classified.

Anderson gave two reasons for getting involved in the Freedom of Information Center. One was a personal reason — he was curious about what the government had on file about him. A second reason was because he was a journalist — he is a true believer of the free flow of information.

"I do believe in democracy," he said. "We can't have an open society without free flow of information, without active, free press and without dealing with the culture of secrecy in Washington."

Audience member John Wheeler identified with Anderson's struggle. He was the last American correspondent based in Cuba, and has had a FOIA request for 10 months regarding government information about his time there.

"I was interested in knowing what their assessment of me was," Wheeler said. "There is no reason why they should not release it. It's my own personal records."

Harry Hammitt, editor and publisher of Access Reports, a bi-weekly newsletter on FOIA and open government laws and policies, said Anderson's speech contained some inaccuracies.

"It's not accurate, but it's close enough for audience members who didn't know," Hammitt said.

The government does not have to give an index of documents to Anderson unless he takes the case to court, Hammitt said. And the government does not have to give any information if it's properly classified, he said.

The Freedom of Information Center was founded in March 1958 by Earl English and Paul Fisher, both MU journalism faculty, as a response to the government withholding information from the media during World Wars I and II. The center is open to anyone who wants information concerning government documents.

Missourian staff writers Erica Berardi and Kimberly Speight contributed to this report.

[This story appeared on Page One of the Columbia Missourian on April 10, 1998.]

The lead. This story begins with what was apparently the most important point the writer thought Anderson made: that for years, the government has refused to give him information about the people who held him captive. This is followed by a quote in which he says the CIA told him to get notarized releases from his kidnappers if he wanted that information. Note that the story doesn't start with the quote (or a cliché or question). Instead, the writer sets up the quote with a straightforward, direct lead, then follows it with a couple of paragraphs that explain Anderson's view of why it's wrong that he's being denied that information.

The nut graph. The fifth paragraph explains why the story is important now — that Anderson spoke on campus. It gives the where, when and why of the story. It also says the auditorium was packed.

Remaining themes. The story goes on to explain why Anderson has become an advocate for freedom of information, mentions an audience member who has had a similar experience, then quotes an expert who points out minor inaccuracies in Anderson's speech. The story closes with a paragraph of background information about the organization that sponsored the speech. The story flows nicely from theme to theme, and the themes are arranged in the order of their importance. The paragraphs are in summary form. The story has no chronological sections or lists.

Quotes. Quotes are spaced evenly throughout. The first quote, which recounts an anecdote from Anderson's experience, vividly brings home the irony of his predicament. The second and third quotes are strongly worded statements that reflect Anderson's perspectives on bureaucrats and a growing problem with secrecy in government. The fourth quote is a passionate statement about why Anderson feels freedom of information is important, and it includes the provocative phrase "culture of secrecy." The quote from the person who had a similar experience indicates his support of Anderson's position. The last quote, from the expert, brings up the inaccuracies and puts them into context.

Community as context. Details that give clues to the event's importance include the description of a packed auditorium, which indicates that interest in the speech was indeed high, and an explanation of the university's connections to the organization sponsoring the speech.

Press Conferences

People who hold press conferences usually have something to promote or explain. Such conferences are held to announce big plans, tout achievements or release the latest information about high-profile situations that have caught the public's interest. Holding a press conference is basically just an efficient way to release information to a large number of reporters.

The following is a good example of a story based on information from a press conference.

Police arrest 25 bomb suspects in Jakarta bombings

By Christine T. Tjandraningsih
Kyodo News Service

JAKARTA, Sept. 24, 2000 (Kyodo) — Indonesian police said Sunday they have arrested 25 people suspected of involvement in a series of bombings in the capital over the past two months, including two attacks that left 12 people dead.

The chief suspect, Iwan Setiawan, was arrested Saturday while allegedly on his way to bomb the U.S. Embassy and a department store in Jakarta, Jakarta City Police Chief Insp. Gen. Nurfaizi told a press conference. The 24 other suspects were rounded up after his interrogation.

"He (Iwan) was involved in the bombing of the Jakarta Stock Exchange," Nurfaizi said, referring to the Sept. 13 bombings inside a multilevel parking lot under the bourse that claimed at least 10 lives.

Among the other 24 suspects is Teuku Ismuhadi, an Acehnese, who allegedly manufactured all the bombs used in the attacks.

Nurfaizi did not say whether Ismuhadi is connected with the separatist Free Aceh Movement seeking independence from Indonesia.

However, the spokesman for the national police chief, Sr. Supt. Saleh Sa'af, hinted at the movement's possible involvement.

"We've got information ... there is an armed civilian group that was most probably behind (the bombings)," Sa'af told reporters. "We'll investigate the link between the armed civilian movement in Aceh and the suspects."

Ismuhadi allegedly made the bombs in a car service center in South Jakarta near the private residence of President Abdurrahman Wahid, police said.

On Aug. 1, an explosion ripped through the residence of the Philippine ambassador in Jakarta, killing two people and seriously injuring dozens of others, including the ambassador, Leonides Caday, and his driver.

In another attack, a grenade was thrown into the compound of the Malaysian Embassy, but no one was injured.

Sr. Supt. Harry Montolalu, detective unit chief of the Jakarta Police Headquarters, who accompanied the police chief, told reporters he has not found evidence linking the suspects with Hutomo "Tommy" Mandala Putra, the youngest son of former President Suharto.

"So far, not yet, but it doesn't mean no," he said.

Nine days ago, Wahid ordered police to arrest Tommy for his alleged involvement in bombings at the Jakarta Stock Exchange complex. But after questioning him the following day, police said there was insufficient evidence to arrest him.

Montolalu said the suspects confessed they received between 300,000 rupiah (about U.S. $32) and 400,000 rupiah to carry out the attacks.

No members of the military are among the 25 suspects, Nurfaizi said, referring to claims that the military was behind some of the attacks.

"But everything is still under investigation," he added.

The lead. This is a direct, summary lead.

The nut graph. The first two paragraphs contain the information sometimes set apart in a nut graph; the story is important now because 25 people were just arrested in connection with a series of bombings.

Remaining themes. After giving a summary of who was arrested and the circumstances of the arrests, the story links the chief suspect to one of the bombings and gives details about that attack. It then mentions a possible link between this suspect and a separatist group, gives more details about how he is believed to have been involved in the bombings, describes two earlier bombings, gives an update on the investigation of the possible involvement of the former president's son, and provides more details about the suspects.

Quotes. Quotes are used well to support the allegations made throughout the story. Again, they are evenly spaced, and each is boiled down to essentials.

Community as context. This story would be important to people in or near Indonesia, or who have family, friends or business connections there. Background information that would be important for the reporter to have is knowledge of the separatist movement in Indonesia and the investigation of the former president's son.

Style note. Note that the writer says the police chief "told a press conference" what happened, which indicates that phrase is taken in Indonesia to mean assembly of reporters. In the United States, she would probably have said the chief "told reporters during a press conference," because here the phrase refers to an event.

Press conferences also can be an effective way for people or organizations to present information in a light that is favorable to the presenters. If you are covering a press conference that seems geared to making certain people or organizations look good, don't feel you have to buy the "spin" along with the information. If you spot inconsistencies or information that does not ring true, do independent research before writing your story. If your research reveals errors or gaps, keep checking things out until you're sure you have the facts right for your story. Once again, it's a matter of credibility. And, like the work you do before attending speeches, advance reporting before the press conference can pay off with better questions and more interesting responses.

Community Events

Nearly every veteran reporter can tell stories about covering the living Americana embodied by county fairs, community festivals and parades, and fund-raising breakfasts, lunches or dinners. The people who write the best stories about such events are those who appreciate how such activities bind people together in common pursuits that shape a community's identity, and who understand the value of homemade fun that often serves worthy causes as well.

The following is an example of an advance story about one of these events.

Annual Mud Bug Festival to feature food, music, fun

By Vivian Salazar
Globe-News Features Editor

Supporters of The Bridge Children's Advocacy Center are getting into a Cajun frame of mind as they prepare for Saturday's fourth annual Mud Bug Festival.

Organizers are planning a good-time evening of good food, good music, games and a silent auction for the folks who attend the festival, which begins at 7 p.m. and continues until "howlin' time" (midnight) at the Army National Guard Armory, 2904 T-Anchor Blvd.

Proceeds from the evening's activities will help provide services to young victims of reported physical and/or sexual abuse in Amarillo and the surrounding communities.

Roxanne Carter, executive director of The Bridge, said dress is casual.

Mud bugs, sometimes called crawdads or crawfish, will be the main course. They will be served along with cajun fried turkey, corn on the cob and all the trimmings.

"We're preparing 1,500 pounds of the hottest, spiciest crawfish in town, so we'd like for everybody to come eat all they can," Carter said. "Another thing we have is cajun fried turkey. The turkeys are injected with spicy seasonings and deep fried, and they are wonderful. Everything's just really spicy."

That "everything" Carter referred to includes the fresh corn on the cob, which also is boiled in spices along with the potatoes. Board members have a corn-shucking party the night before the festival and shuck 14 cases of corn, Carter said.

Members of St. Thomas the Apostle Men's Club will set up blackjack, roulette and craps tables, and part of the ticket price includes free chips for everyone to play, Carter said.

Back again this year by popular demand is the band, "Kracker Jack," who will entertain throughout the evening. Other entertainment includes a silent auction, and complimentary beer, wine and setups also will be available.

"We just have a great time. Everybody comes out to bid on items, play the casino tables and dance. We had about 500 people last year and we're hoping for as many or more for this year."

By midweek, festival organizers already had sold 31 reserved tables (about 250 people), Carter said. Tickets are $40 a person or $75 per couple. Gold donor tables are $1,000 (reserved seating for eight); silver donor tables are

$500 (reserved seating for eight); and bronze donor tables are $250 (reserved seating for four).

Organizers would prefer that people make reservations, Carter said, and tickets can be picked up anytime through Friday at The Bridge, 1419 S. Polk St., or at First American Bank at 45th Avenue and Teckla Boulevard. Tickets also will be available at the door.

For further ticket or festival information, call The Bridge at 372-2873.

Table sponsors for this year's festival are as follow:

Gold Sponsors — Northwest Texas Healthcare System, Asarco, Carrasco and Carrasco LLP and United Supermarkets;

Silver Sponsors — Southwestern Public Service Co., Kraft Foods Inc., Affiliated Foods Inc., DeJarnett Sales, Wells Blue Bunny, H&R Block–Plainview, Underwood, Wilson, Berry, Stein & Johnson, Bank of America, Ben Parker Inc., Baptist St. Anthony's Health System, Amarillo Anesthesia Consultants, Amarillo Area Healthcare Specialists LLP, Wal-Mart, Morgan Stanley Dean Witter, McCormick Advertising, Plains Dairy, Corporate Computer Solutions and Tommy Buckley;

Bronze Sponsors — Amarillo National Bank, Amarillo Coca-Cola, Southwestern Bell Telephone and Forms Professional.

The Bridge Children's Advocacy Center opened its doors in Amarillo in 1989 and was Texas' first children's advocacy center. It provides a neutral, home-like atmosphere for videotaped forensic interviews of children following an outcry of physical and/or sexual abuse. The Bridge was created to alleviate the trauma associated with the multiple interviewing process conducted by various government agencies.

During 1999, The Bridge provided services to more than 600 young victims and their families in crisis situations throughout Amarillo and the surrounding communities. The children were referred by law enforcement or Children's Protective Services. The Bridge staff and multidisciplinary team members work together to comprehensively aid the abused child to prevent trauma and re-victimization by the system.

From the Amarillo (Tex.) Globe-News, Sunday, April 23, 2000

The lead. This direct, summary lead picks up on the Cajun theme of the festival.

The nut graph. The second and third paragraphs explain that the event will take place within the week and proceeds will benefit an organization that serves abused children.

Remaining themes. After the first four paragraphs, which lay out the basics about the event, the writer devotes three paragraphs to describing the spicy food, three paragraphs to the entertainment, a three-paragraph update on ticket sales and reservations, followed by a list of sponsors and two paragraphs of background information about the center that will benefit from the festival.

Quotes. This story includes two quotes, each offering one person's comments about an aspect of the event. These quotes are typical of the kinds of things people say about such community events: The food will be delicious and plentiful, and the entertainment will be loads of fun.

Community as context. Most Yankees probably don't call crawfish "mud bugs"; one of the nicest touches in this story is the way the writer turned proper terminology upside down by saying "Mud bugs, sometimes called crawdads or crawfish, will be the main course." The mention of St. Thomas the Apostle Men's Club and the list of sponsors indicate that the Amarillo paper includes thorough information about organizations that are involved in such events, which serves not only to acknowledge these organizations' contribution but also to let people in the community know who might be there. Newspapers vary in how much of this information they include. In general, the smaller the paper, the more names — of both people and organizations — are included.

Overt controversy is rarely part of such community event stories. Occasionally, the organizers of such events must deal with financial concerns such as loss of funding, decreasing revenue from falling attendance, or questions about where the money went. In addition, factions may form among the organizers, resulting in power struggles of varying intensity. Most of the time, however, reporters assigned to cover such events write feature stories about things like 4-H kids preparing their livestock for auction, headline musical acts at the state or county fair, the Blackberry Festival Queen's hectic week, the person who builds all the floats for the annual parade, or the volunteers who peel and cut all the potatoes for the annual fire department fish fry. They also write news stories about what happened at a given event, how many people were there, and what people who attended thought of it.

When covering such events, it is important to allow time to watch, talk to people and nose around. Those are the best ways to find good quotes as well as to get a feeling for the most essential or unusual aspects of the event.

COVERING UNPLANNED NEWS DEVELOPMENTS

The kinds of compelling stories that sometimes win the Pulitzer Prize — stories about people coping with the sudden devastation wrought by extreme forces of nature, intentional destruction or human negligence — are challenging to write. These are stories about people who die or are driven from their homes when rivers flood, hurricanes rage or the tail of a tornado tears through a town; about the massacre of young students at Columbine High School; about a passenger train knocked off the tracks when it collided with a semi that witnesses saw driving around the flashing safety signal; or two airplanes turning the World Trade Center towers into treacherous infernos.

You've read thousands of these stories before. Most probably shared many attributes in common with the following story.

Update: Tornado reminder for Xenia

By The Associated Press

XENIA, Ohio (AP) — A tornado swept through this city that was devastated by a twister a generation ago, killing one person and injuring dozens of others as it heavily damaged buildings, overturned cars and downed power lines.

Authorities searched through the night for other possible victims of the storm that hit around 7:30 p.m. Wednesday.

"We are going home by home to see if everybody is OK," Mayor John Saraga said.

The storm — confirmed as a tornado by the National Weather Service — was a frightening reminder of a twister that struck the southwestern Ohio city in 1974, leaving 33 people dead and millions of dollars in damage. Authorities said the storm moved on a parallel path Wednesday but the damage, while significant, was far smaller.

"This was a major tornado, but it's nowhere near the area the '74 tornado covered," said Charlie Leonard, assistant city manager.

Still, at least 115 people were injured, and 14 were admitted to hospitals. One woman was in critical condition and three people were in serious condition Thursday.

The person who died, whose identity was not immediately released, was in a car that was crushed by a tree near the Greene County fairgrounds, Sheriff Jerry Erwin said.

Ruby Godfrey was in the Dayton Avenue Baptist Church when she heard hail pound the roof, which was eventually torn off.

"We're hitting the floor, getting under pews. You heard the roar. You saw the roof flying off and then it was gone," Godfrey said.

Gov. Bob Taft issued an emergency declaration for Xenia, and he toured the area Thursday.

Crews searched through the night for possible storm victims in the rubble of a grocery store that collapsed, though there were no reports of anyone missing. Nothing was found as of daybreak Thursday, but one more search was planned at the store and other buildings that were hit.

All that remained of the Groceryland was a tangle of steel girders, drywall and insulation. But cans of food still could be seen stacked neatly on a shelf inside.

Substantial damage also was reported at a Wal-Mart store where cars were overturned, utility lines fell and trees splintered. Windows were shattered and walls collapsed.

"There really was no warning," said employee Travis Waddle, 20. "I saw the tiles come down and people running and everybody screaming."

He said some people suffered cuts and bruises, but he saw no major injuries inside the store.

About 75 percent of Xenia remained without power at daybreak, the city manager said. Schools were closed in the city of nearly 25,000 people about 20 miles southeast of Dayton.

"I was tired of being in the dark and I wanted to know what was going on," said Robin Hunter, 44, who spent the night at a temporary shelter set up at a local elementary school.

The tornado that swept through Xenia and southwest Ohio on April 3, 1974, was one of a series of storms over two days that killed more than 300 people in Alabama, Georgia, Tennessee, Kentucky and Ohio. It was one of the worst outbreaks of tornadoes in the past 75 years.

In central Ohio, a second tornado that hit about an hour after the Xenia storm damaged about 15 homes north of Columbus.

Art Sidell, 74, of Xenia, was in a barn when the power went off.

"About the time I headed for the door, the roof went off. I just dove under a table," he said Thursday. "After about 10 seconds it was over. I crawled out from under that table and there was debris everywhere. Not a scratch on me."

Sept. 21, 2000

The lead. Never is a direct, summary lead more appropriate than in stories about devastating events. This one includes all the essential information, and it's constructed extremely well. First, the writer mentions that a tornado struck and that it was the second such catastrophe in recent history. In two subsequent clauses, the writer summarizes casualties and injuries, then physical damage to the town. Note that the date and time of the tornado are left until the second paragraph, in keeping with the idea that you don't have to tell the whole story in the lead.

The nut graph. This story, like most others with direct summary leads, works into the lead the information sometimes contained in a nut graph if delayed, anecdotal or other types of leads are used.

Remaining themes. Immediately after summarizing what happened, the writer describes what officials are doing in the aftermath of the tornado, which is compared to the previous one mentioned in the lead. The writer then gives details about injuries and the one reported death, followed by a quote from an eyewitness. After including further information about the official response and more details

When disasters strike, reporters cover both the devastation and the recovery. Here, journalists covered an effort by teenagers from Xenia (Ohio) Christian High School to bring water and food to volunteers cleaning up after a September 2000 tornado.

Photo by Bill Reinke. Source: Dayton Daily News

about damage, the writer goes on to include more quotes from eye-witnesses, interspersed with details about the effects of the most recent tornado and more facts about the previous one.

Quotes. This story uses quotes well. The first quote, from the mayor, conveys the urgency and hard work involved in situations like this. But the best quotes are those of eyewitnesses, who make it possible for us to picture what it was like to survive such an event, in a variety of settings. The eyewitness quotes in this story are extremely vivid.

Community as context. This story would have the greatest significance to people in or near Xenia, but, as disaster news, it also is the kind of story that tends to be reported nationally. As for what the reporter needed to know about this community, it was certainly important to mention the previous tornado.

No stories are more exciting, difficult or sensitive to report. You must get the facts right under less than ideal conditions, often piecing together fragments of information from several sources at the scene. You must talk to people who are experiencing the range of emotions that naturally follow such cataclysmic events, including anger, despair, grief, panic, and denial. Sometimes you must risk a degree of danger yourself, although editors generally do not put reporters in life-threatening situations. You might find yourself in a situation in which you have an opportunity to help or rescue someone. You might see scenes of devastation that become indelibly etched in your memory. And you might have to report about devastation that has affected you or people close to you.

Through it all, your job is to gather as much information as possible, and that includes not just facts but details that you can use to describe the physical and emotional impact of what has occurred.

You can take several steps to prepare for these kinds of stories long before disaster strikes. You can make sure your paper keeps on file up-to-date copies of disaster plans prepared by governmental agencies in your area and find out where they are kept. In addition, you can keep an emergency kit in the trunk of your car. Your kit might include foul-weather gear, a sweatshirt and jeans, long underwear, spare socks, a pair of sturdy shoes, a flashlight, extra batteries, extra notebooks, extra pens or pencils, a few bottles of water, and maps of area cities, counties and states. You also can carry a cellular telephone (or a long-distance phone card or supply of coins so you can call your editors from pay phones), a notebook computer and other electronic equipment, for which you should also carry extra batteries.

When the unexpected occurs, first try to determine the true scope of the event. When disasters, accidents and extreme weather come up, many people over- or underreact. Sometimes your editor can give you an accurate picture of this emotional climate. If not, and you have the chance, make a call or two to find out what's really going on before you go out to start reporting.

Find out where to go. While your making those phone calls, ask where you will be able to find the appropriate officials at the scene. Have they set up a temporary headquarters or media center? If so, get its exact location. Where are the danger zones, if any? And where are injured people being taken? In addition, look over your maps before you go, to scope out alternate routes in case major highways are blocked.

Buy emergency supplies. Always fill your gas tank before you go. If you're going someplace where you could be stuck for some time, think about what else you might need: food, water, or other supplies. Should you take along packaged food? Blankets? Candles? A sleeping bag and pillow? More changes of clothing? A stocked toiletries kit? Pack whatever you could conceivably need.

Phone home. After you arrive on the scene, phone your editor often. In the chaos that follows such events, information can take many sudden and unexpected twists and turns. Estimates of the number of people killed or injured can be revised dramatically up or down. Only by keeping your editor posted can you be sure your paper will carry the most up-to-date information.

Talk to officials. Find out which agencies are in charge of what. Then go to the appropriate officials to get statistics on numbers of people hurt or killed, amount of property damage, whether anything like this has happened in the past and so on. These officials also can give you an account of what happened, to whom, where, when, why and how. Get as many details from them as possible — the minute-by-minute or hour-by-hour account of what happened, names of survivors or victims and biographical information about them, or population and other statistics about affected towns — for use in some of the visual elements discussed in Chapter 9.

Talk to witnesses, who may also be victims. Officials can give you some information about the human element of the story, but you will do better in that regard to find eyewitnesses who can tell you how people have been affected by what occurred, how they are coping, and what their own personal experiences have been. Approaching people under these circumstances requires a great deal of sensitivity. Remember that everyone you approach may have lost loved ones, their homes, their livelihoods or even just their dignity — and you must overcome the stereotype of the reporter who approaches emotionally distraught people and asks, crassly, "How do you *feel?*"

In such situations, remember these three things: First, many people find it cathartic to talk. Second, give them an out. And, third, be patient. When you approach someone who is clearly in emotional distress, introduce yourself, tell them you're a reporter, express your sympathy or condolences, and say you will understand if they would rather not talk to you under the circumstances — but you think their story might help others understand the emotional toll the event is taking on people. If the person turns you down and you can talk to other people in that general vicinity, stay close by them for a while. Sometimes, they just need time to come around to wanting to tell you their story. Another way of offering an out is a technique developed by Jacqui Banaszynski, a former reporter for the "St. Paul Pioneer Press," who has interviewed many victims of tragedies. She tells people before she interviews them that if, when the interview draws to a close, they don't like the way she has handled things, they can

Sink or Swim: Jumping into the Story

Jyll Upright was gonna get wet today.

A nor'easter was moving up the Atlantic Coast. The city where she lived and worked as a reporter was expecting several inches of rain, 40 mph winds and tidal flooding. Jyll came to work in jeans and duck boots, knowing she would be called out to cover the deluge. She was paired up with a photographer, Fran Hutter, and was told to find flooding on the city's east side. Check out the trouble spots, her boss said.

Jyll found plenty of trouble.

The pair quickly ran into a river of water that should have been a highway underpass. Jyll saw a woman at the water's edge, frantically waving them over. "Save my baby! I can't swim! Save my baby!" the woman screamed, pointing to a sedan buried in the water up to the car doors.

Fran pulled out her camera and started shooting. Jyll dropped her notebook and jumped into the water, waist high but with a wicked current. She got to the car and pulled a crying toddler through the window and back to safety.

Mom was ecstatic. Jyll was soaked but happy and excited. She actually helped save a life today.

Fran was appalled.

They returned to the office so that Fran could turn in her photos of the rescue, which she considered very newsworthy, despite the fact that it was a reporter who was part of the story. But Fran told Jyll that it's not a journalist's role to become part of the action, no matter how noble the motivation. (Besides, Fran said, the police were on the way and could have easily made the rescue.)

Our job, Fran said, is to record the event, not to be a part of it. As soon as we enter the event, we change the story.

Jyll wasn't so sure.

There was a life at stake, she argued.

The cops may have come in time, sure, but what if the car had shifted and the toddler had drowned? It was more important to Jyll that she acted as a responsible citizen first, and as a journalist second.

Still, the exchange bothered her. Had she given up her credibility as a journalist in helping the youngster in trouble? Jyll took her question to her metro editor — and was surprised to find him supportive of Fran's point of view.

"Perhaps you do give up something when you cross that line," the metro editor said. "Perhaps, though, you're asking the wrong question."

"So how do I make sense of this?" Jyll asked, growing more upset. It seemed she was moving from heroine to journalistic goat all in one day.

"Well, think about it not in terms of either/or, but in terms of risks and benefits. In other words, what do I have to give up as a citizen in order to be a journalist? Well, there are company rules about joining political campaigns, for instance. And some journalists — not me — think they must give up their right to vote, so as not to be perceived as biased. But even the most involved journalist agrees that you have to stand a bit apart in order to faithfully report.

"Does that mean you can't coach a soccer team, or be a member of a church, or do many of the things that citizens do every day? Does it — in the extreme case here — require you to stand by while a person's life is in jeopardy?"

"Well, no, but Fran says ..."

"... that you've become a part of the story. She's right, of course. In fact, Fran got some great shots that we'll run tomorrow. But it's OK that you made a different choice, too. Sometimes, becoming part of the story is the only thing you can do."

have her notebook and she won't write anything. No one has ever taken her up on the offer.

Find out how others can help — or protect themselves. One of the most important services journalists can provide is to tell people what they can do to help those who were in harm's way, how they can get

Tips for Talking to Trauma Victims

Interviewing people who have witnessed or been victims of traumatic events such as natural disasters or violent crimes is one of the most difficult things journalists do.

The idea of being assigned to interview trauma victims is repugnant to most young reporters.

But, as CNN medical reporter Elizabeth Cohen found while interviewing family members and friends looking for loved ones in the days immediately after the Sept. 11, 2001, attack on the World Trade Center, many people *want* to talk.

Interviewing victims is an important way of helping people understand the human impact of devastating events. Former Miami Herald crime reporter Edna Buchanan says that can keep us from glamorizing or becoming overly intrigued with those responsible for violent acts.

"Crooks may be colorful, quotable, and even likable, but they are not nice people. When you tell their stories, it always helps to give the victims equal space," Buchanan wrote in "The Corpse Had a Familiar Face."

Giving victims that space, however, presents many challenges to reporters.

"What we now know about trauma can make a difference in how journalists do their jobs and their relationships to the people they cover. We know that the interviews, the stories, and the photographs all have the potential to either add to the injury or to help in the recovery," William Coté and Roger Simpson wrote in their book "Covering Violence: A Guide to Ethical Reporting about Victims and Trauma."

Coté and Simpson offer the following suggestions to reporters covering the aftermath of violence:

• Think through how interviewing victims can be of value. Plan coverage with those considerations in mind. For example, reporting about victims can increase awareness of the human costs of violence, give people empathy for others' suffering, and provide information and insight that affects public policies and programs that aid in recovery or protect against future violence.

• Learn about how trauma affects people. Get to know the differences in people's reactions to natural disasters, for which no one is to blame, and human-caused violence, which is more likely to cause anger and bitterness. Be aware that children are far less able to cope with trauma than adults. Understand that people go through several stages in the aftermath of a traumatic event. One experienced disaster worker says it's typical for disaster victims, for example, to respond immediately by helping one another survive, then spend some time taking care of basic needs for food, shelter and safety. Usually a period of disillusionment follows, as people experience frustrations with agencies involved in the recovery and realize how slowly recovery occurs. Eventually, usually long after the event, they settle into rebuilding and begin to feel better in stages, as they make progress; however, symptoms of the initial trauma still may appear.

• Make sure your newsroom has a

(cont.)

plan for covering major accidents and disasters. Such plans should include what to do (and not do) during the first few minutes and hours, as well as what you should do over time.

• Weigh every decision to interview or photograph a victim in light of what you know about trauma's effects. If it seems that the interview or photo would harm someone, consider finding other approaches to the story. You always have two choices: to interact sensitively with victims or to leave them alone. Only you can make that call.

• Use great sensitivity in approaching and interviewing a traumatized person. Say "I'm sorry" — sorry for the person's loss, or that they had such a devastating experience. Give the person time to tell the story in his or her own way. Listen carefully and patiently. Expect emotional responses. Encourage the person to ask a friend or family member to be there during the interview for support. Develop policies to reduce the possibility that you will be the first person to announce a death to a survivor.

• Don't take at face value people's immediate assumptions about the causes of their anger, grief or shock. Things can be very confusing in the wake of traumatic events, and people can place blame only to find out later that blame was misplaced.

• Avoid damaging clichés in your reporting. In your efforts to cover the human side of tragedy, don't just focus on "the shocked survivor" or "the grieving relative." Be careful not to exaggerate displays of panic, anger, grief or shock. Look also for people who are helping or exhibiting courage, resilience or determination.

• Involve editors, reporters, photographers and graphic artists in discussions about what information and photos (or news footage) to publish or air, and how often to print (or broadcast) it. Remember that children may be inadvertently exposed to images in newspapers left lying around or on unmonitored televisions. Again, be aware that children are less able to cope with violence, including visual images of violence.

• Understand that, as a reporter, trauma can have the same effects on you as it has on anyone else. If you're witnessing a traumatic event, you can have an unexpected emotional response just like any other victim. If you interview other victims, your empathy can take an emotional toll on you. Over time, you might find yourself experiencing recurring mental images of some part of the event; feeling emotionally numb; becoming unusually fearful, jumpy or irritable; or forgetting things. The common belief that journalists' training and experience enables them to set aside emotion is being disproven by a growing body of research.

• Ask a compassionate editor to debrief you after you have covered a traumatic event, allowing you to talk about your reactions to what you were covering as well as the decisions you made in covering the event.

• After you have finished covering a violent event or interviewing victims, take some time to restore yourself through such activities as exercising, listening to music, praying, seeking counseling, or whatever works for you.

Here are some additional tips for interviewing trauma victims, taken from an article by staff of the Victims and the Media Program at Michigan State University, published in the fall 1996 issue of Nieman Reports:

• Take care with first impressions.

(cont.)

Approach the person without your notebook. Exude poise, confidence — and caring. If you seem too pushy, people in these situations will not want to talk to you. Once you make contact, ask them if you can take notes and if you can quote them.

• Be aware that you may be the first to deliver the bad news. On some occasions, you may arrive to interview a crime victim's family or neighbor before they know the person has been hurt or killed. Think through how to handle such a situation — before it happens.

• Express your sympathy with a simple phrase like, "I'm sorry for your loss," "I'm sorry this happened to you," or "I'm glad you weren't killed." But don't say "I know how you feel," because you don't, even if you've been in a very similar situation.

• Establish ground rules up front. To give people a sense of power and control, let them know that they can stop or take a break from the interview at any time. Tell them to let you know any time they want to tell you something they don't want you to use. Tell them what you need and ask if they have any questions.

• Be accurate. Minor errors that normally seem annoying can seem monumental to people who are traumatized. In addition, be careful about imputations of blame — especially suggestions that victims were at fault.

• Be sensitive to the special impact of photos, graphics and other visual elements. Avoid using overly gory photos or illustrations that stereotype people.

help themselves or protect themselves from harm. Always track down this information and be prepared to include it with your story.

People unaffected by the trauma can help, for example, by donating blood, money or supplies, or by volunteering their time. A word of caution, however, about how you present pleas for help; news reports about disasters can inadvertently cause harm. In their book "Covering Violence," for instance, Coté and Simpson tell stories of how offhand or incomplete comments contained in news reports have resulted in relief shelters being flooded with donations they don't need, requiring relief workers to turn their attention away from helping victims to figure out to do with the unneeded supplies.

As for ways reporters can help people take care of themselves, they can direct them to government agencies, charities and other agencies offering relief, or give them information about things they should do or not do — like not opening suspicious-looking mail or packages, boiling their water if there's a chance a storm contaminated their water supply, taking alternate routes when bridges or roads have been damaged, or staying or leaving their homes (depending on what kind of threat is looming).

Think visually. Imagine that you're trying to draw a diagram of what happened — because that's what the graphic artist at your paper probably will do, with your help. Get details and exact measurements. How many yards did the train travel after it hit the semi, for example? What path did the gunmen take through Columbine High School? How close together were the homes damaged by the tornado? If possible, collect maps and photographs that will help you and the newspaper's graphic artist create an accurate visual representation of what occurred.

Be wary of speculation. Take care in reporting early speculations as to what caused accidents or disasters, especially from unofficial sources, and in reporting off-the-cuff comments about how the current situation compares to similar situations in the past. In the aftermath of such crises, it is natural for people to want to know how something like that could happen, which usually leads to the question of who is responsible. However, causes of such events are often complex or impossible to determine conclusively and require time for investigation. Absence of concrete evidence does not stop people from speculating — and such speculations can damage innocent people when not sufficiently verified. The key is to make sure any determination of cause is based on factual evidence, and that any historical information used to place events in context is accurate.

OTHER COMMON ASSIGNMENTS

Neighborhood News

Neighborhood news stories run the gamut from those about new businesses, churches or other organizations to profiles of people in the neighborhood to coverage of events as straightforward as school bake sales or as complicated as citizen-initiated programs for addressing serious problems in the area.

To cover neighborhood stories well, it's best if you can spend time there, soaking up the sights, sounds and even smells. In addition to gathering information about the subject of your story, talk to people about the neighborhood to get a sense of what knits residents together. Ask them questions about anything you've seen that has made you curious. Whenever possible, try to impart a sense of place — of what makes the neighborhood unique — in these stories.

Helping with Major Projects

As a general assignment reporter, you can count on helping with major stories that come up. These usually are the kinds of in-depth stories you will read about in Chapter 13. In such cases, your editor or another reporter either will give you a specific assignment or include you in a planning process in which you can take part in creating story ideas and determining what stories you write.

Such major stories include ongoing coverage of elections. Generally, political reporters cover breaking news stories about who has decided to run for office, what they do on the campaign trail, and how much money they're receiving and spending to get elected. General assignment reporters usually get drawn into campaign coverage in the last few months before the election, when most papers prepare some sort of voter's guide. They also usually write stories on election night, helping to track election results, people's reactions to the results, and what comes next.

Voter's guides usually include stories about candidates' backgrounds and their positions on various issues, initiatives or referenda that are pending. Sometimes stories in these sections summarize positions on issues laid out by the candidates as political platforms during their campaigns. Many newspapers also do research to determine which issues are important to voters, then ask candidates to respond to questions based on that research. Methods for uncovering these issues include formal, scientific polls (usually conducted only by larger newspapers with research departments); small-group discussions (sometimes called focus groups); and paying attention to issues raised by the public in interviews for news stories, public events, phone calls to the newspaper and letters to the editor.

Working with Wire Stories

General assignment reporters also are asked to "localize," or add local information to, international, national, state or regional stories that come to their newspaper via various wire services. Sometimes the story may have a direct local connection — someone mentioned in the story formerly lived in the area, or local people are likely to be affected by developments elsewhere. A good example of such a story would be one announcing that a retail chain with a store in your area is planning to close some of its stores. The obvious question is whether your local store is on the list and, if so, what the impact will be. When localizing stories, it's best to include some local information in the lead, so readers know how it affects (or will affect) them.

Enterprising reporters can turn wire stories around by doing enough local reporting that the wire information ends up as an insertion into the local story. Don't stop at finding out how many stores might be affected. Find out who in the community might be affected, and how — the people employed at the store, the neighborhood that frequents it, the local stock firms that invested in that store's corporation, etc. By putting a local lens on a national or international wire story, you'll be adding context and relevance to the issue for your readers.

EXERCISES

1. Call an organization on campus or in your community and ask how the organization promotes the events it sponsors. Find out how the organization gets the word out about its activities, what materials it prepares for reporters, and how often it contacts news organizations to request news coverage.

2. Choose a speaker or performer who is coming to your campus or community. Find out everything you can about him or her, from whatever sources you can locate in print or online. Call the organization that is sponsoring the local event and ask what kinds of background information, photos or posters of other materials they received about the person for promotional purposes. Based on your research, make a list of sources for gathering background information about noteworthy people.

3. With the sound of sirens as your cue, seek out the scene of an accident, fire or other emergency. Go to the scene and observe, taking notes about who does what. Pay attention to people on the fringes (those who direct traffic or set up first aid stations, for example) as well as those in the middle of the action. How many people come just to see what's going on? How do they behave? Do they help? Get in the way? Make notes about your observations.

4. Look through a print or online newspaper for a wire story about an issue affecting college students. Type the story into your computer, then interview two other students from your journalism class about how that issue affects them. As a writing exercise, modify the lead and add their quotes and other local information to the story.

Further Reading

ON THE WEB

Festivals.com lists festivals across the country and includes feature stories and other information: www.festivals.com

Pew Center for Civic Journalism, "Where's Grandma?" by Mike Jacobs, about the newspaper's coverage of flooding in Grand Forks, N.D., published in Pew's Civic Catalyst Newsletter, Winter 1998: www.pewcenter. org/doingcj/civiccat/displayCivcat.php3?id=27

The Poynter Institute for Media Studies, "'Who Said That?': Guidelines for Evaluating Sources," by Bob Steele and Al Tompkins: www.poynter.org/ dj/tips/ethics/et_sourceguide.htm

The Victims and the Media Program, Michigan State University School of Journalism: http://victims.jrn.msu.edu/victims.html

IN PRINT

"Associated Press Coverage of a Major Disaster: The Crash of Delta Flight 1141," by Thomas Fensch, published by Erlbaum, Hillsdale, N.J., 1990.

"Covering Violence: A Guide to Ethical Reporting about Victims and Trauma," by William Coté and Roger Simpson, Columbia University Press, New York, 2000.

"Festival and Special Event Management," by Ian McDonnell, Johnny Allen and William O'Toole, published by Wiley & Son, New York, 1999.

"Ordinary Life, Festival Days: Aesthetics in the Midwestern County Fair," by Leslie Mina Prosterman, published by Smithsonian Institution Press, Washington, D.C., 1995.

"Under the Whelming Tide: The 1997 Flood of the Red River of the North," edited by Eric Hylden and Laurel Reuter, published by the North Dakota Museum of Art, Grand Forks, N.D., 1998.

Chapter 12

Covering a Beat

Police reporters always appreciate a moment like this one — a baby being dramatically rescued from a burning house by Richmond, Ind., firefighters. Writing about such moments provides balance against the many stories about death and destruction these reporters must write.

Photo by Steve Koger. Source: Palladium-Item

████████████████ **Key Concepts** ████████████████

- Expertise is the most valuable characteristic for any beat reporter.

- Getting to know your beat is like a scavenger hunt. Gather as many contacts and as much information about the beat as possible to help make sense of the most important issues and best possible stories.

- Newspapers define beats in many ways. Four universal beats are government, public safety, education and sports.

██

Someone chopped Guillermo Mendez into pieces. A torso and dismembered arms and legs were found in the county landfill; the head was left in a cemetery.

Tim McGlone, then the police reporter for the Schenectady, N.Y., Daily Gazette, was gathering information along with reporters from other media. It was a frustrating day. Police weren't saying for sure that the body was that of Mendez. And they weren't admitting that an unidentified man questioned at the police station was a suspect.

So McGlone started working his beat. The day led into an all-nighter. By 4 a.m., he knew the identity of the man in police custody. Just after dawn, he interviewed the suspect — just as the police dropped the man off at his apartment. And by noon, McGlone was home in bed after having filed an exclusive story that would run in the next day's Daily Gazette.

The story began this way:

SCHENECTADY — Nelson Estrella told police at the end of 16 hours of interrogation that he did not kill and dismember his friend Guillermo Mendez, Estrella said early Friday morning.

Estrella said police told him during the interrogation that the dismembered body found in the Rotterdam landfill was Mendez.

He said that toward the end of the 16-hour session police accused him of killing Mendez, but he denied it.

Police officials and District Attorney Robert M. Carney have not said publicly that Mendez is the same man as the victim, but the similarities are striking. (Aug. 22, 1992, Page One)

McGlone got the story through persistence, old-fashioned shoe-leather reporting and a little luck. He started with the most obvious sources: the police detectives and other officials within the department. But he didn't give up when the official pipeline of information shut down. He talked to people on the street to help him find the section of town where the suspect lived. He spent the evening "staking out" the police station and searching the neighborhood. Finally, at 4 a.m., he saw detectives drive to an apartment that he would later confirm as the suspect's. Under the apartment was a little grocery store. McGlone waited until the store opened, and then interviewed the store owner, who confirmed that Estrella had been picked up the day before for questioning. As McGlone and the store owner were talking, Estrella walked in, tired, nervous and excited. "He's chattering," McGlone would later say. "He says, 'Oh yeah, they kept me there for 16 hours, under the hot lights, and I didn't do anything.'"

Although McGlone didn't make friends at the police station, he got the information to write an important story involving a particularly brutal murder while holding police accountable for the way they were conducting their investigation.

Like a cop on patrol or a doctor making rounds, McGlone was working his beat. The beat is the basic organizing structure of any newsroom. Beats provide road maps for the newsroom and for each reporter. Whether defined by geography, institutions or themes, reporters' beats help give sense and direction to their reporting.

Beats tell reporters what areas of public life they are responsible for covering — what stories they should go after as well as what to stay away from. Beats sometimes overlap; a city council reporter may write about a school district budget if the council ultimately must approve the spending, for instance. A single story may cross over several beats: The wreck of an Amtrak train in Newport News, Va., involved a half dozen beat reporters for The Virginian-Pilot. The transportation reporter researched deadly train crossings. The city hall reporter gathered comments from area officials. The police reporter wrote down observations and interviewed people at the scene of the accident, then ran a database search on other wrecks at that intersection. Several general-assignment reporters conducted interviews in the neighborhood of the accident, at the hospital where the injured were taken, and with the families of passengers. Each reporter brought to the story some specialized knowledge acquired through becoming familiar with people and agencies on each beat. Each knew, before the accident occurred, the names and phone numbers of people who could provide information about certain things. Each also knew the location of public records, databases or other informational sources. Even the general assignment reporters had unique knowledge about various neighborhoods.

In fact, expertise is the single most important characteristic of any beat reporter. Becoming a beat reporter means developing a body of knowledge that is useful in understanding and interpreting news developments for the rest of us. Most news organizations don't expect the person who covers the judicial system to have a law degree, but they do want that person to know the difference between burglary and robbery, prison and jail, and bail and bond. Education and government reporters need not be fiscal experts, but they must know how to read and understand schools' and governmental agencies' operating and capital budgets.

HOW BEAT STRUCTURE INFLUENCES NEWS COVERAGE

What gets defined as a beat gets covered. Even the largest newspapers don't have enough reporters to cover every possible government agency, community group, neighborhood or field of endeavor. In setting up the beat structure, upper-level editors decide where to put their reporting muscle. It's often an agonizing process, involving choices and trade-offs. Should the paper have an education reporter for every city in the area, even it means less coverage of higher education issues at the state Capitol? How important is it to have an environmental reporter? If the newspaper only has the budget for one new position, should it be a full-time religion reporter or a full-time arts writer? You can learn a lot about a newspaper's values by knowing the beats it creates.

Generally, though, most newspapers maintain several traditional beats around core issues in any community. Residents expect a newspaper to tell them about public safety issues, or what many journalists call "cops and courts." They expect the paper to tell them what their government is doing, how those actions are connected to the public's concerns and whether the government is operating as it should. Government-related beats, then, may include reporters covering public life at the local, state or national level as well as political reporters covering campaigns. Education is another typical beat, usually going beyond coverage of kindergarten-through-12th-grade (K–12) schools to include colleges and universities.

Beat reporters usually report to a particular "desk," so named because the rotating crew of editors who are scheduled to be on hand to supervise reporters' work at various times of day usually sit at or near a particular desk. Typically, daily newspapers have a "metro" or "city" desk, which supervises coverage of what journalists call "hard news," or the most important stories of the day in the geographic area where the paper is read. In smaller papers, local hard news stories usually appear in the front section of the newspaper. Newspapers in larger cities usually run these stories in what might be called a "metro," "city" or "local" section. Most daily newspapers also have sports, business and features sections. Most reporters who work in each of these areas are generalists — government reporters, business reporters, sports reporters or features writers. Others might specialize in covering such subsets as technology (usually included the business section), college sports (in the sports section), or music (in features or arts sections).

Many editors also create specialized beats determined by the unique characteristics of a community — yet another way that community creates the context for news. The Elizabethtown, Ky., newspaper has a military beat because of its proximity to Fort Knox. The Sun in Myrtle Beach, S.C., has a tourism writer because of that industry's importance to the financial health of the area. Some news organizations in New York have subway or transit beats, because public transportation issues are important to commuters who depend on them to make it to work each day.

Another factor that can affect beat structures is a change in the editors' views about what is important. When The Lincoln (Neb.) Journal Star, for example, identified a need for a science and environment reporter, it created the position by rolling together the city and county government beats, which formerly were divided between two reporters. When The Orange County (Calif.) Register recognized that many innovative citizens were doing important things without much public recognition, it created a "people making a difference" beat to put the spotlight on their valuable achievements.

Changes in our society also can bring about changes in beat structure. Among the beats newspapers have added most often in recent years are neighborhood and minority community beats; technology beats, focusing on various aspects of the burgeoning use of technology in our country; and religion beats, in response to the growing personal spirituality movement as well as continuing interest and changes in organized religion.

Another increasingly common beat involves coverage of non-profit organizations and related issues. Cox Newspapers, for example, which publishes the Atlanta Journal Constitution, Dayton Daily News and several other papers, created a Washington-based philanthropy beat in June 2000.

"We see it as an opportunity to do some fresh reporting on something that rarely gets covered," Cox senior editor Ron Martin told AJR/American Journalism Review.

Among stories philanthropy reporter Rebecca Carr sees coming out of that beat are welfare reform that has affected charities, the alliance between for-profit and nonprofit groups, and what's involved in applying for grants.

"Most people think of [charity] as just the do-gooders of the world, and there are plenty that are doing wonderful things," Carr told AJR. "But there's so much out there that it warrants taking a hard look. If people are giving money in good faith, but then it's being abused — that's a problem."

The Poynter Institute for Media Studies responded to increasing interest in philanthropy coverage by holding its first seminar on coverage of the nonprofit sector in June 2000.

"There are almost 2 million nonprofit and philanthropic organizations," Poynter Institute president James M. Naughton told AJR. "They do billions of dollars of investments, but there's just a handful of people covering them."

Nothing is sacred about creating a beat. A newspaper can have as many as it has reporters, and then some, if reporters cover more than one beat. And the ideas around which beats are organized are limited only by editors' imaginations and reporters' ability to find stories tied to those ideas. Beats have been created to cover shopping malls, teenagers, farmers and fishermen.

Some newspapers have revised the way they conceptualize even the most traditional beats. Their goal is to shake up staid routines and get away from news coverage that focuses more on institutions than on the citizens those institutions serve. Simply naming the beat can sometimes affect how a reporter frames the coverage. For example, a "cops reporter" might do things differently than a "public safety reporter." If the reporter thinks of herself as a cops reporter, she might tend to focus on the activities of police and their efforts to catch the bad guys. If, instead, she thinks of herself as a public safety reporter, she might think of her responsibilities a bit differently, conceiving stories on ways to prevent crime or on factors that lead to crime. If a reporter is assigned to the learning beat (instead of education), it might mean he is responsible for writing about employee training programs and Saturday morning workshops at the arboretum as well as things that pertain to public schools.

No matter what the name of the beat, however, the challenge for reporters and editors is to define the beat structure in a way that yields stories that cover the events and issues that are most important and meaningful to the community. Beat structures also should minimize overlap between beats and ensure that reporters are covering the most important stories for the paper.

HOW REPORTERS STAY INFORMED

Covering a beat is a matter of getting into and staying "in the loop" without allowing yourself to become complacent. The best reporters set up systems for making sure they get the information they need to track developments on their beat, while always questioning whether they are missing important stories or becoming too reliant on the same set of sources.

Venturing Out on Your Beat

When you're new to a beat, first get to know the territory. Before you write even a single story, visit the places where things happen on that beat and seek out the people who make those things happen and the people who are affected. Keep an eye out for less obvious locations and news sources: Visit the holding area for prisoners at a police station, the garages where city- or county-owned vehicles are serviced, the maintenance supervisor at City Hall and cafeteria workers in schools, for example. Knowing these places and people can help you be in the best place at the best time to get the information you need.

During your travels, read postings on bulletin boards, walls or windows, and pick up copies of any brochures, maps or other information available to the public. Ask people to give you tours. If you catch them when they're not pressed for time, many people love to show a new reporter around. You'll not only see new departments or buildings, you'll see them through the eyes of the tour-giver. Imagine, for example, convincing a city council member to show you around the city. You will learn a lot about the city — as well as a lot about the people, places and issues valued by that council member.

You're on a scavenger hunt of sorts, trying to piece together as many contacts and bits of information about the beat as possible. You can start with suggestions from the previous reporter on your beat. But don't stop there. Create your own list of government agencies, organizations, businesses or other groups you are responsible for covering, and go over it with your editor to make sure you haven't missed anything. Compile names, job titles, phone numbers and other contact information for key people in those organizations. Make sure your list includes like secretaries, assistants and clerks — who often end up being the most valuable sources on your beat.

Sometimes talking to those people away from professional settings helps. If your newspaper allows it, take a source to lunch. The relaxed atmosphere should help you learn more about the person.

Build professional relationships with regular sources. You aren't looking to get or give special favors. But a beat reporter should nurture a relationship of trust. Your sources should be able to trust you to report accurately and fairly and to get their response if accusations are leveled at them. For those people you will interview regularly on your beat, it helps to establish understanding early: They need to know the ground rules for unpublished or off-the-record information. Then, when sensitive or unpleasant stories come up later, you will have that foundation and knowledge as your foundation. As you build contacts on your beat, you will no doubt find yourself gravitating toward people who seem friendlier or more helpful than others. Very often, these are people who are assigned to respond to questions from the media. Sometimes, however, they are simply people who consider it their job to be as helpful as possible to you and other citizens. Cultivate these relationships — but keep them professional. It is not ethically sound, for instance, to develop romantic relationships with your sources. Nor is it ethical to accept gifts that could be construed as payoffs for printing or not printing certain information.

The Pitfalls of Payola

Jyll Upright was anxious to hit the ground running in her new beat. She wanted to make an impression. Fast.

The former general assignment reporter had been picked to cover the police and courts beat. As a GA, she had covered a number of accidents and a few crimes. But Jyll had never covered a trial. So, in addition to reading as much as possible, she set a goal to take a court official to lunch at least once a week. Jyll wasn't looking for quotes; instead, she wanted to understand the ins and outs of the system, to learn what she needed to pay attention to and what to ignore.

Jyll's metro editor approved — encouraged, in fact — lunches with sources. The metro editor knew it was an important way to develop relationships with the people reporters regularly covered.

So Jyll took an assistant district attorney to a popular diner across the street from the courthouse. They ate submarine sandwiches, sipped iced tea and talked. It was an informative and enjoyable outing, until the bill came. The attorney insisted on picking up the tab at the end of lunch.

Jyll insisted that her paper, the Yourtown Tattler pay for lunch. Eventually the source shrugged and let Jyll pay, but only after Jyll promised that next time he would pick up the bill. And he presented her with a Cross pen with the name of the district attorney on it. It was an awkward moment, but Jyll wasn't sure what to do except to stuff the pen in her purse and leave.

She went directly to the metro editor, hoping to hear that the paper has a policy to address the situation. The paper did. But the policy didn't make things easier.

The Tattler's policy said conflicts of interest — or the appearance of conflicts — should be avoided. As for monetary gifts, the policy said reporters could not accept gifts with a dollar value of more than $10.

"So I could have let him pay," Jyll said.

"Perhaps," the metro editor said.

"But the policy is clear: Lunch cost $7, which is under the $10 limit."

The metro editor nodded. "Yes, that's true. But keep in mind that the policy also says you should avoid the *appearance* of conflict at all times. No one would suggest that a D.A. has bought favorable coverage through the purchase of a submarine sandwich. But what if he bought your lunch once a week? Would that make a difference? Would people notice?"

"Of course, but ..."

"Or what if it was during the trial of a murder suspect he was prosecuting, and you were covering it? Would that make a difference?"

"Yes, but ..."

"The point is that no policy can make up for good judgment. You have to deal with these people every day. It's your reputation at stake, as well as the newspaper's. Sometimes it's easy to know when taking 'payola' violates company policy or personal ethics — receiving free legal services, for example, or taking money from a candidate during election season. That's easy. It's the muddy middle that gets, well, muddy."

Now Jyll was frustrated. The metro editor wasn't giving her a straight answer. She wanted to know — up or down, yes or no. The metro editor refused something so simple.

"Let me give you another one: Remember that feature you did on the 90-year-old woman who was quilting pillows for kids at the hospital? Well, she gave you a pillow after the story ran, right? What if I told you that pillow would retail for more than $10? Would you risk offending this old woman for the sake of the policy limit?"

"Well, no. That wouldn't be right. She was so happy to give it to me ... "

"Exactly. That's why I didn't tell you to take the pillow back. There was no danger that the gift would affect your coverage, and all we would do would be to upset that poor old lady. Now, what about that Cross pen?"

"Well, it would offend the attorney, wouldn't it, if I didn't accept?"

"Maybe. Maybe not, if you explain about the policy. But the pen's worth more than 10 bucks, the attorney is a regular source, and it's possible that, consciously or unconsciously, he hoped that giving you the pen would get him something in return: favorable coverage."

Jyll's shoulders slumped. She knew she would be facing another awkward moment this afternoon. But she knew the pen had to go back.

As you get more comfortable with your beat, you'll no doubt develop a routine. Just as nurses on a ward "make the rounds" each day, you should get into the habit of seeing key people on a regular basis. Choose these people well. Include a mix of sources, much as you seek out a mix of sources for individual stories. This may evolve into a standing appointment with some sources — daily, once a week, or at whatever interval seems appropriate. For others, the contacts can be intermittent or made as needed. Typically, your "rounds" should include regular visits to:

• Key people who can tell you about official developments on your beat. These usually include people in charge, who often are the only people authorized to give you on-the-record comments (elected and appointed officials, directors of organizations, business owners or CEOs, citizen leaders, union representatives, etc.) as well as administrative assistants, secretaries, clerks and others who often are not authorized to speak for their organizations but who can clue you in to new developments.

• Places where public records are filed, so you can check recent filings to see if anything newsworthy has been recorded or initiated through document filings.

• A time-tested array of "listening posts" or "third places," where you can talk with, or eavesdrop on, a broad cross-section of citizens, so you can stay in touch with how the public views events and issues on your beat as well as pick up on news stories before they hit public officials' radar screens.

Beat reporters need to develop routines such as these to stay in tune with the people and issues. At the same time, the routine can become a trap, keeping the reporter from meeting new people and being exposed to fresh ideas. Setting small goals to make sure you stay "awake" can help. For instance, you could set a goal of adding one new person to your source list every week. Or each month ask three "regular citizens" their impressions of the things you're writing about. You might find new stories — or new ways to approach old ones.

Other Tips for Beat Coverage

Track stories over time. Set up some kind of method for tracking issues and events. Some reporters mark a calendar with important dates. Others prefer a "tickler file," in which they file press releases, clippings of past stories or other useful information by the month or week. Include regular meetings of decision-making groups — a school board or chamber of commerce may meet every Monday, for instance, or the first and third Mondays of each month. Courts often hear specific types of cases on specific days each week.

Get on mailing lists. Find out if any of the groups on your beat regularly send out announcements, press releases or newsletters. Make sure you're on mailing lists for anything that seems likely to keep you informed of new developments.

Learn the rules. In some settings, you will have to follow procedures or rules for security purposes. During some court trials, onlookers may need to pass inspection with metal detectors, and cameras may or may not be allowed. Many schools require visitors to wear badges issued from the front office. At some public meetings, a special area is set aside for reporters. For some events, reporters are expected to arrange for tickets or passes in advance.

Learn about the professional culture. Find out what kind of education people on your beat must have to do which jobs. Find out if they must be licensed and, if so, whether they must update their skills to stay licensed. Learn a bit about the tools of their job. If you cover the police department, learn something about the cars the police drive and how they're equipped, for example. If you cover the health beat, find out what kinds of diagnostic equipment the local hospital uses.

Pay attention to relevant wire stories and stories in other media. Scan the wire for international, national, state or regional developments that pertain to things on your beat. If you're the police reporter and you read a story about dwindling numbers of volunteer firefighters in part of the country, it would probably be a good idea to check your area. You can then insert a few paragraphs into the wire story to "localize" it, or you can write your own story and pull in some information from the wire story. You can also borrow story ideas from other newspapers, magazines, radio and television broadcasts and online publications.

Attend workshops and join professional organizations. The state judges association may offer a seminar for court reporters, for instance, just as the Society of Professional Journalists offers workshops organized by beats. And there are beat-specific organizations, such as the Education Writers of America. Another approach is to take college courses in the discipline you cover. Some newspapers will even help pay your tuition for such job-related courses.

THE EDUCATION (OR LEARNING) BEAT: THE UNIVERSAL TOPIC

Education affects almost everyone — like you, for instance, taking this class in journalism, and perhaps your parents, who one way or another helped you get to this point. But getting an education is only one aspect of the learning experience. Bus drivers get kids to school so teachers can educate them. Construction workers build schools. Janitors clean them. Taxpayers — most of the adults in any community — foot the bill for public education whether or not they have children. In most places, education takes up the largest portion of the local budget.

In this country, education has been viewed as everyone's responsibility. In 1642, the Massachusetts Bay Colony made education

Public meetings about school-related issues are among the best-attended by citizens. At this meeting in Richmond, Ind., parents listen to school administrators' plans to close several schools.

Photo by Joshua Smith. Source: Palladium-Item

compulsory in the primary grades and required towns to establish public schools. Public education has been viewed as central to our democracy. Education issues are linked to our hopes and fears for our children's future and, as such, they are a focal point in any community.

Education coverage can involve K–12 public schools, private academies, colleges and universities, trade schools and other institutions. Education writers must be part academician, staying abreast of learning trends; part community feature writer, covering interesting achievements of teachers and students in the schools; part political reporter, following school board candidates on their campaigns; and part fiscal analyst, looking for trends in massive building and operating budgets. The education writer must assess the ability of a community to effectively educate its youth and hold the institutions of education accountable.

Perpetual issues include overcrowding and class sizes; standardized city, state and national testing; the teaching of evolution, sex education, prayer in schools and other church–state issues; nine-month versus year-round schooling; inequities between rich and poor schools or school systems; and gender and cultural diversity issues such as differing expectations of various groups of students in math and science.

Decisions about these issues are made by school boards, most of which are elected. Some school board members are political appointees. The boards, usually led by a chairman, are charged with setting overall policy for the school system and deciding (or at least recommending) how tax dollars should be spent. The school superintendent and staff run the day-to-day operations, overseeing individual schools, making purchases and so on. Universities and university systems have similar systems. A board of regents, for instance, might set policy while the university president runs the university.

Good education coverage focuses on more than just the obvious

How to Read a Budget

If you work any beat involving a public institution, odds are you'll need to report on the proposal or passage of different budgets.

Bureaucrats and politicians of all sorts use budgets to allocate simple day-to-day expenses like pens and paper and also to set the priorities for a community. How much a school district decides to pay its teachers, or fund technology, or pay for a new gymnasium says a lot about that district's priorities.

You generally will encounter two types of budgets. An operating budget describes the daily expenses an institution expects to spend in the coming year. Phone bills, computer ink, maintenance on vehicles, service agreements for the copiers, contracts with private companies to maintain the grounds — the budget likely goes on for pages, and each department has its own list. Generally, though, a cap is placed on individual purchases. For instance, any purchase under $2,000 might be considered part of the operating budget. Anything over would then fall as a capital budget item. This budget describes all the major building or equipment purchases — new cars for a police department, new schools for a district, new libraries or roads for a city. The capital budget usually describes the institution's "wish list" for spending beyond just a single year — it

may stretch out three, five or even seven years. The list is reviewed regularly. Just because a new library is on the capital budget one year doesn't mean it will be there the next. The shift, of course, is fodder for stories. Some tips for surviving your first budget process:

• *Review last year's budget stories.* They can give you clues about what's new this year. Compare the stories to the actual budget documents from that year to understand where the information originated.

• *Interview key people.* The finance director or other people directly responsible for compiling the documents can help you understand the intricacies.

• *Know the process.* A budget generally requires public hearings and several votes before final approval.

• *Read the fine print.* You may need to rely on the executive summary initially, but find the time to look at the budget department by department, line item by line item. Good stories can be found there.

• *Consider the stakeholders.* Almost every line item in the budget represents another group of people with an interest in the outcome. Ask yourself who will feel the impact, then interview those people.

activities of school boards, schools, colleges and universities. In fact, "Readers have told us for years they want less coverage of school board politics and more coverage of education," Linda Grist Cunningham wrote in "The Local News Handbook," published by the American Society of Newspaper Editors.

Many newspapers fail to cover areas and issues that are important to the public: school safety and order, the effectiveness of various curricula and education reform programs, and the important relationship between public education and democracy.

"... sorting through the alphabet soup of educational reform — what works, what doesn't and why — should be the newspaper's role. When a new model is recommended in our schools, we should do the homework, the original research. Relying on what board members, the superintendent, the consultant and the teachers say is just plain lazy. Yet, all too frequently, that's just what happens," Cunningham wrote.

She recommends that reporters who cover education take the time to stay on top of trends in education by reading publications such as Education Week and The American School Board Journal and by doing research using Web sites maintained by the Education Writers Association, the U.S. Department of Education and Public Agenda Online.

One of the most important efforts an education writer can make is to talk with the people who are most affected by all this research, money and debate. Too often in covering controversies, writers forget to ask the school children about their views. That's not as simple as it might seem. Talking to a third-grader or 12-year-old requires a different set of interviewing skills. A good approach to such interviews is to use the language of the child — ask about those tests they took yesterday, not "the state-mandated standardized skills assessments." Get on their level, literally. A first-grader will find talking to you much less daunting if he or she can see you eye-to-eye. In addition, some of the best material for stories can come from observation, not one-to-one interviews, especially with younger children. When you do talk to kids, don't talk down to them, but also don't ask them questions that they aren't qualified to answer. Kids have important things to say, if you let them.

If you don't limit yourself, you can find education stories everywhere. Cunningham quotes Pittsburgh Post-Gazette news editor/education Jane Zemel: "The best way to cover education, in my opinion, is to integrate the coverage into every area, every aspect of life. ... education should not be relegated to a once-a-week education page. Education issues are found in sports, national news, local news, Page One news, international news, the arts, entertainment, even the food section. Education, like health, is a universal topic."

THE POLICE (OR PUBLIC SAFETY) BEAT: TRACKING CRIMES AND THE PEOPLE WHO TRACK CRIMINALS

Covering the police and courts is one of the most demanding jobs a reporter can undertake — emotions run so high so often in the cases handled by police, fire departments and the legal system. In a given week, a cops and courts reporter might talk to a family whose home is being destroyed by fire even as they speak, to a woman whose purse was stolen from a grocery cart in what has become a series of

The Lighter Side of Police Reporting

Fortunately for reporters on the police beat, people are sometimes as good at doing silly things — which can provide some much-needed comic relife — as they are at hurting one another.

Take the young man who convinced an entire sawmill town in Northern California that he was a high-level Navy officer overseeing a top-secret installation in the coastal foothills nearby.

He ran up a tab at a local market and acquired a sidekick — an older man who had a large van the young man was fond of borrowing.

He was found out when he drove his sidekick to the beach, told him his mission was to keep a lookout for black holes in the sky, then took off in the man's van — and didn't return.

Here are some other examples of odd stories from the police beat, as compiled by Reader's Digest:

• The "Police Beat" column in the Fort Bragg, Calif., Advocate-News contained this item: "A caller reported that there was a man at her house forcing her to exercise. It was determined that the man in question is a physical thera-

pist assigned to the woman on doctor's orders."

• From the Maui (Hawaii) News "Crime Watch": "A Wailuku woman said someone entered her Liholiho Street unit and ate a piece of chicken from her soup between 7:30 a.m. May 9 and 8 a.m. May 21."

• From The Islander, Sanibel, Fla.: "An alligator basking in the sun in front of the church at 2050 Periwinkle Way was relocated Friday because people wanted to be able to get into and out of the church."

• In the Sonoma, Calif., Index-Tribune: "Police were called to a residence after a woman complained that someone has been entering her house, taking down her doors and rehanging them in a crooked way."

• From the Medford, Ore., Mail Tribune: "Someone at the Mark Antony bar reported three men walking naked northbound on East Main Street about 2:30 this morning, police said. Officers were unable to locate anyone matching that description."

such thefts over the course of several days, to a doctor who says she's being unfairly sued for malpractice, to someone whose spouse was seriously injured in a convenience store robbery and to someone who witnessed that robbery. None of those events bring out the best in people. Indeed, they often are the most traumatic experiences the people involved ever undergo.

Although such situations call for greater sensitivity and interviewing skill on the part of the reporter, the day-to-day techniques for covering public safety stories are deceptively simple. Let's say you are asked to cover a serious traffic accident. You would find the officer in charge to learn the details, including whether anyone has been charged in connection with the crash, how many people were injured or killed, what time the accident occurred and the names of the drivers or others involved. Sometimes police and fire departments have public information officers who might be able to fill in some of those facts. You also would look for witnesses to the accident and check with nearby businesses or homes for other details about both the accident and the site. Do accidents occur there often, for instance? Has anything about the location changed recently in a way that might have made it more hazardous? Usually within hours after the accident, written reports will be filed by officers who were at the scene, and hospitals will be able to give you a one-word description of an injured person's condition ("good," "fair," "stable," "serious," or "critical" are the standard categories). Some time later, information about the accident also might be entered into a database that tracks traffic incidents in the area.

If a crime is involved, even more official documents will become available. Thesemight include reports by the arresting officer, investigating officers' reports, search warrants, indictments, and jail log entries. In such cases, the number of possible sources also increases to include officials at the district attorney's office, the defendant's attorney, court clerks, and more.

The easy access to official sources, though, can become a trap. Officials of all kinds — police included — tend to put a positive "spin" on the news. That spin can manifest in many ways, but typical examples include occasional attempts at covering up or downplaying misdeeds or serious omissions, failing to give sufficient credit to citizens who helped solve a case, and offering rhetoric instead of fact. Similarly, in trial coverage, reporters who rely on attorneys to give them the account of that day's proceedings can get so caught up in reporting on the lawyers' strategies for winning that they lose sight of the facts — not to mention the broader context in which crimes are committed. The media — television in particular, but newspapers and radio as well — can overemphasize the violence in our communities. Author Matthew R. Kerbel captured this tendency in the somewhat cynical title of his book about broadcast journalism: "If It Bleeds, It Leads: An Anatomy of Television News."

"Newspaper and television reports on crime are the most serious cause of exaggerated public fears," according to a Freedom Forum report by Wallace Westfeldt and Tom Wicker. "By contributing to public anxiety, moreover, these reports tend to fuel politicians' fondness for measures to ease the fear of crime, such as tougher prisons and longer sentences — remedies that take effect after the fact of crime." The assault of crimes in our daily news leaves citizens feeling helpless and fearing that the system is out of control.

Westfeldt and Wicker cite additional causes for tabloid-style coverage: Police and prosecutors — the "good guys" — get quoted more often than defense lawyers — the "bad guys" of the system; reporters don't always understand why juries or lawyers act the way they do; and rulings of law, when favoring the defendant, are framed as being based on legal technicalities and not as decisions that uphold the rights of the accused.

Beyond that, a public safety reporter who only plays out "cops and robbers" reports is missing great stories. Covering the criminal justice system touches on some of the most sensitive issues in our country, such as race, the death penalty and gun use.

• *Race.* Westfeldt and Wicker cite a Bureau of Justice Statistics study that showed that the incarceration rate for black men in 1996 was eight times the rate for white males. "Not even the most virulent racist could believe that blacks are that much more criminally inclined than whites, particularly when they're only about 12 percent of the national population." In 1998, more black men were in prison than white men.

• *The death penalty.* Better investigative techniques, such as DNA testing, and disparities in race and income of those incarcerated have led more people to question the validity of state-sanctioned executions. In Illinois, journalism professor David Protess and his investigative reporting students uncovered evidence that persuaded the courts to dismiss several death penalty cases. The governor there later put a moratorium on all executions until the entire system could be evaluated. And in 2000, both the liberal ACLU and conservative television evangelist Pat Robertson called for a nationwide moratorium.

• *Gun use.* Debate has increased in recent years over controlling handgun purchases and restricting the use of all guns. This issue is a particularly sticky one because emotions run high between people who believe passionately in their right to bear arms and those who feel the number of senseless killings in this country would be drastically reduced if fewer people had guns. Parental oversight, Second Amendment rights to bear arms and free trade all come into play here.

Journalists who reframe their thinking to focus on issues of public safety rather than "cops and robbers " will find different stories. They also will report traditional police and courts stories in different ways.

One approach, advocated by journalist Jane Stevens, suggests that we frame violence as a public health problem. What if, Stevens says, crime were treated as an epidemic, in the same way we think of polio or AIDS or even automobile fatalities. Traffic accidents once were blamed solely on "that idiot behind the wheel." Now, many other factors — the condition of our highways, the ability of vehicles to withstand crashes, laws that mandate seat belt use, social issues such as drinking and drug use — are considered. In the same fashion, if crime were considered an epidemic, Stevens says, it wouldn't be enough to simply blame the person who does something that harms others, although that certainly is part of the problem. Instead, we would recognize — as we do with many diseases — that no one factor is the cause. "Each type of violence in a particular community results from a unique combination of social, cultural, biological and economic risk factors and thus requires a unique combination of preventive measures," Stevens says. The problem, then, becomes larger than the court system. It involves doctors, researchers, community organizers, social workers, parents, teachers and citizens.

And it prompts different questions for journalists covering crime, Stevens says. How common is this crime in this community? What are the risk factors? (If alcohol was involved, for instance, how many alcohol outlets exist in the area, and how does that compare to other parts of the community?) Does the suspect or victim have a job? What type of gun was involved, who made it and how available is it on the street? What are the health costs from the crime? Are there community groups working to reduce violence in the area? If not, why not?

Deputy District Attorney Natalie Luna said the jury convicted Vasquez as the gunman, no one else.

GOVERNMENT BEATS: POTHOLES, SEWERS AND THE PUBLIC LIFE OF A COMMUNITY

Decisions made by local governments affect citizens' lives in ways that are much more tangible than most decisions made in Washing-

Shifting the Focus from "Crime" to "Public Safety"

In the online handbook "Reporting on Violence: A Handbook for Journalists," Jane Stevens rewrote several crime stories to show how they would be different if they were framed from a public health perspective.

Here's one, with Stevens' additions (in italic) and questions (bracketed, in italics) in the rewritten version.

BEFORE

TEARFUL TEEN GETS 15 YEARS TO LIFE FOR 1993 SLAYING

John Henry Vasquez was 16 when he killed another teenager at a party over a momentary insult. At his sentencing Wednesday in Sacramento Superior Court, Vasquez pleaded for the family of the victim to forgive him. They were unforgiving.

"I made a mistake. There are no excuses," said a tearful Vasquez, who was given a 15-years-to-life sentence for the second-degree murder of Robert Maisonet, 19.

Maisonet was shot dead in an apartment living room in the early morning of July 24, 1993. Vasquez is 2½ years older now, but appearing in court with his round face and brass-rimmed glasses, he looked like a boy. A boy dressed in jail-issue sweats.

"I know you said I will burn in hell. Please forgive me. That's all I want is for you to forgive me," Vasquez said in a quivering voice to the Maisonet family.

Though Maisonet's girlfriend, Veronica Bursiga, and his sister, Ana Rodriguez, sat only 20 feet away, neither Vasquez's words nor his tears touched the angry young women.

"You had no right to take the life of the father of my kids," Bursiga said. "I am grateful the jury came back the way they did, but the ultimate price which you will pay will be something between you and God," she shouted.

While Rodriguez was speaking, Vasquez turned away to avoid her glare. "Why did you take my brother?" Rodriguez yelled at Vasquez. "You still have your life. You can still see your family. All we can see is a headstone."

According to trial testimony in August, Vasquez and two companions went to a party on 24th Avenue. At the door they were rebuked by party participants, including members of a rival street gang.

Vasquez and a friend returned to the party 15 minutes later and as his friend pushed open the door, Vasquez pulled out a gun and fired multiple shots. Two bullets struck Maisonet, one piercing his aorta.

Vasquez's sentence includes a special gang enhancement that means he must serve at least 15 years in prison before becoming eligible for parole. Defense attorney James Carroll asked the judge to run the gang penalty concurrently so that Vasquez could be considered for release in about seven years.

Vasquez's companion at the time of the shooting, "who was equally if not more culpable," is now walking the streets as a result of his plea bargain in the case, Carroll said.

While in custody over the past 960 days, Vasquez continued his high school studies and now has a high school diploma, the defense attorney added.

Deputy District Attorney Natalia Luna said the jury convicted Vasquez as the gunman, no one else.

"He wants absolution. He wants people to forgive him and make things OK. He has no remorse," Luna said as Vasquez's family and friends sat in the audience.

Judge Jack Sapunor said he agreed with a study done in the case from the California Youth Authority that found Vasquez unsuitable for the treatment and rehabilitation of a youth correctional facility.

"This offense occurred for no reason at

(cont.)

all. In this gang lifestyle, this brief moment of humiliation became a catalyst for violence. This gang lifestyle leads to nowhere except prison, and Mr. Vasquez, that is where you are bound," Sapunor said.

AFTER

TEARFUL TEEN GETS 15 YEARS TO LIFE FOR 1993 SLAYING

John Henry Vasquez was 16 when he killed another teenager at a party over a momentary insult. At his sentencing Wednesday in Sacramento Superior Court, Vasquez pleaded for the family of the victim to forgive him. They were unforgiving.

"I made a mistake. There are no excuses," said a tearful Vasquez, who was given a 15-years-to-life sentence for the second-degree murder of Robert Maisonet, 19.

Maisonet was shot dead in an apartment living room in the early morning of July 24, 1993. Vasquez is 2½ years older now, but appearing in court with his round face and brass-rimmed glasses, he looked like a boy. A boy dressed in jail-issue sweats.

Maisonet's death is typical of a growing trend in California and across the nation. One of the record-breaking 97 homicides that occurred in Sacramento County in 1993, this one featured a victim and a killer who knew each other. That's the case in 78.3 percent of all homicides nationally.

Their ages are also typical in California, where juvenile homicide rates have exceeded adult rates since 1989 and where almost 20 percent of alleged killers are 11 to 17 years old. Nationally, death by homicide ranks as the second leading killer among juveniles, right behind motor vehicle accidents.

"I know you said I will burn in hell. Please forgive me. That's all I want is for you to forgive me," Vasquez said in a quivering voice to the Maisonet family.

Though Maisonet's girlfriend, Veronica Bursiga, and his sister, Ana Rodriguez, sat only 20 feet away, neither Vasquez' words nor his tears touched the angry young women.

"You had no right to take the life of the father of my kids," Bursiga said. "I am grateful the jury came back the way they did, but the ultimate price which you will pay will be something between you and God," she shouted.

While Rodriguez was speaking, Vasquez turned away to avoid her glare. "Why did you take my brother?" Rodriguez yelled at Vasquez. "You still have your life. You can still see your family. All we can see is a headstone."

According to testimony in August, Vasquez and two companions went to a party on 24th Avenue. *[What were the blood alcohol levels on Vasquez and Maisonet? Had the other partygoers been drinking alcohol? Was there evidence of other drug use?]* At the door they were rebuked by party participants, including members of a rival street gang.

Vasquez and a friend returned to the party 15 minutes later, and as his friend pushed open the door, Vasquez pulled out a gun *[What type of gun was used? Who is the manufacturer? Was it a "crime" gun — a Saturday night special or a 9mm handgun? Did Vasquez own the gun? If he bought it, for how much did he purchase the gun? To whom was the gun registered?]* and fired multiple shots. Two bullets struck Maisonet, one piercing his aorta.

Three of every four homicides in California involve guns, 88 percent of which are handguns. Gang activity, for which Vasquez received a special sentence enhancement of at least 15 years in prison, also featured prominently in this case, as it does in one of every four homicides in California, according to the Legislative Analyst's Office. Nationwide, the figure is about 6 percent, according to the U.S. Department of Justice. Defense attorney James Carroll asked the judge to run the

(cont.)

gang penalty concurrently so that Vasquez could be considered for release in about seven years.

Vasquez's companion at the time of the shooting, "who was equally if not more culpable," is now walking the streets as a result of his plea bargain in the case, Carroll said.

While in custody over the past 960 days, Vasquez continued his high school studies and now has a high school diploma, the defense attorney added.

"He wants absolution. He wants people to forgive him and make things OK. He has no remorse," Luna said as Vasquez' family and friends sat in the audience.

Judge Jack Sapunor said he agreed with a study done in the case from the California Youth Authority that found Vasquez unsuitable for the treatment and rehabilitation of a youth correctional facility.

"This offense occurred for no reason at all. In this gang lifestyle, this brief moment of humiliation became a catalyst for violence. This gang lifestyle leads to nowhere except prison, and Mr. Vasquez, that is where you are bound," Sapunor said.

It will cost taxpayers $20,000 to $22,000 a year to keep Vasquez in prison in California, where juvenile incarceration is expected to increase more than 29 percent in the next decade. Risk factors identified with juvenile crime include failure in school, family problems, substance abuse, conduct problems, gang membership and gun possession.

Stevens' suggestions for accompanying graphics:

- U.S. victimization by age group, race, sex per 1,000
- Victim/offender relationship in solved homicides

(The information for these graphics is in the online handbook.)

Her suggestions for accompanying sidebars or follow-up stories included:

- how the change in choice of weapons and the increased availability of firearms has increased the rate of homicide
- how some former gang members are joining together to prevent guns from getting into the hands of gang members

ton. Local officials' decisions determine the condition of the roads on which you drive, where new subdivisions spring up and how many cops are on the street.

Consider the case of sewer systems. Perhaps nothing would seem duller than a story about the city council's decison to lay new sewer pipes to a section of the city. Although many a dull story certainly has been written about such decisions, in many suburbs, they are some of the most important actions a council takes.

Expanding the sewer system isn't simply a matter of moving wastewater; it involves decisions about how the council wants the city to grow. With sewers come housing developments, which in turn mean jobs for people in the home building industry. New houses also mean more cars and kids, which increases demands on roads and schools and libraries and parks. So a "sewer story" may be the most important story of the year — if you see how it ties in with other important issues.

Whether you're covering a town council, the state legislature or the governor's office, handle your assignment with the same attention to context and meaning that is vital to any beat. Look for the interesting and important aspects or ramifications that may be hidden behind seemingly boring and dreary issues. Jargon or technical language also can conceal story gems; getting help figuring out how to translate those obscure words into simpler terms that you — and most other citizens — can understand might yield a better story than you expected. Because of the complex language used in official proceedings, no beat provides more opportunities for writing deadly dull prose than the government beat. For that reason, it's important to cultivate the ability to boil things down to their essence. If the County Council approved an ordinance Monday asking that a local income tax be levied on county residents at a rate of 1 percent and withheld by employers, you might simply write, "County residents soon will have a little more money withheld from their paychecks. The change will result from County Council's approval Monday of a 1 percent local income tax."

One way to ensure that you will be able to adequately communicate the news from the government beat is to make sure you talk to a variety of people who are involved in government. Generally, that includes at least three groups of people: politicians, bureaucrats and citizens.

The Politicians

Reporters who cover government usually are responsible for covering politicians running for election. For some politicians, such as U.S. representatives, campaigning is almost a year-round job because they are up for re-election every two years. Elected officials generally want to talk, and they'll forgive many journalistic sins as long as reporters spell their names right.

The three roles of a journalist — as watchdog, as storyteller and as convener of communitywide conversations — all come into play in elections coverage.

A reporter must constantly check politicians' credentials and claims. Campaign finance reports can tell you where the politicians' money is coming from, and how it's being spent. Reporters regularly monitor campaign advertising for truthfulness in what might be called "truth squad" or "ad watch" projects. They point out ads that exaggerate opponents' statements or outright fibs on the candidates' record. Reporters do the same with candidates' resumés — as occurred when a candidate for county prosecutor in Indiana, for instance, stretched the truth by calling himself a "graduate of Harvard" when he'd attended only a seminar there.

Government reporters who cover campaigns also have an opportunity to tell stories about the people involved in the campaigns. Citizens want to know about the candidate as a person — what drives the candidate, what influences shaped the person, and how he or she got to this place in life. Great storytelling can bring out the human factors behind the platforms and policy speeches.

More than any other point, however, reporters should understand that a campaign is an opportunity for a community to discuss its most pressing problems. A reporter who can articulate those issues and make sure candidates address them is advancing an important discussion that needs to be held. This level of quality coverage requires more than listening to candidates and writing "stump" stories from the campaign trail. A reporter might press candidates for written responses to specific questions about those issues, so that the newspaper can run all candidates' responses side by side on a grid for comparison. A reporter also might attend community forums or devote extra time to listening to people in third places to find out how nonpoliticians are talking about key issues in the election (the words they use, which tend to be different than the words used by politicians; the stories they tell, which illustrate how those issues affect their lives; and the connections they make between those issues and others) as well as to identify any issues the candidates might not be addressing.

The Bureaucrats

The very word *bureaucrat* summons stereotypes of faceless automatons whose job is to give citizens the run-around with endless forms while projecting the attitude, "It's government's business to know and citizens' business not to find out." Sometimes the stereotype is accurate. For example, a coalition of seven newspapers in Indiana conducted an investigation in 1999 to determine the availability of public records in that state. That investigation showed that numerous government officials routinely refused to release public records, thereby violating laws permitting public access to those records. The newspapers also found that people who requested public records were threatened, harassed, lied to, questioned repeatedly and told to get court orders or subpoenas if they wanted to see the records. (That report prompted the creation of a new state office to ensure that these circumstances would change.) More and more, though, government bureaucracies are being forced to run like businesses with a "customer service" focus and an emphasis on efficiency.

Reporters also have to face the challenge that, unlike politicians, few bureaucrats like to have their names or pictures in the paper. If you misquote them, it could cost them their jobs, so they are understandably wary around new reporters. Treat them fairly and honorably and they or their staffs may become your best sources. Remember that many have been there for years, watching politicians come and go.

Of course, sometimes the bureaucrats are the bad guys. Tom Turcol of The Virginian-Pilot won a Pulitzer in 1985 for his series of stories on the spending habits of an industrial development director in a suburban community. The official, a regular source of off-the-record news tips to reporters, was convicted of using taxpayers' money to enhance his collection of antique whiskey bottles.

The Citizens

Most citizens don't care much about the internal politics of city offices or the political strategies of a legislator. They want to know if the schools are getting a big enough share of our tax dollars to educate their kids. They care about parks and potholes. They expect reporters to ferret out what went on in the secret meetings they heard about at the last PTA meeting they attended. Good journalists check with politicians and bureaucrats to find stories, but they know that the final — and most important — check is with the citizenry. Write what people care about and your stories will be read.

The biggest hurdle to overcome in covering public life is not finding stories. Journalists can think of a dozen story ideas in no time flat. The biggest challenge is figuring out which of the multitude of possible stories you should write. Governments hold numerous official meetings, press conferences and other media events. They also generate many, many press releases, reports and other written materials. Reporters must cull the wheat from the chaff.

A few tips follow.

• Choose what meetings and events to attend. Some editors expect reporters to attend every meeting of a public decision-making body. Others would rather that you pick and choose which meetings to attend, or be present for only part of the meeting — especially if the time of the meeting conflicts with another important event on your beat. Keep in mind that it sometimes can be more valuable to go to a nonofficial event like a festival or luncheon than to attend a meeting you could cover by making a few phone calls after the fact. Of course, you might be taking a risk that you will miss something — but it's sometimes a risk worth taking.

• Get hold of agendas as soon as they're available — and make sure you understand what's in them before you go to the meeting. Most groups prepare agendas at least several days in advance. By studying the agenda and talking to key players well before the meeting, you can get a sense of how important the meeting will be, how long, and what background research would be good to do before the meeting. Perhaps more importantly, you can determine if there's a story worth doing in advance of the meeting, giving the public an opportunity to act as citizens.

• Finally, always try the "outside-in" approach. Look for stories that start with a problem faced by citizens, and then ask what government is doing to help solve the problem. Get out of the newsroom — the best stories aren't there. The newsroom shouldn't be where you work; it should be the place where you pick up your paycheck. Then, get out of City Hall. The best stories usually don't start there either.

SPORTS: NUMBERS, CHARACTERS AND GREAT STORYTELLING

Not too long ago, sports writing was considered a simple, pleasant occupation in which reporters could see the game for free, then spend an hour or so after it writing a straightforward, play-by-play story about who won. All you needed to qualify for the job was ability to type, some basic knowledge about sports and a respectful appreciation for an accurate box score.

No more. Sports reporters today are aware that fans already know who won by the time they get their newspaper — because they watched the game on TV or heard the highlights on ESPN. So newspaper sports writers have learned to be more creative and to take fresh approaches to game coverage. In addition, more and more sports reporters have begun covering the "hard news" stories in sports — stories about undercover payments to all-stars or athletes accused of crimes or academic cheating.

In recent years, we as a society have become more willing to acknowledge that coaches and athletic heroes are real people who sometimes do bad things. Some sports figures seem to have made it a personal mission to shock or outrage us with their bad behavior or disregard for anyone but themselves.

In the past, hard-hitting stories about such matters usually were

Covering high-school sports is the mainstay of the majority of sports reporters' jobs. Only a few — and most of them at metropolitan newspapers — get to focus exclusively on college and professional sporting events.

Photo by Joshua Smith. Source: Palladium-Item

investigated and written by cops or courts reporters and printed on the news pages, enabling the sports writer to keep his treasured friendship with the coach and the team. But in many newspapers, that is changing. A sports reporter today might spend time checking public records or attending hearings about errant athletes who face charges that are far more serious than being off sides or committing a flagrant foul. And stories about athletes' bad behavior is much more likely to end up on the sports pages.

However, fear of losing a good working relationship with a coach or a player still keeps many newspapers from digging much below the surface in writing about famous people in sports. Unlike most politicians, who can take many a hit from a reporter without holding a grudge, people in sports tend to be somewhat sensitive and unforgiving. Make a blunder about a football coach and he may punish you for it for years. Write a basketball story that says a player's recent outings indicated his mind wasn't on the game and you could end up with a 7-foot giant looming over you in the dressing room after the next game, uttering a stream of profanities while shoving his index finger in your face.

Most athletic officials and players, from youth leagues to the colleges and pros, expect "their" sportswriters to back the team — and some do. Cover a big-time football game and the home team's writers utter many a heartfelt cheer in the press box. But if you aren't the cheering type, or you're writing some of those hard-hitting stories, some teams, players and fans will accuse you of being "against them" or otherwise malicious.

The best advice from veteran sports writers is to make it clear to coaches and players on the first day on the beat that you're a reporter, not a fan. Promise to be fair to everyone, to be accurate, and to check controversial stories with all those involved. They may not like you, but they'll respect you.

One thing you will discover, with pleasure, is that the higher you go in covering sports, the easier it gets. The usual entry-level job is covering high-school sports, where the lighting is bad, the crowded press box leaks, the programs are colorful but unreliable, soft drinks and sandwiches are across the field and everyone is counting on you to file the perfect box score.

Survivors who advance to a major college sports beat will be offered fried chicken, French fries, hamburgers and soft drinks in a cozy, roomy press box limited to your writing colleagues. A continuing stream of play-by-play printouts of the action is distributed so you don't have to keep statistics. Immediately after the game, box scores and written quotes from winners and losers are handed out.

You'll survive those tough early years and land a job in the big leagues, say the experts, by always remembering that you are writing for the reader, not the coach or the team.

OTHER BEATS

Public safety, education, government and sports are four core beats found in almost every newsroom. But many other beats are very common as well. Each has its own quirks and its own areas of expertise. Among the most common are business, environment, health care, religion, features and arts and entertainment.

Business. Reporters covering business depend heavily on relationships built with sources; little public information is available. The public information that is available — stock market totals and reports that publicly traded companies must file with the Securities and Exchange Commission, for instance — require reporters to become experts at interpreting them. Some newspapers have business reporters who specialize in as coverage of workplace issues, technology, unions, banking, real estate and the retail industry.

Environment. Environmental reporting involves some of the most technical expertise of any beat. Reporters who cover the environment also must draw on information from government, law, and private sector reporting. It's not enough to know the laws about asbestos, for instance; the environmental reporter must know why asbestos is so harmful, why and how it has been used in ways that no longer are allowed, what the trade-offs are for using it in permitted ways, where asbestos products are manufactured and who stands to gain from their continued use. Stories on the environment beat often deal with environmental groups' clashes with building interests, factories and high-yield farms.

Health care. The health care industry, including health insurers and health maintenance organizations (HMOs), has been a rich beat for years. Potential stories abound: personal health topics such as the latest fitness craze; medical science developments, including treatments for cancer or gene therapy and even cloning; federal and state legislation, from regulating doctors to universal health insurance and paying for Medicare and Medicaid; preventative health care measures; geriatric and pediatric specialties; child abuse as a health concern; the drug industry; and more. Like environmental reporting, health and medicine reporters must be able to decipher highly technical information. Doctors are notorious for communicating in ways understandable only by other doctors. Health care reporters frequently must evaluate research results. Important questions to ask about such studies are: Who paid for the study to be done? Why? Who benefits? What are the limitations or weaknesses of the study?

Religion. The importance of covering religion as a beat may seem questionable, but remember: Most of the great conflicts of the past 2,000 years have some roots in religion. Morality and religion, even in this "enlightened" age, continue to tear at the hearts and minds of families, communities and countries. Religion reporters can cover institutions such as local churches, the area Roman Catholic archdiocese, or the Southern Baptist Convention. Or they may approach the beat more thematically: How do people of faith deal with ticklish issues like abortion or gun control? How has the role of women changed in traditional churches? Where are church–state issues impinging on others' rights? In recent years, many newspapers have added religion reporters who sometimes write for entire sections devoted to the subject.

Features. Many newspapers have reporters with the rather generic title of "features reporter." This can mean practically anything, depending on the paper. In many cases, especially at smaller newspapers, features reporters are basically general assignment reporters who also might write weekly stories about arts or entertainment events, or about cooking, gardening or travel; however, at larger papers, reporters can work full-time covering any of these areas. Some features reporters also write personal columns. Most metropolitan newspapers and smaller papers have a standing features section that runs daily. Some also have other sections that usually run on Sundays and focus on any of the previously mentioned areas of specialization generally considered part of a newspaper's features department.

Arts and entertainment. Of all features beats, arts and entertainment are the most specialized. These beats vary dramatically from newspaper to newspaper, usually reflecting the priorities of the news organization and the community. Some papers may have writers devoted exclusively to covering classical music or art exhibits. Some may focus more on community theater or local entertainers, while larger newspapers have reporters who cover the film industry, television and/or nationally known performers. As with most beats, the depth and breadth of entertainment coverage depends on how many reporters are assigned by senior editors to cover these parts of public life, and how many pages the paper is willing to devote to such coverage. Reporters who cover entertainment and the arts must be experts at writing sharp profiles and news features. Their skills and abilities should include an eye for detail, an ear for new trends or genres, and a nose for quirky and off-beat stories.

EXERCISES

This is a four-part exercise.

1. Think about the city or neighborhood where you grew up, or the community where you now live. Spend a few minutes jotting down notes about what makes that place unique. What kinds of people live there, in terms of age, income, racial and ethnic heritage, marital/family status, etc.? What language(s) do they speak? Where do they live? What are their living conditions? What are their lives like? What do they eat? What do they wear? What do they do during the day? Where do they work? How do they get to work? What do they do during the evenings and on weekends? What do they do for fun? What's the area like during the middle of the night? What are the buildings like? What are the area's geological features (mountains, lakes, rivers, etc.)? What kinds of wildlife or domesticated animals live in the area? What kinds of plant life are prevalent?

2. Now make a second list. Think about events and issues you have heard people talk about. What past and present events stick out for people? What things are happening that could make people's lives better or worse? Are any governing bodies about to make any big decisions? What businesses or industries are important to people there? What do people say about things that are happening in the community? What kinds of public issues — things like education, traffic, racism — do they commonly discuss? What is the relationship, if any, between the events and issues that are important to people in the community?

3. Now think about how the local media cover that community. What stories usually are covered? Do the local media cover areas that are important to you and the people you know best? What stories do they usually cover? Make a list of 10 to 20 typical stories that might appear in a week's

worth of newspapers. What stories do they miss? Make a list of 10 to 20 "missed" stories you think would really interest people.

4. Using the techniques outlined in Chapter 4 and this chapter, list ways a reporter might build in routines in the way they cover a beat to make sure he or she is covering not just the obvious stories but also the kinds of stories you had on your "missed" list.

Further Reading

ON THE WEB

Education/Learning Coverage

CJR/Columbia Journalism Review: Article in the Expert Witness series, "Covering Education: What's Our Grade?" — an interview with educator Gene Maeroff by Ari L. Goldman, an assistant professor at Columbia's Graduate School of Journalism, about trends in covering education: http://cjr.org/year/00/3/maeroff.asp

Education Writers Association: www.ewa.org

Public Safety Beat Coverage

CJR/Columbia Journalism Review, "Should the Coverage Fit the Crime? A Texas TV Station Tries to Resist the Allure of Mayhem," by Joe Holley: http://cjr.org/year/96/3/coverage.asp

Cops and Courts Reporters: www.reporters.net/ccr/

Criminal Justice Journalists: www.reporters.net/cjj/

"Handcuffed Reporting: Is Crime Coverage Race-Based?" — transcript of a 1994 Freedom Forum panel discussion: www.freedomforum.org/Freedom Forum/resources/media_and_soc/race/handcuffed.html

"Reporting on Violence, a Handbook for Journalists," by Jane Stevens, Berkeley Media Studies Group, 1997: www.pcvp.org/pcvp/media

Government Coverage

Campaign Finance Information Center: www.campaignfinance.org/

Regional Reporters Association — an association of Washington, D.C., reporters who write for regional newspapers: www.rra.org

The Brechner Center for Freedom of Information — "Indiana Newspapers Win 1999 FOI Award," Nov. 15, 1999: www.jou.ufl.edu/brechner/news.htm

The Poynter Institute for Media Studies — campaign/election coverage resource file: www.poynter.org/Research/elect.htm

Sports Coverage

Association for Women in Sports Media: http://users.southeast.net/~awsm/

CJR/Columbia Journalism Review — cover story on sports journalism, January/February 2000 issue: http://cjr.org/year/00/1/index.asp

Business and Technology Coverage

Association of Area Business Publications: www.bizpubs.org

Computer Press Association: www.computerpress.org

Society of American Business Editors and Writers — publishes a newsletter called The Business Journalist: www.sabew.org/sabew

Health Care Beat Coverage

Association of Health Care Journalists: www.ahcj.umn.edu

Environment and Other Science-Related Beats

International Federation of Environmental Journalists: www.ifej.org

National Association of Science Writers: www.nasw.org

Society of Environmental Journalists: www.sej.org

Religion Coverage

Religion Newswriters Association: www.rna.org/home.html

Other Beat Coverage Resources

AJR/American Journalism Review, "Charity Beat: Newspapers Are Devoting More Attention to Covering Philanthropies," by Kent German, September 2000 issue: http://ajr.newslink.org/ajrkentsept00.html

Investigative Reporters and Editors' "The Beat Page": www.reporter.org/beat/

Knight Center for Specialized Journalism: Useful information for people covering a variety of beats: www.inform.umd.edu/EdRes/Colleges/JOUR/Knight

National Press Foundation — useful for a variety of beats: www.nationalpress.org

"Reader Friendly: Their Futures Uncertain, Newspapers Are Undergoing a Profound Change in the Way They Carry Out Their Missions," by Carl Sessions Stepp, July/August 2000 issue: http://ajr.newslink.org/ajrcarljul00.html

The Poynter Institute for Media Studies — tip sheets for many beats: www.poynter.org/dj/tips/index.htm

IN PRINT

Public Safety Beat Coverage

"Covering Campus Crime: A Handbook for Journalists," published by the Student Press Law Center, Arlington, Va., 1996.

"The Local News Handbook," published by the American Society of Newspaper Editors, Reston, Va., 1999. (For more information, see the listing under "Kiosk," then "Reports" at the ASNE Web site: www.asne.org)

Features Coverage

"The Complete Book of Feature Writing," edited by Leonard Witt, editor, published by Writer's Digest Books, Cincinnati, 1991.

Arts and Entertainment Coverage

"Reviewing for the Mass Media," by Todd Hunt, published by Chilton Book, Philadelphia, Pa., 1972 (out of print, but available in many libraries).

Religion Coverage

"Reporting News about Religion: An Introduction for Journalists," by Judith M. Buddenbaum, published by Iowa State University Press, aMes, Iowa, 1998.

Chapter 13

In-Depth Stories

Weekly newspaper editor Goodloe Sutton and his wife Jean received death threats when they reported on corruption in the Marengo County Sheriff's Department.

Source: Photo provided by Goodloe and Jane Sutton

When former Marengo County Sheriff Roger Davis and his sergeant Wilmer "Sonny" Breckenridge were arrested in 1997, the county's weekly newspaper covered it with more than the usual journalistic interest. For Goodloe Sutton and his wife Jane, the owners–editors of The Democrat-Reporter in Linden, Ala., the arrests confirmed a series of exposés they had written about Davis' financial improprieties and Breckenridge's involvement in drug dealing.

Davis had taken office in 1991 and immediately embarked on an aggressive campaign to rid the county of drugs and drug dealers. The Suttons published a story revealing that Davis used county money to buy a $3,000 all-terrain vehicle for his 16-year-old daughter during his first year in office. Later they reported that Davis was ordered by an auditor to repay county funds earmarked for undercover drug buys, and that he had asked a mental health center to make out "donation" checks to him personally whenever his deputies transported the center's patients, then cashed those checks at local markets. The Suttons also reported that Breckenridge had planted marijuana during a drug raid.

Their stories triggered an investigation that eventually revealed that Davis had offered a deal to a couple who owned a bail-bonding business: The sheriff would close down competing businesses in exchange for a share of the couple's profits. The investigation also showed that Breckenridge had offered a drug dealer protection from police interference in his drug operations in exchange for payment of a $1,000-a-month fee, that he sold confiscated drugs to the protected dealer, and that he and another deputy arranged to buy marijuana elsewhere to sell to the dealer.

The Suttons had persisted in their reporting in spite of scathing letters to the editor; angry, anonymous telephone calls; abandonment by their friends and neighbors; financial setbacks that resulted from advertisers pulling their ads; and even threats of violence against them and their sons.

In the end, Davis was convicted of federal charges of extortion, tax evasion and bribery, and Breckenridge of conspiracy to distribute illegal drugs and one count of possession. Circulation of The Democrat-Reporter has increased, and most of its advertisers have returned.

The investigative reporting conducted by the Suttons went beyond the basic information of daily events that forms the basis for the majority of news stories. They continued a tradition of "muckraking" that is more than a century old in journalism. The late publishing giant Joseph Pulitzer Jr. said a journalist should "never lack sympathy with the poor, always remain devoted to the public welfare, never be satisfied with merely printing news, always be drastically independent, never be afraid to attack wrong. ..." Davis and Breckenridge were arrested because the Suttons decided to dig beyond the official version of guilt and innocence and speak for those who could otherwise not speak.

Basic coverage of high-school events and commissioners meetings, of arrests by police and proclamations by politicians, may form the body of a daily newspaper, but in-depth reporting provides its soul. Journalists working on in-depth reports build upon the tools of daily reporting with solid interviewing skills, judgments as to where to get the right information and how to make sure the various stakeholders are represented. The reporting is usually more intense, involving more interviews or documents over a longer period of time. The work often involves the use of special reporting techniques, such as computer-assisted database searches, polling or facilitating community focus groups. The need for an eye for detail increases; the importance of protecting yourself against libelous statements grows. Everything is under a microscope — from the anticipated reactions of the public to the demands for excellence from editors.

In-depth stories vary greatly in both tenor and scope. The best approach for a given in-depth story is determined by the subject matter and the perspectives of the journalist. Coverage designed to more fully inform the public about important issues or news developments is commonly written as *explanatory journalism* and comprises sets of related stories that describe, for example, the impact and expected long-term consequences of a natural disaster or the details of a community's new comprehensive plan.

Stories of wrongdoing, usually by a public official or government agency, most often are approached as *investigative reports*. In the case above, the Suttons were tipped off to public records that proved that an elected official — a county sheriff — and his hand-picked deputy were misusing public funds and abusing their power for personal gain.

That same story, were it conceptualized from the tradition of *literary journalism* or *creative nonfiction*, could be written as an epic tale of deceit, corruption and, ultimately, justice being served. The writer would use literary writing techniques to draw the reader into the story, while illuminating universal truths about the human condition.

If the story were written as *civic journalism* or *public journalism,* the nature of the conversation within the community would take precedence. In the Marengo County story, civic journalism could begin where investigative reporting left off, with stories that address such questions as: Now that the corruption has been revealed, what can the county learn from it? How could this criminal behavior have happened? What's the best way to move toward ensuring such a deception never happens again? All four approaches use similar interviewing and research tools to different ends.

In-depth stories typically focus on the following categories:

- conflicts or controversies
- social problems
- health and public safety issues
- public policy issues
- unjust, unexpected or devastating events or situations
- changes, trends or events that have long-term, far-reaching effects
- wrongdoing by people in positions of public trust (public officials, business leaders, medical professionals, clergy, school teachers, journalists, etc.)
- historic or highly unusual, noteworthy events

Surely you've seen in-depth reports on domestic violence, illiteracy, drug or alcohol abuse, the AIDS epidemic, affirmative action, welfare reform, the long-term effects of natural disasters or corruption by elected officials. Sometimes such stories are reported and written by one person; sometimes several people work on the story. Such reports can be written either as one long story or broken up into several related stories. If broken into several stories, all may be published in an existing section of the newspaper or as a special section. They also may be published as a series of stories over the course of several days. Follow-up stories then may be written about any further activity or action that occurs after the report appears.

HALLMARKS OF IN-DEPTH STORIES

The main difference is in the reporting. Researching in-depth stories takes much more time and uses a wider variety of techniques than getting the facts for less complicated stories. Reporters must dig deeper to help people more thoroughly understand complex issues or to see troubling truths that were not previously apparent. Sometimes reporters must overcome others' efforts to hide these truths. Sometimes they must spend a lot of time and employ great skill and persistence in gathering and analyzing bits and pieces of scattered information that reveal the problem.

Although it is possible for a group of experienced reporters to create a credible in-depth report in a day's time, that is the exception. In most cases, the reporter (or reporters) doing in-depth stories spend weeks or months gathering substantial amounts of information using a variety of techniques.

It should be the goal of every reporter to employ as many lessons from in-depth reporting as possible on a daily basis. In Chapter 2 we described reporter Jack Cutter's attempts to generate a daily story on a person filing for elected office. Although he didn't have time to check out the candidate fully, he still managed to check with police for outstanding tickets or past arrests — a common technique used by investigative journalists. Cutter framed the announcement beyond the arena of winners and losers, asking instead what issues the candidate brought to the campaign debate — a technique employed by public journalists. He also had little opportunity to use description and other detail to enrich the writing in the story, but he knew that he could use the small details and personal reflections on the candidate gathered from his interviews in a later, more in-depth profile.

Some of the more specialized techniques of in-depth reporting include:

- Interviewing numerous people, usually for longer periods of time and sometimes repeatedly
- Conducting polls or surveys
- Analyzing the information found in stacks or databases of public records or other documents

Writing Deep Stories

Many beginning reporters can hardly wait to sink their teeth into meaningful, in-depth stories. But such stories usually are more difficult than they seem.

"You can't explain what you don't understand," says writing coach and Poynter Institute associate Don Fry.

Experienced journalists say that an understanding of the community is essential for reporters doing in-depth stories.

Chicago Tribune reporter Bill Gaines is one such journalist interviewed by James S. Ettema and Theodore L. Glasser for their book "Custodians of Conscience: Investigative Journalism and Public Virtue."

"Gaines worried that young reporters often lack the opportunity to develop a keen sense of the community and its values," Ettema and Glasser wrote.

Without that sense, Gaines said, as well as knowledge about how things work in that community, in-depth stories can miss the mark.

"You have to know how government is supposed to work before you can criticize it," he told Ettema and Glasser.

The following list, developed by Fry for a National Institute for Advanced Reporting Seminar in 1994, can help reporters avoid common mistakes in developing what Fry calls "deep" stories:

What makes a deep story succeed?

- Reporting deep enough for understanding
- Finding substantial characters to illustrate the story
- Finding narrative elements for explanation
- Interviewing to produce information and illuminating quotes
- Collecting visual materials to make the story graphic, and to make the graphics
- Organizing to promote understanding and to frame difficult materials
- Writing in clear and compelling ways
- Editing and laying out to enhance understanding
- Editors who demand, encourage, and reward depth

What makes an attempted deep story fail?

- Thinking that numbers are stories
- Reporting that seeks only facts and quotes
- Reporting that is too easily satisfied
- Focusing on things and abstractions rather than on people
- Interviewing that stops with easy-to-handle quotes
- Creating graphics from the words of the story
- Failure to organize for the readers
- Writing based on assumptions, and to suit the editors
- Copy editing and layout at the last minute
- Easily satisfied editors

- Acquiring and inputting data into computer programs for analysis
- Immersion in the day-to-day life of a group of people over a period of time
- Recording much more detail for use in stories, including dialogue and descriptions of the physical characteristics of people and places
- Gathering information and insights from people who form a representative cross-section of the citizenry

- Researching not just public problems or issues but also a wide range of proposed and possible solutions to those challenges

These techniques have grown out of the four approaches to in-depth reporting already noted: explanatory journalism, investigative reporting, literary journalism/creative nonfiction and public or civic journalism. All four spring from a commitment to the public service function of journalism, and each can be applied to almost any story but is especially suited for certain kinds of stories, as you will see. Please be aware that this chapter is designed only to introduce you to these approaches, each of which can draw on reporting and writing techniques that are quite complex. Entire books have been written about each approach, and those books are listed in the "Further Reading" section at the end of this chapter.

EXPLANATORY REPORTING

Explanatory in-depth stories are basically informative articles that go deeper and wider than a typical newspaper story. They embody an exhaustive compilation of known facts related to a significant news development or ongoing public affairs issue. Such stories involve extensive interviewing and research that draws from readily available published materials, including poll and survey results. These stories usually appear as two or more interrelated articles, accompanied by the types of elements described in Chapter 9.

Explanatory in-depth stories might provide useful information and perspective in the wake of a factory closing, for example, or take an in-depth look at the challenges faced by women who survive breast cancer. Stories might focus on a beloved local figure who is, for some reason, in the news or part of a news development, such as a natural disaster or a proposal for a new public building that has had or will have widespread impact.

Three examples of explanatory in-depth story packages are described in the following paragraphs.

- The New York Times series "How Race Is Lived in America" presented three-dimensional portraits primarily of blacks and whites whose lives were affected daily by issues of race (some stories included Hispanics). A team of reporters began working on the series in April 1999. It ran during a six-week period in June and July, 2000, as a series of 14 stories, some more than 7,000 words long — many times the usual length of a news story. Articles included a story about a black entrepreneur and his white friend and former business partner, a story about racial prejudice among employees of a slaughterhouse, and a profile of a man with a white mother and black father who described his experiences living in a segregated society. The stories were accompanied by numerous photos and graphics.

- The Palm Springs, Calif., Desert Sun spent four months gathering information for a special report on athletes and eating disorders. That effort culminated in a package of six stories: a Page One story about the overall problem, plus articles on pages inside the Local section that covered opinions from coaches, trainers and athletes about the problem and its severity; a profile of a high-school wrestler who developed an eating problem; practical advice for coaches, parents and friends who want to help athletes avoid eating problems; and warning signs and complications of anorexia, bulimia and compulsive overeating.

- The Chicago Tribune ran six related stories about film critic Gene Siskel in the paper's "Tempo" section immediately after his death. The cover story focused on Siskel's influence as a critic and ran with a recent portrait. Columnist Bob Greene and Tribune movie critic Michael Wilmington wrote reminiscences about Siskel, who had started at the paper as a young reporter the same year Greene had. Wilmington's story ran with a photo of Siskel talking to movie star Jack Nicholson. Television columnist Steve Johnson wrote a story about what would happen to the popular television show "Siskel & Ebert," which ran with a photo of Siskel and co-star Roger Ebert sitting together in a theater. And Owen Youngman, director of Tribune Interactive Media, wrote about how Siskel had become a movie critic. Also included was a list of Siskel's top five movie picks for the past 30 years, illustrated with photos from many those movies.

The hallmarks of explanatory reporting are extensive interviewing, compilation of information from other readily available sources, and the synthesis of all that material into a cohesive, well-organized story or set of stories that gives readers a greater sense of "the big picture." Although explanatory reporting and writing techniques are used in the other three forms of in-depth reporting, pure explanatory journalism doesn't seek to dig out information in the same way that investigative and civic journalism do, nor is it usually written as artfully as literary journalism. It relies on readily available, known facts gathered from numerous sources.

The Wall Street Journal is well known among journalists for its daily in-depth reports about a variety of topics. Stories written in what many journalists call "the Wall Street Journal model" might fo-

Anecdotal/
storytelling
lead

Nut graph ties
anecdote or story
to current issue

Supporting quotes,
facts, anecdotes

Explanations,
opinions, other
contextual
information

Ending brings
story full circle;
can bring back
subjects of
opening graph,
describe next
step(s), etc.

The Wall Street Journal pioneered a type of story journalists often call "the Wall Street Journal model." This figure illustrates how such stories typically are organized.

cus on such issues as the marketing and distribution practices that have caused a shortage of flu vaccine, how brokers kidnap young Vietnamese women and sell them as brides in China, or how a battle between two competing medical products companies caused the cancellation of trials of an experimental treatment that appeared to have great promise in saving children with terminal leukemia. Each such story has an anecdotal lead that focuses on one person whose story serves to put a human face on the problem described in the article. This lead is followed by a nut graph that ties that person's experiences into the broader issues raised in the article, then it goes into additional detail in chapter-like segments about various aspects of the issue. These segments might be organized around issues or written in a chronological fashion.

Here, for example, is the beginning of the story about the China bride trade, which appeared Aug. 3, 1999.

———————————— Double Crossing ————————————

They Don't Say "I Do," These Kidnap Victims Taken from Vietnam

One Woman's Ordeal Shows How Brokers
in China Deal With Bride Shortage

THE NGS HAVE MIXED FEELINGS

By Samantha Marshall
Staff Reporter of The Wall Street Journal

HANOI, Vietnam — Jobless and destitute, Nguyen Thi Hoan felt her luck was about to change. She had just arrived here one sultry June morning two years ago, and almost at once a kindly woman offered her a job in a candy factory.

It was a trap. Within hours, Miss Hoan was spirited across the Vietnam-China border at Lang Son, 100 miles away, by one of the gangs that kidnap young women and sell them to be brides in China.

For several days, the 22-year-old was trucked and traded around southern China, changing hands four times before finally meeting the man who

would be her husband. "I am writing while wiping away tears," she told her family in a letter she mailed secretly. "Please come here and save me."

Bride-buying, a Chinese tradition that the Communists largely stamped out, has seen a resurgence with the country's surging economy. Starting in the 1980s, "women were taken from poor areas, and sold to some areas that had recently gotten richer," says Ding Lu of the All-China Women's Federation, a Chinese nongovernmental organization. In the 1990s, another factor contributed to the bride shortage. Chinese statistics often are unreliable, but Chinese demographers agree that more women than men have abandoned Chinese villages for big-city jobs, leaving the countryside brimming with bachelors.

The story goes on to quote a demographer at a Hong Kong university who explains that the shortage of women is likely to get worse, adds more facts from Ding Lu about the number and origins of kidnapped brides, then quotes a Vietnamese official who adds that only the pretty women are sold as brides. "The ugly ones go to brothels," the official says. Then the story breaks into segments that describe in more detail the compelling story of Hoan's kidnapping, attempted escape, her brother's eventually successful efforts to rescue her, and the shame that prevented her from returning to her family.

The reporting techniques used for this type of story are no different from those used for even the most basic, informative story, with the exception that the reporter must identify and interview at length one person whose experience typifies or symbolizes the subject of the story.

The Wall Street Journal model is longer than the usual newspaper story. In many newspapers, the story above might be divided into two or three articles. One way to divide it would be to keep the anecdotal lead and comments about the bride trade together as one "overview" story, then make the story of Hoan's kidnapping and eventual rescue another story. A third story might focus on the shame she experienced upon her return, with additional comments from experts about the cultural conditions that would cause her to feel that way.

Stories typically are divided in the following ways.

• *Overview or summary story.* This states the focus of the story package and lists the central events, issues, people or other elements of the package. For example, in a package of stories about a proposal to build a new sports stadium, the overview usually would lay out the proposal along with the expected advantages and disadvantages to the community. In stories about a natural disaster, the overview would focus on the overall impact of the storm, tornado, flood, hurricane, earthquake or other calamity.

• *Detail and context stories.* These provide more detail and context about events, issues, people or other elements that are especially significant. To continue the two examples in the item above: The stadium package might include a story about other cities that have built new stadiums, a description of the current stadium's good and bad points and a story about the people or group behind the stadium proposal. The disaster package might give a step-by-step account of how the disaster unfolded, a description of what happened in an area that was particularly hard hit, and a look at the volunteers who came to help. Detail and context stories also include profiles of key people, comparisons of how political candidates stand on policy issues, and excerpts from key documents or transcripts.

• *History.* This story focuses on past developments that have a connection to what's happening now. It usually includes quotes from longtime community members or historians and sometimes is accompanied by a timeline. The stadium package might include a story about when the current stadium was built and/or renovated, how it got its name, and key people in its history. The disaster package might include a description of similar past disasters in the area, region or country, and whether steps had been taken in response to those disasters to reduce the risk or impact of future occurrences.

• *Future story.* This story focuses on what's expected or likely to happen. In the stadium package, this story might lay out the expected timetable for decisions related to the proposal, which in most cases would have to be approved by various city agencies as well as by voters. In the disaster package, this story might state whether additional relief is expected, including financial relief for people whose homes, businesses and crops were damaged.

• *"What you can do" stories*. These stories give readers a way of getting involved, either by volunteering their time or by contributing money or needed goods. They usually are written in list form. Readers interested in the stadium issue might be told which officials to contact to express their views about the proposal or when public hearings will be held to air those views; they might also be given an address to send contributions, either for construction of the stadium or for organizations working for or against the stadium. Readers who want to do something in response to the disaster might be told where to take blankets or canned food for distribution to disaster victims; where to send money; where to go to spend a few hours, a day or several days helping; and/or how organizations they're part of can get involved in relief efforts.

Again, the techniques used in explanatory reporting and writing are no different from those used in writing basic, informative stories — the reporter just does more interviews, gathers more information and works on the stories over a longer period of time.

For most reporters, explanatory reporting is the first approach they take when they are ready to begin tackling in-depth stories. It's easy to get lost in such stories because the tendency is always to go ever deeper and wider. The best advice is to start small. If you want to write a story about domestic violence, for instance, start by writing an overview, one detail story about a family affected by domestic violence, and a "what you can do" story about how to get help if you are being abused.

Beware of common pitfalls: losing your focus, extreme overreporting and underreporting.

Losing your focus. Be careful not to let your story get "too big." If you're writing about deteriorating housing conditions in your community, don't stray off into tangents about the shortage of good workers in the construction industry or the proliferation of do-it-yourself home repair stores over the past 10 years. One sign of a story that has gotten "too big" is when you start to think in terms of numerous "related" stories over several days. In such cases, take time out to refocus and make a list of ideas for future stories that have come out of your reporting. In the housing conditions story, for example, set aside for later stories the information about the construction worker shortage and do-it-yourself stores. As you refocus, keep the following in mind: In either one-day packages or series that run over several days, the stories, photos and graphics must work together to constitute one comprehensive report, not a smattering of loosely related items. Just as the overall story has a beginning, middle and end, each day's installment in a series must advance the issue. A series in The Virginian-Pilot on the prison building boom, for instance, began the first day with an overview of the problem. On the second and third days the series detailed specific hot spots (the increase in population of nonviolent drug users, the disparity in race, the increasing numbers of geriatric prisoners) and ended on the fourth day with legislators' responses to the problem and possible prescriptions for solutions. Decisions on when to run which stories should never be made solely on the basis of what will fit into the space available in the paper from one day to the next.

Extreme overreporting. For nearly every story you write, you will gather more information than you actually use. However, don't talk to so many people that you have seven or eight times more information and quotable material than you need. Overreporting is usually a function of a loss of focus. Be aware that, in reporting about complex issues, you will see many, many connections and overlaps between and among related issues. If you were to keep expanding your story to include all of those related issues, you eventually would find yourself wondering how you're ever going to explain all of humanity's triumphs and struggles in a single package of stories.

Underreporting. At the other extreme, if you don't talk to enough people and gather enough detail, your story might come off as overly simplistic, unfair or confusing. If you're not sure the story is "there" yet, ask other reporters or your editor to look it over and give you feedback. If people in your story relate to you the words, actions or motives of others, make every effort to confirm those statements or get a response to them. Make sure there are no "holes," or missing information, in your story.

A word of caution about polls and surveys. In many in-depth stories, reporters quote from surveys, polls or various kinds of studies. Sometimes the newspaper does this research itself, but more commonly it is done by professional polling organizations or nonprofit groups which then publicly release the results.

No matter where the data comes from, it's important to evaluate it critically. In-house surveys and polls are best done by trained researchers who know how to conduct a poll in such a way that the results are reliable. Few reporters and editors have such specialized training and therefore should avoid doing slipshod research that lays the paper open to criticism for using faulty research methods. Research data from outside organizations should be considered just as critically. Independent polling organizations such as The Gallup Poll, Public Agenda and the Pew Research Center for the People and

Twelve Steps to Un-"hole"-y Reporting

Techniques to make sure your story is complete:

- Overreport, to a degree. Gather more information than you need, but remember that you won't use it all.
- Don't be afraid to call people back if you discover a hole while you're writing.
- Have a list of questions going into a story, and make sure you answer them.
- Make a general checklist if you're prone to holes; check it over before you write and before you turn in your story.
- Ask yourself whether there's another side to the issue. Make sure you talk to that side.
- Self-impose a multi-source rule. Don't ever write a one-source story (except a speech or something similar).
- Make sure you ask lots of follow-up questions in an interview, so that the speaker adequately explains and develops his or her points.
- Make sure you talk to officials *after* the meeting and ask them to explain the points they made during the meeting.
- Never write a story you don't understand. Call somebody back.
- It is all right to ask a dumb question — better that than writing a dumb story.
- Don't "write around" a hole, hoping the editors won't notice. They might not — and then your holy story will wind up in print. If you've got a hole and can't fill it, ask your editor for help. Sometimes you may have to write around it, but at least it's a mutual decision.
- It's OK to report that the information was not available. (For example: "The committee's report didn't list reasons and the chairman couldn't be reached for comment.") It shows you tried to get the information.

Source: Kent State University journalism professor and former newspaper editor Carl Schierhorn

the Press are considered reliable sources of polling data, as are polling arms of media organizations such as television networks and major newspapers.

Many surveys, polls and studies presented as nonpartisan and unbiased are released by special interest organizations that have a vested interest in furthering their cause. Although much of this research is reliable, some is not. Be sure you evaluate whether the research methods were sound. You also should do a background check on the sponsoring organization: Who funds it? Who belongs to it? What is its agenda? Then weigh the reliability of the research methods and the sponsoring organization when evaluating the credibility of the research data. Always include information about whether the research was done in a scientific or nonscientific manner and the name and brief description of the organization(s) that funded and carried out the research.

In addition, always remember that poll results are not absolute, unchanging truths but only "snapshots" of public opinion at the time the polls are conducted. The significance of poll numbers should not be overdramatized. "Polls are valuable but only if they're used in context," Barbara Cochran, president of the Radio and Television News Directors Association, said at the January 2000 conference on "Media Coverage of Polls and Primaries" sponsored by the Freedom Forum, the National Council on Public Polls and the American Association for Public Opinion Research.

Journalists should be more skeptical about numbers and be wary of interpreting poll results as being more precise than they are, Kathy Frankovic, director of surveys for CBS News, said at the conference. She also urged journalists to look over the questions that were asked in the poll and think about what kind of response they personally might make before reaching hasty conclusions about the meaning of the poll results.

INVESTIGATIVE REPORTING

In 1976, Arizona Republic reporter Don Bolles went to a hotel to meet a source promising information about land fraud. The source didn't show, but a bomb planted in Bolles' car exploded as he left. He lingered for days before dying.

In response, a fledgling journalism organization, Investigative Reporters and Editors, descended on Arizona with 38 journalists from 28 news organizations. The group produced a 23-part series demonstrating the depth of corruption, land fraud and links to organized crime in the state. The organization, which was criticized at the time for crusading, set out not to find Bolles' killer but to show organized crime leaders that killing a journalist would not stop the reporting. In fact, it only increased the scrutiny.

What became known as the Arizona Project demonstrates the heart of investigative journalism, for which the motto might be that of former Virginian-Pilot editor Ron Speer: "Good deeds are rarely done in the dark." The investigative journalist's goal is to ferret out information that otherwise would remain hidden. It is especially appropriate for stories involving neglect or wrongdoing on the part of people in positions of public trust. But investigative journalism can go well beyond simply "catching the bad guys." Its purpose also is to explain or expand public understanding of a relatively well-recognized public problem. The rationale behind this kind of reporting is that the reporter's job is to provide information about the problem, and it's the public's job to decide whether or how to act on it.

Perhaps the most famous example of investigative journalism began as a simple daily story. Washington Post reporter Alfred E.

Lewis was writing a story on deadline about an early-morning break-in at the Democratic National Committee offices in the Watergate Hotel. Two relatively inexperienced reporters — Bob Woodward and Carl Bernstein — were listed at the end of the story as two of the eight staff writers who helped gather information for that story. Two days later, Woodward and Bernstein shared a byline on a follow-up story that identified one of the burglars as a Republican security aide. Through tenacious digging, they established that the break-in was part of a widespread campaign of political spying linked to then-President Richard Nixon's reelection effort and that Nixon tried to cover up the details surrounding the break-in. Their coverage prompted an investigation that resulted in impeachment proceedings against Nixon, who resigned Aug. 8, 1974.

It was during the Watergate years that the name investigative reporting came to be used to describe this kind of journalism, but it was hardly a new kind of reporting — which critics of investigative reporting were quick to point out when that name was coined during the 1970s. Decades earlier, a group of American writers who today would be called investigative journalists were branded as muckrakers after Theodore Roosevelt in 1906 pejoratively compared them to "the Man with the Muckrake ... who could look no way but downward" in John Bunyan's "Pilgrim's Progress." At the time, the United States was becoming rapidly industrialized, and journalists Lincoln Steffens, Ida M. Tarbell, Edwin Markham and Charles Edward Russell wrote well-researched accounts of corruption and social hardship caused by big business. Although the muckraking movement faded out between 1910 and 1912, many of its values and traditions persisted in journalism.

Some critics also claimed that investigative reporting embodied a kind of crusading and advocacy that put it at odds with the American journalistic value of objectivity. "The essential energy of investigative reporting is still best characterized as 'righteous indignation,' a term coined by Ida Tarbell a century ago as the anthem of the muckrakers," James S. Ettema and Theodore L. Glasser wrote in their book "Custodians of Conscience: Investigative Journalism and Public Virtue." "But this unmistakable tone of moral engagement stands in apparent opposition to the presumed objectivity of news." Most journalists reconcile this apparent conflict by judging whether the news value of information uncovered through investigation violates the values or moral standards commonly held by people in the community they serve, Ettema and Glasser found.

Despite such criticisms, the investigative approach to in-depth reporting has become a well-respected specialization among journalists. Some newspapers have "investigative reporter" positions that

THE WHITE HOUSE
WASHINGTON

August 9, 1974

Dear Mr. Secretary:

I hereby resign the Office of President of the
United States.

Sincerely,

Richard Nixon

11.35 AM

HK

The Honorable Henry A. Kissinger
The Secretary of State
Washington, D.C. 20520

*Republican President Richard Nixon resigned after
Washington Post reporters Bob Woodward and Carl
Bernstein exposed his involvement in the cover-up of a
break-in at the Democratic National Committee
Headquarters in the Watergate Hotel.*

Source: National Archives

are considered plum assignments for experienced journalists. Others select beat reporters to concentrate on investigative stories, freeing them from writing smaller, episodic stories on the beat.

Like Woodward and Bernstein, reporters taking an investigative approach seek to bring to light, through original research, things people don't know yet. These reporters often have to dig deep for information that a number of people would rather not see published. They may spend hours, days or weeks poring over public records and other documents. They may receive information anonymously or from people who are willing to be interviewed but do not want to be named in the story because they fear they could suffer consequences. The reporters then must find ways of unearthing or verifying that information through other sources they can quote. Sometimes they can find public records that serve as verification; sometimes they find people who are willing to take the risk of being quoted.

The Rules for Confidentiality

As a reporter, you will inevitably encounter someone who is willing to provide information — so long as you keep either the information or the person's identity confidential.

The need for confidentiality differs from most interviews, which are presumed to be "on the record." That means the reporter can use the information and quotes the person provides, and name him or her.

People who want confidentiality usually want to do one of the following three things:

• Talk "on the record" on the condition that you neither name them nor give sufficient information for them to be identified. In such cases, it's common to use a fictional first name in describing the person's involvement in the highly stigmatized situation (such as rape, alcoholism or domestic abuse, or in illegal activity for which they wish to avoid prosecution).

• Talk "off the record," which means you can neither use the information nor reveal its source. Technically, you should not even mention the information to anyone else. However, such information can clue you into angles you might be able confirm by witnessing something, conducting a document search or interviewing other sources.

• Provide background or "deep background" information you can use without attributing it to them by name.

Accepting information under any of these conditions always involves risks — both for you and the person you're interviewing.

If you use incriminating information without naming its source, you run the risk that prosecutors or defense attorneys will issue subpoenas to try to get you into court to reveal where you got the information. You then may have to choose between revealing your source or going to jail on contempt of court charges if you protect the person's identity.

In 1972, the U.S. Supreme Court ruled in the case of Branzburg v. Hayes that reporters can be compelled to testify only if (1) they clearly have information about specific violations, (2) the information cannot be obtained in other ways, and (3) the public has an overriding interest in the information. This ruling limits how often reporters can be called into court. However, it doesn't stop a lawyer from issuing a subpoena your newspaper then has to pay its lawyers to fight. That is one of the biggest reasons most newspapers either have policies against using unnamed sources or strict procedures for approving their use.

In addition, the courts consider a promise of confidentiality to be a binding contract. In the 1991 court case of Cohen v. Cowles Media, the U.S. Supreme Court ruled that journalists who break promises of confidentiality can be sued for damages.

Los Angeles Times media critic David Shaw uses a simple technique in dealing with people who request confidentiality.

"If a source asks to go off the record, I try briefly to keep him on the record," Shaw wrote in the Spring/Summer 1998 issue of Media Studies Journal. "If he resists, I relent — 'on one condition,' I always say: 'When I've actually written my story, I want to call you and read your quotes to you and try to persuade you to go on the record. It will be your decision. But I want you to agree to at least take my call and consider my arguments.' In 15 years, I've never had a source refuse that deal. And in 15 years, I've only had one source reject my subsequent argument and insist on anonymity. In that case, I threw out the quote rather than use it anonymously."

Sticky situations sometimes develop

(cont.)

when news sources decide after the fact that they want to take something off the record. Technically, you have a right to use the information if the person was speaking on the record when they said it. However, in deciding whether to honor their request, it is always wise to consider things like how important the information is to the story, whether the person was aware of the rules about on- and off-the-record information, and whether you need to maintain an ongoing reporter–source relationship with the person. Be sure to explain the rules about off-the-record information so that this problem doesn't come up again with you or any other reporter.

Occasionally, news organizations decide to print information from unnamed sources, as The Washington Post did with the source still known only by the code name "Deep Throat" in the Watergate story. In most cases, such sources are described with phrases like "a source close to the investigation" or "a company employee

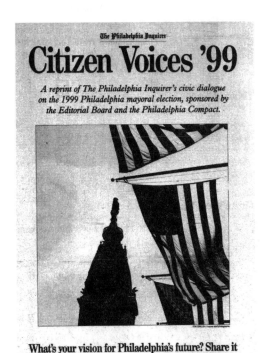

The Philadelphia Inquirer used public journalism techniques to create a civic dialogue on the 1999 mayoral election in that city. Instead of focusing solely on the candidates and their positions on issues, the paper drew out the voices of citizens as a way of enlarging the conversation beyond the topic of who should get the job as mayor.

Source: The Philadelphia Inquirer

who asked not to be identified." This is usually done only after all other options have been exhausted and after consultation with the newspaper's attorney, because using unnamed sources can lead to legal complications such as reporters being placed in the position of having to go to jail rather than reveal the identity of their sources.

The use of unnamed sources raises other issues. In recent years, a number of journalists' supposedly anonymous sources have turned out to be fictional. The most famous such source was the nonexistent 8-year-old heroin addict in a Washington Post story titled "Jimmy's World," for which reporter Janet Cooke won the Pulitzer Prize in 1981. She returned the prize after admitting the story was fiction. More recently, Boston Globe columnists Mike Barnicle and Patricia Smith, and Arizona Republic columnist Julie Amparano were fired on grounds that they included fictional information in their articles. Such cases, which were cited in the ASNE newspaper credibility study described in Chapter 3, have increased the public's skepticism about the legitimacy of unnamed sources. The study found that most citizens (77 percent) are concerned by the media's use of unnamed sources; 45 percent would rather the media not run a story in which no one is willing to go "on the record," and to 28 percent said they would rather the story run with unnamed sources than not run at all. As a result, newspapers have become more reluctant to use sources who don't want their identities known.

Although people are important to an investigative journalist's story, the most valuable source in many investigative reports is the "paper trail" — documents that can prove the reporter's case. Which trail you take depends on the subject being investigated (and in our digital age the trail may take you through electronic records as well). Following are examples from "The Reporter's Handbook: An Investigator's Guide to Documents and Techniques," edited by Steve Weinberg and Investigative Reporters and Editors (IRE), a professional association for investigative reporters.

• Want to know where your charity donations are going? Some charities have been found to be grossly inefficient or even corrupt. The Orlando Sentinel found that a fund-raising organization for a local children's hospital made an $81,000 profit, but none of it actually went to the hospital. Not-for-profit organizations don't pay federal taxes, but they still have to file statements with the IRS. These are known as Form 990s. Any not-for-profit — a church, the cancer society, the local community hospital — must file these annually as long as they bring in at least $25,000 a year.

• If you're wondering how specific businesses spend their money or what CEOs are paid these days, you can check reports that corporations are required to file with the Securities Exchange Commission: unaudited quarterly financial reports (10-Q), audited annual financial reports (10-K), reports pertaining to ownership and stock sales (13-D, 8-K and S-1), and proxy statements, which are annual reports sent to shareholders.

• Universities are huge cash machines. Follow the dollars and you might find stories, especially during times of a budget crunch or tuition increase. Where is the money going? Is more money going into athletics than classrooms? Most budget documents are public. Even foreign gifts to universities must be reported to the Education Department as part of legislation to track foreign influence.

• Find out if the local police department is accredited under the Law Enforcement Accreditation Association, which describes standards for police procedures. If the department is not accredited, find out why.

• Congress and legislators in many states are required to file financial disclosure forms annually. The forms can point reporters to potential conflicts of interest or interesting trends. For instance, at one point, a third of the U.S. House Agriculture Committee members owned farms.

Access to information varies from state to state, because each has its own access laws, which also regulates when government meetings are open to the public. Local, state and federal documents often are requested under what is known as the Freedom of Information Act. At the federal level, the act was first approved by Congress in 1966. The act, as Weinberg says, "places the burden on agencies to show why information could be withheld; requires them to publish in the Federal Register procedures for filing FOIA requests; instructs them to maintain reading rooms with indexes for locating information; tells them to establish uniform, reasonable fees for locating and duplicating records; sets time limits for responding to requests, appeals and lawsuits; and allows recovery of court costs by a prevailing requester."

The quest for documents to hold governments accountable and to make these news stories more authoritative has been augmented by the power of the personal computer and has led to a subspecialty known as "computer-assisted reporting."

LITERARY JOURNALISM (CREATIVE NONFICTION)

British journalist Nicholas Tomalin was a well-respected "hard news" reporter who arranged to go on a helicopter mission in which an

American general and two machine-gunners shot and gas-bombed Viet Cong during the Vietnam War. His story about the experience started like this:

After a light lunch last Wednesday, General James F. Hollingsworth, of Big Red One, took off in his personal helicopter and killed more Vietnamese than all the troops he commanded.

The story of the General's feat begins in the divisional office, at Ki-Na, twenty miles north of Saigon, where a Medical Corps colonel is telling me that when they collect enemy casualties they find themselves with more than four injured civilians for every wounded Viet Cong — unavoidable in this kind of war.

The General strides in, pins two medals for outstanding gallantry to the chest of one of the colonel's combat doctors. Then he strides off again to his helicopter, and spreads out a polythene-covered map to explain our afternoon's trip.

It's hardly your run-of-the-mill inverted pyramid. Instead, Tomalin uses a narrative writing style that most journalists call "literary journalism" and many other writers call "creative nonfiction." Stories written using this approach tend to be intimate accounts of people as they live their day-to-day lives. The significance of such stories is embedded in vivid descriptions of universal human characteristics and experiences that range from inspiring to perplexing to disturbing.

The rest of Tomalin's story, for example, paints a troubling portrait of a general who gleefully guns down people, dismissing any concerns about whether some of them might be civilians. Other well-known works of literary journalism describe such events as the lives of America's early astronauts and how a new type of computer was invented.

Tomalin wrote his story in a single day for the Sunday Times, a weekly newspaper. Many daily newspapers run stories written with a literary approach. Often they take the form of personal columns; sometimes they are single news articles; and sometimes they are part of a larger package of stories.

The St. Petersburg Times, for example, ran a series of compelling stories titled "Three Little Words," by Roy Peter Clark. The stories were written in serial form and appeared in daily installments over the course of 29 days. They described how a Florida woman coped with her husband's death after hearing him utter three little words very different from what most people would assume from the serial's title. His three words: "I have AIDS." Clark describes, with great detail and emotion, how Jane Morse dealt with the feelings of betrayal that came from her husband, Mick, telling her he got AIDS from having sex outside their 21-year marriage, his refusal to reveal anything more about how he got the disease, his insistence that his illness be kept secret from their three children — David, Meghan and Erin — for two years, the pain of watching him gradually succumb to the disease, and the challenge of building a new life for herself after his death.

Here's an excerpt:

They sat around the family room. Jane and Meghan were on the couch. David sat on a chair with his guitar. Little Erin, now 12, sat on the floor, playing solitaire. Mick sat on a footstool apart from the others.

"There's something I need to tell you," said Mick.

"You guys are getting a divorce, right?" said Meghan.

Mick's voice started to break with emotion. "I've got AIDS." And then, "I am sorry." Tears came to his eyes. It was the first time Jane had ever seen him cry.

David knew the secret, but hearing it from his Dad was different. His first instinct was to take his guitar, that instrument of the musical gift he had inherited from his father, and bash it against the wall.

In his mind everything moved in slow motion, the words of his father stretched out so slowly: that — he — would — die — from — AIDS because he had never heard of anyone who didn't die from it, that he would continue to work for as long as he could, that he would do whatever he could for them.

Then David saw something that snapped him out of his trance. Erin, his little sister, sitting on the floor, looking down, stone cold, silent as a Morse. Then a single teardrop fell from her eye and splattered down upon the Ace of Spades.

These stories illustrate the two basic approaches to literary journalism: writing about things the writer has experienced and recorded in great detail, and writing about things the writer has researched extensively, gathering such detailed information that the writer can depict things as accurately as if he or she had been there.

The techniques of literary journalism have been used for centuries. Among the many writers whose works are now regarded as classics, and who have written nonfiction works with literary flair are Charles Dickens, Walt Whitman, Jack London, George Orwell, Norman Mailer, Ernest Hemingway, John Steinbeck and John Hersey. During the 1970s this approach to journalism was heralded as "New Journalism" in a book by the same name edited by Tom Wolfe. Since then, authors who have written in this genre have included Hunter S. Thompson, Truman Capote, James Agee, Rebecca West, Jimmy

Breslin, Joan Didion, John McPhee, Sara Davidson, Rex Reed, George Plimpton and Tracy Kidder.

As with investigative reporting, critics have said that literary journalism was really nothing new, and they have decried its lack of objectivity, especially in stories that use personal points of view — be it the writer's or the subject's. But literary journalists counter that accusation: "There is no such thing as objective reportage," John Hersey wrote. "Human life is far too trembling-swift to be reported in whole: the moment the recorder chooses nine facts out of ten he colors the information with his views." Tom Wolfe took it one step further, suggesting that literary journalism was so thorough and accurate that it offered the reader "more of the truth than he is likely to get any other way."

Just as with investigative journalism, criticism has not prevented most newspapers from embracing literary journalism. And, though many newsrooms encourage writers to take creative approaches to writing news stories whenever possible and appropriate, literary journalism in the true sense is more than a writing style. Extensive reporting, greater use of personal voice (interpretive reporting), use of literary writing techniques and storytelling by building scenes are the hallmarks of literary journalism.

Extensive reporting. This includes careful recording of dialogue and what writer Tom Wolfe called "social autopsy," or recording the most minute details about someone (their gestures, vocal inflections, facial expressions and details of their life such as day-to-day activities, surroundings, and relationships). The writer may seek either to become saturated with information or to be immersed in a given situation over a long period of time.

Use of personal voice, or interpretative reporting. Literary journalism goes beyond the facts to draw from readers an emotional reaction similar to that of the writer. Nicholas Tomalin, for instance, wrote in the first person in his story about General Hollingsworth.

Use of literary writing techniques. This form of journalism makes conscious use of literary techniques to create an element of drama or storytelling. Such techniques include realism, irony, rhythm, foreshadowing, characterization, plot, dialect, dialogue, mood, description, imagery, metaphor, satire and interior monologues or stream-of-consciousness. Although these techniques are used, to a certain extent, in many news stories, they are employed to a much greater degree in literary journalism.

Storytelling by building scenes. Writers of literary journalism use of the technique of realism, including scene-by-scene construction, actual or realistic dialogue, a subjective point of view (usually the point of view of another person but sometimes incorporating bits and pieces of the writers point of view) and descriptive details. Literary journalists also consciously juxtapose the parts of a story, and they experiment with form.

These techniques generally are used in writing stories that fit into three categories: narrative, narrated and stylistic experiments. In narrative works, the reporter recreates what happened as though he or she were writing narrative fiction. This includes stories about processes, such as Tracy Kidder described in "The Soul of a New Machine," about the invention of a computer. In narrated stories, the reporter serves as narrator — which is tricky, because the temptation is for the reporter to fall into making him- or herself the center of the story instead of remembering that he or she is simply the means to the story. It is this type of literary journalism that has been most strongly criticized for its lack of objectivity; however, Nicholas Tomalin's story about the general shows that reporters can be characters in their stories without making the story seem overly subjective. In the last type of story — the stylistic experiment — the writer uses voice, structure, chronology or syntax in ways that would be considered experimental even in fiction writing. The only difference is that the subject matter is nonfiction.

The vast majority of literary journalism appears in monthly magazines or books. However, most newspapers run occasional stories that take a literary journalism approach, usually in their features sections or Sunday magazines. Most such stories in newspapers would fit into the narrative category, although some are first-person, narrated stories in which reporters write from personal experience about a news event or social issue.

Newspapers rarely run the kind of attention-getting stylistic experiments that contain the well-developed points of view for which literary journalism has been most heavily criticized. In such experiments, writers strive to go beyond the facts to draw from the reader an emotional reaction similar to the writer's own. Some of the best-known examples of this include "Fear and Loathing in Las Vegas," by Hunter S. Thompson, which first appeared in two parts in Rolling Stone magazine in 1971; a 1970 Scanlan's Monthly article, "The Kentucky Derby Is Decadent and Depraved," also by Thompson; and "The Electric Kool-Aid Acid Test," by Tom Wolfe.

Here's an excerpt from "The Electric Kool-Aid Acid Test," in which Wolfe experimented with both stream-of-consciousness and point of view in describing author Ken Kesey's paranoia as he hid out in Mexico, convinced that his arrest on California charge of marijuana possession was imminent:

The Truth about "Gonzo Journalism"

If you've heard the phrase "gonzo journalism" used to describe some of the more extreme examples of literary journalism, you've probably heard it in the same sentence with the name Hunter S. Thompson.

Thompson didn't invent the phrase. Former Boston Globe reporter Bill Cardoso did, according to Thompson's comments to Rolling Stone writer P.J. O'Rourke in 1996.

Cardoso wrote Thompson a note about

his article, "The Kentucky Derby Is Decadent and Depraved," in which he said, "Hot damn. Kick ass. It was pure gonzo," Thompson told O'Rourke.

It's an Italian word, and "... it translates almost exactly to what the Hell's Angels would have said was 'off the wall.'" Thompson said. "Hey, it's in the dictionary now. ... That's one of my proudest achievements."

Haul ass, Kesey. Move. *Scram. Split flee hide vanish disintegrate.* Like *run.*

Rrrrrrrrrrrrrrrrrrrrrrrrrrev revrevrevrevrevrevrevrevrev or are we gonna have just a late Mexican re-run of the scene on the rooftop in San Francisco and sit here with the motor spinning and watch with fascination while the cops they climb up once again to come git you —

THEY JUST OPENED THE DOOR DOWN BELOW, ROTOR ROOTER, SO YOU HAVE MAYBE 45 SECONDS ASSUMING THEY BE SLOW AND SNEAKY AND SURE ABOUT IT

Kesey sits in a little upper room in the last house down the beach, $80 a month, on paradise-blue Bandarias Bay, in Puerto Vallarta, on the west coast of Mexico, state of Jalisco, one step from the floppy green fronds of the jungle, wherein flourish lush steamy baboon lusts of paranoia — Kesey sits in this little rickety upper room with his elbow on a table and his forearm standing up perpendicular and in the palm of his hand a little mirror, so that his forearm and the mirror are like a big rear-view mirror stanchion on the side of a truck and thus he can look out the window and see them but they can't see him —

COME ON, MAN, DO YOU NEED A COPY OF THE SCRIPT TO SEE HOW THIS MOVIE GOES? YOU HAVE MAYBE 40 SECONDS LEFT BEFORE THEY COME GET YOU

Wolfe based his writing on Kesey's very detailed letters to his friend Larry McMurtry, which captured much interior monologue, as well as on tapes Kesey made while hiding out and interviews with Kesey and those who knew him.

Most literary journalism in newspapers is very much like what The Washington Post Magazine writer Walt Harrington calls "intimate journalism," because it focuses on "how people live and what they value." In his book, "Intimate Journalism: The Art and Craft of Reporting Everyday Life," Harrington suggests several reporting techniques that are very much in line with the essence of most literary journalism. Among them:

• Think, report and write in scenes. It's not enough to simply "gather facts."

• Capture the "emotional realities" of the subjects — "in other words, writing from inside the heads of our subjects."

• Gather telling details of the subjects' lives. Involve all five senses. Don't use detail for "color" in a story; use it as the foundation for the reporting and writing.

• Collect real-life dialogue. Quotes in a piece using literary journalism often don't belong, because they are not addressed to anyone in particular, except the reporter. Harrington says fictional stories don't work that way. Instead, novels create dialogue between characters.

• Find a beginning, middle and end. Or, put another way, the literary story should have a dramatic problem or tension that must be resolved by the end of the story.

• "Always remember: Scene, detail and narrative bring a story to life, while theme and meaning imbue it with soul." Inexperienced reporters may get so caught up with the techniques of writing for detail and scene that they forget the "eternal verities of love, hate, fear ambition, dedication and compassion are still our bread and butter."

PUBLIC, OR CIVIC, JOURNALISM

If you think of Minnesota as the land of polite, hard-working, fair-haired Scandinavians who say "ya" instead of "yeah," you're not unlike a lot of Minnesotans. But not too long ago, journalists who work at the newspaper in the state's capital city recognized that Minnesota's demographics were changing and decided to report on that trend — as well as growing public apprehension about it. From the beginning, the paper's editors wanted to be sure the stories included voices of newer immigrants as well as longtime residents, most of whose ancestors had been immigrants long ago.

"Instead of finding out what Minnesotans think of immigrants, we decided to do a poll about what immigrants think of Minnesota," the St. Paul Pioneer Press's projects editor, Kate Parry, told Pat Ford in an interview for an article in the Pew Center for Civic Journalism's Civic Catalyst quarterly.

Coincidentally, at the same time the paper was considering how to write about the immigration, the League of Women Voters of Minnesota was planning a series of community discussions around the state on the same topic. The two coordinated their efforts.

As the league began holding its discussions around the state, the Pioneer Press ran a series of articles about new immigrants and their experiences. The paper profiled the five largest immigrant groups, ran lists that told readers how to learn more about current immigration issues as well as about their own ancestors' immigration earlier in the state's history, and how to participate in current efforts such as the league's discussions or outreach programs for immigrants.

The series of stories that resulted, which ran under the title "The New Face of Minnesota," was an example of an approach to in-depth reporting commonly known as public or civic journalism, in which reporters draw on a much broader range of citizen perspectives than occurs in traditional reporting. This approach is extremely appropriate for covering stories about public issues or problems that can be addressed most successfully through input or action by a broad-based group of people. It is also especially valuable when public discourse about a problem or issue has become so volatile or polarized in response to a single proposed solution that people have lost sight of other viable options.

Like investigative reporting, public or civic journalism seeks to bring to light, through original research, things people don't know. But whereas the goal of investigative journalism usually is to expose previously hidden problems or wrongdoing, the goal of public or civic journalism is to put public problems into context and to encourage all citizens — "ordinary" people as well as public officials and community leaders — to weigh the advantages and trade-offs of a range of possible solutions to those problems.

Ironically, advocates of this approach are divided about which title they prefer: *public* or *civic* journalism. Still other titles suggested for this approach include "community journalism," which is more often used as a misnomer for small-town journalism, and "outcome-based reporting" or "solutions journalism." For the sake of simplicity, we're going to call it public journalism, because, as Stanford University Professor Theodore L. Glasser says in his preface to the book "The Idea of Public Journalism," "... it resonates with the history and rhetoric of modern American journalism," in which journalists endeavor to serve and inform the public.

As with investigative and literary journalism, the work came before the name. The Columbus, Ga., Ledger-Enquirer's "Beyond 2000" project in 1988 is generally acknowledged as the first example of public journalism. It involved gathering public input at forums about the community's plans for the future. At that time, many other newspapers around the country also were gathering public input for various types of news stories, and from a more diverse cross-section of people. Formal methods of gathering citizen input included polls, surveys or focus groups conducted by qualified researchers. Less formal methods usually involved group discussions facilitated by the journalists themselves, who called them focus groups, forums, or "community conversations."

Not long after the Columbus project, reporters and editors from the Wichita (Kan.) Eagle surveyed citizens to find out what issues were important in the 1990 governor's race. The paper then focused much of its election coverage on candidates' positions on those issues in a project called "Your Vote Counts." That project became the first of many public journalism projects that have changed the way newspapers throughout the country cover political campaigns: by increasing the focus on issues instead of reporting "sound bites," mudslinging and which candidate was ahead in the latest poll. It is the area of election coverage that public journalism has had the greatest influence.

In reflecting on "Your Vote Counts" in his book "Public Journalism and Public Life: Why Telling the News Is Not Enough," now-retired Eagle editor Davis "Buzz" Merritt said voter turnout and voters' understanding of the issues were measurably higher in areas where people read the Eagle. But a change also occurred among the journalists involved in that project.

"We had deliberately broken out of the passive and increasingly detrimental conventions of election coverage. ... It was also a liberating moment, for me and the journalists at the Eagle. We no longer had to be victims, along with the public, of a politics gone sour. We had a new purposefulness: revitalizing a moribund political process," Merritt wrote.

That statement reflects two key commitments that serve as the philosophical foundation for public journalism: First, that good journalism should benefit, not damage, our democracy, and second, that because news reports inevitably influence events, even when that is not the journalists' intent, journalists should become more aware of how their work influences public life and hold themselves accountable for using that influence constructively.

The ways in which journalists live out these commitments were articulated by longtime journalism educator and ethicist Edmund B. Lambeth in an essay on"Public Journalism as a Democratic Practice," which is part of a book he co-edited, "Assessing Public Journalism":

> ... public journalism can be viewed as a form of journalism that seeks to:
>
> 1) listen systematically to the stories and ideas of citizens even while protecting its freedom to choose what to cover;
> 2) examine alternative ways to frame stories on important community issues;
> 3) choose frames that stand the best chance to stimulate citizen deliberation and build public understanding of issues;

4) take the initiative to report on major public problems in a way that advances public knowledge of possible solutions and the values served by alternative courses of action;

5) pay continuing and systematic attention to how well and how credibly it is communicating with the public.

The first item on Lambeth's list — listening to citizens systematically — generally involves two efforts: defining a broader group of citizens to contact and listening to them differently, in settings (often in group discussions of some sort) that allow for a more free-flowing discussion than the usual reporter-directed interviews.

To broaden their list of citizen sources, reporters with The (Norfolk) Virginian-Pilot sometimes use a "stakeholder exercise" developed during seminars by the four-year Project on Public Life and the Press. In that exercise, a group of journalists brainstorms about who in the community has what stake in a particular issue, event or problem they plan to write about. This focus yields both a more complete source list and a deeper understanding of who is affected and how. Other journalists broaden their sources using techniques described in Chapter 4, such as civic mapping.

The second challenge in listening to citizens — creating a more free-flowing discussion — requires journalists to accept three conditions. First, that there is much they don't know about what's on citizens' minds; second, that they can learn from the ideas citizens express; and, finally, that they must create a different kind of conversation to learn more about and from citizens' points of view. "Typically, newspapers depend upon some combination of letters to the editor, phone-in lines, polls, overheard conversation, and brief interviews as forms of public listening, but — to be honest — rarely does the information gleaned from these snippets do more than get editors and reporters started," journalist Arthur Charity wrote in his book "Doing Public Journalism." To get beneath the surface, he says, journalists must ask different questions, allow more time to talk to people and listen more carefully. By doing so, reporters can flesh out what he calls a "public agenda" — a list of issues the public considers important. "Expressed in the language of traditional journalism, it is simply listening carefully and intelligently to people in order to develop a better news judgment," Charity wrote. He also describes situations in which reporters or editors moderate public forums or focus groups, or collaborate with others who moderate such discussions. Although all journalists can benefit from listening to citizens' responses, the job of moderating forums usually is attempted only by experienced journalists.

The next two items on Lambeth's list — about how stories are framed — center on a concept that is not unique to public journalism. All journalists frame stories. But public journalists have devoted a great deal of thought to how stories traditionally are framed and how they might be framed differently, as New York University Professor Jay Rosen wrote in his book "What Are Journalists For?" "We frame stories all the time, albeit without thinking about how we do it or why," Rosen said. "Story 'angles' or ideas are simply the ideas that should click on deeper questions. What is the frame that drives these story ideas? How are we positioning the players?" A thorough discussion of the elements of story framing is included in Chapter 7.

The fourth item on Lambeth's list addresses public journalists' commitment to fostering citizen engagement through their reporting. If reporters are more aware of public concerns, and more aware of how citizens discuss those concerns, they are more likely to write and frame their news stories in ways that resonate with the public and encourage citizens to become involved in addressing issues in their communities, states, nation and world. Many insights for how they might do this were gleaned from a research project described in the Kettering Foundation report, "Meaningful Chaos: How People Form Relationships with Public Concerns."

The fifth item on Lambeth's list address public journalists' com-

The "Meaningful Chaos" Queries

Many public journalists say that the ideas in "Meaningful Chaos: How People Form Relationships with Public Concerns" greatly influenced their thinking about journalism. Here are some of those ideas adapted into queries journalists can ask themselves about their stories.

• *Connections.* Do our stories reflect an awareness that citizens enlarge, rather than narrow, their views of public concerns, making connections among ideas and topics that journalists fragment and oversimply? Have we made enough connections among public concerns so that our stories reflect the way most people view and experience those concerns?

• *Personal context.* Does our reporting reflect how citizens relate to concerns that "fit" with their personal context — not only their own self-interests, but also issues that matter to them or that they can imagine? Do our stories tap into these interests, values and possibilities as a way of challenging people in our community to move from a private to a public perspective?

• *Coherence.* Have we told the "whole story" on public concerns — with explanation, history, and a sense of overview? Have we helped people to understand those concerns and why they matter? Are we creating a sense of coherence about how and why events and issues fit together today and how they evolved over time?

• *Room for ambivalence.* Have we looked beyond the polarized, politi-

(cont.)

cized extremes in presenting public concerns? Do our stories create room in the public debate for ambivalence — for questioning, discussing, testing ideas, and gaining confidence about views. Do we include more moderate and less sharply focused views?

• *Emotion.* Do our stories accurately reflect the emotions that surround public concerns by tapping into the emotional energy that is vital to people in forming and sustaining relationships with public concerns? Are we unwittingly dampening citizens' interest in public life by stripping away emotions from public discourse in an effort to make it seem more rational?

• *Authenticity.* Do the information and individuals in our stories "ring true"? Are we inadvertently exaggerating or underplaying anything or anyone to make the story more interesting? Will people get the sense from our stories that we're squaring with them?

• *Sense of possibilities.* Do our stories give people a sense of possibility that they personally can do something about public concerns? Have we shown them roles they can play to bring about change so that discussion of public concerns does not seem so isolated from action?

• *Catalysts.* Have we gone beyond interviewing the experts and elite groups? Have we included comments from and about everyday Americans who can be catalysts for others to get more interested and involved in public life?

• *Mediating institutions.* Have we told people about key institutions and places where people can come together and talk and act on public concerns?

Adapted from "Meaningful Chaos: How People Form Relationships with Public Concerns," prepared for the Kettering Foundation by The Harwood Group, published in 1993.

mitment to their own accountability, both *as* citizens and *to* citizens. For many public journalists, a key element of their reporting reflects a shift in their own thinking about their role as journalists. Instead of seeing themselves as detached observers or mere conveyors of benign information, they now recognize that they make many choices in their work that affect how citizens feel about public life and whether they participate in it. These journalists generally see themselves as citizens first and journalists second. As a result, they recognize that they, too, have a stake in the well-being of their communities, and they approach their work with the honesty and integrity that are traditional in journalism, but also with an open sense of caring about the community they serve — "like a candid friend," as longtime newspaper editor Gil Thelen put it. They also make a point of telling readers what they are "up to" when they take a public journalism approach, which Art Charity calls telling "the story behind the story." For instance, in launching the Wichita Eagle's "People Project," a series of stories about how citizen involvement brings about change, Buzz Merritt wrote a front-page essay that keyed readers in to what was essentially a challenge the paper issued to both itself and the public: "At the end of [this project], we'll know an important thing about ourselves: whether we have the will, given the opportunity, to take responsibility for our lives and our community."

A newspaper whose work has reflected the elements of public journalism for a decade now is The Charlotte (N.C.) Observer, which first used the public journalism format in covering the 1992 presidential election. In addition to continuing to take a public journalism approach in election coverage, the paper investigated and published a five-week series on education that touched on crime, discipline, academic quality, busing and parental involvement and resulted in the creation of an education reporting team; a series called "Taking Back Our Neighborhoods," which was a six-month initiative involving news coverage, town meetings and coordination of community efforts to solve problems in the city's most violent areas; and a 1999 project titled "Hunger in the Land of Plenty," an examination of the city's hunger problem and how it can be addressed.

The Observer is only one of what has grown to be a long list of news organizations across the country that has taken a public journalism approach to a wide variety of both in-depth and daily news stories. Even The New York Times, which has taken a firm stand against public journalism, has drawn information for some of its news stories from a technique championed by public journalists: group discussions between reporters and citizens.

As with investigative and literary journalism, critics have argued that public journalism is, at its best, nothing more than good, old-fashioned journalism done as it should be and, at its worst, a betrayal of what they see as the journalist's duty to convey "just the facts."

Rosen describes public journalists as having realized that "it was possible to experiment with the daily news product and the power of the press, turning both to more civic ends, however vaguely this was defined. Journalists could break out of established routines, step into another role, find a different aim for their efforts. And they could learn from what they tried."

Some of the learning experiences have been more controversial than others. In "Beyond 2000," for instance, the Ledger-Enquirer eventually assumed an activist role that drew heavy criticism. In their coverage of the 1998 elections, several North Carolina newspapers — including The Charlotte Observer — were criticized for erring too far on the side of reporting about issues important to citizens at the expense of covering matters of concern to the candidates.

Jennie Buckner, editor of The Charlotte Observer, says much

criticism of public journalism is ill informed. "I have been astonished by the stark ignorance of much of the criticism of public journalism. I am particularly astonished by the number of journalists who seem offended by the suggestion that they might learn something valuable by listening to citizens," she wrote in an article in the Observer (Oct. 19, 1996). "At The Observer, public journalism is simply this. When writing about public life, we have a goal: to provide readers the information they need to function as citizens. We expect politicians to address issues they consider important; but we also expect them to address issues the public considers important. We want to keep people informed about opportunities to become involved in public life — an important service, we think, in our fragmented society. We try to confine advocacy to the editorial page. On both opinion and news pages, we value citizen voices."

COMPUTER-ASSISTED REPORTING

Computer-assisted reporting allows reporters to develop stories by analyzing and interpreting vast amounts of data. Once the purview of university or government programmers, this kind of analysis can be done by reporters who use database programs to analyze anything from the frequency of violent crimes within the military ranks to the time of year that most babies are born in a given city. Relatively simple, off-the-shelf spreadsheets such as Microsoft Excel or Access can be used by reporters for an array of tasks.

Consider, for instance, the people in your reporting class. By gathering information and inputting it into a database or spreadsheet program, you could find the average age or grade point average for your class. You could input additional information about how much time, on average, each of you spends working, participating in student organizations or athletics, studying, or using the campus computer labs. When you use the software to crunch the numbers, you might find support for a story about the correlation between age and grade-point average, or grade-point average and some of those other factors. What if, for instance, you were to discover that students who spend the most time in the computer labs actually get the worst grades? Further investigation might show that it's because a fair amount of that time is spent waiting in line for computers, which might serve as the basis for a story about the need for more computers on campus. Or it might show that students in the labs get distracted by such things as browsing the Internet or socializing with others in the labs, which would form the basis for yet other stories.

This kind of reporting requires basic tools: the raw data, the right equipment and software to access the data, and equipment and software to analyze the data. Mistakes are most likely when the wrong information is entered into a spreadsheet, or when the data is analyzed incorrectly. One of the biggest challenges can be the format in which you receive information: Although government agencies are required to give you the information, they are not required to give it to you in the form you prefer. In other words, if they use an antiquated computer with equally antiquated software, nothing says they have to translate the information and give it to you on disk in a form you can read on your newspaper's more up-to-date PCs using the latest spreadsheet software. This may mean you have to get the information in paper form and enter it by hand. In addition, some government agencies are reluctant to release whole databases, partly because of privacy concerns that often can be addressed by deleting sensitive information such as Social Security numbers or income data. However, as our world becomes increasingly digitized, government agencies are more comfortable dealing with paperless exchanges of information.

Computer-assisted reporting also requires reporters to have the expertise to understand and interpret the data, as well as keen reporting skills that are needed to determine whether the data analysis rings true and can be substantiated through interviews and other traditional reporting techniques. Let's say you want to find out whether the number of violent criminals being sent to prison is going up or down in your area. First, you have to get the data from the local courts. You also have to make sure you know how those courts define violence — some localities include burglary and child pornography as violent crimes along with murder, assault and rape. If you don't check that key point, the information you enter in a spreadsheet could be mischaracterized. But don't stop there — recognizing a trend means analyzing data over a long period of time. Be sure you know whether the courts define violent crime the same way today as they did a year ago, or five years ago. Otherwise, your analysis will be flawed.

Once you've done your analysis, you then need to interview people whose expertise and experiences give them a sound basis for responding to what you've uncovered through computer-assisted reporting. Numbers alone are not sufficient. Sometimes this post-analysis reporting will alert you to important factors you had not considered in your analysis, which will require you to go back and re-analyze your results taking those factors into consideration. These interviews also will lead you to examples you can use to illustrate your findings. If you uncover something that is particularly disturbing, your findings might also trigger denials or an official investigation. That is why it's so important for your numbers to be accurate and your conclusions sound.

The following list is taken from the Web site of Investigative Reporters & Editors (IRE), where they are presented as good examples of computer-assisted reporting.

• *Early Childhood: A Growing Concern*. Courier-Journal, Dec. 5–9, 1999. In this four-month investigation, the (Louisville) Courier-Journal found that the futures of tens of thousands of Kentucky's poorest and youngest children will remain in grave doubt unless the state moves boldly to improve their care. The newspaper's investigation included thousands of state inspection records for child-care providers, interviews with more than 150 people and a review of recent research.

• *Managed Care & Doctors: The Broken Promise*. Newsday, Nov. 14–19, 1999. Newsday's 10-month investigation shows that despite promises of high quality and rigorous screening, New York's biggest managed health care networks offered to their customers doctors who were disciplined for serious — even fatal — wrongdoing. Even though health insurers are fully aware that these doctors have been punished for botched surgery, sexual misconduct, drug abuse, cheating government insurance plans or other offenses, they never tell their millions of customers. The six-part series incorporated computer-assisted reporting and research on the Internet.

• *Pittsburgh in Crisis*. The Pittsburgh Tribune-Review, Feb. 20, 2000. This special report analyzes Pittsburgh's financial crisis using 10 years of city and state audits and other financial data. The newspaper's investigation found that the city is $1.68 billion in debt, far more than other cities of similar size.

Each of these stories was complex and time consuming. But not all computer-assisted stories have to be that involved. Simpler stories exist for the taking. For instance:

• Want to know how many marriages in your area are likely to end in divorce, and whether it's different now from five years ago? Go to the courts' database and get the numbers of marriage licenses and petitions for divorce for the past five years.

• Want to know which older neighborhoods are becoming the "hip" places to renovate homes? Check the number and types of building permits that have been filed over time and look for patterns. If permits tend to be concentrated in certain areas, it might tip you off to renewal efforts in those areas. Or you might end up chasing an entirely different kind of story if you notice something else —

like a lot of permits to replace roofs in the area surrounding a new chemical processing plant, for example.

• Curious about how heating costs have risen over the past five years? The local public utilities keep records you can use to determine typical heating bills in the past as well as the average annual increase — which, in turn, can be used along with comments from utility company officials to predict this year's typical heating bill.

More and more databases can be found on the Internet — everything from a complete listing of sex offenders to U.S. census figures can be found. State and federal government sites are numerous, but many local governments also post information once available only at City Hall. As with all information, reporters must take great care to verify the source of the information.

One of the challenges in computer-assisted methods is finding valuable sites without wasting hours culling through useless information. A good place to start is with the sites maintained by journalism associations or universities. IRE's "The Beat Page," for instance, lists useful (and reputable) Web sites by beats, such as transportation, health, etc. An education reporter can find links to the National Center for Education Statistics and the U.S. Department of Education at the same site.

WHERE TO START

Each of these approaches — wholly, in part or in combination — can be used in writing about a wide variety of topics. As you begin writing more complex stories, you may feel drawn to one approach or another. You might find that one approach leads to another. The Asbury Park (N.J.) Press, for example, embarked on a public journalism project in which reporters, listening to citizens, pieced together information about what investigative reporting then showed to be an illegal conspiracy to jack up real estate prices. Or you might use techniques from each approach in a single package of stories. For example, to write an explanatory set of stories about student drinking and its impact on campus, you might talk to college and community officials, experts, students and parents. You might use an investigative approach in searching through campus and city police records, looking for patterns in alcohol-related arrests involving students. You might hang out in a popular bar near the campus to record dialogue and other detail to use in writing a literary-style story about the bar scene and its place in students' drinking patterns. You also might use the public journalism technique of inviting faculty, staff, students and residents of the surrounding community to participate in public forums about student drinking.

Each approach to in-depth reporting carries its own unique challenges. If you mention someone's dog in a literary story, you need to know the name of the dog, who it belongs to, its breed, how old it is, whether it knows any tricks, how its owner treats it — all details that can be useful in writing the story. Tracking the "paper trail" in an investigative report can lead to documents that some people would rather not be made public. Stories that accuse people or organizations of wrongdoing often require at least three sources or two independent documents as backup. Getting people to admit you into their lives as fully and candidly as they must for you to write a compelling piece of literary journalism requires that you first earn their trust. Determining the varied stakeholders in thorough public journalism means the reporter needs to talk to as many as possible and use their views in the story. If you want to have forums or roundtable discussions, finding enough citizens to give up their time for that purpose can be daunting.

No matter which approach you use, in-depth reporting requires sound analytical and organizational skills, as well as the support of your news organization. It requires thoroughness, persistence and precision. Here are some tips to get you started.

- *Develop a "T-chart."* A T-chart is nothing more complicated than a line drawn down the middle of a piece of paper. One side has the heading "What We Don't Know" or "What We Need to Find Out." The other heading is "What We Know." The left column might have simple notes such as "the mayor's response" or "the # of houses 30 years old or older in the city." The goal is to move the "don't knows" into the "know" column. This is a disciplining device to make sure you are chasing the right pieces of the puzzle. T-charts are particularly useful for investigative stories but can be used in all complex reporting efforts.
- *Write outlines, memos and budget lines.* The "story" and its many parts can change several times over the course of the reporting. Writing a memo or a budget line forces you to articulate the story to that point.
- *Take your editors out on the limb with you.* Senior editors almost always inspect the most sensitive stories. Few like to be surprised. John Uhlmann, the first director of Investigative Reporters and Editors, liked to say that if the top editors are out on a limb with you, they'll be less likely to saw it off. Let them know, early on, what you are planning, what the risks are, who else might need to be involved and how much time you might need. And then keep them informed along the way.

• *Space kills.* If you don't have a reasonable expectation of how much space the story is worth (or how much you can get), you can be in for a painful experience. It's important to know that, unlike other mediums, space is a newspaper's most precious commodity. Taking "a page or two" in most newspapers constitutes a major investment of time and money and tells something about the weight the newspaper feels the story deserves.

• *Back it out.* Somewhere between the midway part of reporting and the beginning of the writing, commit to paper a series of deadlines: completion of the first draft, editors' comments, final draft, graphics information to the designer or graphics artist, all photo assignments, first approval from senior editors, all pieces of the project to the designer, and more. This is sometimes called a "backout schedule" because it begins with a target date for publication, then "backs out" all the other activities and dates that need to make the project ready for publication. Sit down with your editor at some point to determine all the pieces and people required. Remember to include all the people who will need to see your story along the way. Some of the most painful experiences on projects can come at the end of the process, when, after long and detailed reporting and writing by the reporter and assigning editor, the project is assumed to be "finished" — when it isn't.

EXERCISES

1. Think of something that you and your friends are obsessing about right now. Grades? Money? A job or volunteer position? Problems in your love life? A campus-wide problem? A problem at home? A new course requirement? Pick one of those topics and try to imagine a package of in-depth news stories that would help you sort out the selected issue. What questions would the stories answer? What information would they give you? Is there anything about the situation that makes you wonder if people are concealing information or being less than forthcoming? Where's the drama? Do you know of compelling personal stories or situations that are tied to the topic you've chosen? Is it something that affects a large percentage of a given population and/or cannot be addressed without participation from lots of people? Think about how, if you were a reporter, you might apply the in-depth reporting approaches to get at various aspects of the story.

2. Find an in-depth reporting package in any newspaper and analyze it. Make a list of the stories that are part of the package and, for each story, jot down a brief summary of what it says, who was interviewed, and what approach the journalists appear to have taken in that story — explanatory, investigative, literary or public. If only one of those approaches appears to have been taken in the entire package, imagine how the stories might have been done differently, using one of the other approaches.

3. Explore what it's like to do a public records search by choosing a topic, going to a public agency, asking to see the records related to your topic and requesting a copy of one of the records. For example, research the

growth of the neighborhood or area of the city where you live (county offices keep plat books and real estate transaction records that can tell you this). Determine crime rates in your part of the city (some police or sheriff's departments issue annual reports that break down crime by neighborhood; more recent statistics are available by looking through police reports). Or find out where new buildings are going up (go to the city or county planning department and ask to see filings for building permits). Take notes about your experience. How easy was it to see the records you requested? How efficient was the agency's record-keeping system? How easy was it for you to get a copy? What did you notice about the records themselves?

4. Write a verbal virtual reality clip. Find a spot on (or off) campus that you find interesting and sit there for a half hour, taking notes about everything you notice while you're sitting there. Make note of sensory details — what you see, hear, smell, touch and taste. If you plant yourself in a campus lounge, what do you see as you enter? Do you head for a comfortable-looking chair? Is the furniture colorful, drab, firm, worn down, modern, or old-fashioned? When you sit down on it, do you sink in or does it feel hard? Is the upholstery smooth or rough? How about the walls — what's on them? And the floor — worn lineoleum, drab carpeting, plush carpeting? What do you smell and hear? Who else is there, and who passes through? Use your notes to write something that comes as close as you can to conveying to someone else the experience you had in that spot.

5. Ask a group of friends to join you for a discussion about a topic that interests or concerns all of you. Make it clear that this is a class exercise, not just for fun, and you will expect them to share their ideas and thoughts as a way of helping you flesh out your ideas for an in-depth story package. Ask how the topic affects them and make note of their personal stories. Ask what things they think are good, bad and so-so. Ask what they think can be done to improve things — or to make sure things either don't get worse or stay as good as they are.

6. Get together with a group of other journalism students, identify an area of concern and do the "stakeholder" exercise to identify possible sources you might use if you were to write about that concern. Go beyond the obvious answers. If your topic is the quality of campus food service, for instance, it isn't just students who have an interest in that. So do the food service workers, the vendors who supply food to the campus, the people who sell and maintain the equipment used in cooking and serving the food, parents who pay for students' meal plans and so on. Make two lists during your discussion: people who are affected, and what concerns they might have about the topic you have chosen.

Further Reading

ON THE WEB

Poll Results

www.freedomforum.org/professional/2000/1/6pollsters.asp

Use of Confidential Sources

AJR/American Journalism Review, "An Unwelcome Encore," by Carol Guensburg: http://ajr.newslink.org/ajrencoreoct99.html

Roanoke Times: Policy on unnamed sources: www.roanoke.com/roatimes/ethics/ethics10.html

The Poynter Institute for Media Studies, "Guidelines for Interviewing Confidential Sources: Who, When, Why?" by Al Tompkins and Bob Steele: http://poynter.org/dj/tips/ethics/whowhenwhy.htm.

Investigative Reporting

Dean Tudor's CAR/CARR Links Page: A page chock full of computer-assisted reporting links, including resources, examples, associations, course syllabi, and discussion groups: www.ryerson.ca/journal/mega11.htm

IRE/Investigative Reporters and Editors: www.ire.org the Arizona Project. Examples of computer-assisted reporting: www.ire.org/data-library/online.html

The Poynter Institute for Media Studies, "Sample Protocol for Ethical Decision-Making in Computer-Assisted Journalism," by Bob Steele and Wendel Cochran: http://poynter.org/dj/tips/CAR/car_prot.htm. Bibliographies for investigative and public journalism: www.poynter.org/research/index.htm

The Washington Post: June 1997 story package commemorating the 25th anniversary of the Watergate burglary: www.washingtonpost.com/wp-srv/national/longterm/watergate/front.htm

Literary Journalism/Creative Nonfiction

Creative Nonfiction — An online journal devoted to creative nonfiction: www.cnf.edu

"Literary Journalism: Newspaper's Last, Best Hope," by Paul Many: www.utoledo.edu/~pmany/litjournal.html

The Poynter Institute for Media Studies, "Narrative Journalism: Ride the River, Scan the Banks," by Chip Scanlan: www.poynter.org/centerpiece/121100.html

Public/Civic Journalism

"Beyond the Public Journalism Controversy," by Judith Lichtenberg, a report from The Institute for Philosophy and Public Policy at the University of Maryland: www.puaf.umd.edu/IPPP/winter98/beyond_the_public_journalism_con.htm

Civic Practices Network, journalism section: www.cpn.org/sections/topics/journalism/

Ernie Pyle Memorial Bookstore's public journalism shelf: http://www.duff.net/ernie/shelf09.htm

"Ethics and Public Journalism," by James Fallows: www.theatlantic.com/unbound/jf-npr/jf605-07.htm

National Conference of Editorial Writers, public journalism page: www.ncew.org/civic.html

Pew Center for Civic Journalism: www.pewcenter.org

The Poynter Institute for Media Studies, public journalism bibliography: www.poynter.org/research/biblio/bib_pj.htm

"What Is Public Journalism? A Brief Description," by Jay Rosen: www.nyu.
edu/gsas/dept/journal/Faculty/bios/rosen/public_journalism.htm

IN PRINT

Polls and Surveys

"Coming to Public Judgment: Making Democracy Work in a Complex
World," by Daniel Yankelovich, published by Syracuse University Press,
Syracuse, N.Y., 1991.

"Newsroom Guide to Polls and Surveys," by G. C. Wilhoit and D. H. Weaver,
published by Indiana University Press, Bloomington, 1990.

"Qualitative Interviewing," by H. J. and I. S. Rubin, published by Sage,
Beverly Hills, Calif., 1995.

"The Voice of the People: Public Opinion and Democracy," by James S.
Fishkin, published by Yale University Press, New Haven, Conn, 1995.

Explanatory Reporting

"Advanced Reporting: Discovering Patterns in News," by Donald Lewis
Shaw, published by Waveland Press, Prospect Heights, Ill., 1996.

"Getting the Story: An Advanced Reporting Guide to Beats, Records and
Sources," by Henry H. Schulte and Marcel P. Dufresne, published by
MacMillan, New York, 1994.

"Public Affairs Reporting," by Michael Killenberg, published by St. Martin's
Press, New York, 1992.

Investigative Reporting

"All the President's Men," by Carl Bernstein and Bob Woodward, published
by Touchstone Books, New York, 1994.

"Custodians of Conscience: Investigative Journalism and Public Virtue," by
James S. Ettema and Theodore L. Glasser, published by Columbia University Press, New York, 1998.

"Power Journalism: Computer-Assisted Reporting," by Lisa C. Miller, published by Harcourt Brace Jovanovich, New York, 1997.

"The Reporter's Handbook: An Investigator's Guide to Documents and Techniques," edited by Steve Weinberg and Investigative Reporters and Editors (IRE), published by St. Martins Press, New York, 1995.

Literary Journalism/Creative Nonfiction

"Creative Nonfiction: Researching and Crafting Stories of Real Life," by
Philip Gerard, published by Story Press, Cincinnati, Ohio, 1996.

"Intimate Journalism: The Art and Craft of Reporting Everyday Life," by
Walt Harrington, published by Sage Publications, Thousand Oaks, Calif., 1997.

"Literary Journalism: A New Collection of the Best American Nonfiction," edited by Norman Sims and Mark Kramer, published by Ballantine Books, New York, 1995.

"Professional Feature Writing," by Bruce Garrison, published by Erlbaum Associates, Hillsdale, N.J., 1994.

"The Art of Creative Nonfiction: Writing and Selling the Literature of Reality," by Lee Gutkind, published by Wiley & Sons, New York, 1997.

"The Art of Fact: A Historical Anthology of Literary Journalism," edited by Kevin Kerrane and Ben Yagoda, published by Touchstone, New York, 1997. An extensive anthology, with selections dating back to 1725. Includes examples of literary journalism from times before the phrases "new journalism" and "literary journalism" were coined.

"The Fourth Genre: Contemporary Writers of/on Creative Nonfiction," edited by Michael Sternberg, published by Allyn & Bacon, Boston, Mass., 1998.

"The Literary Journalists: The New Art of Personal Reportage," edited by Norman Sims, published by Ballantine Books, New York, 1984. An in-depth look at how literary techniques have been applied in a variety of longer stories. (Also available in Spanish: Los Periodistas Literarios: O El Arte del Reportaje Personal, published by El Áncora Editores, Bogotá, Colombia, 1996.)

"The New Journalism," by Tom Wolfe, with an anthology edited by Tom Wolfe and E. W. Johnson, published by Harper and Row, New York, 1973. Out of print, but available in most large libraries. The manifesto of "new journalism," which came into its own in the late 1960s and early 1970s.

"Writing Creative Nonfiction: The Literature of Reality," by Gay Talese and Barbara Lounsberry, published by Longman Publishing Group, New York, 1996.

Public/Civic Journalism

"Assessing Public Journalism," edited by Edmund B. Lambeth, Philip E. Meyer and Esther Thorson, published by University of Missouri Press, Columbia, 1998.

"Doing Public Journalism," by Arthur Charity, published by Guilford Publications, New York City, 1995.

"Public Journalism and Public Life: Why Telling the News Is Not Enough," by Davis "Buzz" Merritt, 2d ed., published by Erlbaum, Mahwah, N.J., 1998.

"The Charlotte Project: Helping Citizens Take Back Democracy," by Edward D. Miller, published by The Poynter Institute for Media Studies, St. Petersburg, Fla., 1994.

"The Idea of Public Journalism," edited by Theodore L. Glasser, published by Guilford Publications, New York, 1999.

"What Are Journalists For?" by Jay Rosen, published by Yale University Press, New Haven, Conn., 1999.

Chapter 14

Journalists' Rights and Responsibilities

The First Amendment in the Bill of Rights provides for freedom of the press.

Source: National Archives

Key Concepts

- In the United States, journalists enjoy a great deal of freedom. They can publish whatever they want to publish.

- Although nobody can stop journalists from publishing something, the courts can make them pay for any mistakes after the fact.

- Accuracy and thoroughness are the best protections against being sued for libel or slander, because truth is the best defense against libel.

- Good journalists also hold themselves and one another to a set of ethical standards.

- Good journalists also view themselves as serving a valuable role in supporting our democracy by providing information and a public forum that helps citizens be engaged and interested in public life.

Ah, freedom of the press! In this country, we can rant in public about college administrators and politicians, we can expose corruption, and we can go to any public library and get books that some people think are so offensive that they ought to be burned. As journalists, we can write or say anything about anybody, right?

Wrong. The law says you can't write or broadcast false, damaging information about someone without running the risk of being sued (and possibly ending your career as a journalist). You can't break the law to get a story, which means you can't trespass onto private property or illegally access electronic files like voice mail or computer records without risking criminal charges as well as a lawsuit. If you promise news sources you'll keep their identity secret, then identify them in a story, you also run the risk of being sued. And if you're a broadcast journalist, there are certain words and images the Federal Communications Commission won't let your station put on the air.

Journalists must live by other rules as well. Many are not enforced by law but dictated by journalistic ethics, which have developed over time into tradition. Journalists shall not lie. They shall not take others' written words as their own. They shall not take money or gifts in return for favorable coverage. They shall not belong to a political party or special interest group, especially when their jobs might require them to report less than flattering truths about that party or group. They shall not make up quotes or people, or make up "composite" people out of several sources. They shall not purposefully misrepresent themselves or their news organizations.

The reason for these "shall nots" is simple: As with other occupations, one factor that marks the development of a craft from a simple trade into a profession is the emergence of credos and ethics. Professionals carefully control the standards of their occupation and form associations to regulate themselves. Doctors and dentists and lawyers and therapists all have, over time, developed rules of conduct. The rules restrict access to the profession and help members of the profession to establish trust with the people they serve. For example, you make several assumptions when you sit down in your dentist's chair — that he or she has advanced knowledge about teeth and how to keep them healthy, that he or she won't injure you, and that he or she won't perform unnecessary work. Similarly, when people buy a newspaper or listen to a news broadcast on radio, they are aware of the credibility of the news organization and how well it accurately represents an event or issue. If you buy a national newspaper like The New York Times, The Washington Post, or USA Today, or listen to a network news broadcast, you probably expect a high degree of professionalism in the way news is presented. If you buy a supermarket tabloid, tune in to talk radio or watch one of those afternoon talk shows that makes spectacles of unusual or bizarre interpersonal situations, you probably have somewhat different expectations, especially with regard to the reliability and news value of the information. It is the degree of trust you place in a given news organization that differentiates it from the cacophony of publications, broadcast programs and Web sites that journalists would agree don't qualify as professional journalism.

As we mentioned in Chapter 4, a news organization cannot earn public trust without credibility. When the Associated Press Managing Editors released the results of the organization's three-year credibility study, ASNE's then-president, Manhattan (Kan.) Mercury editor Edward L. Seaton, articulated the link between professionalism and credibility. "The most fundamental expectation of the press is truth-telling," he said. "Our watchdog role is secondary, at least to the public. It values 'the facts' and truth-telling over interpretation and drama — even including holding stories until both sides can be contacted. ... Credibility is about the quality and integrity of our news report. It is about understanding, articulating and applying high professional standards."

As mentioned in previous chapters, reporters can contribute to a newspaper's credibility in a number of ways: by getting to know the community they're covering, reporting the news without errors, writing with an eye toward detail that makes their stories more believable and engaging, and framing stories in a way that reflects what's really going on and why it matters to people. No universal, foolproof formula exists for developing trust with readers, listeners or viewers — it is a relationship that is slow to build and easy to damage or even destroy. Yet day after day, journalists attempt to do just that with every story, every headline, every picture or graphic. "Like teachers, soldiers, nurses or parents, journalists perform a job whose full value is not represented in their pay," journalist James Fallows writes in his book "Breaking the News: How the Media Undermine American Democracy." "When they do their jobs well, many people benefit. When they do their jobs poorly, when they are irresponsible about their power, the damage spreads further than they can see."

Fallows and others believe that it's not enough to stop at the "shall nots" of professional conduct. He articulates a compelling case for the "we wills" — that is, for journalism to have a purpose, it must foster public discourse. Journalism must increase not just the volume but the quality of talk in the communities journalists write about.

The First Amendment gives journalists freedom. It says, quite simply, "Congress shall make no law ... abridging the freedom of speech, or of the press. ..." Journalists such as Fallows believe that with that freedom comes the responsibility to protect and nurture democracy. In this case, democracy isn't just an act of running a government. It's an act of everyday life.

Even then, and above all, the best journalists have an attitude of humility in regard to the realization that they hold great power to harm and only partial ability to help a community. The media is just one place people turn for understanding. Citizens "place journalistic input alongside their own life experiences and input from families, friends, co-workers and neighbors," says Cole Campbell, former editor of the St. Louis Post-Dispatch. "They sort through all this to come to an understanding of the world, to complete their own acts of synthesis. ... We should recognize that we always will be contributors to understanding and never providers of it."

Journalists have a responsibility to inform citizens with stories whose hallmarks are honesty and integrity, and to engage the public in a way that helps communities work better.

LEGAL RESPONSIBILITIES

The good news is that the only ways you can end up in jail as a journalist (in the United States, anyway) is if you refuse to divulge where you got unattributed information you used in your story and a judge cites you for contempt of court, or if you are so driven to get the story that you commit a crime to get information (in which case, it's the crime for which you'll be prosecuted, not your work as a journalist). That means, if you've taken the advice in earlier chapters about being forthcoming while you do your reporting, avoiding trespassing or other property violations, and carefully considering whether to quote anonymous sources, you'll either stay out of trouble or understand the risk you're running by using unattributed information.

If you do end up in jail, you'll probably get your 15 minutes of fame, courtesy of other journalists who either rally to one another's defense when journalists are jailed for protecting their sources or feel obliged to report other reporters' violations of the law as diligently as they report such violations by others. But in the United States, unlike some other countries, you cannot be thrown into jail for writing something somebody (especially a powerful official) doesn't like.

You also cannot be prevented from publishing the information you have gathered. Except in unusual circumstances (most notably, during times of war), the Supreme Court consistently has ruled that governments or individuals have no right to "prior restraint" — restraining journalists from making information public. The reasoning goes like this: If a government can stop a journalist from publishing something unfavorable, then that government could hide behind the shield of prior restraint without ever being held accountable for its actions.

The most famous case that addresses this issue is one we mentioned briefly in Chapter 1, the Pentagon Papers case. In 1967, during the Vietnam War, the secretary of defense commissioned a history of the United States' involvement in Indochina. The work was classified as top secret. One of the contributors, Daniel Ellsberg, made a copy of the report, and eventually it came into the hands of The New York Times and The Washington Post. The government tried to stop the newspapers from publishing the Pentagon Papers. But the Supreme Court, in a 6–3 ruling in June 1971, said, "any system of prior restraints of expression comes to this Court bearing a heavy presumption against its constitutional validity." Justice Potter Stewart, in a separate statement, pointed to the great responsibility of the press by describing the enormous power of the executive branch of the federal government. Stewart said that the only effective restraint upon "executive policy and power in the areas of national defense and international affairs may lie in an enlightened

The New York Times' Pentagon Papers story.
Source: The New York Times

citizenry — in an informed and critical public opinion which alone can here protect the value of democratic government. ... For this reason, it is perhaps here that a press that is alert, aware, and free most vitally serves the basic purpose of the First Amendment. For without an informed and free press there cannot be an enlightened people."

Stewart, then, weighed the costs of possible damage to the country that might come from publishing unfavorable information — young men were fighting and dying in Vietnam as the Supreme

Although hers was a rare case, writer Vanessa Leggett, center, spent more than five months in the Federal Detention Center in Houston for refusing to give federal prosecutors her research about a murder case. Here, she speaks to reporters after being released in January 2001. She is joined by her lawyer, Mike DeGeurin, left; her husband, Doak Leggett, back; and U.S. Rep. Sheila Jackson Lee, right.
Source: AP/Wide World Photo

Court was deliberating this case — versus the potential danger of a government unchecked by a vigilant press.

Other Supreme Court rulings have gone so far as to say that even rumor and falsehood can be published, as we mentioned in Chapter 1. Remember the case of the newspaper that maligned the Minneapolis police chief in 1931? At the center of that controversy was Jay M. Near, a Minnesota reporter and editor who thrived on scandal and bigotry. His pen was a weapon for hire, "a means of scratching out his living as a sort of scavenger of the sins and political vulnerability of others," historian and First Amendment lawyer Fred W. Friendly wrote in his book "Minnesota Rag." "He had basic writing skills and a quick-on-the-draw sense of outrage."

Near had joined with Howard Guilford in 1927 to publish the Saturday Press in Minneapolis. Guilford was known to accept cash from one politician to write malicious items about a rival. The partners' first issue of the Saturday Press, which included attacks against the rival newspaper and the police, was taken off the streets by the city's chief of police. The next week Guilford was shot and critically wounded while on his way to work. Near continued to pound out stories linking gambling syndicates to police — often not as news but as his own opinions. He and Guilford, from his hospital room, wrote scathing reports full of hatred against minority groups as well. Finally, the newspaper was formally banned using a Minnesota gag law that allowed a judge to bar publication of any newspaper found "malicious, scandalous or defamatory."

The Supreme Court struck down the Minnesota law. In Near v. Minnesota in 1931, Chief Justice Charles Evans Hughes wrote, "The fact that the liberty of the press may be abused by miscreant purveyors of scandal does not make any the less necessary the immunity of the press from previous restraint in dealing with official misconduct."

These landmark Supreme Court rulings make it very difficult for courts to prevent journalists from making information public, but the protections are not absolute. Court battles are waged frequently. In 1998, for instance, a trial judge ordered the Knoxville News-Sentinel not to run a story that included information about lawyers' fees in the case of an accused serial killer. The paper ran the story in spite of the judge's order, which was actually the courts' second attempt to stop that information from being published. An earlier order prevented the paper from obtaining records of lawyers' fees in a case about an accused serial killer. The newspaper obtained the records from an anonymous source.

Still, for the most part, reporters are allowed to write newspaper stories or create broadcast news segments that say just about anything. But there's a catch: You can be punished later if the information is determined to be false and damaging. In broadcast journalism, your station also can be fined or even have its license revoked if it violates Federal Communications Commission content regulations.

False and damaging information goes by two names in the legal world: If it's published it's called *libel* and if it's broadcast it's called *slander*. Libel and slander laws exist to protect the reputations of individuals. A person is *defamed* when an untrue news item subjects that person to hatred, contempt or ridicule by a substantial and respectable group. Many differences exist from state to state, but generally these are components of libel: It's false, and it causes the person to lose face publicly.

Look in any newspaper and you will find potentially defamatory information — stories about people charged with crimes, for instance. But, remember, the story must be defamatory *and* false to be libelous or slanderous. If you read carefully, you'll see that stories about arrests and criminal charges usually say something like "he was arrested on a murder charge" or "she is accused of robbing ... " rather than "he was arrested after he murdered ... " or "she was arrested for robbery," because the latter phrasings essentially say someone is guilty. Such precise wording ensures that the stories are truthful — and truth is the best defense against a libel or slander charge. If the journalist can prove that the defamatory information is true by producing documents or sources who are willing to testify on the journalist's behalf, the lawsuit will be dismissed.

To get a sense of how this works, imagine that you're a reporter who has written a story about a local home builder who, you've learned, has paid off building inspectors and other government officials to overlook shoddy workmanship. You have based your stories on interviews with four current or former inspectors, but none wants his or her name published in the story. The only people who have gone on the record are homeowners who are understandably upset about the workmanship but can offer no proof of the bribes. If the story is published, the newspaper runs a much higher risk of being sued for libel than if the inspectors spoke "on the record." However, your editors might decide it's worth the risk to prevent the builder from continuing to sell defective homes to unsuspecting buyers. First, they would need to be confident that the inspectors were being truthful. They also would want you to find out, before the story runs, if the inspectors would be willing to testify if the newspaper were sued over the story.

As you can imagine, those decisions are never easy. Most journalists, however, consider it an important part of their mission to shed light on wrongdoing. The challenge is to be sure that if you plan to run a story that damages a person's reputation, you make a conscientious effort to make sure the information you have is true. No responsible journalist will casually cast aspersions on someone's good name.

Now, let's imagine the story about paying off building inspectors has a different slant. Let's say you learned that the planning director has been demanding payoffs from a couple of high-volume builders whose work tends to be of somewhat questionable quality. In that case, the courts have declared a tougher standard for proof of libel. Public figures such as people who are elected or appointed to high-profile positions, like planning directors, and people who seek out the spotlight, such as movie stars and sports figures, must prove not only that the information was defamatory and false — they also must prove what that the courts have called *actual malice*. That is, the public figure must prove the information was published "with knowledge that it was false or with reckless disregard of whether it was false or not," according to the landmark 1964 Supreme Court ruling in the case of The New York Times v. Sullivan.

That case concerned an advertisement by the "Committee to Defend Martin Luther King and the Struggle for Freedom in the South." Sullivan was a local official in Alabama. Lower courts, in granting Sullivan a $500,000 judgment, agreed that the ad contained errors in fact. But in ruling on that case, Supreme Court Justice William J. Brennan cited 19th-century social philosopher John Stuart Mill when he wrote that "even a false statement may be deemed to make a valuable contribution to public debate, since it brings about 'the clearer perception and livelier impression of truth, produced by its collision with error.'"

So the test for public officials or public figures is whether the journalist wrote the story with *knowing falsity* or *reckless disregard* for the truth. You can't be successfully sued for libel if you innocently publish something false about the town's mayor or the country's president. You must know in advance that the information is false, or you must have so little regard for the truth that you don't check out the claims being made. The test for actual malice, the high court said in a later ruling in the case of St. Amant v. Thompson, was "sufficient evidence to permit the conclusion that the defendant in fact entertained *serious doubts* as to the truth of his publication."

Other tests for libel have evolved through Supreme Court rulings. The most common deals with where the information was obtained. Statements made in court trials and legislative meetings carry an "absolute" guarantee against defamation. The courts call this *ab-*

solute privilege. The intent, generally, is to foster public dialogue and debate unfettered by fear of retribution.

A journalist, then, can report what was said in a trial in which a defendant in a lawsuit is called a crook and a liar as long as the reporter faithfully relays what was said in court. But the newspaper would be at risk if the reporter wrote the same allegations based on an interview outside the courtroom, in which one of the defendant's former coworkers called him a liar and a crook.

Every journalist should be versed in libel laws and should be sure to learn what his or her news organization's policies are regarding what to do if someone threatens to sue over a story. Too often, though, it is carelessness, not ignorance, that gets journalists in trouble. Stupid mistakes can prove costly. Some examples:

- Using the wrong photo in a story about an alleged murderer, or juxtaposing the story and photo so it looks like the person in the photo is accused of murder.
- Making an error in spelling the name or in the address of a person accused of a crime, so that you inadvertently identify the wrong person as the suspect.
- Mistakenly inserting someone's name under the bankruptcies heading in the public record listings, when it should have been listed under building permit requests (he's adding onto his store, not filing for bankruptcy).

So, once again, we stress the importance of accuracy to both news organizations and individual journalists. If you're careless, you can lose your credibility — and your news organization could lose a whole lot of money if you wind up without a good defense in court.

HOT ISSUE — COLD TYPE

Reporters and their editors usually know when they're dealing with sensitive stories. In such situations, responsible journalists guard against inflammatory language. They let the facts tell the story, in plain English. To put it another way, the hotter the story, the cooler the type.

The most sensitive stories — reports about wrongdoing, either ethical or legal — command the most attention. For that reason, if you make mistakes in those stories and are sued, judges and juries can be very sympathetic to the people who have sued you — and, as a result, punish the news organizations and journalists heavily by awarding huge sums of money to the plaintiffs. To avoid being sued,

One-Minute Libel Guide

(Well, maybe two minutes ...)

WHAT IS LIBEL?

Libel is a written or printed defamation — an expression that tends to damage a person's standing in the community. (*Slander* is the proper term for spoken or broadcast defamation.) Defamation cases are taken to civil rather than criminal court, which means that the penalty for people and/or organizations found guilty of libeling someone involves paying what are called monetary damages, not serving time in jail or prison.

Individuals and organizations, including businesses, can sue for libel; governments cannot.

For the record, most news organizations carry libel insurance that covers the costs of defending the organization and the reporter against libel suits.

HOW IS LIBEL PROVED?

To receive monetary damages from news organizations for libel, the person who claims his or her reputation has been damaged must prove all four of the following:

- *Defamation* — the story contained defamatory language.
- *Identification* — the defamation clearly was about the plaintiff.
- *Publication* — the defamation was disseminated.
- *Fault* — the defamation was published as a result of negligence or recklessness.

In order to receive monetary damages, the plaintiff also must prove that the defamation caused personal harm, such as damage to reputation, emotional distress, or the loss of business revenue. The plaintiff must prove that a publication has held them up to hatred, ridicule, or contempt.

WHAT ABOUT PUBLIC OFFICIALS?

In three other types of cases, people who file suit also must prove that you published your story with what the courts call "malice."

Public officials must prove "actual malice," which is defined as publishing a false statement when you know it's false or haven't bothered to check it out.

Businesses that file "trade libel" suits in which they claim you disparaged their product(s), and people who claim you libeled them by innuendo (called "libel per quod"), must prove "common law malice," which is defined as intending to harm someone by publishing a false statement.

WHAT KINDS OF STATEMENTS RESULT IN LIBEL SUITS?

Most of the time, libel suits involve words and phrases that state or suggest criminal activity, serious moral failings, or incompetence in business or professional life. Both businesses and business products can be libeled.

Other dangerous phrases:

- Words that imply a person is unpatriotic, mentally incompetent, an alcoholic, infected by a loathsome disease, dishonest or otherwise lacking in character, a member of a discredited political organization, has vicious motives, behaves antisocially, or has/has had sexual conduct that deviates from generally accepted norms (like being pregnant and unmarried, making improper sexual advances, being homosexual, or being the victim of a sex crime).
- Imprecision in crime reporting.
- Allegations of occupational incompetence, unethical practices, criminal activity, or failure to fulfill marital or familial obligations.
- Disparaging comments about a business product.

(cont.)

Words that are always defamatory (called "libel per se"): *unethical, adulterer, thief, drunkard,* and *cheat.*

Words to watch in business reporting: *fraud, cheated, ripped off, gypped.*

DID YOU KNOW ...?

Advertisements can be libelous, if they imply that competitors have been incompetent or irresponsible.

Photos can be libelous, if they do not reflect what the photographer saw, or if the photos are altered.

The juxtaposition of a photo and headline can be libelous, if the average reader would get the wrong (read: *defamatory*) impression of a person in the photo, based on what the headline says.

People who can show they can be recognized as characters in defamatory works of fiction may succeed in suing for libel.

You can libel all members of a group of fewer than 100 by making defamatory statements about the group.

"Publication" of libelous statements can occur via press releases, interoffice memos, conversations, interviews, and business letters. In other words, if you write a memo containing a libelous statement and circulate it among several people, you effectively have published that information. If you make libelous statements in the course of asking questions during an interview, you have published that information — even if it never appears in the paper.

The fact that you're quoting someone else in print saying something libelous is no protection against a libel suit.

WHAT THINGS *ALWAYS* ARE PROTECTED FROM LIBEL SUITS?

Government officials acting in their official capacity can say whatever they need to say to do their jobs, without fear of being sued for libel. That's why we can report what police or court officials say, but we can't report potentially libelous allegations made by ordinary citizens.

People who initiate or authorize publications that damage their own reputations cannot successfully sue.

Political candidates also can say whatever they want, so long as it pertains to the election and/or their opponents.

WHAT THINGS *USUALLY* ARE PROTECTED FROM LIBEL SUITS?

Comments made in public meetings, court trials, other official proceedings and public records fall under what is known as "reporter's privilege." That means those comments can be reported, so long as they are reported fairly, accurately, with attribution, and printed without ill will.

Comments made outside official proceedings (before, after, or privately to the reporter) are not privileged. This does not mean they cannot be used, only that a suit can be successful if the person who files it can prove the statements qualify as libel, as outlined above.

People with common interests who are members of an organization can communicate openly about mutual affairs without the threat of being successfully sued. That is why, for instance, if you work for a newspaper that is part of a chain, your editors will communicate to other editors in the chain about your interest in moving to another paper in the chain. If your job search takes you outside the chain, however, your editor might avoid any possibility of being sued for slander by confirming only the dates of your employment.

People also can't sue for libel if they uttered the first libelous remarks, and the defamatory remarks about which they are unhappy were made in reply to things they said first.

Opinion is constitutionally protected from libel suits, except if the writer makes statements that are provably false.

Source: "The Law of Public Communication," 2nd Ed., by Kent R. Middleton and Bill F. Chamberlin, published Longman Publishing Group, New York, 1991.

news organizations often conduct libel reviews of sensitive stories prior to publication. These reviews typically involve staff attorneys and senior editors along with the reporter and assigning editor. The lawyers give advice, but the decision whether to run the information is ultimately that of the senior editor in charge. More often, discussions center not on whether to publish a story but on specific words or paragraphs.

Regardless of whether a formal review is conducted, reporters should constantly run mental libel checks on the stories they write.

Here are guidelines for "libel proofing" a story.

• Get at least two documents or three sources. In stories alleging wrongdoing, it's important not to rely on just one source. Confirm the information. In the case of anonymous sources, most newspapers require that at least three sources independently verify the information. Because unnamed sources so severely threaten the credibility of a newspaper report, a few newspapers have banned their use entirely; make sure you check with your editor before you promise anyone anonymity.

• Remove derogatory words and phrases. Look for words that characterize people in ways that would hurt their business, accuse them of a crime, or hold them up to ridicule. Don't assume the story is libel free just because a person's name is not in the story.

• Consider the source's point of view. How will that person respond to the information? One way to answer this is to mentally insert your name in place of the source. How would you characterize the information from this vantage point? In a story that accuses someone of wrongdoing, it's essential to make every attempt to get a response and put that response early in the story.

• Consider other sources. In making accusations about one person, does the story imply wrongdoing by a larger group? In the example of the crooked home builder, if the reporter writes that the crooked builder isn't the only major builder who paid off government officials, then the potential for defaming other home builders grows. If there are only three or four home builders in the area, the risk grows even more. It lumps the builders doing an honest job with the crooks.

And remember the checks from Supreme Court libel rulings:

• Is the story provably true? Are there documents (ideally) or sources to back up the claims in the report?

• Is the subject a public person or private one? If the person is private, then the reporter cannot rely on the test of actual malice as a defense.

- Is the information covered by "reporter's privilege"? Court documents and legislative hearings are the reporter's best friend, because they come closest to being "libel-proof."

CREATING A PUBLIC SQUARE

Overall, the Supreme Court has been reluctant to rule against anything that impinges upon a person's First Amendment right to free speech. The court has held to the notion that the truth can emerge only if citizens have the right to express views freely and hear the freely expressed opinions of others in an open marketplace of ideas — where, as 19th-century philosopher John Stuart Mill said, ideas "collide" to produce a clearer perception of truth.

A journalist must, in all cases, get the facts right. But the conscientious journalist knows that's not enough. Journalism also bears the responsibility of representing multiple perceptions of the truth — covering all sides of a debate; reflecting the wide diversity of a community; bringing forth competing ideas of the solutions as well as the problems.

Any time a journalist presumes to know the truth, he or she suppresses the possibility of other truths. Instead, the journalist should work to create the printed equivalent of a public square, in which a community can work through its fears and problems and dreams for the future.

Social researcher Daniel Yankelovich describes in his book "Coming to Public Judgment" the way in which this idea of a public square works in day-to-day decision making. Yankelovich differentiates *mass opinion,* a snapshot of thousands or millions of individual opinions, from *public judgment,* in which a community or country has made a collective decision. "Public judgment," he says, "is the state of highly developed public opinion that exists once people have engaged an issue, considered it from all sides, understood the choices it leads to, and accepted the consequences of the choices they make."

Yankelovich says there are three stages in the process of forming public judgment: consciousness raising, working through and resolution.

Consciousness raising is what journalists spend most of their time attempting to accomplisht. It's the state in which "the public learns about an issue and becomes aware of its existence and meaning," Yankelovich says. This happens every time a newspaper brings to

Social researcher Daniel Yankelovich's theories about how the public comes to an informed judgment (rather than a superficial opinion) are outlined in his book "Coming to Public Judgment."
Source: Syracuse University Press

light a problem, and people begin to worry about that problem. Media researchers often call this stage "agenda setting" — the media sets an agenda by describing problems that a community needs to address. Yankelovich cites as an example the dangers of AIDS, which at one time was little understood by the public and thought to be a threat only to select groups of drug users and homosexual men.

Working through is the messy part. Here the community recognizes a problem has to be faced and is sorting out competing values. People may differ with each other on how to solve the problem, or, more likely, have conflicting thoughts within themselves about which way to go. For example: It's a good thing to clean up the environment; it is also a good thing to keep taxes low and to allow businesses to operate freely. In the working through stage, these conflicts about choices are weighed and debated. Second and third thoughts are considered. Too often, journalists ignore this stage of deliberation because there are no clear victims or villains, winners or losers in this process. Beat reporters, in particular, find it difficult to report the same issue with a new twist or development. But the working through stage is where the most important work of democracy occurs. What this means for reporters is that they should look for other pieces of an issue — search for many more opinions than just two sides, report on possible solutions that may not be debated by the majority, and independently check the validity of ideas pushed by the governments or other institutions.

Finally, *resolution* is the product of all that deliberation, when the public has completed its journey and decided on a plan of action. "The public" can be any group working on the issue, and it's often the stuff of Page One news: when a town votes on a referendum; when a city council kills a road plan because of pressure from the larger community; when Congress kills the health bill, or the Supreme Court weighs in on a suspect's Miranda rights.

The implication for journalists, then, is to make sure they do a great job on all three stages of decision making. It's not enough to clang the bells about a problem or report the outcome at the end; journalists must ferret out the competing choices to be made in finding solutions to the problem.

How does this idea that a journalist's job is to foster democracy by presenting the public square play out in day-to-day reporting and writing?

Consider these questions.

* *Have I listened to all sides?* Ask yourself whether there's a third or fourth opinion on an issue. Often there is, especially in politics. Although the political parties in a two-party system may present two polar opposites, someone else may hold a different and important view.

* *Have I included the viewpoint with which I most disagree?* Christian conservatives often accuse the press of ignoring them, while giving more sympathetic coverage to such liberal issues as welfare or animal rights. There may be few born-again Christians in most newsrooms, and so their views may seem radical outside the norm of reporters' personal and professional worlds. That doesn't make the views of conservative Christians less valid. Although journalists don't like to admit that they carry biases into the newsroom, it's human nature to do so.

* *Have I characterized "rights" and "wrongs" when they don't exist?* If the building inspector is taking bribes, it's safe to describe it as unethical or illegal. But when a city council is debating what to do about potholes in the street, then it's usually about making choices. The choice to be made between competing goods can be just as compelling, and often more difficult for a community, as one between

good and evil. Don't put the journalistic equivalent of black hats or white hats on public figures unless they truly merit them.

OTHER ETHICAL CONSIDERATIONS

In the late 1990s, high-profile lapses in professional conduct reinforced the need for journalists to do more than simply avoid lawsuits:

- Within a year, "The Boston Globe" discovered two cases of columnists fabricating facts and people.
- The "San Jose Mercury News" retracted a highly publicized investigative report alleging CIA involvement in inner-city drug deals. Its executive editor said that the story oversimplified the issue and used imprecise language and graphics. Contrary evidence also was omitted.
- At "The Cincinnati Enquirer," a reporter illegally obtained voice mails of executives of Chiquita Brands International and then lied to his editors about it. The newspaper ultimately renounced the investigative series the reporter wrote about Chiquita, because it could not stand behind its reporter. The reporter faced criminal charges of trespass and the company that owned the paper — The Gannett Co. — paid $10 million to Chiquita to settle the suit.

These highly publicized cases — along with the more mundane but equally corrosive day-to-day mistakes, inaccurate quotations, misspellings and the like — leave a bad taste in the mouth of the public. An October 1998 Freedom Forum survey found that 88 percent of the public believes reporters "often" or "sometimes" use unethical or illegal tactics to investigate a story; in the same year a Pew Research Center poll found the public evenly split as to whether the press is immoral or not.

In response, many news companies have reexamined their ethical policies or created them anew. In June 1999, The Gannett Co.'s newspaper division released its "principles of ethical conduct for newsrooms." That document has much in common with various other credos and ethics statements by individual newspapers as well as journalism associations, including the Society of Professional Journalists, the "Associated Press" Managing Editors, and the American Society of Newspaper Editors (see Appendix E). And it reflects the aspirations of good journalists everywhere.

- *"Seeking and reporting the truth in a truthful way."* Note the emphasis on how information is obtained. This principle, in essence, says that the ends do not justify the means. It's not enough to report the truth. A reporter must act with honesty and integrity along the way. "We will not lie," the Gannett authors said. "We will not misstate our identities or intentions. We will not fabricate. We will not plagiarize. We will not alter photographs to mislead readers. We will not intentionally slant the news."

• *"Serving the public interest."* This principle declares the journalist's role to "uphold First Amendment principles to serve the democratic process": to be a vigilant watchdog of the government; provide news that empower people as citizens; provide a forum for diverse viewpoints and segments; and shed light on solutions as well as expose problems and wrongdoing.

• *"Exercising fair play."* Like the item on reporting in a truthful way, this principle addresses how a reporter goes about gathering information and distilling it into news stories. "We will treat people with dignity, respect and compassion," the statement said. "We will correct errors promptly. We will strive to include all sides relevant to a story and not take sides in news coverage. We will explain to readers our journalistic processes. We will give particular attention to fairness in relations with people unaccustomed to dealing with the press. We will use unnamed sources as the sole basis for published information only as a last resort. ..."

• *"Maintaining independence."* This principle describes a reporter's relationship with its sources and with citizens at large. The Gannett authors say that their staff will "maintain an impartial, arm's length relationship with anyone seeking to influence the news" and avoid any potential conflicts of interest. The principle suggests that a newspaper shouldn't be beholden to any person or organization for favorable news coverage (or for withholding unfavorable reports).

• *"Acting with integrity."* This principle states, among other things, "we will obey the law." This may seem like common sense. But recall the Chiquita example above, which was the impetus for Gannett issuing the statement of principles. There is a difference between going to jail for protecting a confidential source and stealing records. The principle also describes an intention to observe standards of decency and to "take responsibility for our decisions and consider the possible consequences for our actions. ... We will always try to do the right thing.

EXERCISES

1. Read several newspapers, looking for stories about people accused of wrongdoing. Make note of the language reporters use. What specific words are used to describe the accusations? To whom is the information attributed?

How did the reporters ensure that the information was worded and attributed so as to be accurate and truthful?

2. Use a search engine to look for information on the Internet about one of the issues discussed in this chapter. Read about some of the cases mentioned here, or see if you can locate current cases in which people have tried to stop the media from printing information or have sued successfully for libel.

3. Go to your local law library and read one of the Supreme Court rulings mentioned in this chapter. As you read, make a list of issues the justices address in the majority and dissenting opinions. Think about how those issues might apply to recent cases in which the media has been accused of wrongdoing.

Further Reading

ON THE WEB

Key court cases online: The New York Times v. the United States, The Washington Post Co., et al, 403 U.S. 713, 29 L. Ed. 2d 822, 91 S. Ct. 2140 [1 Med. L. Rptr. 1031] (1971); Near v. Minnesota (Spencer, p. 29) 283 U.S. 697, 75 L. Ed. 1357, 51 S. Ct. 625 [1 Med. L. Rptr. 1001] (1931); The New York Times v. Sullivan, 376 U.S. 254, 11 L. Ed. 2d 686, 84 S. Ct. 710 [1 Med. L. Rptr. 1527] (1964); St. Amant v. Thompson, 390 U.S. 727, 20 L. Ed. 2d 262, 88 S. Ct. 1323 [1 Med. L. Rptr. 1586] (1968).

"The How, Why and What of the New Principles," by Phil Currie and Larry Beaupre, The Gannett Co. News Watch web page, June 18, 1999: www.gannett.com/go/newswatch/ga/june/nw0618-2.htm

For links to Web sites maintained by professional organizations, go to http://newslink.org/org.html

For links to online versions of journalism trade publications go to http://newslink.org/mjou.html

IN PRINT

"Breaking the News: How the Media Undermine American Democracy," by James Fallows, published by Vintage Books, New York, 1996.

"Law for the Reporter," 5th ed., by Dale R. Spencer, published by Lucas Bros. Publishers, Columbia, Mo., 1980.

"The Law of Public Communication," 2nd ed., by Kent R. Middleton and Bill F. Chamberlin, published by Longman Publishing Group, New York, 1991.

"Minnesota Rag: The Dramatic Story of the Landmark Supreme Court Case That Gave New Meaning to Freedom of the Press," by Fred W. Friendly, published by Vintage Books, New York, 1981.

Chapter 15

Getting a Job —
and Keeping It

Working for college media organizations is one of the best ways to prepare for a career in journalism. Here, University of Missouri journalism student Michaella Hammond, left, listens to advice on her traffic story from Gina Henderson, city editor of the university's daily newspaper, the Columbia Missourian.

Source: Columbia Missourian

Key Concepts

- Be prepared to put in the time and effort to find the right job. Do research for your job search as though you were planning to write an in-depth story about current job openings in journalism.

- Editors place great weight on your clippings, or collection of published stories. You can accumulate clippings by writing for your college newspaper, completing internships and doing freelance writing.

- Even after you get the job, learn more about the editors, reporters and others that help shape the values of the newsroom.

Two letters arrived in response to a newspaper's ads announcing a job opening for a reporter. The first began this way:

> "Please accept this letter as application for the general assignment reporter's position ... advertised on Editor & Publisher's Web site."

The other, from graduating college senior Lisa Singh, began like this:

> "He called me his Queen Esther. He confided in me. There I was, a journalism student who had landed an interview with New York's most notorious serial killer. I knew that David Berkowitz, the Son of Sam, had declined similar requests from the New York Daily News and Gannett Newspapers. Still, I wasn't about to let gratitude warp my judgment. I would not settle for a generic, rehash interview. Or allow his responses to go unchallenged. Although my only credential at the time was my passion for the craft of storytelling, I knew I had to go further."

Which of those was better at grabbing your attention? Now, imagine that you're an editor who hires reporters and copy editors. You see hundreds, sometimes thousands, of resumés every year. As you're shuffling through the latest batch of applications, knowing you have one job and 75 applicants, which of the letters would you set aside for further scrutiny?

To "make the cut" in applying for jobs in the news business, you must show editors you have learned the lessons of good journalism in everything you do, from the cover letter and resumé to your story samples and interviews. You must demonstrate a mastery of the English language, or at least the ability to write well and conform to Associated Press style. You must show that you can write with clarity and grace. And you must provide samples of your work that show you can write a variety of stories, from informative news stories to personal profiles to feature stories to in-depth reports.

For most editors, you also must be able to demonstrate a passion for the craft beyond the desire for a regular paycheck. Journalists enter the news business for what might be as many reasons as there are reporters and editors. But two attributes tend to stand out: a love for the written word and a desire to improve the human condition — to make a difference in people's lives.

The hunt for a job can be exhausting. Resumés, cover letters, phone calls, follow-up letters, research, interviews — all take time and attention. But good jobs, like good stories, rarely just "happen." Approach your job search as you would an in-depth story. Give it your best effort from the very beginning, and you are likely to get good results.

FIRST STEPS

Experience pays. Editors want to know they have hired reporters, photographers and copy editors who can work their beats and shoot assignments and write headlines from the day they begin work. A college degree with journalism course work helps, of course. But that, by itself, isn't enough. An aspiring journalist must develop a body of work that shows stories or photos or headlines or page designs. This collection is commonly known as a "clip book" or "clip file," which is shorthand for the clippings of your work cut out from the newspaper.

Showing up at an editor's office with a college degree alone probably won't land you a job at a newspaper, small or large. Showing up with that degree and a fistful of copies of published stories could. Many students work at internships, college newspapers or find freelance work. Here are some of the advantages of each of these forms of experience:

• *School newspapers.* Many college newspapers offer an excellent opportunity to get a taste of the real thing. You can take a turn at writing, copy editing, photography, creating informational graphics, page design or even being an editor who supervises people in those positions. You also can develop substantive stories that would be welcomed at any metropolitan daily. Most college newspapers are fiercely independent and pursue stories that describe both the promises and follies of the college administration, campus police, student government, academic departments and individual students. Writing day-to-day news stories, light features and stories about events is excellent training for your first full-time journalism job. But don't forget to look for ideas for in-depth stories that will give you a chance to dig deeper. Stories that stand out among your peers might also stand out in the mind of a recruiting editor.

• *Internships.* You can turn to several sources to find a good internship. Most colleges have placement services or offices that help students get a line on internships and jobs. Some colleges have off-campus programs that involve internships in major cities. You can look for internship listings online, at the Web sites listed at the end of this chapter. You also can select several news organizations to contact directly. Keep in mind that most large newspapers select their summer interns during fall term. Make sure your resumé is on the editor's desk by November *at the latest*. Smaller newspapers may make their decisions later, but it's still a good idea to approach them several months before your summer break. Check for special internships as well, such as programs for minorities or women. Some newspapers have developed partnerships with specific colleges. Your placement office or faculty advisor can tell you if your college has such arrangements. Also ask whether any newspapers make recruiting trips to your college or to other colleges in nearby cities. Check on whether internships are available at other times of year, such as Christmas break or during other free blocks during your college career.

Some newspapers use interns to write obituaries, briefs or calendar items from press releases, or other simple news stories. Other newspapers may use interns to fill in for vacationing staffers, which generally means you'll be given more complex assignments and asked to generate your own story ideas. Pick the internship that fits your own development. Would you feel most comfortable having a relatively low-stress job, as a way of getting accustomed to a newsroom setting? Or are you ready to dig in and do some real reporting? Check with former interns or your college advisors. What's the quality of the editing at the papers your considering? Do interns get any mentoring or other training? Does the newspaper let interns do hard news as well as light features and profiles? Eventually, you will want to get an internship that closely mirrors a professional journalist's day-to-day experience: working a beat, developing sound story ideas and publishing three-dimensional, complex articles that appear on the Page One (or front page of a section).

• *Freelance work.* Some students develop clips throughout the school year by taking on freelance assignments. Newspapers large and small constantly search for qualified correspondents to work on a per-story basis. Check with your faculty advisor for leads. Common sources include large city newspapers looking for stories about college issues, sporting events, guest speakers or visiting artists on your campus. Many smaller local papers also need correspondents to cover town meetings (for this, you'll probably need access to a car) and "stringers" to cover high-school sports events. You can also market your work more aggressively. Think about the number of students you've met on campus, and the number of towns or cities they call home. Each hometown newspaper might love to see a special feature about its native daughter or son.

Many writers make a full-time living through freelance work, often relying on specialty trade magazines or newspapers, in-house company publications or newsletters for their money. It's not an occupation for the faint of heart, though: Your next paycheck depends entirely on the ability to find assignments and deliver on them in a timely fashion. Sometimes you can't afford to be picky — any assignment that pays may be a good one if it's all you've got that week.

If you're thinking about freelancing as a way to build your portfolio, be selective. Make sure the assignments give you the kind of stories you can show off to a prospective employer. A lucrative article for a company newsletter might not be a very good example of what you can do as a journalist, because the information was presumably given to you and only showed one view (the management's) of the company. But an in-depth interview with cartoonist Scott Adams, of "Dilbert" fame, might be of more value, because it requires intense research, good interview techniques, the courage to ask for time from someone who has many requests for interviews and deft writing that separates the person from the personality.

• *Other writing.* There's no substitute for clippings from newspapers or news magazines. But you can develop other writing forms. Short fiction pieces, technical or persuasive writing, even articles written for church newsletters can help you show an editor how you organize information and relay it to an audience. These clippings also can demonstrate your diversity of writing interests.

APPLYING FOR A JOB

Before sending out applications, take some time to consider where you want to go and what you want to accomplish. List all the factors you need to consider and then prioritize them. Is it important that you be near family? If it's a top priority, that may severely limit your choices, because few cities have more than one newspaper these days. What do you need to grow as a writer and reporter? Good editing is always a consideration. Do you need the breadth of experience provided by a general assignment position, or do you need the experience of a more defined beat like cops and courts? Where do you eventually want to go? Think about the steps needed to get there and list them.

Be realistic. Your first job won't be as a music reviewer or columnist or foreign correspondent. It doesn't matter if you graduate *cum laude* with a master's degree and a personal letter from the dean. Editors expect reporters to pay their dues in the working world first. Other specialty jobs, such as covering the environment or religion, may be out of reach at large metropolitan newspapers. Smaller newspapers, though, often provide more opportunities to do those kinds of reporting. Sometimes smaller dailies can't afford full-time specialties but allow a general assignment reporter to spend extra time on subjects such as the environment or religion.

The size of the newspaper is an important consideration. Generally, bigger newspapers have better-paying jobs, more job opportunities within the paper, more training and more intense editing. Smaller newspapers often allow you to try all kinds of work — even column writing or reviews, on occasion — more than a reporter could ever hope to do at a larger newspaper.

It's important to know these generalities but not be trapped by them. Bigger doesn't always mean better — and doing lots of jobs, if done poorly with little editing, may not help you grow over time.

Several sources can help you figure out where to apply and whom to contact. Trade magazines such as Editor & Publisher and Quill run classified ads with job listings. Most state press associations list openings, as does the Society of Professional Journalists. Some professional groups such as the Associated Press Managing Editors, host regional job fairs. Other trade groups, such as the National Association of Black Journalists, hold fairs during their annual conferences.

Many job postings or notices of job fairs can be found on the Internet, and many allow you to send resumés and cover letters directly to recruiters' Web sites. Your college may have a placement service, and recruiters may make campus visits.

Contact the editors you worked with during any internships; if they don't have openings, they may know of others who do.

Editor & Publisher also has a yearbook that contains information you'll need, such as correct addresses, circulation figures, and contact names and phone numbers. Even then, it's a good idea to double check the names and spelling of contacts at the newspaper — it's what any good reporter or editor would do.

Submit four items when applying for a job: a cover letter, resumé, references and clips. In each case, your job hunt will end quickly if you don't get correct information.

The Cover Letter and Resumé

It is amazing how often otherwise good reporters and editors seem to check their journalistic hats at the door when applying for a job. Resumé packets land in the trash can when a name is misspelled on the cover letter. The recruiter assumes you can't get correct information in a job if you can't get it right in a cover letter.

The first three rules of journalism — accuracy, accuracy and accuracy — apply. Whatever you do, don't make a mistake in the name of the contact person or the name of the newspaper. Is it the Inquirer or Enquirer? Does the Register-Bee have a hyphen or not? Is the word *the* capitalized in the name of the paper? (It's The New York Times but *the* St. Louis Post-Dispatch). It's easy enough to

Web sites offer job listings that can help beginning reporters find internships and jobs.

Source: Newslink

check out. Call if you can't find out from another source. Inaccuracies are inexcusable and will result in your application ending up in the garbage.

Editors also view grammatical errors as grounds for your application to take the fast track to the trash. If grammar isn't your strong point, have a friend who's an excellent writer read over your cover letter before you send it out. Even the best wordsmiths need someone to read their copy.

Business texts or materials from your college placement office can show you standard forms for cover letters and resumés. Follow the formats as much as possible, but remember to make your letter more lively than the examples you're likely to encounter there. Follow the advice that usually suggests you limit cover letters and resumés to one page. If you must, use two pages. Whatever you do, don't copy them on front and back — editors miss things when they're rushed, and they might not notice there's a second page to your resumé.

When in doubt, be true to journalistic forms and practices first. If the resumé template calls for Indiana to be abbreviated as IN, follow the "Associated Press Stylebook" instead (it says you should use "Ind."). Work, not education, should come first on the resumé. Journalistic tradition and temperament place a higher value on hands-on experience (just a few generations ago, most reporters were not college-educated).

The cover letter doesn't have to be a "Queen Esther" type story, but it wouldn't hurt. Consider your audience: an editor or editors with very little time, looking at dozens of cover letters from people just like yourself. Always keep it short and to the point. Don't use flowery or inflated language. Do tell a story — a story about yourself. Try to give the editor a sense of who you are, why you want to be a journalist, and what you've done to get to this point.

The References

Applicants traditionally include three to five references. Again, business texts or your placement service can provide formats. Don't just list your preferred editors or professors. Ask their permission first. It's common courtesy — not to mention sound strategy. Make sure you get their current phone numbers and addresses, and list e-mail addresses, if available. Also ask them what they might say about you: What would they describe as your strengths and weaknesses? Whenever possible, choose people whose titles indicate they know something about journalism and who can speak knowledgeably about you. (That's another benefit of internships — they often give you contact with editors who are happy to give you a good reference, if you've earned it.)

The Clippings

Spend some time compiling and preparing your clippings. They are the most important item you will send. More than anything else, the clips will give editors insights into your abilities. So, what should you send? Consider these variables.

- *Range.* Just how varied are your clips? As much as possible, your packet should contain many different story types and lengths — breaking news, issue stories off a beat, profile writing, news features, etc. When applying for several jobs, tailor the clip packet to each application. If the open position is for a police reporter, you might send more breaking, hard news stories. Even then, make sure there's more range than just cops reports — editors want to know you can do it all when the need arises.
- *Number.* Editors have different opinions here. In general, include no fewer than eight and no more than 12 clippings. There should be enough to show a good range but not so many as to overwhelm a recruiter trying to plow through them. And send only your best — it's better to have fewer clips of the highest quality than to include mediocre or mundane stories.
- *Enterprise.* One of the highest values of a reporter is his or her ability to find stories that don't come from official sources, events or public information releases. Which clips demonstrate your ability to "dig up" stories — to search out information from records and sources and analyze that information clearly? Which clips show you didn't just wait for a story to be given to you? Reporters who can write a story off a press release are cheap; those that can discover the pulse of a community and find stories there are precious.
- *Analytical skills.* Look for clips that "connect the dots," drawing out links between distinct events. Be careful, though, that the analysis isn't your opinion by another name.
- *Writing.* Include your best efforts at storytelling. Ask yourself which news stories boast of clear organization, active verbs and smooth transitions. Think about how you mixed direct quotes with paraphrasing.
- *Timeliness.* It's OK to include special stories done a year or two

ago, but try to keep your stories as current as possible. Don't include anything more than two years old unless, for example, the opening is for a police beat, and the last significant crime story you did was three years ago. Under the "what-have-you-done-for-me-lately" mindset, editors who see "old copy" will suspect that you haven't done anything worthwhile recently.

Editors will consider all these variables as they read. It's important to send your best and to be able to analyze the qualities of those clips when asked by other journalists.

Some reporters never get that far with their packets. Too often, a job candidate will spend hours deciding which stories to include and minutes actually producing the copies. If an editor can't easily read a story, he or she won't. Here are a few tips:

• Your clippings must look neat and be legible. Use white paper when copying clips. Pretty colors only reduce legibility. Don't reduce the print size too small in an effort to fit neatly on an 8-by-11 sheet of paper. It's better to slice apart the newspaper article, paste it on paper and then copy it. But keep the pages tidy. Articles that are copied torn or at odd angles give the impression that you're sloppy and careless.

• The clippings must say where they were published and when. Make sure the date and publication are noted, either by clipping out the information from the folio line and pasting it next to the story or by printing it out on the page before you mount the story.

• Make your packet easy to share. Recruiters often will make copies to share with other editors. Keep everything on 8-by-11 or 8-by-14 sheets of paper. Keep the size consistent and don't wrap your clips in fancy presentation folders (chances are they'll just get thrown away anyway, so the editor can stack your resumé neatly with the rest).

THE INTERVIEW

Successful interviews in newsrooms don't vary much from interviews you might have had for other jobs. You should be prepared to talk about what you want to accomplish as a journalist and how you hope to reach your long-range goals. Mere aspirations, though, won't count for much. Be ready to describe your past successes — in your schoolwork, in internships or other summer jobs, even in particular stories that demonstrate your best qualities.

Before You Arrive

Research the newspaper. Find out whether it publishes in the morning or the afternoon, and how many papers it circulates. Learn the names of the managing editor or other newsroom leaders. Find out who owns the newspaper. Look up articles that mention the newspaper. You can learn a lot about the organization's philosophies and reputation before you arrive. Use that information to ask intelligent questions during the interviews.

Remember: A job interview works two ways. As much as you should sell yourself to the editors, you should also shop. The job and the newsroom must meet your career goals and personal values.

Editors don't need to see another dozen clips. But it doesn't hurt to ask, before you arrive, whether the editor would like to see further examples of any kinds of stories. You might want to bring along any article you're particularly proud of that was published after you sent your packet. Finally, it doesn't hurt to bring a few copies of your resumé to the interview.

Newsrooms are notorious for casual clothes, or at least for ill-fitting business attire. Don't follow suit. The reporters you'll see there already have a job; you don't. Dress as if you are serious about getting a job.

Interviewing the Interviewers

Consider the following questions when applying for a job.

• Does the newsroom have a mission or purpose statement? If so, how does it fit with any written goals of the newspaper? Does it fit with your ideas of the kind of journalism you want to do?

• How much "turnover" occurs in the newsroom? Turnover refers to the number of people who resign or are terminated and then replaced during a given period. Some turnover is expected, and even can be a good thing. But alarm bells should go off if 30 or 40 reporters out of a complement of 80 or 90 have left in the past year.

• What are the backgrounds of senior newsroom managers? What is their philosophy of the news? Does it fit in with the written goals? How many managing or executive editors have there been in the past three or four years? What is the relationship between the newsroom and the newspaper's publisher?

• Who owns the newspaper? If it's a family, what is the family history and current ownership like? If it's a corporation, how has the company performed financially and in its responsibilities to cover the news?

The Interviews

Every newsroom has its own style of interviewing. You may interview with a dozen editors, one at a time, or with groups of three or four. You might be asked to take copy-editing tests or write headlines from that day's stories. Some newspapers also include tests that probe a reporter or editor's interests and motivations or require a tryout of one or two days, in which you would be given one or more assignments to turn around quickly and for publication. Newspapers generally pay applicants for the tryouts.

The questions asked by editors vary as well. Be prepared to talk about yourself — your likes and dislikes, your motivations for entering journalism, even the last book you read or movie you watched. Think about specific examples: What was your favorite story? Why? What was your worst mistake in reporting or editing? What did you learn from that mistake? Talk about a time you had to deal with a difficult source, colleague or editor. Describe competing stories you were working on and how you resolved which had the higher priority. Have you ever written a correction?

From your research, you should have ready some questions of your own for the editors. It's OK to ask specific questions about the job — for whom you would be working, the job's pay range and benefits, the start date, the size of the work group, the expectations (is a specific number of stories expected per week?). Don't forget to ask when a decision will be made as well.

After the Interview

Patience and persistence are required after you leave. Don't expect decisions to be made in a day, or even within a week or two, unless the hiring editor has given you a timetable. Send a thank-you note as soon as possible after the interviews, including any points you want to underscore or clarify. If, for instance, you believe you mangled an answer during the interviews, don't hesitate to give a better response in a letter. It's OK to call for an update, especially if the editors' stated deadline for a decision has passed.

Finally, learn from your rejections. If a newspaper passes on you, ask the editors how they assessed your strengths and weaknesses. Ask what you could do differently with the cover letter, references, resumé and clips. Ask how you came across during the interviews. Usually, if you have demonstrated enough skills to make it to face-to-face interviews, the question is not whether you are qualified for the job but how you fared with others competing for it. Whatever you do, don't get defensive. Learn from the experience.

THE VALUES OF A NEWSROOM

It's important to identify the enduring values of the newsroom and its parent company; current tensions within the newsroom or between the newsroom and other departments; the philosophy and passions of senior managers; and the commitment of the company to its public service role in the community.

Don't rely on whether you like the editor for whom you would be working. That's important, of course, but remember that newsrooms, like people, constantly change. A favorite editor today might be reassigned tomorrow. He or she might leave to follow academic pursuits or be recruited by another newspaper.

Instead, consider the total picture — the whole story. It will help you find the right job. And it will help you as you begin work. Although writing is often a solitary pursuit, you are not alone in this journalistic factory you are preparing to enter.

Many people shape the values of a newspaper: the paper's owners, including stockholders in publicly traded companies; the publisher and editorial board; senior editors who define the general direction of the newsroom; assigning editors who supervise day-to-day production; and fellow reporters, copy editors and photographers. Even senior leaders in production or advertising can subtly or directly influence the operations of the newsroom, especially when it comes to competition for scarce resources.

And the community in which it operates helps shape the newsroom's values. The residents of Portland, Maine, may have different expectations of their newspaper than the residents of Portland, Ore.

THE INFLUENCE OF PUBLISHERS AND OWNERS

Upon learning of orders to cut the newsroom staff, a senior editor first got angry, then turned philosophical. He shook his head and said, "Well, you know, we'll put out the best newspaper that the publisher can pay for."

Despite its unique role in American democracy, the newspaper industry is, first and foremost, a profit-making business. Corporations that control dozens or hundreds of publications, in addition to television, radio and other communications outlets, own most newspapers. Other newspapers, from as small as the 8,300-circulation Coastland Times in Manteo, N.C., to the massive national newspaper The New York Times, are owned or primarily run by individual families.

Many of the newspaper-owning companies are publicly traded

and therefore beholden to stockholders, who reasonably expect their investments to pay off. Critics charge that this attention to short-term returns prevents long-range thinking and investment. But supporters often say that any company held accountable will operate more efficiently.

What does the attention to "the bottom line" mean to you? Depending on its corporate philosophy, a newspaper may make severe cuts during a newsprint cost increase or with the loss of a major advertiser.

The publisher makes those decisions. If he (there are few female publishers in the industry) also owns the paper, he operates autonomously. If the paper is owned by a corporation, the publisher controls expenses and makes decisions about strategic investments based on mandates from the corporation. On any given week, a publisher could decide whether to spend millions on a new press or on an Internet Web operation, buy an alternative weekly in the area, set the salary budget for next year's raises or sign off on the hiring of additional reporters. The publisher may or may not directly control the newspaper's editorial board. He likely directly supervises the newsroom's senior editor, as well as the leaders in advertising, production, circulation and other departments.

The publisher's commitment to the news can greatly influence the newsroom. A publisher who sees the value of news to his readers, his advertisers and the community at large will understand (if not always agree with) the values of the newsroom.

THE INFLUENCE OF EDITORS

Editors are the people who have the greatest direct impact on a newspaper's content, day in and day out. Top editors generally direct

Fewer Companies Now Own More Newspapers

The two-newspaper city is almost extinct. According to media critic Ben Bagdikian, 99 percent of the 1,500 daily newspapers in the country are the only dailies in their cities. Corporations have swallowed all forms of media. In "The Media Monopoly" (1997) Bagdikian says that the number of mega-media corporations with dominant power in society has shrunk from 50 corporations in 1984 to "closer to 10" in 1996: "This means few choices for citizens looking for genuine differences. ... At issue is the possession of power to surround almost every man, woman, and child in the country with controlled images and words, to socialize each new generation of Americans, to alter the political agenda of the country."

the newsroom's goals and policies but may have less involvement in the actual production of the newspaper. The size of the newspaper determines how many editors stand between the top editor and the journalists who create the stories, photos, graphics and page designs that show up in print.

At some large papers, the top editor may rely on a managing editor to implement policies with the assistance of several deputy managing editors who, in turn, supervise the editors of various sections of the paper. At smaller papers, the section editors may be supervised by either the top editor or by a single assistant managing editor.

Changes in top editors can have a tremendous impact. If an editor with a strong emphasis on day-to-day local news is replaced by an editor whose primary interest is in-depth reporting, the change can result in a reallocation of resources that affects the internal organization and the paper's content. The new editor might want to establish an investigative reporting team by pulling several reporters from daily beat coverage. That action might result in fewer daily stories but more in-depth reports. Your professional life will definitely change if you are chosen for the new team or left behind to pick up some of the stories once covered by a coworker.

No editor, however, has as much direct effect on a reporter than the assigning or section editors who directly supervise your work. That person will help you understand your role in carrying out the paper's policies and achieving its goals. The assigning editor also will give you assignments, edit your work and evaluate your performance.

Although higher-level editors sometimes become involved in the hands-on editing of certain reporting projects — especially in-depth stories involving high-profile issues — most of your work will go into the paper with only your supervising editor's changes.

You can ensure your short-term sanity and long-term success by establishing a good working relationship with your editor. Expect to have a different kind of relationship with each editor. Some editors will want you to update them on nearly everything you're working on. Others would rather you come to them only if you encounter problems. Some will edit your work heavily. Others will barely touch it.

Differences between editors stem from differences in personality and management styles. The stereotypical editor is gruff and curmudgeonly — but many editors with more supportive management styles can be just as demanding. The keys to productive relationships with your editors are no different from those that help you work well with anyone: Value their strengths, work around their limitations, and always do the best work you can. Talk to your editor

Editor
Reports directly to publisher; develops long-range plans, works with other departments of the newspaper (marketing, advertising, etc.)

Editorial page editor
Usually reports directly to publisher; sets direction for editorial section, supervises writers

Managing editor (ME)
Responsible for implementing plans and policies, overseeing editors who supervise various aspects of producing the paper

Deputy or Assistant ME for news
Oversees preparation of daily "hard" news report; supervises editors below who, in turn, assign stories and supervise reporters

Deputy/Assistant ME for features
Oversees preparation of features, arts and "lifestyle" news; supervises editors below who, in turn, assign stories and supervise reporters

Deputy/Assistant ME for design
Oversees preparation of non-text elements and assembly of pages; supervises editors below

Metro editor

Politics editor

Public safety editor

Education editor

Regional editor

Business editor

Sports editor

Features editor

Arts editor

News editor
Supervises layout of the paper

Photo editor
Assigns photos, supervises photographers

Graphics editor
Supervises graphic artists

Many editors at this level also have assistants who help them directly supervise the work of reporters, photographers, graphic artists and copy editors.

An example of a typical metropolitan newspaper's management structure.

Managing Editor (ME)
*Reports directly
to publisher; develops long-range plans,
works with other departments of the
newspaper (marketing, advertising, etc.)*

↓

Assistant ME
*Responsible for implementing plans
and policies, overseeing editors who
supervise various aspects of producing the paper*

**Editorial
page editor**
*May report directly
to the publisher
or top editor; sets
direction for
editorial section,*

City editor	**Features editor**	**Sports editor**	**News editor**	**Photo editor**	**Graphics artist**
Assigns "hard" news stories, supervises reporters	*Assigns feature stories, supervises reporters*	*Assigns sports stories, supervises reporters*	*Supervises copy editors who proofread stories, write headlines and lay out pages*	*Assigns photos, supervises photographers*	*Prepares graphics and other artwork*

An example of a typical small daily newspaper's management structure.

about things that bother you in as constructive a way as possible. Only if you feel you have differences you cannot work out should you take your problems to that person's supervisor — and, ideally, you and your editor would go to that person together.

THE INFLUENCE OF JOURNALISTS

If you've watched many movies, it may seem like most journalists are grizzled white guys with drinking problems, ambitious young women who bollix careers by getting romantically involved or feckless lechers who delight in pawing through people's trash.

Journalists who have been in the business a long time get cynical if they have come to view the news business as nothing but drudgery. They may feel like all they do is cover meetings, at which boring people say boring things, or that, after a while, all murders look alike. Maybe they feel like they've worked under a series of hot-shot new editors whose only goal is to move up the food chain while keeping them squarely at the bottom.

As in every profession, the newsroom has its share of burnouts, and they often make a beeline for the new reporter who hasn't heard their tale of woe again and again. The real world contains both drama and drudgery — and often it's the drudgery that leads to the drama.

Your skills, attitude toward your job, willingness to learn new things, and an understanding that what you don't know will always exceed what you do — as in most professions, these are the attributes that will determine how well you do in the news business and how happy you'll be.

Working journalists hold a tremendous influence over the content of their newspapers. Although editors sometimes dole out assignments and often alter their work, even beginning journalists have a certain degree of latitude in selecting information that will be submitted for inclusion in the paper. The newspaper that hires you places its trust in your ability to report and write honestly, fairly and completely.

Every reporter makes choices about whom he or she interviews, which facts and quotes to use and how those nuggets of information are arranged in a story. Likewise, photographers decide which photographs to shoot and how to frame them, and people who lay out newspaper pages select which material to highlight or downplay. These are the choices that provide the raw material from which the newspaper is made; as a result, they are fundamental in setting the direction of the paper.

In addition, editors are always open to good ideas. Prove yourself, and they will be more willing to let you take on more complicated stories or other responsibilities. However, beware of the trap you will set for yourself if you say you want to change jobs or take on new challenges when you're not doing particularly well in your current job. It can send a message that you tend to look outside yourself for solutions, rather than finding the motivation within to keep doing your present job to the best of your ability — no matter how routine it has become for you.

EXERCISES

1. Buy several copies of the same newspaper and pick a writer whose byline appears often. Clip out a selection of his or her stories that reflect a range of writing styles, story formats and subject matter. Imagine that you are an editor looking at those clippings. What's missing? What kinds of stories would you like to know how he or she would handle?

2. Write a resumé and have at least two people critique it.

3. If you've written stories that have been published, clip them out and mount them as though you were preparing to send them out as part of a job application packet. If you have written enough stories to include a range of stories that show depth, variety and enterprise, do so. Ask at least two other people to critique the clippings. (Your journalism professor or an editor with the student newspaper are good choices, if they have the time.)

Further Reading

ON THE WEB

An ever-changing array of Web sites lists jobs and internships in journalism or provides support for working journalists. These include:

AJR/American Journalism Review job listings: www://ajr.newslink.org/joblink/. Lists of professional organizations for journalists: http://ajr.newslink.org/spec.html

Corporations that own multiple newspapers, such as The Gannett Co. (www.gannett.com) and Knight-Ridder newspapers (www.kri.com)

Pew Center for Civic Journalism's job board: www.pewcenter.org

TVJobs.com — lists jobs in broadcast journalism: www.tvjobs.com/index_a.htm

IN PRINT

"Editor & Publisher Yearbook," published by Editor & Publisher, New York, Updated annually; lists virtually every established newspaper and wire service on the planet.

"The Student Guide to Mass Media Internships," published by the Intern Research Group of the School of Journalism and Mass Communication, University of Colorado, Boulder, 1996.

The Life of a Reporter

DECONSTRUCTING THE NEWSROOM

It's a world where the story and the work have long predominated.
But maybe there's room for a life as well.

By Sharyn Wizda
Features Editor
Austin (Texas) American-Statesman

They say it's adrenaline that keeps it all going.

Every day, this thing we call a newsroom brings together the thrill of the hunt and a race against time. Cinematically speaking, it's "His Girl Friday" for the senior set, "All the President's Men" if you're thirtysomething or "The Paper" for newbies — a collection of smart, just-this-side-of-eccentric scribes on a mission to get the hottest stories for the next day's paper.

But, alas, life isn't always quite as glamorous as the movies. The real newsroom culture has over-long hours, the kind where you're steeped in exhaustion and stress, not tossing off acerbically witty barbs at your deskmate over one more cup of coffee. There are freakish editors who don't suddenly make the right decision in the last reel, as well as certain peculiar-to-journalism expectations thrown into the mix. Is that environment the best for producing a great paper? Talk to the people working in newsrooms now and ones who have left, and some common themes — and questions — emerge. Come inside the newsroom culture, deconstructed.

The Story reigns supreme.

Sharyn Wizda, 30, has survived the vagaries of newsroom culture for more than a decade now, fortunately breaking into laughter more often than tears. When not trying to decide who would play her in the next generation of newspaper movies, Wizda writes and edits in the features section of the Austin American-Statesman. Reprinted with permission from the September 2000 issue of AJR/American Journalism Review.

Yes, The Story is valued above all else, and if you write good ones, the kind that get on the front page, you're at the top of the food chain.

This makes sense, of course, since The Stories fill up The Paper, and it's difficult to persuade people to pay 50 cents for several blank sheets of newsprint. Stories are what win readers (we'd like to think, anyway) and are the vehicle by which newsrooms actually fulfill their mission — to inform, to entertain, to provoke. They inspire change, they teach us something, they win awards. They're probably the biggest measurement journalists use when judging the relative clout of any given newspaper, and they arguably play the biggest role in judging the relative clout of any given reporter.

So ideally, you write good stories — ones with colorful detail, surprising information or news you can use — and your bosses tend to appreciate you, because you're helping the cause.

What's "good" gets a little fuzzier when you look at the newsroom as a whole, where the stories are judged on a bigger stage and with more competitors. In fact, there's an unspoken pecking order in most newsrooms based solely on the perceptions about what kinds of stories each section produces.

Work in metro or national? You're at the top of the hierarchy because you write what generally makes up the bulk of A1. Business usually comes next. Then the serious points start to wane. Features? Fluff chicks on parade (they're never here past 6). Sports? Guys who are fun to banter with but not, shall we say, of a certain caliber to make it in a real section. Despite the move in many newsrooms toward increasing the mix on A1 to include more stories from these sections, folks in these departments often are taken less seriously.

Nancy Lofholm now writes everything from straight news stories to features as the Denver Post's western Colorado correspondent. But in the early 1990s, at the Daily Sentinel in Grand Junction, Colorado, she found she had to combat opinions that she was, somehow, backsliding when she switched from metro to features because the schedule meshed better with her child-care needs.

"The other people in the newsroom were shocked. I had people come and say, 'Are you sure? Do you know what you're doing? I think you're making a big mistake. You won't be taken seriously if you do features.' ... I think there was still a throwback attitude that features was still looked at as the women's page." Lofholm went on to win several national and state awards for her feature writing.

But The Work is what gets you noticed.

Coming in a close second to The Story is The Work, and you'd better put in a lot of it. The pervasive message reporters get from the second they step into a newsroom is that this workplace is a caste system, with those at the top writing the most stories or writing the biggest-clout stories — or, in unusual cases, knocking themselves out doing both. The assumption is that you better either be turning out at least several stories a week or writing the kinds of A1 projects that win so many awards it's all right that your byline shows up only twice a year. Work hard, and you'll be rewarded. Work harder, and well. ... Hey, can you make another call before you walk out the door?

Consider Laura Wisniewski, now an assistant metro editor at the Detroit Free Press, who started her career straight out of college at the Oakland Press in Pontiac, Mich. "I really felt like the harder I worked, the more I could prove myself," Wisniewski remembers. "The longer my days, the more I wrote, the more stories I came up with on my own, the better it was. I really had a sense of proving myself."

On one level, there is a reassuring order to such a dues-paying mentality: It's clear what's expected, and there's a certain scrappy appeal. But without careful editors to help spread the load — or the ability to say "no" — reporters can quickly get buried in a mountain of work that they're afraid to admit is a mountain.

Wisniewski went from the Oakland Press to the Associated Press's Detroit bureau, where she was the day rewrite reporter for two-and-a-half years, juggling stories all day long on eight screens at a time. It's experience she calls invaluable, but she also says she knew she couldn't keep up that pace indefinitely.

"It was very draining. I was there during the [Persian] Gulf War. There's a large Arab community in Dearborn, and I was sent knocking at 6:30 a.m. on doors. They have a very set schedule at the AP — that's probably the only way you could survive working at the wire. You could easily get so addicted and caught up in the news that you don't leave."

Harder is better.

This kind of runs in tandem with the idea that the more stories you write, the better you are. Newspaper folks take a sort of perverse pleasure in how hard it was to get something done. (If you're one of those special-projects reporters or the like, the ones who only write one story every few months or so whether they need to or not, the people churning out the whole metro front every day envy your status but secretly pooh-pooh your work ethic.)

"I think what we fear mostly is our colleagues," Wisniewski says. "You don't want them to think that you're a slacker."

Underscoring reporters' sense of pride in the sheer quantity of work they're doing is the real-life messages they're getting from bosses (the annual byline counts, the pleas from desperate assistant city editors to already-overloaded reporters: "Please, I really need you to do just this one thing," and the romance of the ideals of journalism — the underdog reporter filing against some kind of impossible deadline or circumstance). It's as though the worse your situation is, if you manage to pull a halfway decent story out of it, it's actually better. It gets put into your war chest of stories for one-upmanship at happy hours. The message is clear — not only do you not complain, you're supposed to relish the pell-mell nature of the beast.

"I felt like in news, you could never turn in enough copy," says the

Denver Post's Lofholm, who has worked in news and features sections at smaller papers in Colorado and Nebraska.

Longer hours are the norm, rather than the exception. Few reporters expect to be working eight-hour days routinely — an aspect of newsroom culture that was hammered home to usatoday.com's Christine Montgomery when she came to the Web site in June 1999 from a reporting job at the Washington Times.

"There's sort of a shift mentality, for lack of a better word," says Montgomery, the site's features editor. "Here, we have to have people here all the time, round the clock. So if you come in at 6, you leave at 2. That took some getting used to: The 9 a.m. person left right at 5. I was like, 'This isn't journalism! What the hell are these people doing?'"

Of course, if you're going nonstop — as Montgomery points out the site's staff needs to — eight hours is pretty much all you can take. Well, a newsroom isn't the most placid place, either. And so inevitably the question arises: Is the quality of your work in the newsroom the same when you're writing three stories a day routinely, coming in at 10 and leaving at 8 or 9, as when you have the evenings and weekends to recharge?

"There is a certain signal you're sending off when you work that hard, but it can have a dulling effect on your creativity," says Rebecca Goldsmith, who covers aging for Newark's, N.J., Star-Ledger. Without a recharge, she points out, the work can suffer.

The hard part is that since you're inculcated in the fast, frantic pace pretty much from Day One (and most everyone else is doing the same), it can be difficult, if not impossible, to figure out when you're going too hard.

"With being so busy and working from 9 a.m. to 10 at night and getting paged on the weekend, you just don't have time to think about how crazy your life is," says Brian Reilly, who left journalism after covering crime for four years at the Washington Times. "It seemed normal at the time."

How we cope: The people are pretty funny.

Of course, if it was all hell, all the time, nobody would stay in the newsroom. The upside is that newsrooms generally tend to attract smart, engaged, funny people. There's cynicism, sure — but that shouldn't be surprising for folks who get paid to check out everything before putting it in the paper. In off moments, that spirit often gets funneled into controlled craziness — the parody e-mails, the happy hours — that makes the frenzy a little easier to bear.

"You're surrounded by bright people. You know, when things are working well you move fast, you often work long hours and there's a sense of camaraderie," offers Stephen Buel, a reporter and editor at the San Jose Mercury News until recently.

"I like the idea that I can go to cover a story and newspaper reporters identify with one another," says P. J. Huffstutter, who covers technology for the Los Angeles Times. "I like the humor."

It's part of what makes Jonathan Gaw — who reported for Cleveland's Plain Dealer, Minneapolis' Star-Tribune and the L.A. Times before joining IDC, an Internet marketing firm in Mountain View, Calif., in January — sometimes miss the newsroom atmosphere.

"You know what a newsroom is," he says. "You look up from your desk and some guy's shouting into the phone at some poor secretary — you kind of miss that. ... Journalists are just different people. For example, as a going-away gift a friend of mine got me a crystal ball, a real crystal ball" — Gaw now predicts Internet trends — "which, of course, is extremely amusing. Some of the people here kind of chuckle, and then some look at it and almost frown."

I'm sorry. Did you say you wanted to have a personal life?

When you're 25 and don't have people waiting at home, the newsroom pranks and craziness can make up for the long hours. But what about when you're of the age when you're getting married and starting a family? How difficult is it to reconcile the demands of, well, having a life and having it all in the newsroom?

If a newspaper is to reflect its community as a whole, the newsroom's community needs to be more than a group of workhorses in their early 20s who have never grappled with a Diaper Genie or struggled through buying a house. Aside from the obvious perks of having some reporters who have longevity and wisdom on their beats, it's crucial to bring to the newsroom the different life experiences of the 45-year-old married mom with two kids or the 32-year-old dad of a toddler, as well as the early-20s hungry recruit who can work 12 hours and then come back early the next day to do it all again. But does the way the newsroom is organized encourage or even support such diversity?

"I don't think it's that you can't be a married woman and be a reporter," says the Star-Ledger's Goldsmith, who is slated to join the ranks of married woman reporters at the end of this year. "It's more what you're going to do. It's hard to be a daily reporter who has to leave at 5 every day. There are women here who have to leave at 6 every day. They don't have the greatest beat assignments. ...

I think a lot of it is how you get along in the newsroom culture — if you're likable and try your best, or if you're a nervous Nellie and you're only thinking all day about when you leave."

In other words, if your parameters are that you must leave at 6 every day come hell or high water, you simply can't be assigned to a high-profile city hall beat on which there are night meetings twice a week. But as others point out, it's more a matter of finding that balance for yourself.

"There are committed, hardworking reporters and there are less committed, less hardworking reporters, and some of the most committed, hardworking reporters I know have kids and try to get out of the newsroom at 4:30," says Buel, who spent nearly 17 years at the Mercury

News and other papers in California and Arkansas before going to a dotcom.

"Occasionally that can pose a daily challenge in trying to find a way to get a specific story covered, but I tried to view people more in their sense of the real hunger for the story. I'm thinking of a specific reporter who worked for me — she had two kids and tried to get out of the newsroom every day at 4:30. She got to the paper every day at 8:30 and she kicked butt. She covered deregulation of electric utilities better than anybody ... and she, I think, was a great example of how it is possible to be really dedicated and dogged and hardworking and beat the competition and be human and have a life, and I think she did a better job than myself by drawing the line."

Don't ever leave me.

So what happens if you commit the worst sin of all — you think about leaving? Unless you're heading out for another (better) newspaper job, the reaction tends to be vague suspicion of your motives.

"I think newsrooms are very much a clique. They're very much like, prove yourself the hardest worker, or have the best ideas, or something sharp. You really have to show who you are," the Free Press' Wisniewski says. "So when you leave, it's like quitting the fraternity. And you think they're bailing out, or selling out."

"Everybody figured that Reilly was still gonna be a reporter," says Reilly, now a second-grade teacher in New York City. His former co-workers at the Washington Times simply couldn't fathom that he wouldn't want to come back.

Traditionally, people who left the newsroom went into public relations, the death star of jobs after journalism. (What reporter hasn't shuddered on the other end of the phone when a PR person has said, "Oh, I used to be in newspapers!") And once you left, you left. Rarely would a person who had switched into PR make it back into the newsroom.

But is all that changing, with the growth of the dotconomy that is sucking more and more reporters from newsrooms into Web ventures? Some who have made the jump think so.

"There's this whole 'You've left the brotherhood' kind of thing — that's changed," says IDC's Gaw. "I'm fairly confident that I can go back. That's actually one of the things I asked when I left: 'Can I come back?' ... Some of my colleagues are now calling me and using me as a source. If I'm good enough as a source, then I'm good enough to go back and report on it."

Buel — who recently founded vox.com, a Web site that's a division of a company called Cybergold at which freelance writers, musicians and artists can post their work — says when he announced his departure from the Mercury News earlier this year, there were those who initially expressed the suspicions usually reserved for the PR defectors.

"A friend of mine at the Wall Street Journal sent me a one-word e-mail that was just, 'Cybergold?' And he was clearly dumbstruck by the concept that I would go to work for an Internet marketing firm." But, Buel goes on to say, "It used to be that if you wanted an exit strategy from newspapers, PR was it. Now it turns out that the Internet is an exit strategy, because journalistic skills are highly valued."

Are people leaving because the pay is better? Certainly, no one's turning it down. And over the past few years, the stories of young reporters doubling and tripling their salaries have become legion — as have other financial perks that are strangers to even experienced scribes.

"We had people being offered salaries that we could compete with, but stock options that we really couldn't compete with," says Susan Goldberg, managing editor of the Mercury News, which has lost about 11 staffers to Web sites in the last year. "I think that ... people who went into journalism didn't do it with the expectation of getting rich, but all of a sudden content producers for the first time ever seemed to be in demand. I think a lot of people understandably thought, 'Wow, I'm not going to let this gravy train go by without me on it.'"

Many who've jumped to the supposed cash cow (and even some who haven't) say that's not why: It's the chance simply to do something different. "Money's not the reason I got into journalism," says the L.A. Times' Huffstutter, "and hopefully money won't be the reason I get out."

OK, maybe you should have a life.

Still, could the exodus of some of their best and brightest to the dotcoms make newsrooms rethink their culture like never before? Certainly, there's a time-honored newsroom tradition of getting what you want only after job offers from elsewhere are dangling. In some newsrooms — particularly ones near high-tech meccas — that's meant a recent shift from a mind-set that espouses for-God-and-country motivation to staying for perks that are a little more concrete.

"That's why you're starting to see at both mid-size and larger papers a rush to make the reporters feel that they are more valued," Huffstutter says. "There are more flexible work hours. They are starting to roll out stock options, be more flexible with beat structures and more flexible with projects and with dailies."

Robert Rosenthal, editor of the Philadelphia Inquirer, says that papers are "absolutely" trying to be more responsive. "It's happening — we have a lot of people working four-day weeks, things like that," he says. "You have to adjust when talented, smart people are going elsewhere. Rigidity is death."

And in some cases, it's happening even when there isn't a contingent jumping to the dotcoms. Tiffini Theisen, who covers workplace issues for the Orlando Sentinel, says staffers there are enjoying more flexible work hours, a relaxed dress code and elevated titles — in part because they've had the leverage of a job offer elsewhere. "I think they're definitely doing things to keep people here," Theisen says.

The Mercury News' Goldberg says many of the changes are happening simply because newspapers are paying attention to good management as a way to retain employees.

"All over the country, companies are figuring out that the way to keep people working for you is to manage them properly and try to figure out a way to accommodate people's lives in their work lives," she points out. "We are doing more with flextime. We do let people work from remote offices. We do let people work from homes. Newspaper salaries traditionally have been very low. I think the value of what good journalists do has increased, and salaries are going up, and I'm darn happy about it. It's just a very competitive market for good people."

And keeping good people is worth making some adjustment, says Michael Oreskes, The New York Times' Washington bureau chief. "It's not the way newsrooms used to work," says Oreskes, who nearly a decade ago as the Times' metro editor rejiggered some reporters' work hours and beats to accommodate their needs as new parents. "Obviously, newsrooms have always been somewhat informal ... but there tends to be this presumption in the newsroom that you're always available. But you can still get good work from people who have other priorities and who are not always going to be available.

"It makes it harder to manage, harder to run things. But I think the upside is that you get incredibly talented people ... and you maintain people's careers during phases during their lives when doing other things is just as important."

That's got to be welcome news for those wary of going wired in the wake of high-profile Web waverings, such as the recent layoffs at Salon and the implosion of APBnews.com. (See "Surviving in Cyberspace.") Theisen is one who decided to stay put in the newsroom rather than take an offer from a startup — even though the job would have involved an exciting move to Brussels and a more prestigious title. "There just wasn't enough stability," she says.

Sites linked to a reputable content provider — aka "Your Daily Newspaper" — seem to be weathering the recent dip just fine. "I do think the party's over for the startups," says usatoday.com's Montgomery. "But those closings don't make me worried for usatoday.com. I think it's just kind of a natural shakeout of the industry. I imagine it's much like the early days of TV, when anybody was putting anything on the air. Then there's a chance to mature."

A change is gonna come.

Part of the joy of workplace culture, of course, is that it can change. There's likely always going to be an element of the newsroom that values the commitment of a long day, and an element that relishes that rush of writing four stories in one day on a laptop that keeps breaking down. But as viable alternatives to newspaper jobs crop up just a mouse-click away — and if managers like Goldberg are right about her colleagues paying attention to the life demands of their employees — it seems that newspapers could be poised on the brink of what would be a big culture shift. The challenge is to preserve the aspects that make it good to work there, while getting more flexible and realistic about the parts that drive smart, talented people elsewhere.

So what still makes the newsroom a worthy place to work?

"I think of the creative surge in the sense of anything can happen at any time, and a boring day can become fun at any time," says the "Inquirer's" Rosenthal. "We'll get a breaking story on [our] Web [site], and we beat somebody, and it's exciting. It's like, 'Hello sweetheart, get me rewrite' — it's that romantic thing."

"Every day is a brand-new opportunity to get it right, to do it better, to shy away from yesterday's mistakes," says Melinda Johnson, features editor at the Santa Barbara, Calif., News-Press. "It's always a challenge, always an opportunity to reinvent, to reshape, to kind of cast off yesterday's mistakes, and just take another chance, come charging back."

Get me rewrite? A big comeback?

Sounds like surely it can be like the movies, at least part of the time.

Newspaper Jobs

The word *journalist* is used to describe people who have a variety of jobs within in a newsroom. Although every newspaper is different, most have people in the following roles.

PEOPLE WHO CREATE ORIGINAL MATERIALS FOR THE NEWSPAPER

Writers

Journalists who write for newspapers fall into several categories:

General assignment reporter. A journalist who writes whatever stories need to be covered on a given day. Although this title usually is given to interns and entry-level reporters, it also can be given to experienced reporters who excel at finding stories off the beaten path.

Beat reporter. A writer with specific expertise. Some common beats include cops and courts, government, politics, business, education, environment, health and medicine, ethics and religion, military life and sports.

Correspondent or bureau reporter. A reporter who works and usually lives at a distance from the newspaper's main office. Some of these are entry-level jobs; others, such as correspondents in Washington, D.C., or foreign countries, are considered plum jobs awarded to only experienced, accomplished reporters.

Senior reporters. Experienced, accomplished reporters may have titles like *features writer*, usually specializing in narrative writing and profiles of famous as well as everyday people; *investigative reporter*, concentrating on big stories that require several layers of research and often involve uncovering misdeeds by officials; *database reporter*, specializing in reporting techniques that involve complicated statistical analysis; or *public life reporter*, specializing in citizens' interests and points of view, so as to cover the news about politics and other aspects of public life in ways that resonate with citizens' experiences.

Columnist. An experienced reporter or nonjournalist with expertise who writes periodic personal or themed columns and sometimes news stories as well.

Critic or reviewer. An experienced reporter who critiques or reviews various works of art; most specialize in a particular area, such as classical or popular music, film, opera, art, etc.

Editorial page writer. Any journalist on the "editorial board" responsible for researching issues and writing unsigned editorials. This writer also might write regular columns for the "op-ed" page.

Photographers and Artists

Photographer. In the course of a day, photographers may be asked to cover breaking news, take candid photos to accompany a feature story, shoot a variety of photos for a special story package, and take studio-style portraits for use as mug shots.

Graphic artist. Graphic artists create informational graphics, maps, illustrations and cartoons.

Illustrators. Some large newspapers have illustrators (or graphic artists who also serve as illustrators) who create original artwork for use in the newspaper, usually accompanying stories that appear on the front pages of various sections of the paper.

Editorial cartoonist. Some larger newspapers have editorial cartoonists who create illustrations for use on the editorial page.

Others Who Contribute to the News Report

Librarian. The newspaper's archivist is increasingly a sophisticated news researcher. A librarian may use a variety of sources, including the Internet and nationwide newspaper searches, to assist a reporter's efforts.

Research department. Some larger newspapers have research departments that the newsroom can call upon to do primary research, such as polls or surveys. This information then is used by the reporters and others who prepare material for publication.

News clerks and editorial assistants. People in these essentially clerical roles often compile extremely important but usually routine information, such as calendars, news of personal events (weddings, engagements and anniversaries, etc.), and court filings (real estate transactions, building permit requests, bankruptcy filings, marriage licenses issued, divorce petitions, births, etc.).

EDITORS WHO SUPERVISE PRODUCTION OF ORIGINAL MATERIALS

The size of the newspaper determines how many people serve in this capacity. The larger the paper, the more layers of editors. Following are the basic categories in ascending order of rank.

Assigning editors. These editors work directly with reporters, photographers and graphic artists determining what — and what not — to cover. They also are the first people to edit reporters' and graphic artists' work, and to view photos and cutline information. At times, they might send back stories or information graphics for additions and/or revisions, or ask photographers to re-shoot a photo or provide more or different cutline information. Small papers might have one editor who hands out all assignments. Slightly larger papers might have a city editor who hands out all news assignments, a features editor who assigns human interest stories and coverage of cultural events, a sports editor who supervises sports coverage, and a chief photographer who oversees all photo assignments. Even larger papers might have editors in additional categories, such as business, food, travel, books, graphics, etc. At these larger papers, the preparation of original materials might be supervised by assistant editors who are, in turn, supervised by a top assigning editor in their department. People in these roles usually have phrases like the following in their job titles: metro editor (only at metropolitan papers), city editor (found at papers of all sizes, including metros), features editor, business editor, sports editor, or team leader. The top assigning editors usually are responsible for compiling (or making sure others compile) a list of stories available for the next day's report and presenting that list at daily meetings at which editors discuss the content of upcoming papers. The larger paper's metro editor and small paper's city editor sometimes are described as the hub of the newsroom.

Editorial page editor. The senior editorial writer usually decides, in conjunction with the publisher or a group of people known as the newspaper's "editorial board," what stands the newspaper will take on which issues or candidates in its unsigned editorials. Some editorial boards are composed solely of journalists; a few include a citizen member or two.

Managing editors. Managing editors generally are less involved in hands-on preparation of materials and more focused on management issues, such as ensuring that the paper's policies are followed in day-to-day decision making. They have great influence, for instance, in determining which stories go on A1 or in making decisions about sensitive stories or photos. Again, the larger the paper, the more layers of editors who serve in this capacity. A small newspaper might have one person called "managing editor" who makes assignments, manages the newsroom and serves as top editor as well (see below). A slightly larger paper might have a managing editor who has an assistant managing editor or deputy managing editor (interchangeable titles). A larger paper might have a managing editor who is supervised by a top editor and who has several assistant or deputy managing editors. Divvied up among these editors are responsibilities such as supervising various aspects of the news operation (some newsrooms have deputy managing editors charged with supervising local news, photography or graphics, for example), setting newsroom policy, hiring editors and writers, helping to prepare annual salary and expense budgets and helping with long-range planning.

Top editor. Each newsroom has one top editor whose title and responsibilities vary based on the traditions of the newspaper and the qualifications of the person in the job. This person might be called the managing editor, executive editor, editor in chief, or just "editor." No matter what he or she is called, this editor reports directly to the publisher and is ultimately responsible for all decisions regarding newspaper content, newsroom staffing and spending, and developing long-range plans and strategies for the newsroom. This editor also works with the top managers in other newspaper departments, such as advertising, circulation, accounting, and marketing. Sometimes changes in job title (from managing editor to executive editor, for instance) represent promotions for top editors who assume increased responsibility while essentially staying in the same job.

Publisher. As the top manager of the entire newspaper, the publisher supervises all departments of the paper, including the editorial department. The publisher often (but not always) concentrates on financial matters and leaves the content of the news pages to the discretion of the editors. Publishers usually have extensive professional background in newspapers, but not always on the editorial side. Many are former advertising sales representatives who became top managers of advertising departments before becoming publishers. Former journalists who become publishers do so by working their way up the ladder from reporting or copy editing to assigning editor to managing editor to top editor to publisher.

EDITORS WHO PUT NEWS CONTENT INTO FINISHED FORM

Copy editor. The final editing of stories is done by copy editors. Ideally, they simply polish stories that already have been edited for content, grammar and newspaper style by the assigning editor or editors. Copy editors are expected to be especially good at ensuring that words are used correctly, the grammar is correct, the writing conforms to the "Associated Press Stylebook" (or other specified quite) and that the story contains no factual errors. A copy editor might flag a story if it contains major "holes" (or unanswered questions) or potentially libelous material. Copy editors also write headlines and other display type — the most read parts of any newspaper. In some small newspapers, copy editors also design, or lay out, the newspaper pages.

Page designer. At many newspapers, copy editors also lay out pages for the newspaper. Some larger newspapers have page designers who organize the photographs, graphics, headlines, pullouts and stories into a coordinated and visually appealing page. Usually, page designers work only with the front pages of the sections of the paper (including Page 1 stories) because these are the most prominent pages. Copy editors design "inside" pages. Designers must be editors first, deciding which content is most important and then how best to get the most important information to the readers quickly and efficiently.

Copy desk chief. The chief copy editor, sometimes known as the slot editor, supervises the people who edit copy, write headlines and lay out pages. He or she also usually gives final approval to headlines and other display type on Page One and most other pages.

Design editor. At some newspapers, the visual presentation of the news is overseen by a design editor or managing editors for design or presentation. This person might supervise some or all of the following: the copy desk, page designers, illustrators and photo staff.

Wire editor. This editor monitors state, national and international stories, photos, graphics and illustrations that stream into most newspapers' computer systems, usually via satellite but sometimes via telephone lines. Sometimes this editor flags a story that has a strong local connection so that one of the assigning editors can have a local reporter add to the story — or can add information from the wire story into a story the reporter is working on (and give the wire service credit, of course). Newspapers pay to receive wire services, and what they pay depends on which services and stories they use. The Associated Press wire service is the most universally used. Other wire services, sometimes referred to as "supplementals," include Knight-Ridder, Cox, Reuters, The New York Times and Washington Post/L.A. Times.

Online editor. This editor takes newspaper reports and tailors them for an Internet audience, often adding interactive components that get readers involved in an online conversation about the story.

Television producer. Increasingly, newspapers are forming partnerships with local television stations. The producer identifies potential stories for television from the newspaper's budget. He or she then often acts as reporter and editor to craft video and rewrite the story for television.

Common Mistakes and Unnecessary Words

Following are some of the most common writing mistakes made by less experienced reporters.

GRAMMAR

Punctuation

Don't use apostrophes in possessive pronouns. Possessive pronouns depart from the usual rules about possessives and NEVER are followed by an apostrophe, then "s." An item can be yours, hers, its or theirs, or you may want to know whose it is. But "it's and "who's" are always contractions for "it is" and "who is."

> WRONG: That plane is *their's*, but *it's* engine is not working.
> RIGHT: That plane is *theirs*, but *its* engine is not working.

Keep commas and periods inside quotation marks. In the United States, printing traditions call for commas and periods always to go inside quotation marks. It may help to think of commas and periods as wanting to snuggle up to the word they follow.

> WRONG: "In British books, commas go outside the quotation marks", she said. "It also seems awkward to put the comma inside the quotation marks, especially in single quotation marks like you'd use

around 'Zen and the Art of Motorcycle Maintenance'."

RIGHT: "In American books, commas go inside the quotation marks," she said. "Even though it feels awkward, they also go inside single quotations, which many students say 'seems to go against nature.'"

Capitalize on your use of colons. Capitalize the first word after a colon only if a proper noun or it's the start of a complete sentence. Use lower case if the first word introduces a list or sentence fragment.

WRONG: Remember this: capitalize the first word of a complete sentence after a colon.
RIGHT: Remember this: Capitalize the first word of a complete sentences after a colon.

WRONG: Make sure you understand this: Proper punctuation.
RIGHT: Make sure you understand this: proper punctuation.

Use hyphens only when needed. Take care to know whether something is a compound word, two words, or hyphenated. Sometimes the same concept can be expressed in more than one way, depending on its place in the sentence. The "Associated Press Stylebook" can be very helpful with this. Meanwhile, here are some examples:

Q: Back yard, backyard or back-yard?

A: When used as a noun, it's back yard: *He went into my back yard.* When used as an adjective, it's one word: *He sat on my backyard porch.*

Q: Full time, fulltime or full-time? Not to mention part time, etc.

A: When used as an adjective, it's hyphenated: *He has a full-time job.* When used as an adverb, it's two words: *He works full time.*

Q: Fund raiser, fundraiser or fund-raiser?

A: When used as a noun to describe the activity of raising money, it's two words: *Fund raising is challenging.* When used as a noun to describe an event or someone who raises money, it's hyphenated: *The group is currently planning its 15th fund-raiser, and it hired a professional fund-raiser to handle the arrangements.* When used as an adjective, it's also hyphenated: *The fund-raising campaign was a great success.*

Q: Makeup, make up or make-up?

A: When used as a noun or adjective, it's one word: *She put on her makeup before taking the makeup exam about the nutritional makeup of common foods.* When used as a verb, it's two words: *She knew she needed to make up the exam.*

Q: Teenage, teen age or teen-age? Always hyphenated, whether it's used as a noun or adjective. *The teen-ager had typical teen-age interests.* NOTE: Never used teen-age*d*.

Singular/Plural

A team is an "it." The word *team* is singular, which means it takes singular possessive pronouns. This is also true for a newspaper, a college, a group, or an organization — any single unit composed of many people.

> WRONG: The team had *their* best game of the year. The club had *their* annual meeting. The college will hold *their* commencement ceremony on June 9.
> RIGHT: The team had *its* best game of the year. The club had *its* annual meeting. The college will hold *its* commencement ceremony in May.

Here's and there's. The expression "here's" and "there's" are contractions that stand for "here is" and "there is." Use them only if you are pointing out a single item. Otherwise, use "here are" and "there are." Technically, you can use the contractions "here're" and "there're," but they look awkward in print.

> WRONG: Here's the notes from class. There's the new textbooks.
> RIGHT: Here are the notes from class. There are the new textbooks.

Adverbs and Adjectives

Don't forget to hyphenate multiple-word modifiers. Compound modifiers, or two or more words that express a single concept as an adjective before a noun, should be hyphenated.

> WRONG: She checked the *still boiling* water. A *well known* man was competing for a *full time* job with a *better qualified* woman. Just because he had a *better than average* test score doesn't mean he should act like a *know it all.*
> RIGHT: She checked the *still-boiling* water. A *well-known* man was competing for a *full-time* job with a *better-qualified* woman. Just because he had a *better-than-average* test score doesn't mean he should act like a *know-it-all.*

HOWEVER — don't hyphenate if the first word ends in -ly. Adverbs ending in -ly are never hyphenated with the adjectives they modify. By adding the -ly suffix, you have created a word that automatically modifies the word that follows it.

> WRONG: She had a *purely-innocent* motive. The *badly-damaged* car was *fully-insured*.
>
> RIGHT: She had a *purely innocent* motive. The *badly damaged* car was *fully insured*.

Clauses

When to use who, which or that. If it's a clause about a person or a dog named Spot, it should start with who or whom. Whenever you include a clause in a sentence that talks about about people and animals that have names, start the clause with "who" or "whom."

> WRONG: The man *that* saw the accident was talking to police. His dog, Penny, *which* had run away when she heard the crash, was at his side.
>
> RIGHT: The man *who* saw the accident was talking to police. His dog, Penny, *who* had run away when she heard the crash, was at his side.

If it's a clause that is essential to the sentence, don't start it with the word "which." Clauses that cannot be eliminated without changing the meaning of the sentence should begin with the word "that," not "which." *Which* should be used only for nonessential clauses or to begin a clause within a clause. Most people tend to overuse the word "which" when "that" would be more appropriate.

> WRONG: A big sign *which* announced the store's closing has been taped to the window. The store owner said that the sign *that* is part of the window display was not noticeable enough from the street.
>
> RIGHT: A big sign *that* announced the store's closing has been taped to the window. The store owner said that the sign *which* is part of the window display was not noticeable enough from the street.

When is whom *better than* who? A good way to think through whether "who" or "whom" is correct is to substitute a form of the word "he" in the clause in which you plan to use "who" or "whom." This usually involves a little rearranging of the word order. However, when you get the hang of this trick, it's a foolproof way to determine whether *who* or *whom* is correct: Whenever *him* sounds right, use *whom*. Here's an example:

> TANGLED SENTENCE: He was not sure who [or is it whom?] gave him the note, so he was not sure who [or is it whom?] to contact about it.
> HOW TO UNTANGLE IT: In the first "who" clause, "who gave him the note," if you substitute a form of "he," the clause would be "*he* gave him the note," not "*him* gave him the note" — so *who* would be correct. In the second clause, however, it sounds right to say "contact *him* about it," not "contact *he* about it" — so *whom* would be correct.
> CORRECTED SENTENCE: He was not sure *who* gave him the note, so he was not sure *whom* to contact about it.

WRITING STYLE

Incorrect Word Choices

Creative works are not *entitled* to anything but *titles*. If someone gave a title to something, say they "titled" it, not "entitled" it. *Entitlement* means to have specific rights, like people who are entitled to insurance benefits or heirs entitled to receive part of an estate. Inanimate objects do not have rights, so they cannot be entitled to anything. You'll go farther as a journalist if you further your ability to choose correct words.

Farther/further. Farther and *further* often are confused, but it should be easy to remember: Use "farther" when you're talking about physical distance; use "further" for most everything else:

> WRONG: They went further behind enemy lines. He said the committee needs to look farther into the matter.
> RIGHT: They went farther behind enemy lines. He said the committee needed to look further into the matter.

Discrete/discreet. "Discrete" means separate or detached; "discreet" means being tactful or keeping confidences.

> WRONG: During the presidential election campaign, supporters said President George W. Bush would be more discrete than President Bill Clinton. The city council is considering three discreet proposals for addressing the parking problem downtown.

RIGHT: During the presidential election campaign, supporters said President George W. Bush would be more discreet than President Bill Clinton. The city council is considering three discrete proposals for addressing the parking problems downtown.

Principle/principal. "Principle" refers to a fundamental truth; "principal" means chief or chief official. For example:

WRONG: The school principle said the principle reason for the new policy was the school board's belief in the principal that all people are created equal.

RIGHT: The school principal said the principal reason for the new policy was the school board's belief in the principle that all people are created equal.

Complement/compliment. "Complements" complete one another, but "compliments" are courteous. Remember the word "complete" when remembering the right way to spell complement, compliment, complementary or complimentary. Things are complementary when they complete one another, like complementary colors in art or complementary proteins in vegetarian cooking. Things are only complimentary if they're an expression of appreciation or courtesy, as when someone is complimentary about a story you wrote or offers you complimentary tickets (which most newspapers refuse to let reporters accept for ethical reasons, by the way).

Stationary/stationery. Both come from the same root word, the Latin *stationarius*, and here's how the meanings evolved: "Stationary" means being in a fixed position. A "stationer" was what they called booksellers and publishers who set up shop in fixed, or stationary, locations. So the goods sold by stationers became known as "stationery," or writing paper and envelopes. Keeping that in mind, it may help to remember that "a" comes before "e" in the alphabet — and in this story.

Impact. If you want to talk about how one thing was changed by something else, don't say it "impacted," say it had an impact. If you impact something, it means you force things together or tightly pack them, like an impacted tooth.

Go dog, go. The word "go" simply means to relocate oneself. It does not mean "go to school," "go to church" or "go to the bathroom." Do not say "people who go here" and expect it to be understood that you mean people who *attend* your college or university.

Wordy, Awkward Language

There once was a professor who hated the use of "there was " in all its forms. The phrases "there is," "there was," "there are" and "that was" use passive construction that usually sounds better after rewording. Some examples of how these constructions can be eliminated.

> PASSIVE: There were several students who said there were times during the disturbance that Campus Security should have stepped in. There was a new committee organized that was going to review security procedures. On the left side of the driveway, there was a pasture.
> ACTIVE: Several students said Campus Security should have stepped in during the disturbance. A new committee was organized to review security procedures. A pasture was to the left of the driveway.

Don't engage in *the organization of* news stories — just *organize* them. Some writers get into the bad habit of using the gerund form of verbs (the ones that end in "-ing"), words with multiple suffixes and other forms of wordy writing. Often this style is the result of years of trying to sound more intelligent in academic papers (and often being rewarded for it). But take a look at the following two sentences — which would you rather read?

> WRONG: A discussion of the implementation of the plan for the recylable materials collection program that is in the process of being developed for the entire campus was scheduled by the college's Environmental Action Committee for its subsequent meeting. [Does your head hurt yet?]
> RIGHT: The college's Environmental Action Committee plans to discuss at its next meeting how the new campus recycling program will be carried out.

Go easy on tense. There's no need to say some person or organization "will be coordinating the festival" when "will coordinate" would do. Whenever possible, use simple past, present and future tenses — "plans" instead of "is planning," and "was" instead of "had been" — unless, of course, it changes the meaning of a sentence so that it is no longer accurate.

Go *backward*, *forward* and *toward*, not backwards, forwards or towards. The former is simply more precise.

Keep things *among us*, not *amongst thine ancestors*. Words like "amongst" and "whilst" (and other antiquated forms of words) may sound great in passages written centuries ago or a "Harry Potter" novel, but they sound stilted and affected in journalism. Use the modern words.

WRONG: He stood amongst the flowers whilst his wife watered the garden.
RIGHT: He stood among the flowers while his wife watered the garden.

Avoid unnecessary words. Here are some common wordy expressions and how they can be edited:

WRONG: He stopped at the cafe in order to have breakfast.
RIGHT: He stopped at the cafe to have breakfast.

WRONG: Many different opinions were expressed.
RIGHT: any opinions were expressed.

WRONG: He cleaned up his room, then he served up the soup. Up until that moment, he was hungry.
RIGHT: He cleaned his room then served the soup. Until that moment he was hungry.

WRONG: The musicians will be playing their final concert Saturday afternoon.
RIGHT: The musicians will play.

WRONG: The couple bought 40 acres of land. [*land* is redundant]
RIGHT: The couple bought 40 acreas.

WRONG: Where is she going to?
RIGHT: Where is she going?

WRONG: This attraction was very unique.
RIGHT: This attraction was unique.

WRONG: He seldom ever goes there.
RIGHT: He seldom goes there.

Avoid variation in your attributions. "Don't use fancy words for 'said,'" the professor begged and pleaded. When following a direct quote with attribution, just use the word "said" — not "commented," "pontificated," "remarked," "explained" — just *said*.

WRONG: "I get so tired of writing 'said, said, said'" the reporter snarled.
RIGHT: "But there's such beautiful simplicity in using the word 'said' in attribution," the professor said.

Professional Titles

Be careful when using the title "Dr." that you don't confuse medical doctors with those who have earned doctorates. In a story about an outbreak of typhoid, for instance, it probably would be best to use the title "Dr." only in reference to medical doctors, not in reference to John Smith, who holds a doctorate in political science (and could be rightly referred to as "Dr. Smith" is another context) and is commenting on the political situation in the country where the outbreak occurred.

Capitalization

In journalism, fewer things are capitalized than in other kinds of writing. In general, nouns are not capitalized unless they refer to formal organizations, proper geographic place names or official job titles (but only when used *before* a person's name). It is also important to use capital letters for words that are trademarked names, like Frisbee, Realtor and Kleenex.

> WRONG: All History classes (including American History) are offered through the History Department. Chuck Gates, an Assistant Professor, also serves as Director of the Institute for Foreign Study.
> RIGHT: All history classes (including American history) are offered through the History Department. Charles L. "Chuck" Gates, an assistant professor, also serves as director of the Institute for Foreign study.

Transitions

Avoid lazy or labored transitions — they make for boring stories. Avoid "if–then" constructions, unless you're talking about an actual, concrete cause-and-effect relationship. Consider the following:

> GOOD: If the developer has not paid the fines by the end of the month, the city will take legal action.
> IFFY: If the council (school board, civic league) has its way, the concert will come off with out a hitch.

The second one is "iffy" because the *if* involves wishful thinking, not actual consequences that will definitely result from that thinking. The sentence would be more accurate if it were reworded as follows: "Council (school board, civic league) members hope the concert will come off without a hitch." It's simpler. It's more direct. It's just plain better.

Don't try to fool the reader by relying on a buried transition to signal that you are writing fiction about a contrived event. For example, many agencies stage mock emergencies as training exercises for rescue workers, police and the public, and too often, young writers will begin the story with several paragraphs that describe the scene as though the emergency were real. Then comes a transition, something like: "This didn't happen, but if it did ..." If you succeed in getting readers emotionally churned up about something, then tell them it didn't really happen, you're likely to alienate them.

Don't use "but" for an easy transition — it is common coinage in news stories, to the point of being overused. Use "but" only when a situation is truly oppositional: "A total of 14 residents told county commissioners at their meeting Tuesday that they support the proposal to build a new power substation. But nine other residents said they are concerned about the electromagnetic field that would be generated by the station." A good way to avoid overusing *but* is to reveal your finished stories and consider each time you used the word. Is it really necessary? Or is it simply a cheap transition?

Commonly Misspelled Words

absence
acceptable
accessible
accommodate
accordion
accuracy
accustomed
achievement
acquainted
acquire
acreage
actually
admission
adolescent
affected
affectionately
aisles
alcohol
all right
a lot
amateur
ancestry
annihilate
apiece
appearance
approximately
assassination
atheist
authentic
average

barbarous
bargain
beginning
belief
believed
beneficial
benefited
biggest
boundary
breath
breathe
bureaucracy
cafeteria
calendar
category
cemetery
census
challenge
changeable
changing
characteristic
chief
children
chocolate
chosen
Christianity
coarsely
commitment
committee
conceited

conceive
concentrate
condemn
conscience
conscientious
consensus
consistent
continuous
contradict
convenient
courteous
criticism
criticize
curiosity
curious
dealt
deceive
decorate
definitely
descend
description
desirable
despair
desperate
despicable
different
disagree
disappear
disappoint
disapprove

disastrous
discipline
discussion
dispel
distinct
divine
doctor
dormitory
easily
ecstasy
effect
efficient
eighth
elaborately
embarrass
empty
enemy
entirely
environment
equipment
equipped
escape
especially
evidently
exaggerate
excellent
except
exercise
exhaust
existence
experience
extremely
familiar
fascinate
favorite
February
finally
financially
fluorine
forbear
foreign
foresee
foretell
forty
forward
friend
fulfill

gauge
governor
grammar
gruesome
guaranteed
guard
guerrilla
guidance
happened
happily
harass
heard
height
here
heroes
hindrance
holiday
hoping
human
humane
humorous
hundred
hungry
hurriedly
hypocrisy
hypocrite
ideally
idiosyncrasy
ignorant
imitate
immensely
incalculable
incidentally
incredible
independent
indispensable
individually
influential
initiative
innocuous
intelligent
interrupt
irrelevant
irresistible
irritated
jealousy
jewelry

knowledge
laboratory
laid
led
leisure
length
lenient
liable
library
license
lightning
likelihood
listening
liveliest
lose
luxury
lying
magazine
magnificent
maintenance
manageable
management
maneuver
manual
marriage
material
mathematics
meanness
mere
miniature
minor
mischievous
missile
mortgage
muscle
mysterious
narrative
naturally
necessary
nevertheless
nickel
nineteen
ninety
ninth
noticeable
nuisance
numerous

occasion
occasionally
occurred
occurrence
occurring
official
omission
omit
omitted
opponent
opportunity
opposite
oppression
optimism
ordinarily
paid
pamphlet
parallel
paralleled
parole
pastime
peaceable
peculiar
penetrate
perceive
performance
permanent
permissible
persuade
pertain
physical
pigeon
pitiful
pleasant
poison
politician
possession
practically
precede
predominant
prejudice
prevail
principle
privilege
processes
prominent
pronunciation

prophecy
psychology
pumpkin
quandary
questionnaire
realize
receipt
receive
recession
recipe
recommend
referring
rehearsal
relief
religious
remembrance
reminisce
resemblance
restaurant
rhythm
ridiculous
roommate
sandwich
satellite
saxophone
scarcity
scenery
schedule
secretary
seize
separate
sergeant
several
sheriff
shoulder
shrubbery
sincerely
skiing
sophomore
souvenir
specimen
sponsor
statistics
straight
strenuous
stubbornness
succeed

succession
sufficient
suicide
superintendent
supersede
suppress
surround
suspicious
susceptible
technique
their
therefore
tobacco
tomorrow
tremendous
truly
twelfth
unanimous
unconscious
undoubtedly
vacuum
valuable
various
vegetable
vengeance
vice
villain
violence
weird
wherever
whichever
wholly
yield

A Quick Guide for Covering Emergencies

Some of the most painful mistakes in newspaper writing occur when less experienced reporters are called upon to help cover emergencies such as accidents, violent crimes or disasters. Most such mistakes stem from the reporter's lack of knowledge about the roles people in various professions play in handling such disasters, and what those people's jobs entail.

Following is a brief summary that will help you avoid such mistakes. Much of this material was gathered by Esther Diskin of The (Norfolk) Virginian-Pilot.

GENERAL GUIDELINES

When you go to the scene of an emergency as a reporter, you have a job to do — but so do other people who are working at the scene. Be extremely careful not to get in the way of people who are trying to save lives and reduce trauma. Eventually, you probably will be able to talk to the people who were in the thick of things, but save your questions for them for later.

Instead, start out by taking several minutes to observe. Can you spot anyone who seems to be in charge or who has set up what might be called a "command station" or "base camp"? Sometimes you'll spot one officer who seems to be calling the shots or who stays near his or her car, perhaps talking frequently into the handset of the police radio so as to keep the dispatcher (the person responsible for receiving incoming calls and dispatching officers, as needed) informed of what's going on. Sometimes, you might even spot a tent (when rescue or fire fighting efforts are expected to take 24 hours or more) equipped with tables, portable communication equipment and/or huge plastic coffee urns.

Then, look for people on the fringes near the person or place you have identified. Who's just standing around? Some might be rescue workers who are taking a break. Others might be eyewitnesses. Still others might be gawkers (every emergency seems to attract them). Go stand near them, eavesdrop and observe and start casual conversations with the people nearby.

It's best if you can find eyewitnesses — and be economical with your time. Don't spend too much time with people who don't know much or who want to speculate at length about what might have happened. Also, be aware that eyewitnesses often are connected in some way to what happened — or to someone who has been injured or arrested. That means they may get emotional, so be prepared for that. In addition, be sure to find out about any such connections so you can evaluate the credibility of their statements — and don't be surprised if you hear contradictory (and potentially libelous) versions of what happened. In situations like this, it is not unusual for you to have to make judgment calls about which information to include, which to double-check and what to disregard.

After you've gathered preliminary information from witnesses (or if you can't find any witnesses), start talking to rescue workers on the fringes. Be prepared for them to desert you at any moment if their help is needed — it's their job. And be patient. You may have to wait around, gathering bits and pieces of information from several different people over time before you can get a clear picture of what happened. If you're writing on deadline, spend as much time at the scene as you can — but be sure you allow yourself enough time to write the story.

TYPES OF EMERGENCY PERSONNEL

Police

Police are city law enforcement officers, supervised by a police chief. Police officers work exclusively within the confines of a given city. In most medium- to large-sized cities, officers assigned to patrol are supervised by sergeants who work in shifts and who are called "watch sergeants" (because each of them is the sergeant "on watch" during their shift). Although some police departments have public information or media relations officers, in many cases watch sergeants are the best people to contact for information about breaking news.

These sergeants are supervised by higher-ranking officers (lieutenants, corporals, majors and/or captains) who are, in turn, supervised by the chief. Detectives (including those who work narcotics, vice or undercover) and evidence technicians generally operate independently. They have specialized skills and responsibilities and are called to the scene of an emergency only when those skills are needed.

Evidence Technicians

People who gather evidence at crime scenes may be law enforcement officers or civilians, depending on the jurisdiction.

Deputy Sheriffs

The sheriff is the chief law enforcement officer in a given county. The officers who serve under him or her are called deputy sheriffs, sheriff's deputies or, simply, deputies. Patrol officers in a sheriff's department cover a much larger geographic area than most police officers. Like police departments, sheriff's departments also have watch sergeants, lieutenants, corporals, majors and/or captains; detectives; evidence technicians; and public information or media relations officers. Some sheriff's departments also rely on reserve officers who receive the same training as full-time officers but who work only part-time, usually under the supervision of another officer.

State Police

State police, sometimes called "highway patrol," officers generally patrol and respond to accidents and crimes only on state highways, except when they are called upon to help with specific investigations or arrests (as when a city police department is planning a large drug bust and requests help from the state police). Again, the hierarchy in state police departments is much the same as in police and sheriff's departments.

Firefighters

Firefighters respond to more medical emergencies and car crashes than fires. Many, but not all, firefighters are paramedics. In many communities, fire investigators, not the police, arrest arson suspects. They, too, have the power to make arrests.

When referring to people who fight fires, Associated Press style is *firefighters*, one word. However, firefighters themselves (and their union, the International Association of Fire Fighters) generally prefer *fire fighters*, two words. As a reporter, you must always use AP style.

Firefighters wear tanks of compressed air, not oxygen.

Ambulance Crews

Ambulance crew members have various titles and levels of training. All have been trained to quickly assess the injuries of people who have been in accidents or whose health has taken a sudden turn for the worse, and to administer treatment that will stabilize them for transport to the hospital that can most effectively address their condition. They may be trained as paramedics, emergency medical technicians, or even as nurses. Sometimes they call in medically equipped helicopters to medically evacuate — or "med-evac" — badly injured patients to metropolitan hospitals that specialize in the treatment of children, head injuries or other specific conditions.

Hospitals

If your story will mention any people who are injured and admitted to the hospital, your editor will expect you (or another reporter) to call and find out their conditions so you can include that information in your story. You must have the person's name to get that information. Expect the hospital to give you only a one-word description: *good*, *stable*, *guarded*, *serious*, or *critical*, for example. These words are contained in guidelines developed for hospitals by a national association. Do not expect medical and hospital personnel to go into detail about a person's injuries or give you a prognosis — they are legally required to honor patient confidentiality laws. A tip: If the injured person has been at the hospital for a while and hospital staff refuse to give you a status report, it might be because the person has died; the only two circumstances under which patients' conditions are not released is when they have just arrived and not been seen yet by a doctor, or when they have died and the next of kin has not been notified.

Other agencies

At the scenes of some emergencies, you may encounter officers from numerous other agencies, including the National Guard, the U.S. Marshall's Office, the Department of Alcohol, Tobacco and Firearms, the FBI, the U.S. Forest Service, etc. If in doubt, use the phrase "rescue workers" — that covers firefighters, emergency medical technicians and paramedics.

NOTABLE POLICE TERMINOLOGY

Emergency Jargon

Police and other emergency personnel sometimes say accident victims suffer from "lacerations and contusions." That's medical language for "cuts and bruises."

Other commonly used emergency jargon (and their plain-language translations): *altercation* (fight), *perpetrator* (suspect), *cardiac arrest* (heart attack), and *fractured femur* (broken thigh bone — in other words, translate the name of the bone into a body part).

Guns

A revolver and a pistol are not the same thing. When in doubt, use "handgun."

A purchase permit, which many localities require, is not the same thing as a gun-owner's permit. Carrying a hidden gun requires a concealed weapons permit.

Caliber is the diameter of the bullet. A 9mm bullet is 9 millimeters in diameter. A .38-caliber bullet is 38/100ths of an inch in diameter. Keep in mind the difference between *metric* and *imperial* measurements. For example, a .50-caliber bullet is a half-inch in diameter and can be shot from a handgun. But a 50mm bullet is about two inches in diameter and is more likely to be fired by military aircraft.

Evidence

No one can match with certainty a hair found at a crime scene to the hair of a person. The best science can determine is that the hairs are "similar."

A blood test or blood screen doesn't give a list of all drugs or chemicals present. The basic tests screen for alcohol and the most common drugs, but for anything else, the examiners have to know what to look for. It's sort of a Catch-22: They can't detect a drug unless they know what drug they are looking for.

Medical examiners must be doctors. *Coroners* are elected officials and can be anyone.

Not everyone who dies is subjected to an autopsy. When in doubt, use "examination," as in, "The body will be taken to the crime lab for an examination."

The animal equivalent of an autopsy is called a *necropsy,* as in, "Veterinarians performed a necropsy to determine how the stranded whale died."

Types of Crimes

People are robbed. Homes and businesses are burgled, or burglarized.

> WRONG: While I was on vacation, someone robbed my house.
> RIGHT: While I was on vacation, someone burgled my house.

Killing, slaying, murder, manslaughter and homicide are not inter-changeable words. A *killing, slaying* or *homicide* is any taking of a human life, including police shootings, self-defense and mercy killings. *Murder* is the intentional killing of another human being. *Manslaughter* is the un-intentional or accidental killing of another person through neglect.

Jails, Prisons, Arrests and Sentences

Police don't issue warrants. They can only arrest people on warrants that are issued by judges or magistrates. Police are part of the executive, not judicial, branch of government and have no power to issue warrants for arrest or to search a home. That's the job of a magistrate or judge, de-pending on the state.

> WRONG: Police issued a warrant for the arrest of the alleged bank robber.
> RIGHT: Police obtained a warrant for the arrest of the alleged bank robber.

A person can be taken into custody through a *summons* (a court document that directs an officer to notify the person that a complaint has been filed with the court against him or her), an *arrest* or an *indict-ment* (an accusation handed to the court by a grand jury).

Don't use *bond* in place of *bail*. Bail, according to the Associated Press, is "money or property that will be forfeited to the court if an accused individual fails to appear for trial." The accused can deposit the money or property, or can pay a professional *bail bondsman* a percentage.

Jails are local or regional. In many states, they are supposed to hold criminals no longer than one year, although that rule is rou-tinely bent. People who are not yet convicted always stay in jails. *Prisons* are state or federal, although an increasing number of prisons are privately run. Only people who have been convicted of crimes are sent to prison.

Incarceration just means imprisoned, and it's best to use the sim-pler word possible.

> GOOD: The judge sentenced him to prison for 10 years.
> WORDY: The judge ordered his incarceration for a period of 10 years.

Concurrent sentences are served together. *Successive* sentences are served one after another.

Extradition occurs when one state surrenders to another some-one accused of an offense outside its own territory.

Convicted felon is redundant — there is no such category as a felon who was not convicted.

OTHER NOTABLE TERMS

A snake-bite victim is given *antivenin*, not antivenom.

Cement is a powder that, when mixed with sand and water, forms concrete. There is no such substance as "wet cement." That means "cement truck," "cement shoes" and "cement pond" are really misnomers.

Journalists' Creeds, Platforms and Codes of Ethics

Journalists have written various kinds of statements over the years that embody the goals and ideas to which they aspire. Following are just a few of these.

THE (ST. LOUIS) POST-DISPATCH PLATFORM
By Joseph Pulitzer
April 10, 1907

I know that my retirement will make no difference in [the] cardinal principles [of the Post Dispatch], that it will always fight for progress and reform, never tolerate injustice or corruption, always fight demagogues of all parties, never belong to any party, always oppose privileged classes and public plunderers, never lack sympathy with the poor, always remain devoted to the public welfare, never be satisfied with merely printing news, always be drastically independent, never be afraid to attack wrong, whether by predatory plutocracy or predatory poverty.

THE MARION (IND.) STAR OFFICE CREED
By Warren G. Harding

Remember there are two sides to every question. Get both.
    Be truthful.
    Get the facts. Mistakes are inevitable, but strive for accuracy. I would rather have one story exactly right than a hundred half wrong.
    Be decent. Be fair. Be generous.

Boost — don't knock. There's good in everybody. Bring out the good in everybody, and never needlessly hurt the feelings of anybody.

In reporting a political gathering, get the facts; tell the story as it is, not as you would like to have it.

Treat all parties alike. If there's any politics to be played, we will play it in our editorial columns.

Treat all religious matters reverently.

If it can possibly be avoided, never bring ignominy to an innocent woman or child in telling of the misdeeds or misfortune of a relative. Don't wait to be asked, but do it without asking.

And, above all, be clean. Never let a dirty word or suggestive story get into type.

I want this paper so conducted that it can go into any home without destroying the innocence of any child.

AMERICAN SOCIETY OF NEWSPAPER EDITORS (ASNE) STATEMENT OF PRINCIPLES

Originally adopted in 1922 as the "Canons of Journalism," this document was revised and renamed "Statement of Principles" in 1975.

Preamble

The First Amendment, protecting freedom of expression from abridgment by any law, guarantees to the people through their press a constitutional right, and thereby places on newspaper people a particular responsibility. Thus journalism demands of its practitioners not only industry and knowledge but also the pursuit of a standard of integrity proportionate to the journalist's singular obligation. To this end the American Society of Newspaper Editors sets forth this Statement of Principles as a standard encouraging the highest ethical and professional performance.

Article I

Responsibility. The primary purpose of gathering and distributing news and opinion is to serve the general welfare by informing the people and enabling them to make judgments on the issues of the time. Newspapermen and women who abuse the power of their professional role for selfish motives or unworthy purposes are faithless to that public trust. The American press was made free not just to inform or just to serve as a forum for debate but also to bring an independent scrutiny to bear on the forces of power in the society, including the conduct of official power at all levels of government.

Article II

Freedom of the Press. Freedom of the press belongs to the people. It must be defended against encroachment or assault from any quarter, public or private. Journalists must be constantly alert to see that the public's business is conducted in public. They must be vigilant against all who would exploit the press for selfish purposes.

Article III

Independence. Journalists must avoid impropriety and the appearance of impropriety as well as any conflict of interest or the appearance of conflict. They should neither accept anything nor pursue any activity that might compromise or seem to compromise their integrity.

Aricle IV

Truth and Accuracy. Good faith with the reader is the foundation of good journalism. Every effort must be made to assure that the news content is accurate, free from bias and in context, and that all sides are presented fairly. Editorials, analytical articles and commentary should be held to the same standards of accuracy with respect to facts as news reports. Significant errors of fact, as well as errors of omission, should be corrected promptly and prominently.

Article V

Impartiality. To be impartial does not require the press to be unquestioning or to refrain from editorial expression. Sound practice, however, demands a clear distinction for the reader between news reports and opinion. Articles that contain opinion or personal interpretation should be clearly identified.

Article VI

Fair Play. Journalists should respect the rights of people involved in the news, observe the common standards of decency and stand accountable to the public for the fairness and accuracy of their news reports. Persons publicly accused should be given the earliest opportunity to respond. Pledges of confidentiality to news sources must be honored at all costs, and therefore should not be given lightly. Unless there is clear and pressing need to maintain confidences, sources of information should be identified.

These principles are intended to preserve, protect and strengthen the bond of trust and respect between American journalists and the American people, a bond that is essential to sustain the grant of freedom entrusted to both by the nation's founders.

SOCIETY OF PROFESSIONAL JOURNALISTS (SPJ) CODE OF ETHICS
September 1996

Preamble

Members of the Society of Professional Journalists believe that public enlightenment is the forerunner of justice and the foundation of democracy. The duty of the journalist is to further those ends by seeking truth and providing a fair and comprehensive account of events and issues. Conscientious journalists from all media and specialties strive to serve the public with thoroughness and honesty. Professional integrity is the cornerstone of a journalist's credibility. Members of the Society share a dedication to ethical behavior and adopt this code to declare the Society's principles and standards of practice.

Seek Truth and Report It

Journalists should be honest, fair and courageous in gathering, reporting and interpreting information.

Journalists should:

• Test the accuracy of information from all sources and exercise care to avoid inadvertent error. Deliberate distortion is never permissible.

• Diligently seek out subjects of news stories to give them the opportunity to respond to allegations of wrongdoing.

• Identify sources whenever feasible. The public is entitled to as much information as possible on sources' reliability.

• Always question sources' motives before promising anonymity. Clarify conditions attached to any promise made in exchange for information. Keep promises.

• Make certain that headlines, news teases and promotional material, photos, video, audio, graphics, sound bites and quotations do not misrepresent.

• They should not oversimplify or highlight incidents out of context.

• Never distort the content of news photos or video. Image enhancement for technical clarity is always permissible. Label montages and photo illustrations.

• Avoid misleading re-enactments or staged news events. If re-enactment is necessary to tell a story, label it.

• Avoid undercover or other surreptitious methods of gathering information except when traditional open methods will not yield information vital to the public. Use of such methods should be explained as part of the story.

• Never plagiarize.

• Tell the story of the diversity and magnitude of the human experience boldly, even when it is unpopular to do so.

• Examine their own cultural values and avoid imposing those values on others.

• Avoid stereotyping by race, gender, age, religion, ethnicity, geography, sexual orientation, disability, physical appearance or social status.

• Support the open exchange of views, even views they find repugnant.

• Give voice to the voiceless; official and unofficial sources of information can be equally valid.

• Distinguish between advocacy and news reporting. Analysis and commentary should be labeled and not misrepresent fact or context.

• Distinguish news from advertising and shun hybrids that blur the lines between the two.

• Recognize a special obligation to ensure that the public's business is conducted in the open and that government records are open to inspection.

Minimize Harm

Ethical journalists treat sources, subjects and colleagues as human beings deserving of respect.

Journalists should:

• Show compassion for those who may be affected adversely by news coverage. Use special sensitivity when dealing with children and inexperienced sources or subjects.

• Be sensitive when seeking or using interviews or photographs of those affected by tragedy or grief.

• Recognize that gathering and reporting information may cause harm or discomfort. Pursuit of the news is not a license for arrogance.

• Recognize that private people have a greater right to control information about themselves than do public officials and others who seek power, influence or attention. Only an overriding public need can justify intrusion into anyone's privacy.

• Show good taste. Avoid pandering to lurid curiosity.

• Be cautious about identifying juvenile suspects or victims of sex crimes.

• Be judicious about naming criminal suspects before the formal filing of charges.

• Balance a criminal suspect's fair trial rights with the public's right to be informed.

Act Independently

Journalists should be free of obligation to any interest other than the public's right to know.

Journalists should:

- Avoid conflicts of interest, real or perceived.
- Remain free of associations and activities that may compromise integrity or damage credibility.
- Refuse gifts, favors, fees, free travel and special treatment, and shun secondary employment, political involvement, public office and service in community organizations if they compromise journalistic integrity.
- Disclose unavoidable conflicts.
- Be vigilant and courageous about holding those with power accountable.
- Deny favored treatment to advertisers and special interests and resist their pressure to influence news coverage.
- Be wary of sources offering information for favors or money; avoid bidding for news.

Be Accountable

Journalists are accountable to their readers, listeners, viewers and each other.

Journalists should:

- Clarify and explain news coverage and invite dialogue with the public over journalistic conduct.
- Encourage the public to voice grievances against the news media.
- Admit mistakes and correct them promptly.
- Expose unethical practices of journalists and the news media.
- Abide by the same high standards to which they hold others.

Glossary of Newsroom Terms

Every profession creates its own language, its own jargon. This common language serves as a shortcut — you don't have to explain what you mean to fellow journalists. (Sociologists also would maintain that, like the jargon of any profession, it creates a barrier to entry by those who don't belong to the profession — a secret code, if you will, that distinguishes those who are part of the group from those who aren't. But that's another book.) Although each newsroom uses terms that are unique, the following are often-used terms and their definitions.

advance — A story that describes an event before it happens. Advances can be written about government meetings, community festivals, performances — just about anything that is scheduled ahead of time.

advertorial — A stand-alone section, usually tabloid-sized, that is created by the advertising department to generate revenue. Newspapers vary in their policies, but editorial departments generally keep an arms-length relationship from these sections. Most such sections are labeled clearly as advertising supplements.

agate — Tiny type used for such items as stock listings and sports event summaries. It is much smaller than the type used in the body of most news stories.

attribution — A notation that says where the reporter got information used in a story. Facts usually are attributed to a specific person or organization. Every quote, for instance, is attributed: "Attribute all quotations," the editor said.

background — Material in a story that tells readers what happened before the most recent events, or adds other information that puts the story into a broader context. Sometimes this background is written prior to a scheduled event, especially for an event happening close to the news organization's deadline. Most of an election night story, for instance, can be written beforehand. The reporter can write a description of the candidates and the campaign issues so that all that needs to be added at the beginning is the news of who won. Although a phrase or two of background material might be woven into the lead, most often the sections of background come in the middle or at the end of the story. Sometimes known as "b matter" or a "shirttail."

body type — The style of type used for the body of all stories in a newspaper. This is usually some form of "serif" type, or type that has little curlicues at the ends of the stems of the letters, because studies have found that kind of type is more readable for extended periods of time.

breaking news — An unexpected event such as a fire, a traffic accident, a murder or a sudden announcement by the governor. Breaking news requires quick response by reporters, photographers and editors.

budget — A list of all stories planned for a given day's newspaper, with short descriptions about each and whether photographs or informational graphics are available to run with them. Some newspapers have separate budgets for wire stories, sports, features, etc. Others put them all together on a master budget. The budget is used by editors every day to deliberate about which stories are the most important and where they should run in the newspaper.

budget line — A short description of a story. It usually includes the name the reporter will assign to the finished story document in the computer (also known as the "slug"), the most important facts, why the story is important, the name of the reporter and assigning editor, the finished (or expected) length of the story, and whether it will be accompanied by a photograph, map and/or graphic. The budget line is also sometimes called a "tout" or "pitch," because it is the first and best way to "sell" the merits of a story to senior editors and page designers so they will feature it more prominently in the paper.

byline — The name(s) of the reporter who wrote the story: By Jack Cutter, Staff Writer. Placed at the beginning or end of the story, depending on the newspaper.

chain — A group of newspapers owned by the same company or corporation. Most newspapers in the United States now fall into that category.

circulation — (1) The number of papers a newspaper sells each day, on average. As a newspaper journalist, other journalists will ask you about the circulation size of your newspaper. In general, circulation is an indication of the size of the paper itself as well as its staff. The larger the circulation, the larger the paper, the larger the staff, and the more experience you usually need to get a job there. (2) The newspaper department responsible for getting the paper out to readers. Most newspapers rely on a mix of young newspaper carriers (usually in older residential areas where homes are closer together) and adults who are responsible for "motor routes," or delivering papers by car (especially in spread-out rural and suburban areas) to get newspapers to subscribers. They also have people who put newspapers into vending boxes at locations throughout the area served by the newspaper.

circulation area — The geographic area in which a newspaper is available through home delivery or in vending boxes. In making up each day's news report, newspapers generally give top priority to stories that occur within their circulation area. Decisions about how much coverage to give to certain news developments, and how prominently to feature that coverage, often is influenced by how many readers the paper has in the area in which the development has occurred.

classified advertising — Also known as "the want ads." These ads are sold at an affordable rate, usually with a set price for a maximum number of words and the option of paying more for bold type, small illustrations or other eye-catching elements. They are grouped together in narrow columns, usually in a stand-alone section or at the back of a section that might have news content pertaining to the ads in that section (automobile sections, for instance, sometimes include both news content about cars and classified ads for new and used cars.) These ads are purchased by individuals and businesses with specific needs, such as finding a job (or an employee) or finding a used washing machine (or someone to buy their used washer).

clip — A story clipped from the newspaper. Most newspaper libraries save stories electronically now but still keep "clip files" with stories from pre-computer archive days.

copy — A term for any story or block of information. A reporter might say, for instance, "I'll have a lot of copy for you about that school dedication."

cutline — What nonjournalists call a "caption." A cutline should always include the names of people in the picture, when and where the photo was taken and information that puts the photo in context.

display ads — The larger ads that run on the news pages, usually with big type, photos and/or drawings that call attention to the products or services the ad's purchaser wants you to buy. These are a newspaper's biggest source of revenue.

display type — Big type, like ordinary headlines, or artsy headlines used on the covers of features sections or Sunday magazine sections — anything other than body type (defined above).

double truck — The two connected pages in the middle of most newspaper sections (it's not a double truck if it has a loose page in the middle). Advertising or news stories sometimes run poster-style across this entire expanse of newsprint. Advertisers pay a premium for that kind of space, and editors usually have to request such space well in advance — and reserve such requests only for extremely important, in-depth reports.

ears — Material in the top corners of the front page or the front of a newspaper section, usually promoting stories inside the section.

editorial — (1) All newspaper content that is not advertising. Ann Landers is considered editorial content. So are cartoons, sports articles, feature stories, opinion pieces and everything in between. (2) An opinion piece, written to represent the institutional voice of the newspaper. The editorial is usually, but not always, unsigned and confined to the editorial or "op-ed" page. Editorials usually are segregated from news pages and marked "Editorial" or "Opinion" to signal readers that they include the writers' opinions.

editorial department — The department of the newspaper that includes everyone involved in producing news content.

enterprise — A news story that focuses on a process, not a specific event. Coverage of a house fire is not enterprise reporting; an investigative story on response times by the fire department or a feature about a new program for children is.

fact box — Pertinent information that is set aside in a box or other visually distinctive format. The times, dates and admission prices for a play might be in a fact box, or the key provisions of a peace agreement between countries. Also known as "fast facts" or "factoids."

family-owned — A newspaper that is owned and operated by a family or individual rather than a chain (see definition above). Increasingly fewer newspapers in the United States are family-owned.

file — To turn in a story for editing.

flag — (1) The portion of the front page that contains the newspaper's name in fancy type. Also called the "nameplate." (2) A verb, as in "to flag a libel question" or "to flag a story with problems," as in "red flag." Generally used to describe a major flaw in a story that would prevent its publication.

flush left — A term for type that is lined up, or "flush," along the left side, usually without hyphenated words and with even spacing between the letters. Also called "ragged right," because the right margin usually looks uneven.

flush right — Type that is lined up along the right side, leaving the left margin "ragged." Usually used only in artistic elements in page designs or informational graphics.

follow-up — A story that continues the theme of a previous event or issue. Also called a "folo." Follow-up stories are very common in daily journalism; editors may ask for ideas for "second day folos" even while an event is breaking.

folo — (1) See "follow-up." (2) A sentence or paragraph that follows a recurring feature, such as Dear Abby or a weekly business column. It usually explains a bit about the writer and often gives a postal and/or e-mail address for contacting the writer directly.

graf — Short for *paragraph*. Also can be spelled "graph."

graphic elements — Anything on the page other than the body of the story. Headlines, cutlines, photos, fact boxes, maps and informational graphics all are considered graphic elements.

gutters — The white space between columns of a story or between two pages on the same piece of newsprint.

icon — A graphic device used to help readers instantly recognize parts of a series or a recurring feature. Icons can be used for stories about a specific event, such as an airplane wreck, or a about an ongoing topic, such as election coverage. Also called a "logo."

jump — The part of a story that continues on another page.

jump line — The line of type that tells readers on which page a story will continue. It also gives them a key word or phrase that helps them find the story. For example: "Please see PLANE CRASH, page 6." The headline on Page 6 would include the key words "PLANE CRASH."

justified — Type that is aligned evenly on both the left and right margins of a newspaper column. Most news stories are run in justified type. In the old days, typesetters inserted tiny spacers between words to achieve this effect. Today, computers automatically adjust the space between both words and letters, creating a more even appearance in justified type.

lead — (1) A tip from a news source. (2) The first paragraph, or first several paragraphs, of a story. May also be spelled "lede," to avoid confusion with the previous definition.

lede — See "lead," the second definition.

logo — (1) See "icon." (2) Artistic-looking logos used by businesses or sports teams, sometimes used along with stories about those businesses or teams.

mainbar — The main story in a major breaking news or enterprise story. A mainbar is accompanied by one or more sidebars that include supplementary information to help place the story into context.

mug — A photo, usually about thumbprint size, of a person mentioned or quoted in a story. Mugs help people identify people in the story — the old "putting the face with the name" idea.

nameplate — See "flag," the first definition.

news hole — The amount of space available for news content. This amount usually is determined using a ratio (the industry standard for newspapers is to allocate 40 percent of the space on the pages to news and 60 percent to advertising). Editors usually work with a news hole "budget," in which they know in advance how many columns or column inches will be available for news, based on how much advertising has been (or is expected to be) sold.

nut graphs — A paragraph in a news story that tells the reader why the story is important now.

op-ed page — The page opposite the editorial page.

photo credit — The name of the photographer who took the photo. Some newspapers use a generic photo credit — "Associated Press photo," for example — for nonstaff photos.

pitch — (1) A budget line. (2) The act of convincing an editor of the value of a story idea or finished story. If you pitch a story to editors, for example, you might want them to authorize you to spend extra time on it (and possibly to relieve you of some of your more routine assignments), or to plan for the story to receive special attention in the form of extra space or more than the usual amount of help from other journalists who might write additional stories, create informational graphics or take more than the usual number of photos.

play — Where the story will be placed in the newspaper. An editor might say, "How are we going to play that story on the campus rally that turned into a riot? Should we play it as the lead on A1?" Think of play as the short form of *display*.

pullout — A short sidebar, list or "just the facts" information that runs with a story, usually in a format that offsets it visually from the rest of the story.

ragged right — See "flush left."

refer — Anything that promotes related stories or information elsewhere in the newspaper (or in local television or radio stations with which the newspaper has a media partnership).

series — Any enterprise piece that runs over the course of two or more days.

shirttail — See "background."

shoulder — The story that appears beneath the top story on the page and to one side or the other of the centerpiece.

sidebar — A story of lesser note that accompanies the main story, or mainbar.

skyboxes — A row of graphic elements above the flag (see definition above) that keys readers to articles inside the newspaper. Sometimes these elements actually are surrounded by boxes or by white space or lines. Skyboxes go in and out of fashion.

slot — The chief copy editor, or the place where that person sits. A reporter who wants to find out who will write the headline for his or her Page One story might say, "Who's in the slot today?"

slug — A word or phrase used to identify a particular story. Nonjournalists usually would call this a document or file name.

stand-alone photo — A photo that appears without an accompanying story, with only a headline and cutline.

strip or stripper — The top story on the page, usually "stripped" across the width of the paper.

subheads — Display type (see definition above) that supports the main headline. A subhead often, but not always, goes beneath the main headline.

tag line — A listing of contributors to the report, usually at the end of the story.

tout — See "budget line."

wire — A generic term for the wire services that provide stories for use by newspapers throughout the country. An editor planning coverage of a storm might say, "What kind of wire stories do we have about what's happening in other parts of the state?" Newspapers usually use wire stories to report news developments outside their circulation area, such as news from the state capital (unless, of course, the newspaper is in the state capital), as well as national and international news. Commonly used wire services include independent services such as the Associated Press, Reuters, Bloomberg (business news), and news services run either by large newspapers or by newspaper chains that own multiple newspapers, such as The New York Times, Chicago Tribune, Los Angeles Times, or the Gannett, Knight-Ridder, Scripps-Howard, or Cox newspaper chains.

wrapper — Special pages that cover A1 or another section front. If the St. Louis Cardinals won the World Series, a special championship wrapper might wrap A1, allowing the paper to give special attention to an unusual story while keeping the regular news of the world in A1.

Works Cited

Note: The following works and sources of quotes are presented here in the order in which they appear in each chapter.

Chapter 1

John Steinbeck, from a letter written in the 1950s to the U.S. Information Service, included in "Steinbeck: A Life in Letters," E. Steinbeck and R. Wallsten, eds., published by Viking, New York, 1975, p. 256.

Quotes from the article that prompted the case of Near v. Minnesota, 283 U.S. 697 (1931), included in "Minnesota Rag: The Dramatic Story of the Landmark Supreme Court Case that Gave New Meaning to Freedom of the Press," Fred Friendly, published by Vintage Books, New York, 1981, p. 46.

Pentagon Papers case information from New York Times Co. v. United States, The Washington Post, 403 U.S. 713, 29 L. Ed. 2d 822, 91 S. Ct. 2140 [1 Media L. Rep. 1031] (1971).

Roy Peter Clark quote on Joseph Conrad, from "The American Conversation and the Language of Journalism," "The Poynter Papers: No. 5," Roy Peter Clark, published by the Poynter Institute for Media Studies, St. Petersburg, Fla., 1994. p. 4.

Vaclav Havel, from a speech to the 45th annual Congress of Journalists and Meeting of the International Union of Press Publishers (FIEJ) in Prague May 25, 1992.

Anne Lamott, from "Media Diet," Utne Reader, May–June 1999, p. 110.

James Carey, from "The Struggle Against Forgetting," Columbia Journalism Review, January/February 1996, p. 4.

NATO bombing quotes, from stories by Reuters News Service, July 19 and July 27, 1999.

Cole Campbell, heard by co-author Tom Warhover in The Virginian-Pilot newsroom.

Thomas Jefferson, "[The press] is the best instrument ... ," from a letter to A. Coray, 1823, ME 15:489.

Thomas Jefferson, "I know no safe depository ... ," from a letter to William C. Jarvis, 1820, ME 15:278.

David Mathews, from "Politics for People: Finding a Responsible Public Voice," published by the University of Illinois Press, Urbana and Chicago, 1994, p 106.

Frances Moore Lappe/Paul Martin DuBois, from "The Quickening of America: Rebuilding Our Nation, Remaking Our Lives," published by Jossey-Bass Inc. Publishers, San Francisco, 1994, p. 15.

Tony Germanotta, heard by co-author Tom Warhover in The Virginian-Pilot newsroom.

Chapter 3

Information about a libelous mistake, from "Law of the Student Press," published by the Student Press Law Center, Arlington, Va., 1994, p. 103.

Chapter 4

George A. Hillery Jr., from "Definitions of Community: Areas of Agreement," Rural Sociology 20, June 1955, p. 118.

David B. Clark, from "The Concept of Community: A Reexamination," Sociological Review, 21, August 1973, pp. 397–411.

Michael J. Weiss, from "The Beautiful and the Demmed: You are what you buy, wherever you live," Utne Reader, March–April 2000, p. 54.

Ramon "Ray" Oldenburg, from "The Great Good Place: Cafes, Coffee Shops, Community Centers, Beauty Parlors, General Stores, Bars Hangouts, and How They Can Get You Through the Day," published by Paragon House, New York, 1989, p. 16.

Mary Annette Pember, from the Gannett Co. Inc.'s Editorially Speaking, Vol. 44, No. 8, Oct. 1990.

Dori Maynard, from "Fault Lines: Blindsided," published online by the Robert C. Maynard Institute for Journalism Education, May 21, 2001, at http://www.maynardije.org/columns/dorimaynard/010521_faultlines/.

Jock Lauterer, from "Community Journalism: The Personal Approach," published by the University of Iowa Press, Ames, Iowa, 1995, p. 24

Suggested news values and the story about a gay student's transition to fraternity life, from Rebecca Payne, in "Civic Journalism Interest Group News," Summer 2000, p. 5.

Walt Harrington, from "Intimate Journalism: The Art and Craft of Reporting Everyday Life," published by Sage Publications, Thousand Oaks, Calif., 1997.

Chapter 5

Some questions in the section titled "Asking Effective Questions" were drawn from the "Five Ws of Public Journalism," compiled by Pete

Weitzel after a seminar sponsored by the Project on Public Life and the Press at the American Press Institute.

Edna Buchanan, from "The Corpse Had a Familiar Face: Covering Miami, America's Hottest Beat," published by Diamond Books, New York, 1991, p. 265.

Berkeley High School students' story, from People, March 20, 2000, pp. 89–90.

Chapter 6

Roy Peter Clark and Don Fry, from "Coaching Writers: The Essential Guide for Editors and Reporters," published by St. Martin's Press, New York, 1992, as follows: quote about idiosyncrasies, p. 34; about preparing to write, p. 67; about Saul Pett, p. 34; and about Don Murray, p. 50.

Roy Peter Clark, from "The American Conversation and the Language of Journalism," "The Poynter Papers: No. 5," published by the Poynter Institute for Media Studies, St. Petersburg, Fla, 1994, p. 16.

Chapter 7

Erving Goffman, from "Frame Analysis: An Essay on the Organization of Experience," published by Northeastern University Press, Boston, 1974, p. 39.

Joshua Gamson, from "Incredible News: Tabloids Meet News," Current, Feb. 1, 1995, pp. 3 (5).

John Leo, from "Why Ruin a Good Story?," U.S. News and World Report, May 5, 1997, p. 17.

Suzan Revan, from "Gate Gate," AJR/American Journalism Review, Sept. 1997, archived online at http://www.ajr.org/article.asp?id=1508.

Guido Fernandez, from "Agonía a la Hora del Cierre: El Minuto de Silencio que Puede Hacer Cambiar al Periodismo [The Agony of Deadline: The Minute of Silence that Can Change Journalism]," published by Trillas, Mexico City, and Florida International University, North Miami, Fla., 1994, p. 30.

Davis "Buzz" Merritt, from "Public Journalism and Public Life: Why Telling the News Is Not Enough," published by Lawrence Erlbaum Associates, Hillsdale, N.J., 1995, pp. 10, 20.

Los Angeles man, from "Meaningful Chaos: How People Form Relationships with Public Concerns," the Harwood Group, published by the Kettering Foundation, Dayton, Ohio, 1993, p. 21.

Jay Rosen, from "Public Journalism Theory & Practice: Lessons from Experience," published by the Kettering Foundation, 1997, p. 19.

Danny Schechter, from "Media Matters: Peace Journalism 101," "The Nation," Nov. 9, 1998, archived online at http://past.thenation.com/issue/981109/1109SCHE.HTM.

Chapter 8

Peter Wasson, from The Gannett Co. Inc.'s Editorially Speaking, Vol. 50, No. 9, Nov. 1996.

Jack Hart, from "The Coaches' Corner" newsletter, Sept. 1994, p. 9, originally from the Portland Oregonian's monthly newsletter, Second Takes.

Stephen R. Covey, from "The Seven Habits of Highly Effective People," published by Simon & Schuster, New York, 1990, pp. 239, 240.

Toni Wood, from Writer's Digest, March 1993.

Ken Metzler's story about Nora Villagran meeting Joan Baez, from "Creative Interviewing: The Writer's Guide to Gathering Information by Asking Questions," published by Prentice Hall, Englewood Cliffs, N.J., 1989.

Chapter 9

Edna Buchanan, from "The Corpse Had a Familiar Face: Covering Miami, America's Hottest Beat," published by Diamond Books, New York, 1991, p. 265.

Chapter 11

Jacqui Banaszynski anecdote, from "Writing and Reporting News: A Coaching Method," 2nd ed., published by Wadsworth Publishing Co., Belmont, Calif., p. 491.

Chapter 12

Ron Martin and Rebecca Carr, from Kent German, "Charity Beat," AJR/American Journalism Review, Sept. 2000, archived online at http://www.ajr.org/Article.asp?id=467.

Linda Grist Cunningham, from "The Local News Handbook," published by the American Society of Newspaper Editors, 1999.

Items in the sidebar "The Lighter Side of Police Reporting," from Reader's Digest, Dec. 1996, p. 14.

Wallace Westfeldt and Tom Wicker, from "Indictment: The News Media & the Criminal Justice System," report published by the Freedom Forum's First Amendment Center, 1998, pp. 1, 50.

Jane Stevens, from "Reporting on Violence: A Handbook for Journalists," online handbook, at http://www.pcvp.org/pcvp/media/fore.shtml.

Chapter 13

Joseph Pulitzer, from The St. Louis Post-Dispatch's Platform, printed daily in the Post-Dispatch and carved in granite on its building.

Arizona Project information, from the Investigative Reporters and Editors Web site, http://www.ire.org/history/arizona.html.

James S. Ettema and Theodore L. Glasser, from "Custodians of Conscience: Investigative Journalism and Public Virtue," published by the Columbia University Press, New York, 1998, p. 61.

Examples, from "The Reporter's Handbook: An Investigator's Guide to Documents and Techniques," 3rd ed., by Steve Weinberg, published by Bedford/St. Martin's, Boston, New York, 1996, as follows: from the Orlando Sentinel, pp. 314–316; universities example, p. 171; police department example, p. 185; FOI Act quote, p. 55.

John Hersey, from "The Algiers Motel Incident," published by Bantam, New York, 1968, p. 27.

Tom Wolfe, from New York, Feb. 21, 1972, p. 46.

Walt Harrington, from "Intimate Journalism: The Art and Craft of Reporting Everyday Life," Sage Publications, Thousand Oaks, Calif., 1997, pp. xx–xxii.

Theodore L. Glasser, from "The Idea of Public Journalism," Theodore L. Glasser, ed., the Guilford Press, New York, 1999, p. xxxiii.

Davis "Buzz" Merritt, from "Public Journalism and Public Life: Why Telling the News Is Not Enough," published by Lawrence Erlbaum Associates, Hillsdale, N.J., 1995, p. 83.

Edmund B. Lambeth,from "Public Journalism as a Democratic Practice," in "Assessing Public Journalism," Edmund B. Lambeth, Philip E. Meyer and Esther Thorson, eds., published by the University of Missouri Press, Columbia, Mo., 1998, p. 17.

Arthur Charity, from "Doing Public Journalism," published by the Guilford Press, New York, 1995, pp. 19, 24.

Jay Rosen, from "What Are Journalists For?" published by the Yale University Press, New Haven, Conn., 1999, about framing on p. 148 and about experimentation on p. 6.

Chapter 14

Edward L. Seaton, from "Examining Our Credibility: Why Newspaper Credibility Has Been Dropping," prepared by Urban & Associates Inc. for the American Society of Newspaper Editors, available online at www.asne.org, in the archives under "Reports and Studies."

James Fallows, from "Breaking the News: How the Media Undermine American Democracy," published by Vintage Books, New York, 1996, p. 9.

Cole Campbell, "Journalism as a Democratic Art," in "The Idea of Public Journalism," Theodore L. Glasser, ed., published by the Guilford Press, 1999, p. xix.

Pentagon Papers quote, from "Law for the Reporter," 5th ed., by Dale R. Spencer, Lucas Bros. Publishers, 1980, pp. 29–35, and New York Times v. the United States, The Washington Post Co., et al, 403 U.S. 713, 29 L. Ed. 2d 822, 91 S. Ct. 2140 [1 Med. L. Rptr. 1031] (1971)

Quotes about Near v. Minnesota from "Minnesota Rag: The Dramatic Story

of the Landmark Supreme Court Case that Gave New Meaning to Freedom of the Press," by Fred Friendly, published by Vintage Books, New
York, 1981, first quote from p. 33; quote about Guilford accepting
bribes, p. 35.

Chief Justice Charles Evans Hughes quote about Near v. Minnesota from
"Law for the Reporter," 5th ed., by Dale R. Spencer, Lucas Bros. Pub-
lishers, 1980, p. 29, and 283 U.S. 697, 75 L. Ed. 1357, 51 S. Ct. 625 [1
Med. L. Rptr. 1001] (1931).

Knoxville story information, from the Knoxville News-Sentinel, Jan. 30,
1999, p. 1.

Supreme Court Justice William J. Brennan, from "Law for the Reporter," 5th
ed., by Dale R. Spencer, Lucas Bros. Publishers, 1980, p. 93, and New
York Times v. Sullivan, 376 U.S. 254, 11 L. Ed. 2d 686, 84 S. Ct. 710 [1
Med. L. Rptr. 1527] (1964).

St. Amant v. Thompson, from "Law for the Reporter," 5th ed., by Dale R.
Spencer, Lucas Bros. Publishers, 1980, p. 105, and 390 U.S. 727, 20 L.
Ed. 2d 262, 88 S. Ct. 1323 [1 Med. L. Rptr. 1586] (1968).

Daniel Yankelovich, from "Coming to Public Judgment," published by the
Syracuse University Press, Syracuse, N.Y., 1991, first quote from p. 6,
quote about three stages from pp. 63–65.

Gannett ethical principles outlined in "The How, Why and What of the New
Principles," by Phil Currie and Larry Beaupre, on the Gannett Co. News
Watch web page, June 18, 1999.

Index

About the Authors

Cheryl Gibbs is an assistant professor of journalism at Earlham College. Joining the faculty in 1993, she has served as the faculty advisor to the student newspaper, The Earlham Word, in addition to teaching reporting, editing and design courses. She worked with the Project on Public Life and the Press for many years and with the Charles F. Kettering Foundation of Dayton, Ohio, and the Pew Center for Civic Journalism, since 1994. She has collaborated with journalists and journalism educators involved in civic journalism efforts in Colombia, South America, and has been a guest lecturer in postgraduate courses and seminars for journalists at universities in Bogotá and Medellín. Before joining the Earlham faculty in 1993, Gibbs was a cops-and-courts reporter, arts writer, features editor, regional editor, city editor and weekend news editor at two small daily newspapers. She also has worked on several projects with the Dayton (Ohio) Daily News. She taught at Indiana University East in Richmond for several years while serving in various editorial roles at the Richmond (Ind.) Palladium-Item.

Tom Warhover is an associate professor at the University of Missouri School of Journalism and the executive editor of the Columbia Missourian, a six-day community newspaper edited by professionals and staffed by student reporters, copy editors, designers and photographers. Prior to joining the university, he worked for The (Norfolk) Virginian-Pilot, a 200,000 circulation daily newspaper serving southeastern Virginia and northeastern North Carolina. At the Pilot, he was a copy editor, designer, wire editor and metro editor. He covered city hall as a beat reporter. As an assigning editor in charge of the "public life team," he helped the paper create principles and daily practices for the then-fledgling concept of public (or civic) journalism. He helped guide the long-term strategies of the newsroom as deputy managing editor and the fiscal fortunes of part of the newspaper as the North Carolina general manager.